Values in Psychiatry

Values in Psychiatry

Managing Complexity and Advancing Solutions

Edited by

Robert B. Dudas

Cambridgeshire and Peterborough NHS Foundation Trust

CAMBRIDGE
UNIVERSITY PRESS

CAMBRIDGE
UNIVERSITY PRESS

Shaftesbury Road, Cambridge CB2 8EA, United Kingdom

One Liberty Plaza, 20th Floor, New York, NY 10006, USA

477 Williamstown Road, Port Melbourne, VIC 3207, Australia

314–321, 3rd Floor, Plot 3, Splendor Forum, Jasola District Centre, New Delhi - 110025, India

103 Penang Road, #05–06/07, Visioncrest Commercial, Singapore 238467

Cambridge University Press is part of Cambridge University Press & Assessment, a department of the University of Cambridge.

We share the University's mission to contribute to society through the pursuit of education, learning and research at the highest international levels of excellence.

www.cambridge.org
Information on this title: www.cambridge.org/9781108793117

DOI: 10.1017/9781108883535

When citing this work, please include a reference to the DOI 10.1017/9781108883535

First published 2025

A catalogue record for this publication is available from the British Library

A Cataloging-in-Publication data record for this book is available from the Library of Congress

ISBN 978-1-108-79311-7 Paperback

To my parents, wife, and son, with love.

Contents

Tables

Contributors

German E. Berrios, University of Cambridge
German E. Berrios is Emeritus Professor of the Epistemology of Psychiatry and a Life Fellow at Robinson College at the University of Cambridge.

David Crepaz-Keay, Mental Health Foundation
David Crepaz-Keay is Head of Research and Applied Learning at the Mental Health Foundation in the UK and a Fellow of the Royal Society for Public Health. He is also the vice-chair for the Commission for Patient and Public Involvement in Health, a technical advisor for the World Health Organization, a senior mental health advisor for Public Health England, and co-chair of the Ethics Committee for the International Society for Psychiatric Genetics.

Tom Dening, University of Nottingham
Tom Dening is Professor of Dementia Research at the University of Nottingham and an Honorary Consultant in Old Age Psychiatry for Nottinghamshire Healthcare NHS Foundation Trust. He is an editor of the *Oxford Textbook of Old Age Psychiatry* and has worked on more than 300 publications.

Elizabeth Fistein, University of Cambridge
Elizabeth Fistein is Director of Clinical Studies in the School of Clinical Medicine at the University of Cambridge where she is responsible for delivery of the Professional Responsibilities curriculum. She is also an Associate of the Centre for Law, Medicine and Life Sciences in the Faculty of Law and sits on the Psychology Research Ethics Committee, the University Research Ethics Committee, and the Approved Clinicians appointment panel for the Midlands and East of England.

Ivana Marková, University of Hull
Ivana Marková is a professor and Honorary Consultant in Psychiatry at Hull York Medical School, University of Hull.

John Martin, South Western Ambulance Service National Health Service Foundation Trust
John Martin is the chief executive of the South Western Ambulance Service NHS Foundation Trust in Exeter and a visiting professor in paramedic science at the University of Hertfordshire.

Femi Oyebode, University of Birmingham
Femi Oyebode is an Honorary Professor of Psychiatry in the Institute of Mental Health and School of Psychology at the University of Birmingham. He is an Honorary Fellow of the Royal College of Psychiatrists and has authored extensively on psychiatry.

Malarvizhi Babu Sandilyan, Berkshire Healthcare National Health Service Foundation Trust
Malarvizhi Babu Sandilyan is a consultant old age psychiatrist working for Berkshire Healthcare NHS Foundation Trust, based in Bracknell. She has co-authored chapters on dementia in a number of publications.

Mathew Thomson, University of Warwick
Mathew Thomson is a professor in the Department of History at the University of Warwick and author of three books on the history of mental health in modern Britain. He is currently working on the cultural history of the UK National Health Service.

Benjamin R. Underwood, University of Cambridge
Benjamin R. Underwood is Associate Professor of Applied and Translational Old Age Psychiatry at the University of Cambridge and an Honorary Consultant Old Age Psychiatrist for Cambridgeshire and Peterborough NHS Foundation Trust in Fulbourn.

Toby Williamson, University of West London
Toby Williamson is a postgraduate researcher for the University of West London and an independent health and social care consultant. He has more than thirty years' professional and family experience of mental health issues and has written extensively about values and values-based practice.

Foreword author **Bill (K. W. M.) Fulford** is a Fellow of St Catherine's College and a member of the Philosophy Faculty at the University of Oxford; Emeritus Professor of Philosophy and Mental Health at the University of Warwick; founder editor of *Philosophy, Psychiatry, and Psychology*; and Honorary Consultant Psychiatrist at the University of Oxford (retired).

Foreword

Psychiatry is a polyvalent discipline. The UK's Royal College of Psychiatrists (RCPsych), for example, in addition to its clinical faculties and (welcome) focus on the 'sciences', convenes groups concerned with the 'arts': philosophy, history, literature, spirituality, and many others. Nor do these represent fleeting or minority interests: the philosophy group, as a case in point, was among the first of such groups, established more than fifty years ago, and for much of the intervening period it has had more members than most clinical faculties. Internationally, a similar picture is evident. The World Psychiatric Association (WPA), as a leading exemplar, offers a corresponding range of 'special interest groups'; its journal, *World Psychiatry*, which has held the top slot in the citation ratings among psychiatry journals for the last eight years, regularly publishes articles in areas such as philosophy, phenomenology, and values.

On first inspection, it may seem obvious that psychiatry's polyvalent nature reflects its engagement with the equally polyvalent nature of what the Oxford philosopher of mind Kathleen Wilkes famously called 'real people'. To state the obvious, people are polyvalent too: they are not just 'brains'; still less are they merely objects of the social sciences. Originally, psychopathology, correspondingly, in the work of philosopher-psychiatrist Karl Jaspers, famously sought to combine causal with meaningful connections. This is why the North American psychiatrist and neuroscientist Nancy Andreasen declared herself 'proud' to be a psychiatrist. Why? Because, she said, psychiatry is the one area of medicine in which there is no scope for substituting a concern with persons (Wilkes' 'real people') with a concern for one or more bodily parts or systems (least of all, as neuroscientist Andreasen was aware, a concern for the brain).

Yet herein lies a paradox: psychiatry, notwithstanding its deep connection with 'real people', languishes in both professional and public perceptions, a poor second to bodily medicine. Andreasen's declaration is itself a reflection of this paradox. An academic in literature studies before training in medicine and neuroscience, Andreasen was perhaps uniquely placed to defend psychiatry against stigmatization as a second-class medical discipline: yes, our science is less advanced than are those of many areas of bodily medicine; yes, our very models of disorder are disputed. But this is surely because the challenges we face – scientifically and clinically – are far greater: climbing a mountain takes longer than climbing a hill!

This book confronts the paradox of psychiatry's second-class status head-on. Its editor and lead author, Robert B. Dudas, has assembled a talented polyvalent team, reflecting expertise by experience as well as by training, the latter including authors with expertise not only in psychiatry but in history, literature, and broadcasting. His team, indeed, mirroring contemporary practice, is truly multidisciplinary (one author is a professor of paramedicine). With such a team, the book is unafraid to tackle the big issues, both conceptual (models of disorder and the nature of recovery) and practical (ranging from translation of research findings through economic and management challenges to the co-production of services).

The focus of the book – the particular lens through which it tackles these problems – is values-based practice (VBP). A word on this may be in order as VBP, although concerned with values, has more in common with evidence-based practice (EBP) than ethics. So, while EBP is about the science underpinning medicine, VBP, as this book so ably demonstrates, is about linking science with people. Emerging in the early twenty-first century as a philosophy-into-practice development from the 1990s revival of interdisciplinary work between philosophy and psychiatry, VBP, as Robert B. Dudas points out, actually paralleled the development of EBP. A version of VBP was indeed first proposed by one of the originators of EBP, David Sackett. In his role as Founder Director of Oxford's Centre for Evidence-Based Medicine, Sackett came up with a three-part definition of EBM – EBM, he argued, combined *best research evidence* with *clinical experience* and, note, *individual patient's values.* Of course, now EBM focuses mainly on just the first of Sackett's three elements. But a few years ago, when we launched the Centre for VBP at St Catherine's College in Oxford, Sackett (who by this time had retired to Canada) sent us a good luck message for finally getting back to what EBM was originally all about!

Much of the early work in VBP, as might be expected from Robert B. Dudas's polyvalent book, was fronted by psychiatry in co-production with other mental health disciplines. The first training programme ('Whose Values?') flagged by Dudas in his Conclusion was developed in a joint venture between Warwick University's postgraduate PEMH (Philosophy, Ethics, and Mental Health) programme and a non-governmental organization, the Sainsbury Centre for Mental Health in London: Toby Williamson (Chapter 3, this book) was one of those involved alongside me and a nurse trainer, Kim Woodbridge. The training manual was adopted by the Department of Health and became the basis of a workstream within its (at the time recently launched) mental health policy-implementation body, NIMH (National Institutes for Mental Health). Subsequently, NIMH produced a number of VBP-based policy initiatives, including a Values Statement guiding all its work (co-produced by a multidisciplinary group chaired by service user and academic Piers Allott), the '3 Keys' guidance on mental health assessment (co-produced by Laurie Bryant and Lu Duhig, respectively a service user and a carer lead for NIMH), and a training manual to support implementation of the 2007 revision of the Mental Health Act (co-produced under the leadership of social work trainer Malcolm King).

It is no coincidence that so much of NIMH's work was co-produced. As several chapters of this book make clear, the challenges facing mental health, including the very concept of recovery, are such that teamwork and co-production, tapping into the additional valences offered by diverse perspectives, are essential to progress. In this, philosophy is important. A brief origin story from the VBP Collaborating Centre will make the point. In its early days the centre was focused on practical implementation and as such was supported by a senior advisory board representing expertise in practical delivery on health policy (National Institute for Health and Care Excellence (NICE), NHS (National Health Service) England, the Professional Standards Authority (PSA), RCPsych, and others). At our first advisory board meeting we reported somewhat apologetically on the extent of the centre's commitment to philosophy. But 'Why apologise?' was the board's response; digging into the philosophy underpinning health care, they continued, is essential if VBP, like others before it (and here they mentioned EBM), is to avoid being 'dumbed down' and losing its efficacy! The result was that the centre took ownership of its philosophy, pursuing its work through an ongoing dynamic between theory and practice, with exciting developments in areas ranging from analytic philosophy (semantic logic and relational value theory) through phenomenology to non-European philosophies such as those of Africa, the Caribbean, and South-East Asia.

This book, although, as noted earlier, engaging with key philosophical and conceptual issues, is focused primarily on the practical impact of VBP. Its three main parts explore the values of psychiatry respectively through historical, contemporary, and clinical perspectives, and it adds a final (but vitally important) chapter on research. The historical dimension is illuminating not least in combining chapters by psychiatrist-historians (German E. Berrios and Ivana Marková) with a chapter by an academic medical historian (Mathew Thomson). Together with Dudas's own chapter, Part I amply demonstrates the truth of what Mathew Thomson once pointed out to me, that the history of medicine is a history of medical values. Part II builds on this. Again, chapters by Dudas are complemented by other voices: poet and broadcaster as well as psychiatrist Femi Oyebode explores the image of psychiatry in art and literature; there are chapters from a variety of perspectives representing the multidisciplinary team; 'progressive developments' are reflected notably in a chapter on co-production and recovery by service user and academic David Crepaz-Keay; and the part concludes with insightful examinations of key contemporary challenges, including risk management and care of the elderly. Part III brings the values of psychiatry home with illuminating explorations of the diverse values challenges presented by three exemplar conditions, depression, dementia, and borderline personality disorder.

Dudas's final chapter, on research, although a stand-alone contribution, takes us to the heart of VBP's role in linking science with people. Dudas's starting point is the widely recognized failure of translation of neuroscientific research into improvements in patient care. This, he argues, reflects a failure to engage with values. Dudas supports this claim with concrete proposals (such as 'values mapping') for developing new research designs in which the values of psychiatry are fully engaged. Therefore, the chapter indicates, besides supporting improved clinical care, VBP holds out the promise of new models of research that more effectively bridge 'from bench to bedside'.

The message of the book as a whole, then, is that combining values with evidence, VBP with EBP, is important if psychiatry is to rise to the challenges it faces in the twenty-first century. But this brings us back to the paradox of its second-class status. Psychiatry, I should say straight away, remains active in advancing this new model. The Royal College's new curriculum, as the book describes, highlights the importance of values in all areas of training. Like so many other positive developments in the field, this new curriculum builds on co-production: in this case, the work of the Royal College's lay representative, Veryan Richards. Internationally, the WPA, in addition to accepting articles in *World Psychiatry*, regularly accepts sessions on philosophy and values in its conference programme. Yet all this work notwithstanding, the locus of activity in the Oxford Centre for VBP has shifted back to bodily medicine. The current director is Oxford University's Professor of Vascular Surgery Ashok Handa; under Ashok's leadership, while mental health has remained in play, with initiatives in areas ranging from aesthetics to racism and the abuse of psychiatry, new training programmes have been developed mainly in areas of bodily medicine – in surgery, of course, but also in areas representative of the multidisciplinary team, such as pharmacy, radiography, and paramedicine.

There is a certain logic to this: paramedics, after all, in the terms of this book, know a thing or two about managing uncertainty and advancing solutions (think ambulance drivers); and it is in the very nature of VBP that it should be multidisciplinary. All the same, mental health, and psychiatry in particular, has lost something of its pole position. This book, in charting the scope and potential impact of the values of psychiatry, takes the profession an important step towards resuming its lead role in linking science with people.

Bill (K. W. M.) Fulford
St Catherine's College, Oxford

Acknowledgements

This book was born as a result of a long intellectual journey, and it would be impossible to mention all the colleagues, patients, and other people and institutions that had an influence on the development of my thoughts. I need to mention, though, two of my teachers at the University of Szeged, Katalin Barabas and Zoltan Janka, who – with their wide-ranging knowledge and charismatic teaching – ignited my interest in mental health as a subject in which the natural sciences, the social sciences and humanities, and art can all be relevant. It was German E. Berrios at Cambridge University who drew my attention to specific aspects of descriptive psychopathology and the crucial relevance of the history of psychiatry.

Discussions with Professor Bill Fulford and reading his work on values-based practice inspired me to embark on writing this book. I am also greatly indebted to him for his invaluable help, as series editor, with finding a wonderful team of co-authors and his astute advice at important junctures.

Peter Jones, Simon Baron-Cohen, John O'Brien, and other colleagues at the Department of Psychiatry at Cambridge University have provided the inspiring intellectual environment necessary for such a prolonged scholarly endeavour. Ideas were developed and improved through discussions in the VBP and philosophy special interest groups at the Cambridgeshire and Peterborough NHS Foundation Trust. Cambridge University Library provided a most conducive writing environment and excellent professional help during the process. I am grateful to Kim Ingram and Catherine Barnes at Cambridge University Press for their invaluable support with bringing out this volume. I am also indebted to copy-editor Lori Heaford for her thorough and thoughtful handling of the text.

I thank my parents for instilling in me a curiosity about the world and people. Throughout this whole journey, I benefited from the inspirational intellectual company and loving appreciation of my work of my wife, Julia Paraizs.

Introduction

Robert B. Dudas

Values permeate all aspects of psychiatry from aetiology, through classification, to treatment. This is unsurprising, as psychiatry is concerned with areas of human experience and behaviour in which human values are particularly diverse. Evidence-based medicine (EBM) can be immensely helpful at guiding us about the efficacy and safety of diagnostic and treatment interventions, but it is silent about the personal importance attached to these by patient and doctor, that is, about patients' and doctors' relevant values. This is problematic because these values are of crucial importance when it comes to various aspects of person-centred care, such as patient choice, treatment adherence, recovery, and clinician attitudes. This is where values-based practice (VBP) comes into play.

Whilst VBP is often portrayed through contrasting it with EBM, this can be somewhat misleading because VBP is also evidence-based; it is just that its evidence has a different provenance and format. Evidence-based medicine was developed to replace the use of intuition, anecdotal evidence, and subjective clinical experience with examination of objective evidence from clinical research, using formal rules to appraise it. The gold standard of EBM is the randomized controlled trial (RCT). Results from sufficiently similar RCTs can be meta-analysed to produce an overall statistic, which is considered to be the highest level of evidence in EBM. High-quality meta-analyses, such as those in the Cochrane Library, also provide ratings of the quality of the evidence. By now, EBM has developed into an essential clinical tool, but, for the clinician to be able to make the most of it, another step is required. This next step is to apply the group-level evidence in individual cases in a person-centred way. This is where VBP comes in as it offers a parallel framework of clinical theory and skills through which to do, among other things, exactly that.

The development of VBP started largely at the same time as that of EBM, around the turn of the last century. The pioneering work of Bill Fulford, a British philosopher-psychiatrist, was instrumental in working out the main principles of VBP, including ten pointers to a 'good process', which refers to the inclusion and balancing of the values of those involved during clinical decision-making (Fulford, 2007; Woodbridge and Fulford, 2004). These include four practice skills: awareness, reasoning, knowledge, and communication about values. Two important concepts in VBP are user-centredness and multidisciplinarity. They were originally described in the context of models of service delivery, but we have developed these further in this book in other contexts, such as clinical theory and research. Partnership between the patient and the clinician is also a key principle in VBP. The nature of this partnership in psychiatry and the relevance and impact of other stakeholders on clinical decision-making are examined in detail throughout this book.

Psychiatry is both an academic field and an area of medical practice. Ideally, research should seek answers to the main questions of clinical practice and advances in research should translate into practice. Unfortunately, in recent years there has been an increasing disconnect between academic and clinical psychiatry (de Haan, 2020). Furthermore, despite significant investment in research, progress in our understanding of the pathomechanism and the mechanism of recovery from major forms of mental illness or in the development of new treatments has been slow. At the same time, strong criticisms have been levelled against current psychiatric practice (e.g. owing to the epidemic proportions of benzodiazepine and antidepressant use or the ever-increasing number of detentions to hospital for assessment and treatment in certain countries) and even though many people with mental illness clearly benefit from psychiatry, despite the substantial investment into psychiatric care, rates of mental illness have not reduced as a result (Jorm et al., 2017), a situation known as the treatment–prevalence paradox (Stein et al., 2022). In writing this volume, we wanted to understand what might be at the root of all this and what could help us overcome the current stagnation in psychiatry. We believed that an approach that takes into consideration the hybrid nature of psychiatry in that it combines forms and practices from both the natural and the social sciences holds the key to this. We also believed that there were important opportunities for making progress if we could only capture the role of values all over psychiatry from aetiology, through diagnosis, to treatment. And VBP would provide an invaluable theoretical apparatus for this.

To achieve our goals, we set out to examine the relevant values of the stakeholders, that is, patients, psychiatrists, and others involved in or with psychiatry. Furthermore, we also sought to showcase the positive values and contribution that psychiatry brings. We felt that, in order to achieve any real breakthrough, it was important to do this focussing not just on the here and now but also diachronically and from the different perspectives of not just medicine but also history, social work, art, and philosophy, and to include the voice of those with lived experience of mental illness. Our team of authors represent the multidisciplinarity required for this.

The structure of our book also reflects our intentions. In Part I, we look at the historical origins of psychiatry. To open, in Chapter 1, German E. Berrios and Ivana S. Marková provide an analysis of the birth of psychiatry as a medical specialty, the forces that brought it forth, and the consequences of that for its epistemology and approach to mental illness. In Chapter 2, Robert B. Dudas explores the history of person-centredness and agency in psychology by contrasting some of its main schools of thought, such as psychoanalysis and behaviourism, as well as cognitive and humanistic psychology. Mathew Thomson presents, in Chapter 3, a historical analysis of the social, cultural, and political value context in which British psychiatry has evolved since the late nineteenth century and lays the foundations for future studies of this kind.

In Part II, we turn our attention to value-laden and controversial issues in the present practice of psychiatry as well as some of the current developments that will be influential on the future of psychiatry. In Chapter 4 on ailments of the mind, Robert B. Dudas investigates the role of values in defining mental illness and psychiatry. He also explores the questions of 'Who decides what is pathological?' and 'What determines or influences mental well-being?' from a values perspective. Chapter 5, also by Robert B. Dudas, investigates the values of psychiatry as seen from within the profession at a personal as well as a collective level and also how psychiatry is viewed from outside, in the public discourse. In Chapter 6, Femi Oyebode explores how psychiatry and psychiatrists are portrayed in literature and the usefulness of such portrayals. Chapter 7, written by Robert B. Dudas, Elizabeth Fistein, and Toby Williamson, approaches multidisciplinarity from the perspectives of medicine and neuroscience, the social sciences, and nursing and social work, respectively. The next two chapters describe progressive developments in psychiatry from a theoretical and a practical point of view, respectively. On the theoretical side, Chapter 8 begins with Robert B. Dudas looking at promising new developments in psychiatric treatment, especially existential psychotherapy and motivational interviewing, and what they have to offer in terms of refining our understanding of mental illness and the role of values in it. In the second half of Chapter 8, David Crepaz-Keay provides insight into recovery and co-production and the potential they carry for improving psychiatric care. Then, on the practical side, in Chapter 9, Benjamin R. Underwood and John Martin present an example of using VBP principles in reorganizing clinical services for the elderly by integrating mental and physical healthcare. To round off Part II, Chapter 10 takes a closer look at the current climate in which psychiatry operates, especially in the UK. Robert B. Dudas first examines the value context of specializing and working in psychiatry. This is followed by Elizabeth Fistein's analysis of the recent extreme focus on managing risk, especially preventing suicide, in psychiatry. Finally, in a section on values questioned and debated, Robert B. Dudas contrasts the approaches of anti-psychiatry and critical psychiatry.

Part III of the book focusses on three common psychiatric conditions and the benefits of taking a values-based approach to them. In Chapter 11, Robert B. Dudas describes a philosophically informed approach to understanding depression and its treatment and presents a methodological description of clinical value-mapping, which can facilitate a good process and reduce moral injury. In Chapter 12, Tom Dening and Malarvizhi Babu Sandilyan explore how during the progression of dementia the person's choices and preferences and the clinicians' philosophy of care may change over time, and how VBP can contribute to addressing the challenges this presents. Chapter 13, by Robert B. Dudas, explores value conflicts in borderline personality disorder and further elaborates on the use of clinical value-mapping.

Finally, as VBP has much to offer for research, too, Robert B. Dudas explores this in Chapter 14, a separate chapter at the end of the book. Owing to its richly value-laden nature, psychiatry is particularly well-placed to play a leading role in developing VBP. More than in other specialties, psychiatrists need to know their patients as people in order to arrive at the correct diagnosis or formulation and to be able to develop effective therapeutic relationships. Cultural and social factors can contribute powerfully to the development of psychiatric conditions and to the recovery from them. Consequently, psychiatry needs to call upon a range of cognate fields, such as psychology, sociology, anthropology, and law, and – to navigate this immensely complex, multidisciplinary endeavour – philosophy. This book is about the unique contribution of psychiatry to bringing about this collaboration and managing this complexity.

References

Fulford, B. (K. W. M.) 2007. Facts/values: Ten principles of values-based medicine. In Radden, J. (ed.), *The Philosophy of Psychiatry: A Companion*. New York: Oxford University Press, pp. 205–234.

De Haan, S. 2020. *Enactive Psychiatry*. Cambridge: Cambridge University Press.

Jorm, A. F., Patten, S. B., Brugha, T. S. & Mojtabai, R. 2017. Has increased provision of treatment reduced the prevalence of common mental disorders? Review of the evidence from four countries. *World Psychiatry*, 16(1), 90–99.

Stein, D. J., Shoptaw, S. J., Vigo, D. V., Lund, C., Cuijpers, P., Bantjes, J., Sartorius, N. & Maj, M. (2022). Psychiatric diagnosis and treatment in the 21st century: Paradigm shifts versus incremental integration. *World Psychiatry*, 21(3), 393–414.

Woodbridge, K. & Fulford, B. (K. W. M.) 2004. *Whose Values? A Workbook for Values-Based Practice in Mental Health Care*. London: Sainsbury Centre for Mental Health. https://valuesbasedpractice.org/wp-content/uploads/2015/04/Whose-Values-A-Workbook.pdf.

Chapter 1

The Origins of Psychiatry as a Profession

German E. Berrios and Ivana S. Marková

Introduction

According to a current definition: 'Psychiatry is the branch of medicine focused on the diagnosis, treatment and prevention of mental, emotional and behavioural disorders. A psychiatrist is a medical doctor (an M.D.) who specializes in mental health, including substance use disorders. Psychiatrists are qualified to assess both the mental and [the] physical aspects of psychological problems.'[1] Hence, psychiatrists (1) require a medical degree and specialized postgraduate training; (2) must be members of a legitimizing institution that accredits their clinical competence via examinations and access to specialized journals, textbooks, congresses, and so on; and (3) need to have their practice regulated and protected by legislation.[2] This chapter maps the history of this professionalization process.

The Beginnings

Although medical practitioners have always shown interest in madness,[3] 'psychiatry' (as defined in the 'Introduction' to this chapter) did not exist before the nineteenth century. Throughout the 1800s, these medical interests and views became organized into a recognizable discipline and profession. The word *psychiatrie* was coined in 1808,[4] but for most of the century the profession was called 'alienism' (France) or 'psychological medicine' (Great Britain, Germany).

Since its inception, psychiatry has been bedevilled by (1) boundary disputes (with neurology, psychosomatic medicine, palliative care, etc.) and the need to (2) justify its usefulness and existence vis-à-vis 'anti-psychiatry' and (3) defend its medical status vis-à-vis clinical psychology, mental nursing, sociology, and psychoanalysis. These challenges continue; hence, the future of 'psychiatry' remains uncertain.

Of late, psychiatry has thrown in its entire lot with the neurosciences. This relationship has biased training and new generations of psychiatrists are being formed with a great deal of knowledge about the brain but with little information on philosophy, history, and the social sciences. If madness proves to be more than a brain disorder, then new disciplines with adequate conceptual and hermeneutic repertoires will step in to offer richer and more useful explanatory accounts. Owing to its conceptual poverty, psychiatry will be unable to compete or break away from its current correlational mentality.

Madness before 1800

Transforming Madness into a Medical Object

An old form of human suffering, madness has throughout history attracted the attention of priests, medics, politicians, philosophers, poets, lawyers, and others. Until the eighteenth century these views are found embedded in cultural contexts where the predominant religion provided the permissions and exclusions required to construct their own definition of madness. The religious view of madness, therefore, was not one among many but rather a sort of core belief in relation to which all other views needed to be defined. During the nineteenth century, Comte's model of progress influenced the earliest historiographies of madness and views on madness were lined up in stages: theological (fictitious), metaphysical (abstract), and positive (scientific).[5]

Although rhetorically interesting, this view is not helpful in understanding how the narratives of madness were constructed. For example, based on this linear historiography, the religious accounts of madness must be considered a thing of the past and retrograde. Yet, things are more complicated. Indeed, from the start the concept of madness has combined natural, supernatural, and moral elements which can still be found in the current 'medical' narrative.[6] For example, it is likely that the main cause of what is called the stigma of mental illness is not just 'ignorance of the facts' but the active presence in the current definition of mental disorder of hidden moral and religious meanings.[7]

Up to the seventeenth century, irrespective of whether proposed by medics,[8] philosophers,[9] religious writers,[10] or sufferers themselves,[11] views on madness showed Galenic influence.[12] However, a process of secularization started during the 1600s that in the event led to the so-called scientific revolution and later the Enlightenment. This affected the way in which madness was conceived, leading in due course to its medicalization.[13] It started to be considered as a 'natural kind', that is, as an object collocated in both space (a region of the human body) and time (with a beginning and an end). The development of the functional sciences (physiology, psychology) in the nineteenth century caused a reformulation of madness as a pathological distortion of a 'function', and by the end of that century it had given rise to the psychoanalytical narrative of madness.

Madness as a 'Natural Kind'

During the seventeenth century Thomas Sydenham[14] introduced the view that diseases and plants were similar ontological entities (i.e. 'natural kinds'). This gave rise to a form of 'more *botanico*' nosology, namely, the view that diseases could be classified as plants, as can be seen in the work of Linné, Sagar, McBride, Vogel, Boissier de Sauvages, Cullen, and others.[15] Using 'complaints' as their unit of analysis, they lumped together disease states which currently would be differentiated as disease, syndrome, and symptom.

The same applied to madness and mental symptoms, and clusters of symptoms were listed together. On occasions, listing criteria were used such as the mental faculties, for example, under *mentales*. Linné included Order I: *ideales* (delirium, paraphrosine, amentia, mania, daemonia, vesania, and melancholia); Order II: *imaginarii* (syringmos, phantasma, vertigo, panophobia, hypochondriasis, and sonnambulismus); and Order III: *pathetici* (citta, bulimia, polydipsia, satyriasis, erotomania, nostalgia, tarantismus, rabies, hydrophobia, cacositia, antipathia, and anxietas).[16] In the same vein, under *vesaniæ*, Boissier de Sauvages included Order I: *hallucinations* (vertigo, suffusio, dyplopia, syrigmus, hypochondriasis, and somnanbulismus); Order II: *morositates* (pica, bulimia, polydipsia, antipathia, nostalgia, panophobia, satyriasis, nymphomania, tarantismus, and hydrophobia); Order III: *deliria* (paraphrosine, amentia, melancholia, mania, dæmonomania); and Order IV: *folies anomales* (amnesia and agripnia).[17]

Eighteenth-century nosologists agreed with Linné that only a feature or two (of either a plant or a disease) should be privileged as classificatory criteria.[18] For example, William Cullen chose 'aetiology' as a criterion to group the 'neuroses' (*comata*, *adynamiæ*, *spasmi*, and *vesaniæ*) defined as general disorders of sense and motion in the nervous system. This means that dissimilar conditions such as diabetes, asthma, whooping cough, hallucinations, abdominal colic, diarrhoea, mania, melancholia, and so on were all included in the 'neuroses' class. Not everyone agreed with Linné's method. For example, Adanson[19] proposed that classifications should be based on the analysis of all features characterizing either plant or disease. Implementing this method became possible only after the advent of computers and gave rise to 'numerical taxonomy'.[20]

Madness as a Spatio-temporal Object

In addition to the various narratives available to explain it, the concept of 'madness' up to the eighteenth century was different from the current one in terms of its 'ontology' and 'epistemology', that is, of what its deep nature was believed to be and how it was to be known, respectively. As part of the Newtonian mechanization of the world, the definition of physical objects required that they had space–time coordinates.[21] Up to the 1700s, it was not clear whether the metaphysical status of madness required that it had to be a thing collocated in space and time; indeed, it seemed as if it was an a-temporal form placed outside time. Against this background, clinical remissions needed explanation and the notion of 'lucid interval'[22] was introduced to explain the temporary quiescence of madness.

To be placed in space and time, the concept of madness needed reframing and one such proposal was to reduce it to being an abnormal brain site.[23] This conception must be distinguished from earlier views according to which madness was an ethereal substance floating in the cavities of the brain 'ventricles'.[24] The view that madness occupied a region of bodily space was further developed by David Hartley,[25] who conceived of the mind as a signalling system resulting from changes in the pattern of micro-vibrations of the nerves. Complex thoughts and emotions were just vibrational composites put together by means of Locke's laws of the association of ideas. To Hartley, 'madness' could be used to name eight 'imperfections of the rational faculty': (1) erroneousness of judgement in children and idiots; (2) dotage in the elderly; (3) drunkenness; (4) delirium in acute distempers; (5) recurrence of the same ideas in the course of study; (6) violent passions; (7) melancholy; and (8) madness as such. None of these imperfections corresponds to current clinical categories. This mechanistic view of the mind led Hartley to conclude that there was no absolute demarcation between soundness and unsoundness of mind.[26]

Madness after 1800

Madness as a Disease

Mental Symptoms

Whether medical or mental, individual complaints or clusters thereof were listed side by side by eighteenth-century nosologies. The concept of 'mental symptom' as an autonomous unit of analysis (1) holding a relationship with a specific area/function of the brain and (2) being able to cluster up with different symptoms, thereby giving rise to various mental disorders, was only constructed during the early nineteenth century. This does not mean to say that mental sufferings were not complained about before this period. The issue is that each complaint was treated as a nosological entity and listed accordingly. This was to change during the 1800s when Griesinger started to call such units of analysis *Die Elementarstörungen der psychischen Krankheiten* and suggested that each might be related to a specific mental function (e.g. hallucinations to perception; delusions to thinking; depression to affect; etc.).[27]

Conceptual and social forces led to the construction of the concept of mental symptom. Firstly, there was the new concept of 'medical symptom' constructed as part of the medical discipline of *Séméïologie*[28] or *Séméiotique*.[29] Secondly, there was the popularity in general science of the 'analytical method' (as per Bacon, Locke, Newton, and Hartley) according to which objects and concepts are best understood when teased out into their constituent parts.[30] Thirdly, there was the ongoing linguistic debate on the referential function of names and on the interaction of language and thought (featuring Rousseau, Herder, Monboddo, Humboldt, Dégerando, etc.).[31]

The concept of mental symptom in psychiatry was not free from aporias. For example, if it was the same units of analysis (mental symptoms) that when combined in different clusters gave rise to different diseases, then *what* determined the peculiar nature of each disease? Was it just (1) the *sui generis* nature of the combination or (2) the presence of differences in the quality or quantity of some of the symptoms constituting the disease? The latter option gave rise to what was called 'pathognomonic' symptoms, that is, symptom-presentations whose specific features signified only one diagnosis.[32] But if 'pathognomy' was a clinical reality then: (1) some mental symptoms had to be considered as semantically more important, that is, as *primus inter pares*; and (2) the idea that all mental symptoms had the same analytical value had to be abandoned.

Once the concept of mental symptom had become available, madness itself and its varieties (later called mental diseases, conditions, disorders, illnesses) were redefined as 'clusters' thereof. This in turn gave rise to the problem of having to give an account of the nature of the 'glue' that kept the symptoms together (neurobiological, genetic, statistical, social, symbolic, cultural, etc.). This issue has not yet been resolved. It seems clear that current neuroscientific accounts of schizophrenia, bipolar disorder, obsessive compulsive disorder, and so on do not provide separate explanations for *each* of the symptoms constituting the cluster. One or two are chosen as representative and most of the research effort goes into explaining them; the presence of all others is left unexplained. In other words, for all its predominance, neuroscience has not yet provided a general theory for each mental disease which, starting with its genetics, would then provide accounts for each of the mental symptoms present in the manifold.

Descriptive Psychopathology

Crucial to the professionalization of alienism was the construction of a proprietary language for the description/construction/capture of mental symptoms. This process took place during the first half of the nineteenth century and gave rise to what is now called descriptive psychopathology (DP).[33]

The relationship between DP and madness can be conceived in two ways. One is to consider DP as merely carving madness at its joints and then capturing in neutral words (one of the meanings of 'description') the resulting components (mental symptoms), thereby offering a 'theory-free' picture of madness. Another approach is to consider these stages as being theory-bound because it cannot be claimed that madness has joints to carve and because words, rather than capturing mental symptoms, actually construct them.

In other words, a theory is needed to break up madness in a particular way, and another to construct the mental symptom (prefer certain features to others, etc.).

One of the issues in play here concerns the meaning of 'description'. Started in classical Greece as a metaphorical conceptualization of the amanuensis (ὑπογρᾰφεύς)[34] who is expected to write down exactly what she is dictated, it was translated into the Latin *Descriptio*, which meant write down, transcribe, trace, draw, represent, and prescribe (in the sense of establishing laws).[35] The dimension of metaphysical creativity[36] built into these last two meanings was replaced during the early twentieth century by a 'logical' definition according to which description was a 'theory-free copy'.[37] Whether DP describes in this new logical sense or in the earlier metaphysical (constructive) sense needs to be determined, as all neuroscientific research is based upon it. Given the fact that the objects of psychiatry can be defined as ideal, virtual, and conceptual (rather than as natural kinds), it is unlikely that DP can but contribute to their construction.[38]

The construction of DP was also attended by social and conceptual factors. Driven by philanthropic ideas and in response to scandals affecting the treatment of the insane,[39] early in the nineteenth century a programme for the building of mental asylums was started in various European countries, and as part of this process medical doctors found themselves working in the new mental institutions.[40] Although their primary duty was to look after the physical health of the inmates, to comply with hospital regulations their case notes needed to include comments on mental state. This created the need for a semiology of madness (or DP).

Asylums allowed for the accumulation of patients with similar complaints and this made possible their classification based both on cross-sectional and on longitudinal observation. The latter offered clear evidence that patients got better and this forced a review of the old metaphysical definition of madness. One such change concerned its temporalization, that is, the view that madness needed to be replaced in a 'time' dimension.[41] This in turn allowed for (1) the differentiation between 'acute' and 'chronic' madness, and (2) the uncovering of relationships between mental disorders and infancy, adulthood, and old age.[42]

Like medicine, psychiatry also needed criteria to differentiate the normal from the abnormal. By the 1850s, medicine had developed 'objective' signs and biological markers to do so. Alienists did not have such help, although for most of the nineteenth century some physical signs (fever, pain, tolerance to cold, changes in bowel habit, etc.) were considered to be part of some forms of madness. This led alienists to resort to criteria borrowed from the social sciences and their definition of mental 'abnormality' was based on social deviance (i.e. deviation from what at the time was considered proper, ethical, and socially acceptable). Mad behaviour was primarily demarcated by social criteria and only secondarily by speculative neuroscientific claims as to what was wrong with the patient's brain. This means that DP was from the start based on a hybrid conceptual platform in which the 'descriptions' already carried some clear claims of social deviance (which is a social, not a biological marker). In a way, this has continued to our own day as psychiatry remains bereft of strong biological markers.[43] Neither in the nineteenth century nor since has the diagnosis of madness been based on brain-related criteria alone.

Alienism Becomes a Profession

Each European country professionalized alienism at a different pace and with different resources. By the second half of the nineteenth century, England, Germany, France, Italy, and several other countries had founded professional societies and journals and started training procedures for alienists. In spite of the bellic interruptions, exchanges between nations continued to the point where, by the 1890s, textbooks and classifications in the main European countries carried similar information.

To discharge their duties, alienists (or mad-doctors, as they were called) needed to create for themselves a physical, social, and legal space. It is not surprising then that after the 1820s they participated in all national debates relating to lunacy legislation and the housing and management of the insane.[44] In the asylums themselves, social hierarchies were also established with doctors at the top, followed by keepers (later called mental nurses) and supporting staff, and then inmates at the bottom.[45] Likewise, functional dichotomies were proposed to facilitate patient control: public versus private, male versus female, agitated versus quiet, acute versus chronic, rational versus irrational, continent versus incontinent, epileptic versus non-epileptic, organic versus functional, criminal versus non-criminal, and so on. These categories later influenced asylum architecture.[46] Asylum building was often governed by financial convenience. For example, English counties shared costs by building asylums on territorial boundaries, and, regardless of the local weather, asylums in the colonies were often built on plans used in the metropolises.[47] Fashion was occasionally influential and at least two asylums[48] followed the ideology of Bentham's panopticon.[49]

By accumulating ever-growing cohorts of chronic patients and making possible regular post-mortem examinations,[50] asylums brought about a minor epistemological revolution. This, given the type of neurological patient that was often collected, strengthened the organic theory of madness.[51]

Alienists plied their trade in a complex social and political context and had to use local resources. For example, in Roman Catholic countries, general hospitals and mental asylums were run by religious congregations.[52] Frictions developed when (as happened in France) the alienist in charge was not religious and objected to practices such as regular prayer, overly modest clothing, and other religious duties. Similar frictions developed in the interface between psychiatry and the law. Insanity and dementia were traditional legal categories and lawyers used simple tests for them.[53] Alienists had a less black and white view of such disorders and on occasions this caused major disagreement.[54]

The Fragmentation of Madness

The nineteenth century had inherited Cullen's claim that from an aetiological viewpoint the *vesaniæ* (insanities) were a form of neuroses, that is, 'disorders of the sense and movement of the nervous system without fever or focal lesion'.[55] In other words, madness was just another bodily disease. Cullen's views influenced the French concepts of madness. They also provided the criterion on the basis of which neurology (as a new specialism) started to be constructed after the 1850s by collecting 'neuroses' in which focal brain lesions had been found (e.g. Parkinson's disease, multiple sclerosis, etc.).[56] This erosion of the originally large class of Cullean neuroses continued until the end of the nineteenth century, by which time it contained only the insanities, hypochondriasis, hysteria, anxiety disorders, obsessional-compulsive disease, neurotic depressions, and Raynaud's phenomenon. Soon enough the insanities were reconceptualized as 'psychoses'[57] and removed from the group. Only the remaining conditions continued to be called 'neuroses' but were reconceived as functional diseases, the expression of 'nervous irritation'.[58] Soon enough Freud was to offer yet another explanation, to wit, that the remaining neuroses were symbolic expressions of a psychological conflict.[59]

The old concept of madness (insanity, lunacy, alienation, distraction, vesania, etc.) became 'psychosis' during the nineteenth century. Already in use by the 1800s to name the subjective component of an experience, the word psychosis this time was used to name a cluster of complaints that included hallucinations, delusions, mental confusion, irrationality, thought disorder, and so on.[60] By the second half of the nineteenth century, clinical dichotomies were used to classify the psychoses: functional versus organic, endogenous versus exogenous, and acute versus chronic.

Organic psychoses were used to label those seen in the wake of physical disease (infection, brain tumour, stroke, drug-induced state, alcoholism, neurosyphilis, etc.) and functional psychoses (schizophrenia, mania, melancholia, etc.) named states in which no clear brain aetiology could be identified.[61] On the basis of theory rather than fact, it is nowadays claimed that all psychoses are 'organic' and hence the concept of 'functional psychosis' has been dropped.

During the late nineteenth century, the dichotomy 'endogenous–exogenous' was introduced to refer to psychoses whose aetiology was related to genes, degeneration of the seed and immanent causes in general (e.g. schizophrenia or melancholia), or external causes (syphilis, trauma, etc.) respectively. Once again, the theoretical view that all psychoses must have a genetic basis has led to a reordering of traditional causal factors and the claim that, since all psychoses are 'endogenous', the dichotomy has become irrelevant.

Lastly, and following the introduction of time as a dimension of madness, acute and chronic psychosis started to be differentiated.[62] The adjectives acute and chronic (as applied to disease) are very old but had a different meaning. Up to the end of the eighteenth century, acute referred to a disease of rapid onset and great severity that followed a typical dichotomous path: it either led to death or was followed by a period of crisis and then remission. Chronic meant more or less the opposite. The descriptions of 'acute' and 'chronic' thus referred to characteristic and intrinsic features of different diseases and these two classes did not mix. The current view that a badly treated acute disease could then become chronic was not available at the time. For example, madness belonged to the group of chronic diseases. By the middle of the nineteenth century, 'acute' no longer referred to severity but mainly to short duration, whilst 'chronic' meant the opposite.

Psychiatry after 1900

Challenges and Tributaries

The nineteenth century witnessed the professionalization of psychiatry, the appearance of the alienist (psychiatrist) as an expert in mental disorders, and the introduction of the view that madness: (1) was a natural kind sited in the brain; (2) existed as an object within a temporal-spatial framework; (3) could be classified according to clinical features or aetiology;[63] and (4) resulted from brain factors which could be modulated by external ones.[64]

This narrow view of madness soon clashed with the cultural changes developing in Europe towards the end of the nineteenth century. In addition to the long shadow cast by Hegel, there was the work of Bradley, Lotze, Nietzsche, Dilthey, and the renaissance of the Kantian view that reality (the noumenon) was unknowable and that phenomena (all that man could perceive) resulted from the application to reality of mental categories themselves susceptible to historical change. These historicist and interpretative views of reality called into question the simplistic view that madness was just the expression of brain sites in distress,[65] and propitiated the development of new narratives. Jackson's multilayered model of neuropsychiatric disease[66] was taken up in France by Janet, Ribot, and Dumas[67] and in Austria by Freud and followers, giving rise to a new hermeneutic understanding of madness. In addition to these major challenges, psychiatry had to face new ones such as clinical phenomenology[68] and anti-psychiatry.

Hermeneutics and Psychiatry

Freudian ideas posed an important challenge to conventional psychiatry. Although Freud did accept the medical linear causal model and equivocated in regard to the aetiological relevance of the brain to madness, he offered an original view on the meaning of the symptom itself. Until his time, the simple sign-signifier function of the symptom had remained predominant, that is, the experiential content of the mental symptom was an adequate reflection of the anatomy and physiology of the distressed neural substratum. As against this, Freud proposed that: (1) both the symptom and its content were symbolic and unrelated to their conventional function and surface meaning; (2) special codes and rules were needed for their understanding; (3) such rules could be worked out from a close reading of the history and context of the sufferer; and (4) the decoding process was the beginning of treatment. Although later members of the psychoanalytical movement disagreed on some of the above points, the fact remains that the dynamic model itself seriously addresses the complexity of madness, perhaps more so than earlier or later mechanistic neuroscientific narratives. Countries and their psychiatric culture responded differently to psychoanalysis. In some countries (e.g. the USA), it became for a time the predominant approach both in public and in private psychiatry; in others, like most European countries, psychoanalysis was received with great enthusiasm but only partially incorporated into their clinical practice. In spite of the predominance of the neurobiological accounts of madness, most clinicians have always believed that madness is sited in a psychological and cultural space and hence its successful management requires a modicum of interpretation.

Phenomenology

The phenomenologies are a family of philosophies issuing out of the work of Brentano and Husserl. Developed during a time when psychiatry was already under pressure from psychoanalysis, the phenomenologies presented themselves as a new challenge. Offering a new way of conceiving the ontology and the epistemology of both sufferers and their sufferings, they soon entered into a conceptual coalition with psychoanalysis.[69] In regards to clinical psychiatry itself, it remains unclear whether the phenomenologies have had any lasting effect on it. Since early in the nineteenth century, descriptive psychopathology was adequate enough to satisfy the descriptive needs of clinicians as attested by the work of Emminghaus, Morselli, Störring, Chaslin, Séglas, and so on. Although not a phenomenologist,[70] Dilthey[71] also developed an interesting form of descriptive psychology which some have found useful to psychiatry. The claim that Jaspers achieved a perfect marriage between psychiatry and phenomenology needs further confirmation. Of late, some writers have suggested that by introducing interesting middle-level concepts such as temporality, self, embodiment, and so on, phenomenology has been able to bridge the space that has always existed between the conventional level of clinical description and the new brain narratives.[72]

Anti-psychiatry

'Anti-psychiatry' names heterogeneous views on the meaning and contents of 'psychiatry' as developed in the West after the 1950s by writers such as Basaglia, Szasz, Lidz, Goffman, Laing, Deleuze, Guattari, Foudraine, Breggin, Antonucci, Cooper, Scheff, and Esterson, and by the Scientology movement. Their critique was addressed to: (1) the existence and meaning of the discipline in toto; (2) its objects (mental symptoms and diseases);[73] or (3) its treatments and management routines. Libertarian, spiritualist, existentialist, psychodynamic, religious, and ethical views combined formed the philosophical basis for anti-psychiatry.

Anti-psychiatry held a mirror to psychiatry and its practices, and psychiatrists found that their limited conceptual repertoire did not equip them to deal with accusations that psychiatry was a pseudoscience, 'mental illness' a myth, diagnostic labelling meaningless, illegal and offensive, and mental hospitals total institutions based on moral coercion and violation of individuality.[74] It was also claimed that the experience of madness was a path to self-fulfilment and realization and that biological treatments were brutish, misguided, and coercive.[75] All these criticisms were partially right for, in its desperation to become a 'science', psychiatry had neglected to develop a solid epistemological justification for its own existence and missed out on the obvious fact that it is a hybrid discipline[76] straddling the natural and social sciences.

The Present

The first two decades of the twenty-first century have added next to nothing to the epistemological and nosological and nosographic routines of psychiatry as these were put gradually together during the last two centuries. The neuroscientific narrative still predominates, and the reigning 'classification' is one offered by the American Psychiatric Association via the latest version of its Diagnostic and Statistical Manual of Mental Disorders (DSM-5). Efforts are also being made to harmonize the next version of the classification of mental disorders embedded in the eleventh revision of the International Classification of Diseases (ICD-11) with DSM-5.[77]

Efforts to justify the current neuroscientific narrative of psychiatry have not worked. The predominant 'centripetal' approach makes use of off-the-shelf philosophical views and techniques, such as analytical philosophy, that are alien to psychiatry.[78] This neglects the fact that psychiatry is essentially a historical discipline and instead of auditing the 'findings' of neuroscience it justifies them.[79] Unlike the 'centripetal' approach, the 'centrifugal' approach proposes the construction of a proprietary epistemology based on (1) analysis of the internal problems of psychiatry and (2) its essential historicity.[80] According to this approach, the main function of such regional epistemology ought to be the uncompromising auditing of all the narratives of psychiatry.[81]

Conclusions

The medicalization of madness and the construction of psychiatry as a profession are contingent historical events resulting from the *sui generis* convergence of some social, economic, and political factors. This means that the outcome could have been different. Now, had psychiatry and psychiatrists not come to pass, madness (or mental complaints) would still be around as an important cause of human suffering and society would have needed to find alternative (and probably equally successful) ways to manage it. The point here is that these alternative ways would appear to us to be just as 'natural and true' as the medical approach we privilege now.

It would be reassuring to believe that the arrival of the medical view had some sort of historical inevitability, for it can be no other than the logical culmination of scientific progress. As against this historical determinism, however, it would be more prudent to believe that the medical solution was the best that society could afford at the beginning of the nineteenth century, and leave it there as a contingent fact. For one, it would do away with the questionable belief that its monopoly on madness is based on some eternal scientific truth. It would be far wiser for psychiatry not to rest on its laurels but regularly to endeavour to show that what it does for its patients is therapeutically and ethically superior to what any other approach could do. Psychiatrists must remember that this great privilege has been historically granted and can be easily withdrawn.

Notes

1. American Psychiatric Association 2024. What is psychiatry? www.psychiatry.org/patients-families/what-is-psychiatry.
2. Freidson, E. 1986. *Professional Powers: A Study of the Institutionalization of Formal Knowledge.* Chicago, IL: University of Chicago Press.
3. Some historians have argued that because medics have always shown an interest in madness, 'psychiatry' has always existed. See Ey, H. 1954/2006. La position de la psychiatrie dans le cadre des sciences médicales. In Ey, H., *Études Psychiatriques*, vol. I. Perpignan: Crehey, pp. 67–82 (originally published Paris: Desclée de Brouwer).
4. Marneros, A. & Pillmann, F. 2005. *Das Wort Psychiatrie wurde in Halle geboren.* Stuttgart: Schattauer; Marková, I. S. 2023. What is psychiatry? *History of Psychiatry*, https://doi.org/10.1177/0957154X231197525.
5. Comte's views on the alienism and psychology of his day were negative. He believed that psychology needed to become neurophysiology – see Bodenhafer, W. B. 1923. Comte and psychology. *Papers and Proceedings of the American Sociological Society*, 17, 15–26. He also believed that alienism needed to be 'regenerated'. Interestingly enough, he used the concept of *folie* (madness) as an illustration of his law of the three stages. See Braunstein, J. F. 2008. Auguste Comte et la psychiatrie. In Missa, J. N. (ed.), *Les Maladies Mentales.* Les Cahiers du Centre Georges Canguilhem, no. 2. Paris: Presses Universitaires de France, pp. 259–282. On Comte's law of the three stages of progress, see Hobhouse, L. T. 1908. The law of the three stages. *Sociological Review*, A1, 262–279.
6. Indeed, criteria to differentiate between 'demoniacal possession' and madness have been available from the start in most religions: Preuss, J. 1923. *Biblisch-talmudische Medizin*, 3rd ed. Berlin: Karger; Dols, M. W. 1992. *Majnūn: The Madman in Medieval Islamic Society.* Oxford: Clarendon Press; Johnson, C. V. & Friedman, H. L. 2008. Enlightened or delusional? Differentiating religious, spiritual, and transpersonal experiences from psychopathology. *Journal of Humanistic Psychology*, 48, 505–527.
7. Dijker, A. J. M. 2007. *Stigmatization, Tolerance and Repair: An Integrative Psychological Analysis of Responses to Deviance.* Cambridge: Cambridge University Press; Overton, S. L. 2008. The stigma of mental illness. *Journal of Counseling and Development*, 86, 143–151.
8. Willis, T. 1684. *The Practice of Physick.* London: Dring, Harper and Leigh.
9. Charland, L. C. 2014. John Locke on madness. *History of Psychiatry*, 25, 137–153.
10. MacDonald, M. 1981. *Mystical Bedlam.* Cambridge: Cambridge University Press.
11. Hodgkin, K. 2007. *Madness in Seventeenth-Century Autobiography.* Basingstoke: Palgrave Macmillan; Ingram, A. & Faubert, M. 2005. *Cultural Constructions of Madness in 18th Century Writings: Representing the Insane.* Basingstoke: Palgrave Macmillan.
12. Temkin, O. 1973. *Galenism.* Ithaca, NY: Cornell University Press; Johnston, I. 2006. *Galen on Diseases and Symptoms.* Cambridge: Cambridge University Press.
13. Berrios, G. E. 2012. The 19th century nosology of alienism: History and epistemology. In Kendler, K. S. & Parnas, J. (eds.), *Philosophical Issues in Psychiatry, vol. II.* Oxford: Oxford University Press, pp. 101–123;

Berrios, G. E. 2014. Defining and classifying mental illness. In Bloch, S., Green, S. A. & Holmes, J. (eds.), *Psychiatry: Past, Present and Prospect*. Oxford: Oxford University Press, pp. 180–195.

14. Dewhurst, K. 1966. *Dr Thomas Sydenham (1624–1689): His Life and Original Writings*. Berkeley: University of California Press.
15. López Piñero, J. M. 1983. *Historical Origins of the Concept of Neurosis*. Cambridge: Cambridge University Press.
16. Linné, C. 1763. *Genera Morborum*. Upsala: C. E. Steinert, pp. 12–13.
17. Boissier de Sauvages, F. 1772. *Nosologie Méthodique*, vol. 7. Lyon: J. M. Bruyset, pp. 1–44.
18. Larson, J. L. 1971. *Reason and Experience: The Representation of Natural Order in the Work of Carl von Linné*. Berkeley: University of California Press.
19. Adanson, M. 1763. *Familles des Plantes: Parts I and II*. Paris: Chez Vicent.
20. Berrios, G. E. 1999. Classification in psychiatry: A conceptual history. *Australian and New Zealand Journal of Psychiatry*, 33, 145–160; Sneath, P. H. A. & Sokal, R. R. 1973. *Numerical Taxonomy: The Principles and Practice of Numerical Classification*. San Francisco, CA: W. H. Freeman; Webb, A. R. 2002. *Statistical Pattern Recognition*. London: John Wiley.
21. Dijksterhuis, E. J. 1969. *Mechanization of the World Picture*. Oxford: Oxford University Press.
22. De Villargues, R. 1829. *Jurisprudence du Notariat*. Paris: Bureau de la Jurisprudence du Notariat, Decourchant; Haslam, J. 1809. *Observations on Madness and Melancholy*. London: J. Callow.
23. Willis, T. 1684. *The Practice of Physick*. London: Dring, Harper and Leigh.
24. Reisch, G. 1523. *Margarita Philosophica*. Basel: Sebastian Henric Petri.
25. Berrios, G. E. 2015. David Hartley's views on madness. *History of Psychiatry*, 26, 105–116.
26. Ibid.
27. Griesinger, W. 1871. *Pathologie und Therapie der psychischen Krankheiten*, 3rd ed. Braunschweig: F. Wreden.
28. Double, F. J. 1811. *Séméïologie générale ou traité des signes et de leur valeur dans les maladies*, 2 vols. Paris: Croullebois.
29. Landré-Beauvais, A. J. 1818. *Séméiotique ou traité des signes des maladies*, 3rd ed. Paris: Brosson.
30. Warren, H. C. 1921. *A History of Association Psychology*. New York: Scribner and Sons; Oberg, B. B. 1976. David Hartley and the association of ideas. *Journal of the History of Ideas*, 37, 441–454; Claparède, É. 1903. *L'association des idées*. Paris: Doin.
31. Aarsleff, H. 1983. *The Study of Language in England 1780–1860*. Minneapolis: University of Minnesota Press; Underhill, J. W. 2009. *Humboldt, Worldview and Language*. Edinburgh: Edinburgh University Press; Formigari, L. 2004. *A History of Language Philosophies*. Amsterdam: John Benjamin; Dégerando, J. M. 1799. *Des signes et de l'art de penser*, 4 vols. Paris: Goujon Fils.
32. An old word, 'pathognomonic' has since its inception been used to refer to 'a sign or symptom by which a disease may be known or distinguished; specifically characteristic or indicative of a particular disease' (*Oxford English Dictionary*, 1992).
33. Berrios, G. E. 1996. *The History of Mental Symptoms*. Cambridge: Cambridge University Press.
34. Liddell, H. G. & Scott, R. 1996. *Greek-English Lexicon*. Oxford: Clarendon Press, p. 1877.
35. Glare, P. G. W. 1968. *Oxford Latin Dictionary*. Oxford: Clarendon Press, p. 524.
36. Nobis, H. M. 1971. Beschreibung. In Ritter, J. (ed.), *Historisches Wörterbuch der Philosophie*, vol. 1. Darmstadt: Wissenschaftliche Buchgesellschaft, pp. 838–842.
37. Kaulbach, F. 1971. Beschreibung. In Ritter, J. (ed.), *Historisches Wörterbuch der Philosophie*, vol 1. Darmstadt: Wissenschaftliche Buchgesellschaft, pp. 842–846.
38. Berrios, G. E. 2011. Psychiatry and its objects. *Revista de Psiquiatria y Salud Mental*, 4, 179–182.

39. Parry-Jones, W. 1972. *The Trade in Lunacy: A Study of Private Madhouses in England in the Eighteenth and Nineteenth Centuries.* London: Routledge and Keegan Paul.

40. Jones, K. 1955. *Lunacy, Law and Conscience.* London: Routledge and Keegan Paul.

41. Berrios, G. E. & Marková, I. S. 2016. The temporalization of madness in the 19th century. *Rivista Sperimentale di Freniatria,* 140, 13–27.

42. Kahlbaum, K. 1863. *Die Gruppirung der psychischen Krankheiten und die Eintheilung der Seelenstörungen.* Danzig: A. W. Kafemann; translation by Berrios, G. E. 1996. The classification of mental disorders . . . Part III. *History of Psychiatry,* 7, 167–181.

43. Berrios, G. E. & Marková, I. S. 2015. Towards a new epistemology of psychiatry. In Kirmayer, L. J., Lemelson, R. & Cummings, C. A. (eds.), *Re-visioning Psychiatry.* Cambridge: Cambridge University Press, pp. 41–64.

44. Smith, L. D. 1999. *Cure, Comfort and Safe Custody: Public Lunatic Asylums in Early 19th Century England.* Leicester: Leicester University Press; Scull, A. T. 1979. *Museums of Madness: Social Organization of Insanity in 19th Century England.* London: Viking.

45. Bartlett, P. 1999. *The Poor Law of Lunacy: The Administration of Pauper Lunatics in Mid-Nineteenth-Century England.* London: Leicester University Press.

46. Piddock, S. 2007. *A Space of Their Own: The Archaeology of 19th Century Lunatic Asylums in Britain, South Australia, and Tasmania.* Heidelberg: Springer.

47. Swartz, S. 2010. The regulation of British colonial lunatic asylums and the origins of colonial psychiatry, 1860–1864. *History of Psychology,* 13(2), 160–177.

48. West Riding Pauper Lunatic Asylum (1818) and Middlesex County Asylum/Hanwell Asylum (1831) – see http://thetimechamber.co.uk/beta/sites/asylums/asylum-history/the-asylums-list.

49. Semple, J. 1993. *Bentham's Prison: A Study of the Panopticon Penitentiary.* Oxford: Clarendon Press.

50. Andrews, J. 2012. Death and the dead-house in Victorian asylums: Necroscopy versus mourning at the Royal Edinburgh Asylum, c. 1832–1901. *History of Psychiatry,* 23, 6–26.

51. Berrios, G. E. & Freeman, H. (eds.) 1991. *150 Years of British Psychiatry 1841–1991.* London: Gaskell.

52. Walsh, J. J. 1910. Asylums and care for the insane [listed under 'Insane, Asylums and care for the']. In Herbermann, C. G., Pace, E. A., Pallen, C. B., Shahan, T. J. & Wynne, J. J. (eds.), *The Catholic Encyclopedia,* vol. 8. New York: Robert Appleton Company, pp. 38–41. https://archive.org/details/07470918.8.emory.edu/page/n3/mode/2up.

53. Walker, N. 1968. *Crime and Insanity in England, Vol 1: Historical Perspective.* Edinburgh: Edinburgh University Press.

54. Smith, R. 1984. *Trial by Medicine: Insanity and Responsibility in Victorian Trials.* Edinburgh: Edinburgh University Press.

55. '*Sensus et motus laesi, sine pyrexia idiopathica, et sine morbo locali*', Cullen, W. 1785. *Synopsis Nosologiæ Methodicæ,* vol. 2, 4th ed. Edinburgh: W. Creech, p. 182.

56. López Piñero, J. M. & Morales Meseguer, J. M. 1970. *Neurosis y Psicoterapia: Un estudio histórico.* Madrid: Espasa-Calpe.

57. Flemming, C. F. 1859. *Pathologie und Therapie der Psychosen.* Berlin: A Hirschwald.

58. Leven, M. 1887. *La Névrose: Étude Clinique et Thérapeutique.* Paris: Masson; Axenfeld, A. 1883. *Traité des Névroses.* Paris: Baillière.

59. López Piñero & Morales Meseguer, Neurosis y Psicoterapia.

60. Berrios, G. E. 1987. Historical aspects of the psychoses: 19th century issues. *British Medical Bulletin,* 43, 484–498.

61. Ibid.

62. Lanteri-Laura, G. 1972. La chronicité dans la psychiatrie moderne Française. *Annales,* 3, 548–568.

63. Berrios, G. E. 2008. Baillarger's 'Essay on a classification of different genera of insanity'. *History of Psychiatry*, 19, 358–373.

64. Berrios, G. E. 2000. Historical development of ideas about psychiatric aetiology. In Gelder, M. G., López-Ibor, J. J. & Andreasen, N. (eds.), *New Oxford Textbook of Psychiatry*. Oxford: Oxford University Press, pp. 147–153.

65. Berrios, G. E. & Marková, I. S. 2002. The concept of neuropsychiatry: A historical overview. *Journal of Psychosomatic Research*, 53, 629–638.

66. Berrios, G. E. 2001. Jackson's 'The factors of insanities'. *History of Psychiatry*, 12, 353–373.

67. Berrios, G. E. 1988. Historical background to abnormal psychology. In Miller, E. & Cooper, P. J. (eds.), *Adult Abnormal Psychology*. Edinburgh: Churchill and Livingstone, pp. 26–51.

68. Halling, S. & Nill, J. D. 1995. A brief history of existential-phenomenological psychiatry and psychotherapy. *Journal of Phenomenological Psychology*, 26, 1–45.

69. Ibid.

70. Makkreel, R. A. & Scanlon, J. 1987. *Dilthey and Phenomenology*. Washington, DC: University Press of America.

71. Dilthey, W. 1977. *Descriptive Psychology and Historical Understanding*. The Hague: Nijhoff; Caparrós, A. H. 1986. *Ebbinghaus: Un funcionalista investigador tipo dominio*. Barcelona: Publicacions Universitat de Barcelona.

72. Fuchs, T. 2010. Phenomenology and psychopathology. In Gallagher, S. & Schmicking, D. (eds.), *Handbook of Phenomenology and Cognitive Science*. Berlin: Springer, pp. 547–573.

73. Berrios, Psychiatry and its objects.

74. Szasz, T. 2009. *Antipsychiatry: Quackery Squared*. New York: Syracuse University Press; Kotowicz, Z. 1997. *R D Laing and the Paths of Antipsychiatry*. London: Routledge; Hochmann, J. 2015. *Les Antipsychiatries: Une histoire*. Paris: Jacob; Tantam, D. 1991. The anti-psychiatry movement. In Berrios, G. E. & Freeman, H. (eds.), *150 Years of British Psychiatry 1841–1991*. London: Gaskell, pp. 333–347.

75. Berrios, G. E. 2008. The history of psychiatric therapies. In Tyrer, P. & Silk, R. (eds.), *Cambridge Textbook of Effective Treatments in Psychiatry*. Cambridge: Cambridge University Press, pp. 16–43.

76. Marková, I. S. & Berrios, G. E. 2012. The epistemology of psychiatry. *Psychopathology*, 45, 220–227; Marková, I. S. & Chen, E. 2020. The hybrid structure of psychiatry. *Dialogues in Philosophy, Mental and Neuro Sciences*, 13(2), 36–42.

77. First, M. B. 2009. Harmonisation of ICD-11 and DSM-5. *British Journal of Psychiatry*, 195, 382–390; Jablensky, A. 2009. Towards ICD 11 and DSM 5: Issues beyond harmonisation. *British Journal of Psychiatry*, 195, 379–381.

78. See, e.g., Fulford, K. W. M., Thornton, T. & Graham, G. 2006. *Oxford Textbook of Philosophy and Psychiatry*. Oxford: Oxford University Press.

79. Beaney, M. 2013. *The Oxford Handbook of the History of Analytic Philosophy*. Oxford: Oxford University Press; Bennett, M., Dennett, D., Hacker, P. & Searle, J. 2003. *Neuroscience and Philosophy*. New York: Columbia University Press; Rorty, R., Schneewind, J. B. & Skinner, Q. (eds.) 1984. *Philosophy in History*. Cambridge: Cambridge University Press.

80. Berrios, G. E. 2006. 'Mind in General' by Sir Alexander Crichton. *History of Psychiatry*, 17, 469–497.

81. Hundert, E. M. 1989. *Philosophy, Psychiatry and Neuroscience*. Oxford: Clarendon Press; Natanson, M. (ed.) 1969. *Psychiatry and Philosophy*. Berlin: Springer; Palem, R. M. 1997. *Henri Ey: Psychiatrie et Philosophie*. Paris: Rive Droite; Berrios, G. E. & Marková, I. S. 2002. Biological psychiatry: Conceptual issues. In D'Haenen, H., den Boer, J. A. & Willner, P. (eds.), *Biological Psychiatry*. New York: John Wiley, pp. 3–24; Blanc, C. J. 1998. *Psychiatrie et Penseé Philosophique*. Paris: L'Harmattan.

Chapter 2

A History of Psychology
Values and Person-Centredness

Robert B. Dudas

Introduction

The level of organization with most relevance to the clinician is that of the person. Therefore, the most relevant psychological insights for clinicians come from research that is carried out at the person level or the findings of which can be related to the person in a meaningful and reliable way. However, over its history the interests of psychology have varied and research at the person level has often been neglected. In her 1971 paper titled 'Where is the person in personality research?', Rae Carlson (1971) pointed out a number of important consequences of academic psychology 'adopting the research values of "process psychology"' and relegating the psychology of 'person' to psychiatry, psychotherapy, and literature. Unfortunately, her observation is still relevant today (Fisher et al., 2018; Molenaar, 2004). Carlson felt that personality researchers would be best suited to studying the complexity and the individuality of life but that research the way it was done was incapable of discovering much about these owing to the methodological choices being inappropriate. She found that 'not a single published study attempted even minimal inquiry into the organization of personality variables within the individual' over a year (Carlson, 1971, p. 209). Carlson's verdict was that the goal of studying the whole person had been abandoned. Psychology over the years had been borrowing increasingly from mathematics and physics but would, in her view, have done well to borrow more from anthropology. From a clinical perspective, these were serious concerns because they called into question the usefulness of much ongoing psychology research for clinical psychiatry.

In order to explain mental symptoms, the psychiatrist will seek correlation between the symptom and certain entities, such as a neurobiological variable, or concepts, such as a psychological variable. Therefore, we cannot fully understand the history and the main tenets of psychiatry without understanding the development of its parallel discipline: psychology. Psychology as a discipline was born at a time when there was growing interest in the person and his or her inner experience. Because, for clinicians, the person is at the centre, in this chapter I will explore the history of psychology using the concept of person-centredness and chart the importance of person-centredness in four main schools of thought in psychology: psychoanalysis, behaviourism, cognitive psychology, and humanistic psychology. The way these orientations approached the person (their 'research subject') depended on what they considered 'the proper object of psychological knowledge' (Danziger, [1990] 1994, p. 69). Importantly, this had major consequences for what attributes they were able to notice about them. Psychoanalysis and behaviourism will be of particular interest because they represent the two opposing ends on the spectrum of person-centredness and in terms of epistemological approach. Psychoanalysis, which had an idiographic descriptive approach, saw the person as an individual in their relational context and tailored its methodology accordingly, whilst behaviourism applied an experimental approach and was most of the time too reductionistic to see individuals as persons, or at best saw them as a sum of predictable laws. Cognitive psychology and humanistic psychology are the two schools that feed into today's clinical practice the most. They both tried to address the limitations of behaviourism by putting the mind back into psychology: cognitive psychology by allowing for mental processes and humanistic psychology for the strivings of the individual. What also gives relevance to humanistic psychology here is that person-centredness was considered to be its essence.

To formulate my questions and guide my exploration, I will use the concept of person-centred care, which is one of the ten pointers to good practice in values-based practice (VBP; Woodbridge-Dodd, 2012). Person-centred care includes regarding the patient as a whole person (body, mind, and spirit); using a compassionate clinical approach, based on both values and evidence; and involving the patient in their care and sharing responsibility and decision-making with them and others involved in their life. Importantly, person-centred care uses a model of the person that draws on not just neuroscience but also the social sciences and the humanities, and considers the impact of culture, religion, and social systems (Royal College of Psychiatrists, 2022).

From this perspective, it can be revealing to look at the following:

1. What were the epistemological priorities of these schools of thought in terms of the position of psychology in relation to the natural and social sciences and the humanities?
2. Where was the person in them?
3. How much agency did they afford the person? How much control were individuals believed to have over their own experiences, behaviour, decisions, mental life, or mental illness?
4. In psychotherapy, which is the practical application of these theoretical orientations, how much control or self-determination did the various modalities allow for the patient and, in a different but related way, the therapist? In other words, how much of an active role did they allow the patient and the therapist to meet the patient's needs, that is, to solve the patient's problems and help them make changes in their lives?

It would, of course, be inappropriate to compare past practices to our current standards, but it is illuminating to trace how elements of our current views evolved over time or, to put it differently, and not necessarily assuming relationship or continuity, how certain values appeared, disappeared, or reappeared over time.

To help with this, important criticisms will also be discussed, as they often lay bare the values of the stakeholders. What survived into current theory and practice as the legacy of these main psychological approaches will reveal the value choices of subsequent generations of academics and clinicians.

The Person at the Birth of Psychology: Introspection and the Humanities

Similar to psychiatry, psychology as we understand it today really began to develop from the nineteenth century. During this period, consensus has been reached among psychologists as to what phenomena they consider to belong to their remit and what methodology is accepted to be used to study these.

Certain important developments paved the way for this. The neurobiological variables that are causally relevant to psychiatry are more likely to be found at the behavioural rather than the molecular or the tissue level (Dudas, 2020) and there is a relatively long tradition of *measuring mental phenomena* at the behavioural level dating back to the eighteenth century (Berrios, 1995). This was one of the first major steps in developing a psychological understanding of the mind and mental illness.

Another crucial epistemological advance was that developments in psychological theory made possible the study of inner experience and the content of consciousness using *introspection* (Berrios, 1995). What had facilitated this was the development of the language of the self during the Enlightenment period. Attention in the humanities turned to related subjects, providing an important conceptual basis and methodological tools for the natural sciences. In literature and philosophy, the subject of one's inner experience became the focus of intense study, including in Johann Wolfgang Goethe's (2000) *The Sorrows of Young Werther*: 'Ich kehre in mich selbst zurück, und finde eine Welt! Wieder mehr in Ahnung und dunkler Begier als in Darstellung und lebendiger Kraft' ('I withdraw into myself, and I find there a world! More of a world of forebodings and shadowy desires, rather than of clear ideas and life forces' – my own translation), foreshadowing later psychological concepts, such as that of the unconscious as described by Sigmund Freud, who was well-versed in literature, including Goethe's work (Weckowicz and Liebel-Weckowicz, 1990a).

The branches of psychology most relevant to psychiatry are abnormal psychology and clinical psychology. Abnormal psychology deals with mental disorders and abnormal behaviour, whilst clinical psychology focusses on the assessment and treatment of mental illness and behavioural problems. They really began to develop, respectively, from the nineteenth century and the beginning of the twentieth century, and they used insight from the above-mentioned main schools of thought. The differentiation of these is based, to a large degree, on their specific epistemological orientations. They were not always clearly demarcated from each other in every aspect; nor were they always mutually exclusive. Their evolution was far from independent from concurrent historical developments and prevailing political ideologies.

The earliest schools of thought in psychology were structuralism and functionalism. Their key values centred on establishing psychology as a scientific discipline separate from philosophy and biology. This included adopting an experimental approach and reductionistic principles. Structuralists tried to break down every mental process into its basic components and understand the whole from its parts. They used introspection, which meant a form of rigorous and highly structured self-observation, as an experimental technique. Wilhelm Wundt (1832–1920), a major figure of structuralism, who in 1879 founded at the University of Leipzig what is regarded as the first experimental psychology laboratory, considered psychology to be an empirical science that is between the natural sciences and the humanities. Importantly from a methodological point of view, he combined experimental and statistical methods with interpretative and qualitative ones depending on the nature of the problem, which is rare even today. Functionalists focussed on the relationship between internal states and external behaviour and the purpose of consciousness and behaviour. Functionalism was influenced by Darwinism. William James (1842–1910), one of the main figures of functionalism, was the brother of writer Henry James. Like Wundt, he also studied medicine and was a philosopher and psychologist. His name is associated with the founding, at Harvard University, of one of the first psychology laboratories. Unlike structuralists, and relevant to a person-centred approach, he also took into consideration the environment and the context of behaviour. A student of James's, G. Stanley Hall (1846–1924) was the founder of the first American experimental psychology department at Johns Hopkins University and the first president of the American Psychological Association (APA). In 1909, he invited Sigmund Freud and Carl Jung to speak at Clark University, a visit which played an important role in making psychoanalysis widely known. Hall (1923) was a proponent of eugenics, a then popular but highly controversial and morally questionable movement aimed at improving the genetic quality of humanity through excluding from reproduction people judged to be inferior and promoting those judged to be superior. The fact that thirty-one presidents of the APA between 1892 (Hall's presidency) and 1947 (Carl Roger's presidency) were leaders in various eugenics organizations illustrates its acceptability among the leading minds in psychology of the era (Yakushko, 2019).

In summary, psychology was born at the intersection of the humanities, the social sciences, and the natural sciences roughly at the same time as psychiatry. The humanities and the social sciences, with their focus on the person in their social context, pull psychology upwards, whilst the natural sciences pull it downwards, on the hierarchy of levels of organization where genes are at the bottom and society or humanity is at the top. Ideally, psychology is anchored in the middle, at the level of the person, if it is to generate knowledge that is useful to psychiatry. The values of psychology kept shifting as it was trying to demarcate its boundaries from other disciplines, and this had an impact on how it approached its subject matter: human beings and their mental life in health and illness. Let us examine this from the perspective of person-centredness in two sections, first by contrasting psychoanalysis and behaviourism and then through examining cognitive and humanistic psychology.

Two Extremes of Person-Centredness: Psychoanalysis and Behaviourism

In this section, I will review two main approaches: psychoanalysis and behaviourism. These schools of thought represent two extremes. Psychoanalysis was person-centred and idiographic to such a degree that it was difficult to test its hypotheses with the prevailing methodology of medical science based primarily on natural scientific principles. On the other hand, behaviourism tried to perfect its methodology by moulding it onto natural scientific principles as much as possible, thereby making it difficult for it to capture anything subjective or person-level. My focus in this section will be on these approaches' values in terms of how they viewed human beings and the role and capabilities of psychology in relation to mental illness.

Box 2.1 Psychoanalysis

Key values of psychoanalysis:

- preference for idiographic as opposed to nomothetic description
- understanding the patient as a person with their unique life history and social relationships
- search for the meaning of symptoms and other experiences
- incorporating values and ethics into the epistemology of psychiatry.

The Context in Which Psychoanalysis Developed and the Factors in Its Spread

What gave rise to psychoanalysis? What made its tenets so popular and acceptable at the turn of the nineteenth and twentieth centuries and for several long decades afterwards? Perhaps the pendulum had swung too far in the direction of trying to understand human psychology in a reductionistic fashion, by concentrating on the level below that of the individual, and psychoanalysis was a dialectical response with a focus on the whole rather than its constituent parts. A similar objective drove the development of Gestalt psychology.

It has also been argued that psychoanalysis was a *reaction against the horrors of asylum care and* the *'somatic dogmatism'* of the nineteenth century (Millon, 2004; Weckowicz and Liebel-Weckowicz, 1990a). Psychoanalysis developed during a period when great advances were made in medicine. Leading scientists of the age were trying to understand mental illness using a neuroscientific disease model. In this model, symptoms represented an anatomical or functional defect or adaptation and compensation for this (Millon, 2004). The focus in psychoanalysis was to a large extent on the latter.

It is important to note that *psychoanalysis started in the clinic*, not in the laboratory, and I would argue that this had a major impact on its development and attitude towards the person and thereby its epistemological orientation. Sigmund Freud (1856–1939), the founder of psychoanalysis, was *influenced by two opposing traditions*: positivistic science and the 'Helmholtzian school of medicine', on the one hand, and the philosophy of Leibniz, Kant, Spinoza, and Herbart, the German Romantic tradition, the writings of Goethe, and possibly to some degree the Jewish mystical tradition, on the other (Weckowicz and Liebel-Weckowicz, 1990a). He felt that Darwinism offered hope in terms of understanding the world. The idea that an organic or *biological explanation might be found* one day for the mental phenomena delineated by psychoanalysis was present in major psychoanalytic thought from the beginning, including in Freud (Fonagy et al., 2018). This was the other major influence on the epistemological approach of psychoanalysis.

Until the second decade of the twentieth century, psychoanalysis was practised by a relatively small circle of people, mainly doctors of Jewish origin in Austria. In 1909, Sigmund Freud and Carl Jung (1875–1961) were invited to a conference cycle in the United States by Stanley Hall. By the time another decade or so had passed, to a large extent thanks to its apparent success in healing war neurosis, psychoanalysis had started what has been described as a global takeover (Innamorati, 2017). Its expansion, however, was hampered by two momentous political events, namely, the rise to power of Adolf Hitler in Germany and that of Joseph Stalin in the Soviet Union. In the so-called Eastern bloc (which was far from being a homogenous bloc in many respects, including as regards how much psychoanalysis was allowed to be practised in these countries), psychoanalysis was considered to be too 'bourgeois'; and in Russia, Ivan Pavlov (1849–1936), who described classical conditioning, had a greater influence (Innamorati, 2017).

In Western countries, in a different cultural and political environment, psychoanalysis was embraced more freely and evolved further in different ways. Erich Fromm (1900–1980) suggested the concept of 'social character', referring to personality being strongly influenced by social and historical conditions (Fromm, 1994). Karen Horney (1885–1952) described very different themes and problems in neurotic personalities in Western versus non-Western cultures (Horney, [1937] 2014). Heinz Hartmann (1894–1970) and his pupils tried to develop Freudian ideas into a general psychology, which would allow for these to become more mainstream in academic departments. In more recent times, Leo Rangell (1913–2011) continued this work.

Herzog (2016) argues that one of the most important factors in psychoanalysis becoming so popular was the acceptance of its compatibility with Christian values. Freud saw the importance of this; this was one of the reasons why he hoped that Jung would become his successor.

Why Was Psychoanalysis Such a Major Paradigm Change?

Psychoanalysis changed how we think about normal and pathological mental life in many ways and had an immense impact well beyond psychiatry, including on Western culture. Psychoanalytic ideas exerted a major influence on research in anthropology, sociology, politics, literature, and the arts. In psychiatry, psychoanalysis represented a change in terms of scope, epistemological approach and explanatory level, clinical practice, and moral attitude. Its impact was so significant that many consider it a revolution in psychiatry, on a par with Philippe Pinel's unchaining of the mentally ill and moving them from the prison to the hospital (Weckowicz and Liebel-Weckowicz, 1990a; Zilboorg, 1941).

One of Freud's major contributions was that he brought into psychiatric discourse less-severe forms of mental illness. Before that, eighteenth-century spa doctors and general practitioners treated minor nervous disorders. Major mental illness was 'treated' in asylums, and, although practices varied between places, and good examples existed, asylums were often places where the main task was the control of physical violence (Clark, 1996). By widening the scope of psychiatry and bringing less-severe forms of mental illness under the same umbrella, and especially by describing major conflicts and unacceptable drives in normal development, too, psychoanalysis made the divide between mental health and illness less drastic. Exemplified by the work of Eugene Bleuler (1857–1939) at the Burghölzli, the psychoanalytical movement reduced the split between hospital psychiatry (mainly concerned with psychotic patients and assuming an organic aetiology) and the psychiatry that took place in the consulting office and was concerned primarily with neurotic conditions (Weckowicz and Liebel-Weckowicz, 1990a).

The way in which psychoanalysis treated its subject of inquiry, that is, the person suffering with mental symptoms, shaped its *unique epistemological approach*. Its clinical roots conveyed some clear advantages in comparison to other orientations in this respect.

Whilst biological approaches for the most part relied on measurable data and statistical analysis, psychoanalysis mainly used *idiographic descriptions* (single cases and their individual circumstances and development, described in painstaking detail). As psychoanalysts tended not to run experiments or test their hypotheses systematically using empirical data, though, many viewed their model and theory building as mere speculation (Paris, 2017).

Psychoanalytic thinkers often used mythological and other *cultural references and metaphors* as important tools in their reasoning. Why was this the case? As Otto Rank (1884–1939) pointed out, myths were repositories of cultural norms and values (Rank, 2015). In the absence of a well-worked-out philosophical or scientific understanding of values in this context, using mythological analogies was an elegant and effective way for psychoanalysis to tap into the collective cultural understanding about common human value situations.

According to Millon (2004), 'psychoanalysis focusses on the *unconscious* level because overt behaviours and conscious reports are merely surface expressions of repressed emotions and associated defence mechanisms' that give rise to distinctive symptom patterns. Freud and other psychoanalysts saw childhood experiences as early events in development that led to *defence mechanisms* that could persist into adulthood and become increasingly maladaptive (Millon, 2004). Crucially, according to psychoanalysis, processes in the unconscious cannot be influenced or changed by surface interventions. Therefore, treatments aiming at behaviour modification will not address the deeper causes. Similarly, cognitive modifications can treat only relatively minor problems that can be tolerated consciously, that is, they are not repressed. Repression can be a manifestation of resistance during treatment that protects the individual from the anxiety that facing the issue would cause.

Importantly, psychoanalysis tried to explain the *personal meaning of the symptom*. This was very different from the views of psychiatrists of a neurobiological persuasion, who tended to consider mental symptoms as being mere epiphenomena of organic brain pathology without any intrinsic meaning (Weckowicz and Liebel-Weckowicz, 1990a). In their view, mental phenomena were caused by physical events, but they were incapable of causing anything themselves.

Creating frames of reference whereby psychological processes could be included in the concept of disease was one of Freud's most important contributions (Engel, 1977). A further contribution to understanding the complexity was the realization of the possibility that mental phenomena are often '*overdetermined*', a concept used by Freud (1913) in *The Interpretation of Dreams*, referring to elements of dreams being caused by multiple factors in the life of the dreamer. Overdetermination occurs when there is more than one cause that would be sufficient to account for the effect (for more details, see Chapter 4).

One of the most significant facts from the point of person-centredness is that psychoanalysis represented a divergence from the analytic approach of natural science: instead of trying to understand the whole from its parts (i.e. starting at levels lower than that of the individual), it aimed at studying mental symptoms at the *person (organismic) and social level*, and not only cross-sectionally but also in a *diachronic* fashion. However, unlike Kraepelin who studied groups of patients and sought to classify disorders according to a common course and outcome, Freud placed the emphasis on the unique attributes of the individual patient. By doing so, he inevitably took their personal values (concerns, needs, desires, etc.) into consideration.

Biological approaches tended to investigate simpler aspects of psychological functioning, whereas psychoanalysis looked at the more complex, higher-order ones that are more likely to be influenced in important ways by other people or society (i.e. they are relational or have relational elements). Consequently, psychoanalysis placed more value on *studying the person as a whole, living in their social environment*, and would come much closer to our current-day concept of the person-centred approach.

Our current conceptualization of the causes and treatment of mental illness, which includes – in addition to biological – *psychological, social, existential and contextual factors*, owes much to psychoanalytic thought (see Table 2.1).

Psychoanalysis *integrated values into its epistemology*. As Ruth Macklin (1973) observed in this context, value conflicts are often the reason why patients seek psychiatric help in the first place. Rank (2015) described how values were individually created and relative (see also Menaker, 1984). He used the concept of conformity and differentiation as two opposing forces to explain the interaction between the prevailing social values and individualistic ones (Hecht, 1994, p. 137). Rank illustrated how social values varied with historical time and

Table 2.1 Some of the key contributions by psychoanalytic thinkers

Key figure/author	Contribution	Reference
Sigmund Freud	– 'unconscious' – defence mechanisms	Freud, 1913
Carl Jung	– 'persona and shadow' – introversion and extroversion	Jung, 1923
Alfred Adler	– 'inferiority complex' – mental disorder enabling patients to dominate others in subtle ways	Adler, [1928] 2013; Adler, 1917; Millon, 2004
Harry Stack Sullivan	– psychiatry as the study of interpersonal relations with the psychiatrist as a participant observer – neurosis and psychosis being not diseases but personality developments warped by unsatisfactory interpersonal relations	Sullivan, 1955
Karen Horney	– importance of cultural factors and the present situation	Horney, [1937] 2014
Eric Fromm	– man being motivated by social values rather than instincts – dialectical interaction between man and society – neurosis being cultural in origin – alienation leading to insanity – capitalist society (or authoritarian communism) leading to the whole society being sick versus a humanistic society stressing the dignity and equality of men and encouraging the participation of workers in the decision-making process	Fromm, 1994, 1956/2013

place according to the social group's needs (Menaker, 1984). Maybe because of its clinical origin, thinking about the personal values of both the patient and the clinician – the other major stakeholder in the patient–therapist relationship crucially involved in the (co-)creation of the narrative of the patient – was present from early on in psychoanalysis. Although it has been demonstrated that psychoanalysis incorporated and mixed both the medical and the ethical models (Margolis, 1966) and thereby has a place in the history of ethics and is, in fact, at least in part, philosophy (Harcourt, 2015), the true significance and potentialities of this for psychiatry have been hardly recognized or exploited so far.

Psychoanalysis was the *first systematic psychological talking therapy* (Paris, 2005). By seeing most patients in private consulting rooms, as opposed to hospitals or asylums, psychoanalysts increased the acceptability of mental illness, 'normalizing' mental health problems. It was perfectly possible to have mental health problems and to live in society; conversely, it was possible to be a member of mainstream society and to have mental health problems.

Consistent with the compassionate clinical approach of person-centredness, psychoanalysis also represented a *change in moral attitude*. Freud traced how unconscious instincts and conflicts wove into pathological overt behaviour and realized that this happened in both healthy and ill people. This helped to reduce the gap between normal behaviour and mental illness. Psychoanalysis stayed clear of using degeneration as an explanation for mental illness and emphasized a non-judgemental approach. In contrast to the constitutionally oriented approaches of his contemporaries such as Bénédict Morel, Jean-Martin Charcot, and Pierre Janet, Freud searched for a logical relationship between the patient's symptoms and their psychological experiences.

Our current notion of sexuality developed by the end of the nineteenth century. Prior to that, during the 1870s there was a shift in medical thinking, with many forms of sexuality being increasingly considered perversions and pathological (Oosterhuis, 2012). Freud was 'a militant atheist with liberated attitudes toward sexuality' (Millon, 2004), uninfluenced by Christian ethics. For example, unlike many of his contemporaries, he regarded homosexuality as a variation of sexual function and not an illness, and thought that it was a great injustice and a cruelty to persecute homosexuality as a crime (Lewes, 1989).

Person-Centredness and Agency in Psychoanalysis

Agency is linked to reflection, an ability that brings to light what one cares about, that is, one's values. Let us first consider agency from the perspective of the patient. Psychoanalysis developed ways that enhance the patient's agency through addressing their resistance and thereby *creating new choices* for them (Williams and Levitt, 2007). Yet, psychoanalysis has been criticized for being authoritarian and nurturing reliance on the therapist, for instance, by not sharing with the patient the tools with which the therapist has achieved therapeutic improvement. This could be seen as depriving the patient of certain agency, although it is not clear as to whether the effective elements of the therapy can be taught to the patient in the same way as in some other modalities, for example in cognitive-behavioural therapy (CBT).

Unlike most other orientations, psychoanalysis regards the study of the patient–therapist relationship as an essential tool in both diagnosis-making and treatment. Analysing the *transference and counter-transference* in the room also offers an opportunity to examine the personal values, related beliefs, and emotions of the patient and the therapist. Interestingly, historically psychoanalytic psychotherapy went through three phases in terms of its stance towards the degree to which the *values of the therapist should be made explicit to the patient* and influence the course of therapy, with a non-directive middle period around the same time as Rogers presented his non-directive approach before a return by both psychoanalysis and Rogers to a more active and participating attitude (Macklin, 1973).

It is also possible to think of agency from the perspective of the stakeholders versus psychoanalysis as a therapeutic modality. Different modalities require various degrees of *identification with or adherence to their central models or tenets* from the patient and the clinician. Psychoanalytic *psychotherapists have needed to undergo personal analysis* themselves to become a therapist. Cognitive-analytic therapists usually also need to have their own cognitive-analytic therapy (CAT) treatment to qualify. This is not a requirement with most other modalities. Like their patients, clinicians also have a personal history that leaves its imprint on their preferences, concerns, and expectations (Dudas, 2022) about how psychotherapy should be done and what the outcomes should look like. Some will find psychoanalysis and its requirements a good fit in this respect, and some will not.

Although the *long duration and intensity* of psychoanalytic treatment has been criticized for various reasons, it is also possible to argue that inevitably it requires a certain amount of time and persistence for the therapist to truly get to know the patient. Our current practices do not cater for this, but historically psychiatrists and patients embraced this mode of working.

Who is present with us at the time influences how we think, feel, and act in a given situation. From a VBP perspective, we could ask, 'Who else, in a metaphorical sense, other than the therapist, is sat in the room with the patient in various orientations?'. Who are the *hidden stakeholders*? With psychoanalysis, it may have been some grand narratives created from the amalgamation of natural scientific and arts and humanities themes. They were often reminiscent of Greek mythology with great structural ideas about the mind, such as the id, the ego, and the superego, and powerful driving forces, such as the life instinct (Eros) and the death instinct (Thanatos).

The number of volumes written to critique psychoanalysis bears witness to its strong intellectual appeal. One recurrent criticism with relevance to our question about a natural versus a social sciences and humanities approach is that psychoanalytic concepts are hard to measure or quantify, let alone prove or disprove empirically. Some have argued that this renders *psychoanalysis unscientific*, such as Karl Popper ([1963] 2014) who was concerned about the lack of falsifiability, that is, the testability of its assertions. Popper's view places emphasis on natural scientific criteria; according to Aragona (2020, p. 136, citing Weber, 1904/1949, p. 80), 'in human sciences we are concerned not with "laws" in the narrower exact natural science sense "but with adequate causal relationships". In other words, in this field nomological knowledge derives from the generalization of first-person and empathic experience of regularities observed in 'normal' (i.e. rational) usual reactions. It is a 'knowledge of certain known empirical rules, particularly those relating to the ways in which human beings are prone to react under given situations . . . derived from our own experience and our knowledge of the conduct of others' (Weber, 1906/1949, p. 174). Others have pointed out that the methodology of psychoanalysis can be defensible if the nature of the subject of its inquiry is taken into consideration. As Millon (2004) put it, '[a]lthough these processes are difficult to formulate according to the tenets of scientific objectivity, their existence cannot be denied or overlooked. . . . [T]he search for them is mandatory.' As a brief sidenote, in psychoanalysis it is the individual in a relational context that is the focus. Psychoanalysis's historical lack of interest in testing its efficacy in randomized controlled trials (RCTs) may be rooted in this: RCTs can tell us how relatively homogenously patient populations do in treatment, but they cannot say much about the same tendency in the individual.

Psychoanalysis stopped being a leading framework for psychological research and practice in most places by the late 1970s. Several factors contributed to this, including the seismic shift brought about by the publication of the Diagnostic and Statistical Manual of Mental Disorders (DSM-III) in 1980 with its move towards a symptom-based categorical disease model of mental illness (Mayes and Horwitz, 2005). This new, a-theoretical classification system quickly became popular with those whose priorities lay in categorizing and measuring mental illness objectively and reliably for research, clinical, or financial purposes.

As I mentioned earlier, Freud and other early psychoanalysts envisaged linking their concepts to biological underpinnings eventually. *Neuropsychoanalysis* emerged during the 1990s as a response to the extreme reductionism in neuroscience and biological psychiatry, with the aim of reconciling psychoanalytic and neuroscientific perspectives (Panksepp and

Solms, 2011). Among others, Eric Kandel (1929–), an Austrian-born psychoanalytically trained psychiatrist and biological scientist who held a series of professorships at Columbia University and won the Nobel Prize for his work on the formation of short- and long-term memory at a molecular level, attempted, in a persuasive way, to link psychoanalytic concepts to modern neurobiological ones (Kandel, 1999). Several key concepts of psychoanalysis, such as the unconscious, transference, and attachment, have now been mapped onto modern biological neuroscience research findings (Luborsky and Barrett, 2006; Weinberger and Westen, 2001). This renewed interaction with neuroscience has also led to new theory development in psychoanalysis (Johnson and Flores Mosri, 2016). Although the debate continues as to whether the evidence gathered so far provides sufficient empirical confirmation, this direction in research, especially if it gains traction, holds hope for closing the currently rather large explanatory gap between the biological and the clinical or phenomenological levels.

Until about the First World War, when repeated demonstrations of striking regularities in social statistics led to 'an infatuation with large samples' and the belief that human behaviour could be described with quantitative scientific laws, experimental results were attributed to individual experimental subjects in nearly all published studies (Danziger, [1990] 1994, p. 70). Since then, with the serious and reasoned concerns about the degree to which findings from research deploying the all-too-common scenario of looking at a handful of variables at group level can be generalized to individuals, *calls for a return to the idiographic approach* have been made repeatedly (Carlson, 1971; Molenaar, 2004). Carlson expressed her scepticism about such reforms half a century ago on the basis that these choices were dictated not by scientific considerations alone but also by the 'academic marketplace' and the pressure for quick publication. Has anything changed?

A major surviving clinical legacy of psychoanalysis is the recognition that genuine treatment requires building a therapeutic relationship in which the person can achieve creative reconstruction and recovery. Over the last two decades, there has been *renewed interest in treatments rooted in psychoanalysis* and in research identifying where it is most effective (e.g. de Maat et al., 2009; Leichsenring and Klein, 2014; Leichsenring et al., 2004).

Box 2.2 Behaviourism

Key values espoused by behaviourism:
- extreme preference for a natural science approach (prediction and control)
- objectivism
- radical reductionism
- functionalist, utilitarian approach
- experiments to generate empirical data
- technocratic, social engineering applications.

The Context and the Objectives of Behaviourism

Another main school of thought with lasting impact in the history of psychology is behaviourism. The idea of using reward and punishment to alter behaviour had been present in the *moral treatment movement* and in the idea that temporal connection produces a bond between ideas in *associationism* (Weckowicz and Liebel-Weckowicz, 1990b).

However, it is particularly relevant to mention some of the various forces, such as *changes in preferences regarding epistemological orientation* and methodology, and *needs emanating from the historical context*, that eventually brought forth and led to the popularity of behaviourism.

John Broadus Watson (1878–1958), a pioneer of behaviourism and a professor of psychology at Johns Hopkins University, was very sceptical about what he called subjective or introspective psychology, which he described in the preface of his influential work *Behaviorism* (Watson, 1925) as 'a world of intangibles, a world of definitions'. Instead, he favoured 'behaviouristic psychology [that] deals with tangibles[;] the reader sees no break between his physical, chemical, and biological world and his newly-faced behavioristic world. He may not like the simplicity and severity of Behaviorism, but he cannot fail to understand Behaviorism if he gives it a little honest reading.'

Some behaviourists had no smaller objective than to develop a 'technology of behaviour' that could serve as the basis for social reform (Rutherford, 2017). This was particularly welcome in the 1920s and 1930s when technological progress was felt to be the solution to the Great Depression in America.

As regards what drove the interest in behaviouristic approaches from a clinical perspective, it became increasingly clear that psychoanalysis was not effective for every type of problem or every patient. Hans Eysenck (1916–1997) was believed to have demonstrated that there was an inverse correlation between psychoanalytic psychotherapy and recovery, with the recovery rate reducing with more treatment (Marks, 2015). Marks describes the formation of a Pavlov reading group of practitioners in the 1950s at the Maudsley in London, where both a department of psychiatry and a separate department of psychology were established, making it possible to develop new, experimental treatments and to clinically evaluate them. There was an important shift in the emphasis from treating the mind to treating the nervous system. Unlike psychoanalysts, Eysenck believed that the neurosis was the symptom itself and with the elimination of the symptom the neurosis was cured (Marks, 2015).

Major Proponents and Tenets of Behaviourism

From a theoretical perspective, the main strands that typified behaviourism – a strongly objectivistic and functionalist approach and a focus on behaviour – had existed for a long time, but behaviourism took these to a truly radical degree (Pleh, 2010). Behaviourism was materialistic, positivistic, and causal-reductive. Its main principles were derived principally from the work of Pavlov, Watson, and Skinner.

In his above-mentioned book, Watson said, 'Give me a dozen healthy infants, well-formed, and my own specified world to bring them up in and I'll guarantee to take any one at random and train him to become any type of specialist I might select – doctor, lawyer, artist, merchant-chief and, yes, even beggar-man and thief, regardless of his talents, penchants, tendencies, abilities, vocations, and race of his ancestors' (Watson, 1925, p. 82). Although it is important to note that Watson expressed this opinion in the context of rejecting genetic determinism at a time when degeneracy theories and eugenics were dominant ways of thinking about mental illness, looking at such statements, one cannot help but start to see some of the problems with behaviourism and the considerable potential of it being misused in the wrong hands.

Although their most often quoted experiments and laws focussed on the behaviour of the individual, leading behaviourist theorists tried to establish a link between the individual and society and to create tools for improving society. Behaviouristic principles were also adopted in education to produce 'well-adjusted' children (Weckowicz and Liebel-Weckowicz, 1990b). Burrhus Frederic Skinner (1904–1990), a professor of psychology at Harvard University and one of the most prominent behaviourist psychologists, who aimed to establish psychology as a natural science, believed that designing a culture is like designing an experiment by arranging the contingencies and noting the effects. In his view, the difference was that '[i]n an experiment we are interested in what happens, in designing a culture with whether it will work' (Skinner, 1971, p. 153, cited by Rutherford, 2017, p. 296). Skinner experimented with pigeons and rats primarily. In his utopian novel *Walden Two* (Skinner, [1948] 2005), he described what social reform based on his behavioural principles extrapolated from these experiments would look like. Carefully designed positive reinforcers would lead to a society where individuals behave in ways that increase the chances of survival of that culture, such as having a lower birth rate and more efficiently using the available resources (Skinner, [1948] 2005). His best-known inventions include the *Skinner box*, which has been adapted to study how drugs can modify animal behaviour; the *air crib* to give parents more time and control over their babies' sleep time and crying; the *teaching machine* to improve academic attainment; and the idea of training pigeons to guide missiles (Rutherford, 2017).

In his controversial book *Beyond Freedom and Dignity* (1971), Skinner devoted a chapter to 'values'. He asserted that 'behavioural science . . . [,] to the extent that it is concerned with operant conditioning, is a science of values' (Skinner, 1971, p. 104). Skinner's (1971, p. 104) view was that 'when we say that a value judgement is a matter not of fact but of how someone feels about a fact, we are simply distinguishing between a thing and its reinforcing effect'. Considering value judgements ultimately as statements on evolutionary usefulness, he said: 'Things are good (positively reinforcing) or bad (negatively reinforcing) presumably because of the contingencies of survival under which the species evolved' (Skinner, 1971, p. 104). Talking about moral values, he explained that people tend to attribute behaving well with each other to knowing right and wrong or some sort of inner virtue, whereas in reality, when we behave well, it is owing not to a sense of responsibility, obligation, or loyalty but to effective social contingencies. Similarly, people follow rules or the law because of the attached natural or social contingencies. Conflicts among feelings (values) are conflicts between contingencies of reinforcement.

According to Skinner, we can avoid control by others by questioning the social reinforcers and turning to immediate gratification (where only personal reinforcers remain at play), but this means becoming valueless. Skinner borrows from Maslow in describing this as, among other things, anomie, amorality, anhedonia, and 'the lack of something to believe in and be devoted to' (Skinner, 1971, p. 117). As regards the solution, Skinner says that people will seek education if the link among knowledge and skills and prestige is restored and will seek work if having a good life is made contingent on productive labour. He concludes that a technology of behaviour to successfully maximize the achievements of which the human being is capable is available, but 'the defenders of freedom oppose its use' (Skinner, 1971, p. 124). They argue against it on the basis of values when asking questions like 'Who is to decide what is good for man?' or 'Who will use this technology and to what end?'. His view is that if this technology were to be used to excess, one could challenge it and turn to things that are good only for oneself. The solution would be contingencies that generate behaviours for the good of others. These could be intensified, and previously neglected individual gains, such as security, order, health, and wisdom, could be highlighted (Skinner, 1971, p. 124). Critics have pointed out that Skinner's naturalistic ethics require science to function beyond its scope; they do not provide us with practical guidance, especially in deciding about difficult cases, and their justification of survivability as a criterion for resolving ethical problems is inadequate (Ruiz and Roche, 2007).

Skinner's was 'a view that placed all emphasis on observables, and the locus of control within the environment, not within the putative "mind" of a person' (Rutherford, 2017, p. 298). Taking Skinner's logic further, if all our behaviour is determined by reinforcement, we could argue that there is no need for any moral thinking; concepts like personal responsibility would then become hard to explain.

Person-Centredness and Agency in the Behaviouristic Approach

Unlike psychoanalysts, behaviourist therapists were not interested in the patient's effect on them, only the effect of their intervention on the patient. Even there, their focus was on the 'machine-like' and predictable aspects of human behaviour. Knowing the patient as a person was not a requirement for this. For them, the level of organization of interest was below the level of person. In stark contrast to psychoanalysis, the person was almost a blind spot for behaviourism. The individual was interesting only from a pragmatic perspective as a sum of conditioned responses or a cogwheel in the machinery of society.

It has been argued (Place, 2000, p. 57) that 'the hostility which behaviorism has provoked throughout its history is evidence that it flouts an important convention, the convention that, whenever possible, human beings are treated as and must always give the appearance of being rational agents'. In a strict philosophical sense, the assumptions of behaviourism do not allow for human agency; the environment (stimuli and conditioning) determines human minds and behaviour (Slife and Williams, 1995). Key concepts of VBP, such as choice, option, desire, volition, decision-making, selection, and agency, are closely linked to free will and most behaviourists would find it hard to integrate free will (and thereby these other concepts) into their theoretical frameworks (Slife and Williams, 1995).

Let us return to our earlier question – 'Who else, in a metaphorical sense, other than the therapist, is sat in the room with the patient?'. In behaviourism, it is more of a 'science fetish' and the vision of a 'technocratic society', such as is espoused in Skinner.

In its early version, behaviourism was *highly reductionistic*, treating people like objects, pieces of wood to be worked on or animals to train, beings without agency, aspirations, or preferences, or individuals without a family, community, or other social ties. Also, behaviourism could never prove convincingly the correctness of its ontological stance according to which internal mental processes do not exist. These and other limitations eventually led to researchers moving away from it.

Relevant to our inquiry, behaviourism and behavioural therapists largely *ignored important aspects of mental ill health and recovery*. For example, with a few exceptions, such as studying experimental neurosis in cats and dogs forced to discriminate between reinforced and non-reinforced stimuli (Weckowicz and Liebel-Weckowicz, 1990b), they did not attempt to provide an explanation or treatment beyond the symptom level. They *rejected the idea of disease entities* as they are not directly observable (Weckowicz and Liebel-Weckowicz, 1990b). In the main, they were not interested in or did not satisfactorily consider the complexity of the context in which the symptoms developed (such as the patient's life history or current social, economic, and other circumstances), secondary gain, interpersonal and communication difficulties, volition, or intentionality. Although, in contrast to psychoanalysts, behaviouristic psychotherapists did produce empirical evidence to demonstrate the effectiveness of their interventions, including controlled studies, the scientific quality of their methodology and the reporting of these studies, even in major works by key authors, left a lot to be desired even through the eyes of the observer of the time (Stewart, 1967). Although Eysenck believed that behavioural treatment was effective for almost any type of problem (Paris, 2005), behaviourism, despite reaching a high level of sophistication at its peak, failed to provide a plausible explanation for most forms of mental illness or to produce treatments for more than a few forms of it (Dudas, 2020) that would outlive the heyday of this psychological approach, which spanned more than five decades. As Rutherford (2017, p. 291) points out, in the context of its own time, '[t]his technoscientific attitude quickly led to psychology acquiring a *social engineering function* (italics are mine) that continued to increase as psychologists developed ever-closer ties with the state, especially during and after World War II'.

We need to mention here some highly *controversial applications* of behaviouristic treatments. The 'squeaky wheel' principle of VBP states that values become more apparent when there is a problem. Scandals indicate major problems and serve as a focal point, forcing us to examine and declare our values, and offering an opportunity to learn from our mistakes. Scandals can also signal shifting priorities, lead to public outrage, and catalyse policy changes, be they well-thought-out, proportionate, and helpful or not (Lloyd et al., 2014; Turner et al., 2015). Aversion therapies were used in the 1960s and 1970s for the 'social normalization' of behaviours considered undesirable at the time, such as transvestitism and homosexuality (Marks, 2015), in the main without much effect. Behavioural approaches also became part of common practice outside the sphere of psychotherapy in the criminal justice system, education, and social work, sometimes in controversial ways, for example as documented in the 'Pindown' scandal in the 1980s in Staffordshire where long periods of physical restraint were used in child residential care as a form of behaviour training for children with problematical behaviour (Marks, 2015).

An important surviving legacy of behaviourism is *objective experimenting.* Owing to its laboratory origins, behaviourism generated a large amount of data about animal behaviour (especially learning) in very controlled situations. Some of this data has relevance to psychiatry, but clinical practices that have roots in behaviourism lost their importance in most places. One system that was once popular in hospitals was 'token economy'. This included rewarding desirable behaviours with tokens that could be exchanged for items or privileges that the patient valued and punishing undesirable behaviours by taking away tokens. Despite the evidence-based success of token economies, their use declined very significantly (Liberman, 2000). Many factors played a role in this, including the difficulty involved in implementing and maintaining them in the community after the deinstitutionalization of psychiatric care. Treatments that are still used include *systematic desensitization,* also called graded exposure therapy, for phobias and aversion therapy for alcohol dependence. However, behaviouristic interventions are rarely used in isolation nowadays.

The Roots of Current-Day Clinical Practice: Cognitive and Humanistic Psychology

In this section, I will examine the two psychological approaches that are perhaps the most mainstream in today's psychiatric practice. Interventions of the CBT type are the most often used psychotherapeutic modality in psychiatry today. Humanistic or person-centred psychotherapy forms the basis of many counselling-type interventions. Relevant to VBP, many elements of person-centred care and co-production have their roots in the humanistic approach.

Box 2.3 Cognitive psychology

Key values espoused by cognitive psychology:
- mental models
- empirical/experimental approach
- measurement.

Factors in the Rise of Cognitive Psychology

Although the development of cognitive psychology around the 1960s and 1970s could be conceptualized in some sense as a return to the Wundtian view of the mind, it was also related to certain developments in behaviourism, such as its difficulties with studying language and learning, and it did not mean a return to introspection. Other factors included developments in perception research, recognizing certain limitations of Gestalt psychology, and ultimately the need to invoke the concept of mental models. Experimentation using human subjects to study attention, memory, language, mental representation, knowledge acquisition, and problem solving, among other subjects, characterizes this approach. Progress in cognitive psychology has been facilitated by developments in linguistics, information technology, and computing, and the increasing use of the 'computer analogy'.

The Development of CBT

Around the 1950s, before the rise of academic cognitive psychology, innovators in the world of psychotherapy wanted to develop treatments that were free of what they perceived as the flaws and limitations of both psychoanalysis and behaviourism. They were often psychoanalysts themselves but, instead of working on suppressed childhood memories that were inaccessible to conscious thought, they wanted to focus on the consciously available negative thought patterns, such as in Ellis's *rational-emotive therapy*. Unlike the behaviourists, Albert Ellis (1913–2007) believed that the personal story of the patient was relevant (even crucial) to understanding their neurosis (Marks, 2015). Aaron T. Beck (1921–2021), who had trained in psychoanalysis, wanted to develop a treatment the efficacy of which could be measured more objectively. In 1976, he published his *Cognitive Therapy and the Emotional Disorders*, which was a step-by-step guide for treating the various problem areas in depressive illness through the systematic challenging of the patient's distorted cognitions about themselves, the world, and the future, before replacing them with healthier ways of thinking. In his works, Beck described how frequently occurring negative automatic thoughts revealed the core beliefs of the patient that they had developed through the course of their life experiences. The behavioural elements of his methodology included role-playing difficult situations and preparing a more positive response for when the situation occurs in real life (positive reconditioning). By the beginning of the twenty-first century, CBT had become the psychotherapeutic treatment modality for which we have the strongest evidence base, with a considerable number of meta-analyses supporting its efficacy in the treatment of a variety of psychiatric conditions, and Beck's self-report measure of depressive symptom severity, the Beck Depression Inventory (BDI), one of the most widely used instruments of its kind in psychiatry.

Person-Centredness and Agency in CBT

Teaching patients techniques for recognizing and modifying their own thinking and behaviour (which was believed then to lead to improvement in their mood) was an integral part of these therapies, but they largely ignored important elements of agency, such as motivation and social cognition (see Bandura's (2001) emergent interactive agency). However, it has been argued that by helping them alter their thought patterns, cognitive techniques can activate or promote patients' agency (Williams and Levitt, 2007). Patients gain skills that help them overcome the non-reflective thinking and maladaptive behaviours that restrict their choices and thereby become freer to select from their options.

It is customary to consider the therapies of Ellis and Beck as 'second-wave' CBT, with the 'first wave' referring primarily to the behaviourist roots of CBT. Third-wave CBTs include acceptance and commitment therapy (ACT), dialectical behaviour therapy (DBT), behavioural activation (BA), and mindfulness-based cognitive therapy (MBCT). This evolution has led to these more holistic versions of CBT that look at the whole person with his or her physical, psychological, and spiritual characteristics. They take the context of the person's values into consideration more than their predecessors did and aim at more comprehensive life goals rather than simple symptom reduction. Although CBT can be used with some degree of flexibility and in an 'eclectic' way, combining it with elements of other modalities, it is generally a manualized modality that requires the patient and the therapist to follow a certain structure during the sessions and during the entire course of treatment.

In addition to the above-mentioned limitations, it has been pointed out that CBT is too mechanistic (Radden, 2007) and does not consider some important aspects of mental activity and the whole person (Gaudiano, 2008). In practice, clinicians can (and usually do) consider the patient's values when identifying priorities and setting goals, a previously unacknowledged but potentially crucial ingredient. Although the above-described treatment model, especially applying it too strictly, does not suit every patient and therapist, it has been argued that CBT can be practised in a highly empathic, person-centred way (Brabban et al., 2017; Josefowitz and Myran, 2005). Modern adaptations have certainly moved in this direction.

Box 2.4 **The humanistic approach**

Key values espoused by humanism:
- person-centredness
- autonomy and self-determination
- personal responsibility
- self-actualization
- unconditional positive regard.

The Origins and Major Tenets of the Humanistic Approach

Alfred Adler's theories about 'life styles' anticipated the views of humanistic and existentialist psychologies (Weckowicz and Liebel-Weckowicz, 1990a). Both he and Rank believed that individual development was neither biologically nor socially determined but was – to a significant degree – self-determined (Weckowicz and Liebel-Weckowicz, 1990a). *Rank's ideas* had an influence on Rogers' psychological system and his technique of non-directive, person-centred counselling. Carl Rogers (1902–1987) described his client-centred approach, encouraging positive regard for patients, in his book *Counseling and Psychotherapy* (Rogers, 1942). Other key ingredients included empathy and the therapist's congruence, which means that the therapist is present and authentic during their interaction with the client. Rogers ([1951] 1995) popularized the concept of *unconditional positive regard.* He described the characteristics of a fully functioning person, such as continually aiming to fulfil one's potential; to choose an existential lifestyle; to increase organismic trust, freedom of choice, reliability, and constructiveness; and to live a full life.

In 1954, Abraham Maslow (1908–1970) published his *Motivation and Personality* (Maslow, 1954) in which he described his *hierarchy of needs*, which has become a household term ('Maslow's pyramid'). His work and others' research stemming from it provided important insight into human values. Rokeach (1973) argued that values can be placed on a continuum from lower- to higher-order values according to Maslow's hierarchical theory of motivation, with values pertaining to self-actualization or psychological health being of the highest order.

The third main figure of humanistic psychology was Rollo May (1909–1994). Unlike other humanistic psychologists, he maintained that therapists should not remain value neutral but should express their values openly, thereby creating a choice for the patient to accept or reject these (Millon, 2004, p. 153).

Person-Centredness and Agency in the Humanistic Approach

Various psychological approaches can be placed on a spectrum in terms of how much personal autonomy or self-determination they afford the patient. Genetic determinism or behaviourism would be on one end of the spectrum, with the individual having little or no real control over their choices, whereas humanistic or existentialist approaches would be on the other end, with the individual making their own choices but also carrying the responsibility for these.

Humanistic psychology and psychotherapy concerned themselves with topics of great relevance to us, human beings, including love, intimacy, self-actualization, achieving one's full potential in life, autonomy, responsibility, finding peak experiences, and transcendentality. Some of the questions they explored also had great clinical relevance, such as 'What makes life worth living?'.

According to humanistic psychology, the role of the therapist is to restore the patient's own power (Coleman and Neimeyer, 2015) through creating a supportive environment that facilitates introspective self-examination and allows the patient to develop the capacity for self-direction (Williams and Levitt, 2007). Improving the patient's self-esteem was considered key to therapeutic success. Rogers preferred the word 'client' to 'patient' because the latter put the therapist in an expert position and diminished the agency of the person receiving the treatment (Williams and Levitt, 2007).

The Critique of Humanistic Psychology

Interestingly, although this was one of the main elements of his model, Rogers said relatively little about the capacities that allow people to recognize and formulate their own goals and behave for the sake of them (Slife and Williams, 1995). Millon (2004, p. 157) points out another shortcoming of humanistic psychology, especially in contrast to psychoanalysis: 'There is something grossly naïve in exhorting humans to live life to the fullest and then expecting socially beneficial consequences to follow. What evidence is there that one's inherent self-interest would not clash with the self-interests of others?'

Although humanistic psychology was person-centred and aware of the relevance of the values held by the person and by society to mental well-being, it was not concerned in the main with the causes of mental illness beyond attributing it to a failure of self-actualizing. This failure is attributed to a clash between the individual's strivings and society's values. Humanistic psychology did not particularly concern itself with removing mental symptoms. Millon's (2004, p. 124) view is that its relevant ideas were discursive commentaries rather than systematic theories of mental illness.

Contrasting it with its European existentialist forerunners, Irvin Yalom (1980) points out that from the 1960s humanistic psychology became a broad church. Its emphasis on hedonism, individual fulfilment, and especially on anti-intellectualism (such as in completely denouncing the cognitive approach) led to a divorce between humanistic psychology and the academic community (Yalom, 1980).

Millon (2004, p. 148) tells us how Rogers, 'a perennially optimistic and encouraging man', espoused that people were able to work through their difficulties as long as they were encouraged to believe that they had the means to create their own futures. However, during the time when he developed his ideas, Rogers was working with highly able and generally well-functioning university students in Chicago. When he tried the same approach with patients in hospital wards, his method did not lead to the same success. Critics of humanistic psychology also pointed out the relative lack of empirical support for the insights and observations of its proponents, perhaps with the exception of Rogers' client-centred therapy.

Conclusions

Firstly, looking at the history of psychology one cannot but see some striking similarities with psychiatry. Both disciplines became professionalized during the nineteenth century. Both are concerned with the mind and have clinical applications. There has been a lot of cross-fertilization and psychiatrists and psychologists have often contributed to each other's disciplines. Owing to their nature of inquiry and their relatively undeveloped epistemological foundations, both disciplines favoured polymaths. Just like in psychiatry, many psychologists had detailed knowledge of other fields, such as the natural sciences, mathematics, or the arts and humanities, which contributed to their creativity and helped them develop new theories and invent new methodologies.

The humanities and the social sciences study a different, higher level of organization than the natural sciences do. Their methodology is necessary for the subject matter of psychology (and psychiatry). For some questions, it may even be better suited. Natural laws are objective and true about everybody in the same group, but clinical psychiatry deals with individual patients. Concentrating solely on natural scientific objectivity is also a value choice. The problem for natural scientific approaches in this context is that people are different, and every person has their individual values and personal preferences, and this requires knowledge and understanding of subjectivity. Consequently, psychology benefitted when it tried to embrace more of the humanities.

Secondly, history teaches us that although the choices in scientific methodology are dictated to a considerable degree by the nature of the task, scientific methodology is also influenced by the personality, the education, the set of abilities, and – last but not least – the personal values of the investigator. Like in psychiatry, in psychology several orientations or approaches have vied for primacy over time. Evidently, however, no single approach has managed to provide the full explanation of mental illness, though they all had the potential to advance our understanding and complement each other. The fact that none of these different approaches managed to fully explain all types of mental illness does not mean that none of them is a valid approach, but rather suggests that the explanation of one type of mental illness is different from that of another. History also indicates that overemphasis on one approach will lead, sooner or later, to a demand for the other.

In ideal cases, theory, research, and clinical practice developed simultaneously, supporting each other, but vogues in academic and clinical psychology did not always coincide. As Stephen A. Diamond has observed, by the twenty-first century, after the achievements of depth psychology during the twentieth century, the pendulum has swung back and the biological orientation that was so dominant before psychoanalysis has made a return, in what Freud might call reaction formation and Jung enantiodromia (Diamond, 2018). History seems to have come full circle as regards treatment, too: minor mental illness has been relegated to primary care again, meaning less scientific interest and less help, which is often provided by non-specialists.

Thirdly, in a clinical speciality of a hybrid nature that straddles the natural and the social sciences and the purpose of which is to help patients (i.e. suffering individual human beings), person-centredness and agency are core features. Therefore, the usefulness of any psychological approach for psychiatry is determined to a large degree by how much it can incorporate these core features into its theory and models. This is an area where psychology has again benefitted from more humanities and social science input during its history. Psychoanalysis focussed on the whole person and managed to incorporate values and ethics into its epistemology more than other approaches could and this was its crucial input into psychiatry. Behaviourism reduced values to reinforcement and humanistic non-directive psychology dealt with them but, at least from a psychiatric point of view, in a less convincing way. Psychoanalysis, by focussing on the relational nature of human beings and by combining medical and ethical models in its approach, prepared the way for building a new, *person-centred psychiatric epistemology*. The solution for the future of psychiatry may be not to return to psychoanalysis itself but to embrace and build on its epistemological achievements.

Lastly, a few words about the evolution of the relationship between psychology and psychiatry. Historically, the care of the mentally ill increasingly came under the purview of medical doctors from the eighteenth century onwards. As psychology evolved, psychologists also took an interest in psychopathology and treatment, but as Fishman and Franks (1992, quoted by Marks, 2015) described their feelings in the 1950s in the UK, the recently professionalized psychologist was viewed as a 'diagnostic assistant to the psychiatrist', working within a traditional medical disease model. Although, especially in settings where they work together, this has gradually become more of a partnership of equals, the clinician responsible for the overall care of the psychiatric patient still tends to be the psychiatrist owing to aspects such as risk management, severity of the illness, lack of treatability by psychology, and, in hospitals, custodial responsibilities. If anything, history highlights the inadequacy of either discipline alone and the need for both.

References

Adler, A. 1917. *Study of Organ Inferiority and Its Psychical Compensation*. New York: Nervous and Mental Disease.

Adler, A. [1928] 2013. *Understanding Human Nature*. Abingdon: Routledge.

Aragona, M. 2020. At the origins of hermeneutic psychopathology. In Marková, I. S. & Chen, E. (eds.), *Rethinking Psychopathology: Creative Convergences*. Cham: Springer International, pp. 131–144.

Bandura, A. 2001. Social cognitive theory: An agentic perspective. *Annual Review of Psychology*, 52, 1–26.

Berrios, G. E. 1995. *The History Of Mental Symptoms: Descriptive Psychopathology Since the Nineteenth Century*. Cambridge: Cambridge University Press.

Brabban, A., Byrne, R., Longden, E. & Morrison, A. P. 2017. The importance of human relationships, ethics and recovery-orientated values in the delivery of CBT for people with psychosis. *Psychosis*, 9, 157–166.

Carlson, R. 1971. Where is the person in personality research? *Psychological Bulletin*, 75, 203–219.

Clark, D. H. 1996. *The Story of a Mental Hospital: Fulbourn 1858–1983*. London: Process Press.

Coleman, R. A. & Neimeyer, R. A. 2015. Assessment of subjective client agency in psychotherapy: A review. *Journal of Constructivist Psychology*, 28, 1–23.

Danziger, K. [1990] 1994. *Constructing the Subject Historical Origins of Psychological Research*. Cambridge: Cambridge University Press.

De Maat, S., De Jonghe, F., Schoevers, R. & Dekker, J. 2009. The effectiveness of long-term psychoanalytic therapy: A systematic review of empirical studies. *Harvard Review of Psychiatry*, 17, 1–23.

Diamond, S. A. 2018. Who were the alienists? A new television series resurrects a curious old term. *Psychology Today*, 26 January. www.psychologytoday.com/gb/blog/evil-deeds/201801/who-were-the-alienists.

Dudas, R. B. 2020. The discontents of psychiatry: What can the history of psychiatry and values-based medicine contribute to resolving them? In Marková, I. S. & Chen, E. (eds.), *Rethinking Psychopathology: Creative Convergences*. Cham: Springer International.

Dudas, R. B. 2022. Values-based practice: How can history taking help psychiatrists explore the values involved in clinical decision-making? *British Journal of Psychiatry Advances*, 28, 153–162.

Engel, G. L. 1977. The need for a new medical model: A challenge for biomedicine. *Science*, 196, 129–136.

Fisher, A. J., Medaglia, J. D. & Jeronimus, B. F. 2018. Lack of group-to-individual generalizability is a threat to human subjects research. *Proceedings of the National Academy of Sciences*, 115, e6106–e6115.

Fishman, D. B. & Franks, C. M. 1992. Evolution and differentiation within behavior therapy: A theoretical and epistemological review. In Freedheim, D. K. (ed.), *History of Psychotherapy: A Century of Change*. Washington, DC: American Psychological Association, pp. 159–196.

Fonagy, P., Person, E. S. & Sandler, J. 2018. *Freud's 'On Narcissism: An Introduction'*. London: Taylor & Francis.

Freud, S. 1913. *The Interpretation of Dreams*. New York: Macmillan.

Fromm, E. H. 1994. *Escape from Freedom*. New York: H. Holt.

Fromm, E. 1956/2013. *The Sane Society*. International Library of Sociology (ILS) 252. Abingdon: Routledge.

Gaudiano, B. A. 2008. Cognitive-behavioural therapies: Achievements and challenges. *Evidence-Based Mental Health*, 11, 5–7.

Goethe, J. W. V. 2000. *Die Leiden des jungen Werther - Band 1*. Project Gutenberg. www.gutenberg.org/ebooks/2407.

Hall, G. S. 1923. *Jesus, the Christ, in the Light of Psychology*. New York: D. Appleton.

Harcourt, E. 2015. The place of psychoanalysis in the history of ethics. *Journal of Moral Philosophy*, 12, 598–618.

Hecht, P. J. 1994. The 'fine line' of Otto Rank. Unpublished PhD thesis, University of Rhode Island.

Herzog, D. 2016. The libido wars. In Herzog, D. (ed.), *Cold War Freud: Psychoanalysis in an Age of Catastrophes*. Cambridge: Cambridge University Press, pp. 21–55.

Horney, K. [1937] 2014. *The Neurotic Personality of Our Time*. Abingdon: Routledge.

Innamorati, M. 2017. Review of *Cold War Freud*, *Psychiatry in Communist Europe*, and *Psiquiatría, psicoánalisis y cultura comunista: Batallas ideológicas en la guerra fria* [*Psychiatry, Psychoanalysis and Communist Culture: Ideological Battles in the Cold War*] [Review of *Cold War Freud* by D. Herzog (2016), *Psychiatry in Communist Europe* ed. by M. Savelli & S. Marks (2015), and *Psiquiatría, Psicoánalisis y Cultura Comunista* by H. Vezzetti (2016)] *History of Psychology*, 20, 330–335.

Johnson, B. & Flores Mosri, D. 2016. The neuropsychoanalytic approach: Using neuroscience as the basic science of psychoanalysis. *Frontiers in Psychology*, 7, 1459.

Josefowitz, N. & Myran, D. 2005. Towards a person-centred cognitive behaviour therapy. *Counselling Psychology Quarterly*, 18, 329–336.

Jung, C. G. 1923. *Psychological Types: Or, the Psychology of Individuation*. New York: Harcourt, Brace & Company.

Kandel, E. R. 1999. Biology and the future of psychoanalysis: A new intellectual framework for psychiatry revisited. *American Journal of Psychiatry*, 156, 505–524.

Leichsenring, F. & Klein, S. 2014. Evidence for psychodynamic psychotherapy in specific mental disorders: A systematic review. *Psychoanalytic Psychotherapy*, 28, 4–32.

Leichsenring, F., Rabung, S. & Leibing, E. 2004. The efficacy of short-term psychodynamic psychotherapy in specific psychiatric disorders: A meta-analysis. *Archives of General Psychiatry*, 61, 1208–1216.

Lewes, K. 1989. *The Psychoanalytic Theory of Male Homosexuality*. London: Quartet.

Liberman, R. P. 2000. The token economy. *American Journal of Psychiatry*, 157, 1398–1398.

Lloyd, L., Banerjee, A., Harrington, C., F. Jacobsen, F. & Szebehely, M. 2014. It's a scandal! Comparing the causes and consequences of nursing home media scandals in five countries. *International Journal of Sociology and Social Policy*, 34, 2–18.

Luborsky, L. & Barrett, M. S. 2006. The history and empirical status of key psychoanalytic concepts. *Annual Review of Clinical Psychology*, 2, 1–19.

Macklin, R. 1973. Values in psychoanalysis and psychotherapy: A survey and analysis. *American Journal of Psychoanalysis*, 33, 133–150.

MargoliS, J. 1966. *Psychotherapy and Morality: A Study of Two Concepts*. New York: Random House.

Marks, S. 2015. Psychologists as therapists: The development of behavioural traditions in clinical psychology. In Hall, J., Pilgrim, D. & Turpin, G. (eds.), *Clinical Psychology in Britain: Historical Perspectives*. Leicester: Leicester British Psychological Society.

Maslow, A. H. 1954. *Motivation and Personality*. New York: Harper.

Mayes, R. & Horwitz, A. V. 2005. DSM-III and the revolution in the classification of mental illness. *Journal of the History of the Behavioral Sciences*, 41, 249–267.

Menaker, E. 1984. The ethical and the empathic in the thinking of Otto Rank. *American Imago*, 41, 343–351.

Millon, T. 2004. *Masters of the Mind: Exploring the Story of Mental Illness from Ancient Times to the New Millennium*. Hoboken, NJ: John Wiley & Sons.

Molenaar, P. C. M. 2004. A manifesto on psychology as idiographic science: Bringing the person back into scientific psychology, this time forever. *Measurement*, 2, 201–218.

Oosterhuis, H. 2012. Sexual modernity in the works of Richard von Krafft-Ebing and Albert Moll. *Medical History*, 56, 133–155.

Panksepp, J. & Solms, M. 2011. What is neuropsychoanalysis? Clinically relevant studies of the minded brain. *Trends in Cognitive Sciences*, 16, 6–8.

Paris, J. 2005. A shrinking perimeter. In *The Fall of an Icon: Psychoanalysis and Academic Psychiatry*. Toronto: University of Toronto Press, pp. 92–114.

Paris, J. 2017. Is psychoanalysis still relevant to psychiatry? *Canadian Journal of Psychiatry*, 62, 308–312.

Place, U. T. 2000. Behaviorism as an ethnomethodological experiment: Flouting the convention of rational agency. *Behavior and Philosophy*, 28, 57–62.

Pleh, C. 2010. *A lélektan története*. Budapest: Osiris.

Popper, K. [1963] 2014. *Conjectures and Refutations: The Growth of Scientific Knowledge*. New York: Routledge.

Radden, J. 2007. Thinking about the repair manual: Technique and technology in psychiatry. In Phillips, J. (ed.), *Philosophical Perspectives on Technology and Psychiatry*. Oxford University Press, pp. 263–278.

Rank, O. 2015. *The Myth of the Birth of the Hero: A Psychological Exploration of Myth (with an Introductory Essay by Robert A. Segal)*. Baltimore, MD: Johns Hopkins University Press.

Royal College of Psychiatrists 2022. *Psychiatry Silver Guide: Guidance for Psychiatric Training in the UK*. Version 1.0. www.rcpsych.ac.uk/docs/default-source/training/curricula-and-guidance/silver-guide-final_7-1-22.pdf?sfvrsn=da9c22a2_2.

RogerS, C. R. 1942. *Counseling and Psychotherapy*. Cambridge, MA: Riverside Press.

Rogers, C. R. [1951] 1995. *Client-Centered Therapy: Its Current Practice, Implications and Theory*. London: Constable.

Rokeach, M. 1973. *The Nature of Human Values*. New York: Free Press.

Ruiz, M. R. & Roche, B. 2007. Values and the scientific culture of behavior analysis. *Behavior Analyst*, 30, 1–16.

Rutherford, A. 2017. B. F. Skinner and technology's nation: Technocracy, social engineering, and the good life in 20th-century America. *History of Psychology*, 20, 290–312.

Skinner, B. F. 1971. *Beyond Freedom and Dignity*. Harmondsworth: Penguin Books.

Skinner, B. F. [1948] 2005. *Walden Two (with a New Preface by the Author)*. Indianapolis, IN: Hackett. A reprint of the 1976 Macmillan edition.

Slife, B. D. & Williams, R. N. 1995. *What's Behind the Research? Discovering Hidden Assumptions in the Behavioral Sciences*. Thousand Oaks, CA: SAGE.

Stewart, C. M. 1967. Behavior therapy techniques: A guide to the treatment of neuroses. *Archives of General Psychiatry*, 16, 253–254.

Sullivan, H. S. 1955. *The Interpersonal Theory of Psychiatry*, edited by H. S. Perry & M. L. Gawel. Abingdon: Routledge.

Turner, J., Hayward, R., Angel, K., Fulford, B. (K. W. M.), Hall, J., Millard, C. & Thomson, M. 2015. The history of mental health services in modern England: Practitioner memories and the direction of future research. *Medical History*, 59, 599–624.

Watson, J. B. 1925. *Behaviorism*. New York: W. W. Norton & Company.

Weber, M. 1904/1949. 'Objectivity' in social science and social policy. In Weber, M. (ed.), *The Methodology of the Social Sciences*. Glencoe, IL: Free Press, pp. 50–112.

Weber, M. 1906/1949. Critical studies in the logic of the cultural sciences. In Weber, M. (ed.), *The Methodology of the Social Sciences*. Glencoe, IL: Free Press, pp. 113–188.

Weckowicz, T. E. & Liebel-Weckowicz, H. 1990a. Sigmund Freud: The new dynamic psychiatry. In Weckowicz, T. E. & Liebel-Weckowicz, H. P. (eds.), *A History of Great Ideas in Abnormal Psychology*. Advances in Psychology vol. 66. Amsterdam: North-Holland, pp. 223–282.

Weckowicz, T. E. & Liebel-Weckowicz, H. 1990b. The roots of behaviour therapy. In Weckowicz, T. E. & Liebel-Weckowicz, H. P. (eds.), *A History of Great Ideas in Abnormal Psychology*. Advances in Psychology vol. 66. Amsterdam: North-Holland, pp. 293–314.

Weinberger, J. & Westen, D. 2001. Science and psychodynamics: From arguments about Freud to data. *Psychological Inquiry*, 12, 129–132.

Williams, D. C. & Levitt, H. M. 2007. Principles for facilitating agency in psychotherapy. *Psychotherapy Research*, 17, 66–82.

Woodbridge-Dodd, K. 2012. Values-based practice in mental health and psychiatry. *Current Opinion in Psychiatry*, 25, 508–512.

Yakushko, O. 2019. Eugenics and its evolution in the history of western psychology: A critical archival review. *Psychotherapy and Politics International*, 17, e1495.

Yalom, I. D. 1980. *Existential Psychotherapy*. New York: Basic Books.

Zilboorg, G. 1941. *A History of Medical Psychology*. New York: W. W. Norton & Company.

Chapter 3

Psychiatry and Values

Perspectives from the Social and Cultural History of Mental Health

Mathew Thomson

Introduction

An interest in the relationship between psychiatric theory and practice and the society that encouraged and facilitated those ways of thinking and acting has been at the very heart of the social and cultural history of psychiatry. Such historians have tended to accept the inevitability of a close relationship between psychiatry and the values of the time. On the other hand, because they take that relationship for granted, they have devoted surprisingly little direct attention to the significance and precise nature of this relationship. As a consequence, there are no histories of the relationship between psychiatry and values across time. Historians would be able to provide multiple examples of how particular values were entangled with their histories of psychiatry in different periods and contexts. They would find it far harder to answer the wider question of what the broad history of the relationship between psychiatry or mental health and values looks like. Conceptually, this demands new thinking. This review sets out to begin that process. The central aim of this chapter is to begin thinking about what happens when we bring together existing work in the social and cultural history of psychiatry to reflect on what this tells us about the changing relationship to values across time. In the process, it does its best to avoid judgement on those values, though it highlights that this has been a characteristic of some history of psychiatry and is one of the reasons why the history of psychiatry itself has had an influence on psychiatry's relationship to values. We will see that the idea that psychiatry is inherently value-laden takes us only so far; the more interesting and important story is of some fundamental shifts in the nature of this relationship. Recognizing and understanding such shifts will hopefully be helpful in our consideration of the place of values in psychiatry today.

The review that follows confines itself to historical developments in Britain. The British example should be helpful in thinking about development more generally in comparably developed countries but is clearly less so in relation to lesser developed settings. It reaches back to the start of the nineteenth-century emergence of an asylum system and forwards to the anti-psychiatric debates and shift of policy towards community care in the 1970s. It pays less attention to developments in recent decades. The assumption here is that an understanding of the more recent period will be much better handled in other chapters in this volume and that the main value of this chapter will be to offer a point of contrast and comparison to help us think about our own times historically. But it is also worth highlighting that the history of the last half-century remains under-developed. The chapter moves forwards in time covering four rough periods: the nineteenth century, the early twentieth century, the era of the Second World War, and the post-war era up until the end of the

1970s. In each period I attempt to tease out the relationship of developments to values. A conclusion will return to reflect on this, draw out patterns of development, and attempt more precisely to delineate the different ways in which history can help us think about the position of values in relation to psychiatry and mental health.

The Nineteenth Century

In the late eighteenth and early nineteenth centuries it is anachronistic to talk of either 'psychiatry' or 'mental health'. Both were products of the century ahead. Nevertheless, the history of psychiatry has paid close attention to these years as they were seminal in the emergence of new, specialist institutions – in the language of the time, 'madhouses' and 'asylums' – that for a long time were the defining feature of the field.[1] Not until well into the nineteenth century did the doctors who worked in such institutions slowly begin to organize and identify as specialists in the area with the formation of a professional association – from 1841 the Association of Medical Officers of Asylums and Hospitals for the Insane, renamed in 1862 the Medico-Psychological Association – and its journal – from 1853 titled the *Asylum Journal*, renamed the *Journal of Mental Science* in 1858. That kind of process of professionalization entailed one form of value-making in which these doctors began to assume a corporate identity and their actions began to conform to a set of expectations, principles, and therapeutic and managerial approaches beyond those already assumed as part of the medical profession.

In staking a claim to be those best suited to be superintendents of these institutions and in advancing the benefits of an expansion of such a system of care under medical supervision, these figures aligned themselves with the progressive and humanitarian values of non-restraint and moral therapy. The medical adoption of such an approach is of interest to a history of values in indicating that the challenge of mental disorder tested traditional medical thinking and led to reorientation of thinking about the importance of human relationships in well-being. Such developments figured heavily in early historical accounts that portrayed the emergence of 'asylums' under medical control and now under proper regulation as a progressive and humanitarian act. In that iteration, the birth of psychiatry was driven by the kind of values that inspired a broader movement of social reform in the period, which saw, for instance, legislation to restrict the exploitation of children in factories and mines.[2]

The history of the psychiatry of this era has, however, identified a much broader range of motivation that takes us far beyond professional and medical values. Moral therapy initially had a strong religious impulse, as was the case with the Quaker York Retreat which pioneered the approach, and it would prove much harder to successfully implement in the context of large public asylums under medical control. The setting up of the early 'mad-houses' had often been driven by profit, and well into the nineteenth century private asylum care remained significant, meaning that standards of care were sharply demarcated across lines of class.[3] Care for a very large proportion of the mentally ill was inflected by the less-eligibility principles of the poor law, which carried over into specialized institutions that emerged for the indigent, mentally disordered poor.[4] In huge, overcrowded institutions which had little scope to attend to individuality and in which freedom was still heavily constrained, even if not by shackles, a rhetoric of more moral therapy and the move to non-restraint could in practice constitute little more than a self-justifying gloss. This gap between ideal and practice raises awkward questions for the values of those who presided over the system.

Whatever we may now feel about the inadequate conditions and treatment of those housed in the institutions set up across the nineteenth century, the willingness to fund such major effort has come to seem increasingly striking when we look back from an era that has seen the closure of such hospitals and criticism of the inadequacy of alternatives. The efforts of our Victorian forebears in creating a national system of asylums stand, then, as an example of how the broader values of society can be just as crucial as those of psychiatry itself in shaping mental health care policy and practice, enabling what in the context of the day was radical and innovative action.

Early scholarship may have used the term humanitarian for such ventures, but later historians increasingly argued that this approach obscured as much as it illuminated the underlying values, was too ready to accept at face value claims about motivation, and was 'whiggish' in its disposition towards a progressive history.[5] Instead, new studies appeared that showed that 'humanitarian' action was influenced by a powerful, discriminating morality over the deserving and the undeserving, and often harsh standards of morality. This may have been an era of self-proclaimed humanitarian reform, but it was a humanitarianism that was inflected by the hierarchical and moral values of the age. Subsequent scholarship has also become more critical of the idea that the changes were genuinely liberating. Influentially, Michel Foucault's *Madness and Civilisation* challenged the idea that the 'moral therapy' of pioneering asylums such as the York Retreat should be seen as an unshackling of the mad.[6] Foucault portrayed moral therapy instead as the replacement of one form of coercion for another that was less obvious but ultimately more insidious and in the long term hugely influential for the policing of social norms. Here, liberal values remain central, but this liberalism became the subject of critique. Sociologist Nikolas Rose extended this line of argument into the development of mental health care beyond the asylum in the twentieth century, in which the internalization of mental health values left its subjects 'obliged to be free'.[7] Humanitarianism has similarly come under criticism through work on the nineteenth-century asylum system. Most influentially, American sociologist and historian Andrew Scull argued that such institutions may have had humane, reformist origins, but expansion was driven by the fact that society was increasingly unable, unwilling, or intolerant in coping with the marginal and the socially desperate.[8] Asylums became a kind dumping ground for the incapable and the seemingly incurable. They also began to cater to the social misfits who filled workhouses, prisons, and reformatories: since the deterrent principle upon which such institutions were based seemed unable to deter recidivism, it proved increasingly attractive to explain inadequacy and incorrigibility instead as the result of underlying mental incapacity. In such circumstances, early therapeutic optimism in asylums waned as they filled up with long-stay, chronic cases, and overcrowding encouraged therapeutic pessimism and the fear that a seemingly rising tide of insanity was a sign of a broader process of degeneration of the population.

For a while, the notion of social control held sway in accounts of the expansion of the asylum system.[9] Such histories highlighted how lunacy and new psychiatric labels such as weak-mindedness and mental deficiency operated as tools to support society's moral and social expectations of appropriate behaviour.[10] Yet something rather different and more subtle was evident in work that focussed less on growing numbers and more on the challenges of running this system. Study of the admissions process highlighted that a broader set of social actors, not least families, lay behind the increase in numbers.[11] The medical superintendents were faced by a hugely challenging set of circumstances: their therapeutic armoury was still very limited; they often had to cope on their own and rely on poorly trained attendants in attending to the needs of huge patient populations and a growing number of ageing and long-term residents; and their ability to reach out to more readily treatable mental illness was constrained by the strict legalism of the asylum system that saw admission as a last resort and made it far harder to reach the potentially curable. Working within the severe constraints of the time, these doctors were often by necessity first and foremost administrators – as their title of 'superintendents' indicated. As doctors, much of their time was taken up trying to prevent the spread of infectious illness. Their values could, of course, help in creating a more benevolent asylum regime, but the scope for fundamental reform was limited.[12] They were not uninterested in the individuality of their patients – indeed, there is some evidence of genuine dialogue in the therapeutic relationship – but circumstances were not favourable towards making this easy or common.[13] Occupation of patients therefore performed a dual role: perhaps to a degree therapeutic, but also valuable in management and in the economy of the asylum.[14] But blaming psychiatry and its values to a large extent misses the point. These doctors were trapped by circumstances and limits that were largely beyond their control. In the nineteenth century, the values of the broader society were of primary importance in shaping the system of care.

The Early Twentieth Century

By the end of the nineteenth century, the seemingly inexorable growth of the asylum population was fuelling pessimism about degeneration of the national stock. A further major expansion was to follow with an additional system of care and control for the mentally handicapped under the Mental Deficiency Act of 1913. That legislation even gave a place to 'moral deficiency', a clear indication of the way in which the field could operate as a control on behaviour, even if the implementation of the policy indicates that this diagnosis proved unattractive in practice. Psychiatry, though still a notably low-status field within medicine, was increasingly prominent through its position at the helm of this system. In an era of heightened anxiety about national efficiency and with the rise of eugenics as a popular movement, the profession was dragged into these broader debates. It would be wrong, however, to overstate the field's alignment with eugenics or to interpret this simply in terms of values.[15]

As custodians of institutions that housed populations which were the primary object of concern for eugenics, psychiatrists were called upon for expert analysis on the issue of heritability. But psychiatrists were not numerous within or at the forefront of the eugenics movement. When they did contribute to the debate, it was to offer scientific backing to the hereditary nature of conditions, though, in truth, such assumptions long predated eugenics and the more important evidence came from mathematical and statistical scientists. We also need to bear in mind that in the early twentieth century, eugenics attracted broad progressive support, seen as part of a modernizing agenda of bringing the fruits of science to social policy.[16] The leading advocates of an expansion of segregation, which was a central feature of the British eugenics movement, were not those already struggling to deal with current numbers in asylums but instead groups in the broader community such as charities, social workers, and those working in the penal, poor-law, and education systems who were keen to offload those who made management of these systems difficult owing to their perceived inherent degeneracy.

The majority of the profession remained in often isolated, under-staffed, closed institutions. As such, they were generally more preoccupied by the challenges of managing their hospitals than pontificating in public debate over values.[17] If they had guiding values, these lay more in the realm of ensuring efficiency, order, and as good health as possible on limited resources. It was rare for one of these doctors to openly react against the sacrifices it entailed in terms of the patients' welfare and freedom, and for that they perhaps merit criticism.[18] But, in more limited fashion, they were involved in efforts to adapt the physical space of the institution to humanize life within, through past-times and employment that also added to the efficiency of the institutions. The move towards use of multiple buildings in colony-style institutions can similarly be seen as characteristic of a slow effort to try to humanize the sort of care that could be provided in the vast institutions of the era through hierarchies of care, an ethos of community, and a greater sense of there being a series of stepping-stones that might lead to life outside the institution through licensing, guardianship, or hostels.[19] The same logic could even make some of these psychiatrists sympathetic towards the campaign to introduce sexual sterilization of 'mental defectives' in the 1930s, the view being that this would enable release of milder cases, who would no longer be seen as a potential eugenic threat, and so relieve pressure on the overcrowded institutions.[20] It is tempting to condemn the values of the psychiatrists who headed these institutions that provided so little hope to those admitted and tempting too to condemn those drawn to a policy such as sterilization, but we do need to bear in mind the very difficult conditions that they faced.[21] In other contexts, not just Germany but also the United States and Scandinavia, this logic of using sterilization to ease pressure on institutional care was put in place. The reasons for these differences lie less in the values of psychiatry, which was often open to the policy, than in the broader values and structures of the political system; in Britain, concerns about protecting the liberty of the subject, which had to a degree shackled modernization of institutional psychiatry, again prevailed.[22]

The other avenue for the energies of progressive medical superintendents was to conduct research. This was an era of some progress in scientific efforts in the field, notably at the pioneering Maudsley Hospital.[23] Some of that work, often reporting on the new physical treatments of the era, reached the pages of the profession's *Journal of Mental Science*. At a more mundane level, medical superintendents collated statistics on their patient populations that filled annual reports. The benefit of working in one of these huge institutions was the ready presence of a large, captive population that could be used to test new approaches. It can be argued that there was a move in the direction of scientific values. But other values could be sacrificed in the process: reading some of these research reports highlights serious questions over whether that population consented to being used in this way and whether they received therapies that were really necessary for their own well-being. This era also saw the advance of specialist training for psychiatrists but also mental nurses.[24] Such developments steered this work, and its guiding values, towards a medical and indeed emerging psychiatric frame, in place of one that was merely custodial or managerial. This was symbolized and further encouraged by the Mental Treatment Act of 1930, which saw institutions renamed as mental hospitals and the introduction of voluntary and temporary treatment orders enabling care of patients without legal certification. When it comes to institutional psychiatry, this move from a custodial to a medical orientation was the major value shift of the era, but it should not be overstated. The patterns of everyday life for chronic and long-stay patients remained largely the same for decades to come. Psychiatrists may increasingly have been on the side of exploring new therapeutics and looking to more open-door policies, but the constraints of limited resources, social isolation, and public stigma towards mental illness persisted. In such circumstances, the opportunity to experiment with new therapies found itself sometimes without sufficient constraint of concern over patient rights and welfare; individuality was still sacrificed to the efficiency of the regime, and abuse persisted, hidden from public sight until a series of public scandals in the 1960s.[25]

Engagement with public values was more obvious among those within psychiatry whose work took them beyond the confines of mental institutions. Indeed, to a degree, one can argue that the profession in this period increasingly looked to escape the legalism of the asylum in development of a more therapeutic role.[26] In the first decades of the twentieth century, this was already an exciting area of growth. Such work included private clinical practice, some of which was inspired by new psychodynamic theory and methods such as psychoanalysis. It extended to child guidance work in the inter-war years. There was also growing interest in addressing the 'human factor' in the workplace to ensure happier, more-efficient, and less-illness-prone workers. Perhaps most dramatically, the First World War had seen psychiatry deployed to address the problem of shellshock, treating men who broke down mentally and often physically through the stress and fear of warfare.[27] By the inter-war period, there was a growing emphasis on the prevention of mental illness and cultivation of 'mental health' and 'mental hygiene'.[28] In advancing itself in relation to problems of social adjustment, psychiatry necessarily situated itself in relation to prevailing normative values about behaviour.[29] This included a quite common alliance with Christian thought.[30] Anyone interested in the field's relationship to values would want to look carefully at its ideas about what needed adjustment and what constituted health and hygiene. Certainly, in some cases it continued to play a role in enforcing broader conventions on morality, as in the way that the mental deficiency legislation operated to target action on those who were perceived as a sexual danger or whose behaviour brought them to the attention of the public authorities. But at times the field's positions could be in tension with traditional social and moral values.[31] Psychoanalytic positions on sexuality are a case in point.[32] Indeed, in general, advice on behaviour was now increasingly in line with more progressive and tolerant values, reframing immorality and misbehaviour as something to be understood and worked through rather than condemned.[33] Psychiatry found itself moving into the role of gatekeeper on values, arbitrating, for example, on whether collapse in war was a sign of cowardice or mental strain and on whether soldiers should have access to a pension as a result of mental injury, or, following the return to peace, whether workplace sickness claims were the result of mental strain or malingering.

Scarcity of experts and funding meant that this move beyond the asylum was often dependent on multidisciplinary teams and in particular alliance with psychologists and psychiatric social workers.[34] But this had its limits, too: all of these fields were in embryo. The bold visions of the mental hygiene movement would therefore ultimately depend on the power of advice and on the ability to translate advice into a popular idiom. In practice, the appetite for such writing was often met by an eclectic variety of mental health entrepreneurs who were less tainted by association with pathology than psychiatry was and who mixed psychological theory with religious, spiritual, and even mystical thinking, or more often a strong dose of common sense and an emphasis on practical technique that avoided dependence on experts. This culture was popular, practical, heterodox, and democratizing in orientation.[35] Psychiatry stood only at its more orthodox margins and in tension with unorthodox and lay competitors. But this popular interest did facilitate extension of psychiatry into the community and beyond mental illness to mental health. It provided a platform for paying growing attention to the interplay of mind and body in general practice.[36] It also paved the way for a psychosocial approach that propelled psychiatry into the realm of public values: if mental health involved finding a balance between internal drives and social conventions, this raised the question of whether those conventions, social structures, and values might sometimes benefit from adjustment in the interests of mental health.[37]

The Second World War

As the situation across Europe darkened in the 1930s, there was growing interest in the possibility that psychosocial understanding could be crucial in addressing the phenomena of financial panic, dictatorship, and nationalist aggression. The mass aerial bombardment of Guernica in the Spanish Civil War also directed attention at the likely importance of mental health in any future war, with growing fears that the next war would be decided by the defence of civilian morale.[38] British psychiatrists and psychologists began to write about the psychological causes and effects of appeasement at Munich and the value of democracy to mental health and of mental health to democracy. War, when it came, provided a unique opportunity for psychiatry to advance itself as a tool not just for managing casualties but also for preventing breakdown. Psychiatry was turned to for advice in relation to the maintenance of civilian morale, the policies of the Ministry of Information, the handling of air raids, and the virtues of evacuating children from cities. The Blitz of Britain's cities and the mass separation of children from parents through evacuation provided laboratories for the psychosocial exploration of mental health.[39] And mental health experts were drawn into discussions on the psychosocial benefits of planning for a post-war welfare state, as well as diagnosis of Nazis and advice on denazification.[40] Through the radio, which was now a ubiquitous feature of daily life, figures like John Bowlby and Donald Winnicott had huge reach in advising parents on how to rear the mentally healthy children who would provide the good citizenship that was so essential for a healthy democracy.[41] Concern about the interplay of mental health and values was a striking feature of intellectual life by the time the war ended, projected onto the international stage via the 1948 London Conference of the World Federation of Mental Health with its pronouncements on mental health, world citizenship, and peace.[42]

Post-War

The Second World War was a high point for this belief that mental health was both the basis for and the result of broader public values. Wartime national emergency, existential concern about morale and manpower, and a unique climate of state intervention had all encouraged this. Those conditions faded in the war's aftermath. Development continued but often beyond psychiatry, in areas like social work, marriage guidance, and general medical practice.[43] The psychosocial orientation of the inter-war era also took a turn towards integrating the biological into new work on stress.[44] By this point, the longer-term battle to align the mental health system with medicine had been won and thus, without any significant controversy, these services moved from being under the separate administration of the inter-war Board of Control to being included in the new National Health Service under the Ministry of Health. But the mental health services found themselves, if anything, an even lower priority in this new position. An impulse to humanize care, adopt more open-door policies akin to other areas of medicine, and emphasize therapeutics continued, but so did inadequate staffing and resourcing, overcrowding, and the challenge of long-stay patients. When public attention was drawn to the conditions within these institutions, it could be difficult to maintain the claim that they had truly seen a transformation from their custodial origins. For all the efforts at policy and therapeutic reform, there remained a mismatch between conditions on wards often dominated by elderly and chronic patients and modern medical values that increasingly emphasized the importance of the individual and of cure.

Values, which had been an asset for psychiatry in a period in which it had allied itself with the move from custody to treatment and with a turn to mental health in the broader community, now to a degree bit back. Despite slow progress in improving services, as, for instance, now charted in the area of psychogeriatrics, and a growing public profile for a small number of media psychiatrists, the conditions within mental hospitals were exposed as falling short of modern medical and humanitarian ideals.[45] The challenges of de-stigmatizing mental disorder persisted and continued to affect attitudes towards the field.[46] The idea that psychiatry could be a tool for social adjustment now also found itself under growing criticism in an era in which individual freedom and authenticity began to be prized over social conformity. This dual problem of values was the context for the emergence of what has come to be known as anti-psychiatry in the late 1960s and 1970s.[47] Particularly associated with a small group of radical psychiatrists, most famously R. D. Laing, this phenomenon was characterized by a significance that lay less in the relatively small number of people involved than in the broader interest and sympathy that their actions and writing attracted and the implications of these for public attitudes towards psychiatry.[48] Laing and his anti-psychiatric colleague David Cooper were influential, for instance, in the development of Ken Loach's television drama *In Two Minds*, which was subsequently turned into a film under the title *Family Life*.[49] This drama captured the idea that family, rather than being essential in the bolstering of mental health, could be the key disintegrating force. It also used the symbol of electric shock therapy for psychiatry's violent potential and its focus on biology rather than the individual. The fact that the victim of this psychiatry is a young woman thwarted in trying to break with family and sexual and gendered convention is no coincidence. Whereas, half a century earlier, psychiatry had begun to seem to be an ally of progressive social values, public morality on issues of gender, sex, and individual freedom had radically shifted and psychiatry could now be portrayed as often on the other side to permissiveness. The critique over the values of psychiatry went further through the influence of the second-wave feminist movement of the era, which objected to the way in which ideas about adjustment, it felt, had commonly enforced gender inequality.[50] A third component of this more prominent culture of critique was the emergence of a more formalized movement to represent service users who, for all the progress away from confinement, still often felt acutely their relative lack of liberties and voice within the system.[51] Holding together all these strains of anti-psychiatric critique was a feeling that the rights, feelings, and individuality of patients were being neglected by an overly authoritarian and overly medical profession. Rather like in the popular psychology of the early twentieth century, people were keen to turn instead to a more eclectic body of thought and practice directed at growth, the search for authenticity, and practical strategies of therapy that did not depend on still-difficult-to-access expertise.[52] This anti-psychiatric culture was also, as noted in the 'Introduction' to this chapter, an important influence on the development of the history of psychiatry in these years, attracting social historians to the field and orientating them towards seeing psychiatry as deeply tied to the often authoritarian and illiberal values of its times and as having played a role in what was often described as 'social control'.

The influence of this anti-psychiatric culture in shaping public views and suspicion of the field went well beyond the movement's own achievements. The fact that its heyday coincided with a turn away from mental hospitals towards community care makes it tempting to assume a fundamental impact on policy too, but that turn was already underway, in line with the longer-term reform of institutional care, and was now made much easier by the arrival of new drugs as well as the expansion of allied professions such as social work.[53] Perhaps, however, one legacy of the anti-psychiatric critique was that psychiatry emerged more cautious than earlier in the century about taking a public role on values. Gone to a large extent was the grand ambition of mental hygiene with its vision of making a more mentally healthy society, its bold speculation over how society should be organized, and its forays into the realm of public values. Without this bold reforming vision, community care was instead something that tended to be rather vaguely defined, struggled to capture the public imagination, and was left with the same problems of under-resourcing that had beset the mental hospital system.[54] Only relatively recently has mental health begun to be advanced prominently by governments and political parties as deserving parity with physical health and as a priority for national action. Interestingly, this new moment also seems to have provided fertile territory for a revival of interest in values and thinking about a values-based approach in psychiatry, which is the context for this volume and which has seen the Royal College of Psychiatrists draw up its own statement on values.[55] The question of what lies between that anti-psychiatric era and the present sense of national crisis and interest in values demands far more historical attention than it has received to date.[56] The focus on values within this book should provide a further significant step in helping us build towards some answers.

Conclusion

This chapter began with the proposition that a relationship among psychiatry, mental health, and values has been integral to the cultural and social history of psychiatry but that it is so taken for granted that it has rarely, if ever, been focussed upon in its own right. The central purpose of this chapter has been to offer a review of developments but also existing historical work that can begin to provide some answers on two issues: what changes took place; and what we might mean by values. The scale of the challenge has not made this easy. Surveying development over two centuries has entailed some crude generalization and overlooking many significant aspects of historical development. The result is certainly very far from a definitive picture. The hope is that it helps, nevertheless, to stimulate further reflection about the use of this kind of history for thinking about psychiatry and values.

One central theme of the chapter has been that historical research highlights that the values that shape mental health policy are not just those of the practitioners involved; they are also those of the broader society, whether this be the values that determine why families feel the need to turn to the services, the values that shape why governments support a service, or the social and cultural values that determine understanding of what constitutes mental health. Historically, these broader values have often been just as important as those of what came to be the field of psychiatry. Historical research has also highlighted that mental health practice has often depended on psychiatry allying with other fields and that their values therefore also need consideration. This cultural and social historical perspective also has implications for thinking about values within the profession itself. It highlights that psychiatrists have always been part of broader value systems and that choices in this area cannot be overlooked. However, the chapter has also indicated that decision-making in this area is complicated, shaped by limited resources of finance and staff, professional insecurity, limited knowledge, and the balancing of competing demands of care, cure, and control. Historical judgement needs to bear those factors in mind. Instead of casting sweeping blame over what may now seem to have been bad value choices, it may be more helpful to examine these dilemmas in finer-grained detail so as to learn lessons.

Turning to a second central theme of the chapter, the issue of change over time, the review has provided a picture of a rise, retreat, and possible rise again of confidence in thinking about the relationship between psychiatry and values. In the nineteenth century, psychiatry found itself the beneficiary of a broader values-based impulse to create and radically expand a system of institutional care for the mentally disordered. Those values – whether we see them as humanitarian or driven by social control – had a profound impact in shaping psychiatry. Some psychiatrists assumed public roles as advocates of those values. But this also placed psychiatry in an insecure position, without the therapeutic tools to advance its status within medicine, increasingly confined to its own institutions, and tied down by problems of management. As a result, psychiatry gradually turned away from broader statements on values to focus on more cautious profession-building through training and research. The rise in ambition did continue, but now outside these institutions in a period culminating with the Second World War, which provided uniquely fertile territory for thinking about mental health in values-based terms. That expansion of ambition demanded alliance with other professions and often involved a stronger psychodynamic orientation. The retreat partly stemmed from the post-war ebbing of a sense of national crisis and its heightened anxiety about human nature. It also reflected the continuation of trends of professionalization that entailed a more cautious approach to values. A new climate of opinion around anti-psychiatry was also significant to the retreat, signalling the vulnerability of the field from a values-based perspective. The possibility that there has been a second shift and a new rise is more of a suggestion and a provocation than a claim within this chapter. It provides a potential context for situating the efforts of this volume. It also raises the challenge of explaining such a further shift. If historical precedent is a useful guide, the answer is likely to lie only partly in the actions and aspirations of psychiatry itself.

Notes

1. Porter, R. 1987. *A Social History of Madness.* London: Wiedenfeld & Nicolson.
2. The account that pioneered this reformist, humanitarian interpretation in fact came from the discipline of social administration that was significant in opening up the history of social policy: Jones, K. 1955. *Lunacy, Law and Conscience, 1744–1845: The Social History of the Care of the Insane.* Abingdon: Routledge. For the broader early framework for thinking about this era, see Briggs, A. 1959. *The Age of Improvement, 1783–1867.* London: Longmans, Green and Company.
3. Parry-Jones, W. [1972] 2007. *The Trade in Lunacy: A Study of Private Madhouses in England in the Eighteenth and Nineteenth Centuries.* Abingdon: Routledge.
4. Bartlett, P. 1999. *The Poor Law of Lunacy: The Administration of Pauper Lunatics in Mid-Nineteenth-Century England.* London: Leicester University Press.

5. The critique of 'whig' history goes back to Herbert Butterfield's *Whig Interpretation*: Butterfield, H. 1931. *The Whig Interpretation of History*. New York: W. W. Norton and Company.
6. Though published in French in 1961, it took much longer for this book to influence English-speaking historians. By the 1990s he was a ubiquitous reference point and not just for the history of psychiatry: Bracken, P. 2015. 'On *Madness and Civilisation: A History of Insanity in the Age of Reason* (1961), by Michel Foucault', *British Journal of Psychiatry*, 207(5) 434; Gutting, G. 2005. 'Foucault and the history of madness'. In Gutting, G. (ed.), *The Cambridge Companion to Foucault*. Cambridge: Cambridge University Press, pp. 49–73.
7. Rose, N. 1999. *Governing the Soul: The Shaping of the Private Self*. London: Free Association Books.
8. Scull, A. 1979. *Museums of Madness: The Social Organisation of Insanity in 19th Century England*. London: Allen Lane.
9. Cohen, C. & Scull, A. (eds.) 1983. *Social Control and the State: Historical and Comparative Essays*. London: Palgrave Macmillan.
10. Thomson, M. 1998. *The Problem of Mental Deficiency: Eugenics, Democracy and Social Policy in Britain, c.1870–1959*. Oxford: Oxford University Press.
11. Suzuki, A. 2006. *Madness at Home: The Psychiatrist, the Patient, and the Family in England, 1820–1860*. Medicine and Society 13. Berkeley: University of California Press.
12. Hickman, C. 2009. Cheerful prospects and tranquil restoration: The visual experience of landscape as part of the therapeutic regime of the British asylum, 1800–60. *History of Psychiatry*, 20(4), 425–441.
13. Chaney, S. J. 2016. No 'sane' person would have any idea: Patients' involvement in late nineteenth-century British asylum psychiatry. *Medical History*, 60(1), 37–53.
14. Chaney, S. J. 2016. Useful members of society or motiveless malingerers? Occupation and malingering in British asylum psychiatry, 1870–1914. In Ernst, W. (ed.), *Work, Psychiatry and Society, c.1750–2015*. Manchester: Manchester University Press, pp. 277–297.
15. Thomson, The Problem of Mental Deficiency.
16. Freeden, M. 1983. Eugenics and ideology. *Historical Journal*, 26(4), 959–962.
17. Though there are high-profile exceptions who have attracted considerable attention, such as Thomas Clouston, James Crichton-Browne, and Henry Maudsley, these tended to be doctors whose daily lives were not taken up by the demands of managing a large institution.
18. Soanes, S. 2009. Reforming asylums, reforming public attitudes: J. R. Lord and Montagu Lomax's representations of mental hospitals and the community, 1921–1931. *Family and Community History*, 12(2), 117–129; Harding, T. W. 1990. 'Not worth powder and shot': A reappraisal of Montagu Lomax's contribution to mental health reform. *British Journal of Psychiatry*, 156, 180–187.
19. Westwood, L. 2007. Care in the community of the mentally disordered: The case of the Guardianship Society, 1900–1939. *Social History of Medicine*, 20(1), 57–72.
20. Thomson, M. 1992. Sterilization, segregation and community care: Ideology and solutions to the problem of mental deficiency in inter-war Britain. *History of Psychiatry*, 3(12), 473–498.
21. See also the study of sterilization in California: Braslow, J. 1997. *Mental Ills and Bodily Cures: Psychiatric Treatment in the First Half of the Twentieth Century*. Berkeley: University of California Press.
22. Thomson, M. 2010. Disability, psychiatry, and mental health. In Bashford, A. & Levine, P. (eds.), *The Oxford Handbook of the History of Eugenics*. Oxford: Oxford University Press, pp. 116–133; Roelcke, V. 2019. Eugenic concerns, scientific practices: International relations in the establishment of psychiatric genetics in Germany, Britain, the USA and Scandinavia, c.1910–60. *History of Psychiatry*, 30(1), 19–37.
23. Jones, E. 2014. 'An atmosphere of cure': Frederick Mott, shell shock and the Maudsley. *History of Psychiatry*, 25(4), 412–421; Evans, B. & Jones, E. 2012. Organ extracts and the development of psychiatry: Hormonal treatments at the Maudsley Hospital 1923–1938. *Journal of the History of the Behavioral Sciences*, 48(3), 251–276; Jones, E. 2003. Aubrey Lewis, Edward Mapother and the Maudsley. *Medical History*, 22(suppl), 3–38.

24. Crammer, J. L. 1996. Training and education in British psychiatry 1770–1970. In Freeman, H. & Berrios, G. E. (eds.), *150 Years of British Psychiatry, Vol. 2: The Aftermath*. London: Athlone, pp. 209–242.
25. Hide, L. 2018. In plain sight: Open doors, mixed-sex wards and sexual abuse in English psychiatric hospitals, 1950s–early 1990s. *Social History of Medicine*, 31(4), 732–753.
26. Takabayashi, A. 2017. Surviving the Lunacy Act of 1890: English psychiatrists and professional development during the early twentieth century. *Medical History*, 61(2), 246–269.
27. Shephard, B. 2000. *A War of Nerves: Soldiers and Psychiatry, 1914–1994*. London: Jonathan Cape.
28. Toms, J. 2013. *Mental Hygiene and Psychiatry in Modern Britain*. Basingstoke: Palgrave Macmillan.
29. Rose, N. 1985. *The Psychological Complex: Psychology, Politics and Society in England 1869–1939*. London: Routledge and Kegan Paul; Thomson, M. 2000. Constituting citizenship: Mental deficiency, mental health and human rights in inter-war Britain. In Lawrence, C. & Mayer, A.-K. (eds.), *Regenerating England: Science, Medicine and Culture in Inter-war Britain*. Amsterdam: Rodopi, pp. 231–250; Hayes, S. 2007. Rabbits and rebels: The medicalisation of maladjusted children in mid-twentieth-century Britain. In Jackson, M. (ed.), *Health and the Modern Home*. New York: Routledge, pp. 128–152; Weston, J. 2019. Citizenship, vulnerability and mental incapacity in England, 1900–1960s. *Medical History*, 63(3), 270–290.
30. Richards, G. 2000. Psychology and the churches in Britain 1919–39: Symptoms of conversion. *History of the Human Sciences*, 13, 57–84; Miller, G. 2020. *Miracles of Healing: Psychotherapy and Religion in Twentieth-Century Scotland*. Edinburgh: Edinburgh University Press.
31. Richards, G. D. 2000. Britain on the couch: The popularization of psychoanalysis in Britain, 1918–1940. *Science in Context*, 13(2), 183–230.
32. Looking ahead in time a little, this is explored in Waters, C. 2013. The homosexual as a social being in Britain, 1945–1968. In Lewis, B. (ed.), *British Queer History: New Approaches and Perspectives*. Manchester: Manchester University Press, pp. 188–218.
33. Bar-Haim, S. 2017. The liberal playground: Susan Isaacs, psychoanalysis and progressive education in the interwar era. *History of the Human Sciences*, 30(1), 94–117.
34. Stewart, J. 2013. *Child Guidance in Britain, 1918–1955: The Dangerous Age of Childhood*. London: Pickering and Chatto; Broad, J. 2021. Working in cases: British psychiatric social workers and a history of psychoanalysis from the middle, c.1930–60. *History of the Human Sciences*, 34(3–4), 169–194.
35. Thomson, M. 2006. *Psychological Subjects: Identity, Culture, and Health in Twentieth-Century Britain*. Oxford: Oxford University Press.
36. Hayward, R. 2014. *The Transformation of the Psyche in British Primary Care 1880–1970*. London: Bloomsbury Academic.
37. Hayward, R. 2009. Enduring emotions: James L. Halliday and the invention of the psychosocial. *Isis*, 100(4), 827–838; Hull, A. 2012. Glasgow's 'sick society'? James Halliday, psychosocial medicine and medical holism in Britain c.1920–48. *History of the Human Sciences*, 25(5), 73–90.
38. Burney, I. A. 2012. War on fear: Solly Zuckerman and civilian nerve in the Second World War. *History of the Human Sciences*, 25(5), 49–72.
39. Shapira, M. 2013. *The War Inside: Psychoanalysis, Total War, and the Making of the Democratic Self in Postwar Britain*. Cambridge: Cambridge University Press.
40. Hayward, R. 2012. The pursuit of serenity: Psychological knowledge and the making of the British welfare state. In Alexander, S. & Taylor, B. (eds.), *History and Psyche: Culture, Psychoanalysis, and the Past*. New York: Palgrave Macmillan, pp. 283–304; Bar Haim, S. 2021. *The Maternalists: Psychoanalysis, Motherhood, and the British Welfare State*. Philadelphia: University of Pennsylvania Press; Pick, D. 2012. *The Pursuit of the Nazi Mind: Hitler, Hess and the Analysts*. Oxford: Oxford University Press.
41. Karpf, A. 2014. Constructing and addressing the 'ordinary devoted mother'. *History Workshop Journal*, 78(1), 82–106.
42. Toms, J. 2012. Political dimensions of 'the psychosocial': The 1948 International Congress on Mental Health and the mental hygiene movement. *History of the Human Sciences*, 25(5), 91–106.

43. Hayward, The Transformation of the Psyche; Bar-Haim, S. 2018. 'The Drug Doctor': Michael Balint and the revival of general practice in postwar Britain. *History Workshop Journal*, 86, 114–132; Long, V. 2011. 'Often there is a good deal to be done, but socially rather than medically': The psychiatric social worker as social therapist, 1945–70. *Medical History*, 55(2), 223–239; Chettiar, T. 2016. 'More than a contract': The emergence of a state-supported marriage welfare service and the politics of emotional life in post-1945 Britain. *Journal of British Studies*, 55(3), 566–591.
44. Jackson, M. (ed.) 2015. *Stress in Post-War Britain, 1945–1985*. London: Pickering and Chatto.
45. Hilton, C. 2016. Developing psychogeriatric services in England: A turning point in the 1960s? *Contemporary British History*, 30(1), 40–72; Hilton, C. 2017. *Improving Psychiatric Care for Older People: Barbara Robb's Campaign 1965–1975*. Basingstoke: Palgrave Macmillan; Miller, G. 2015. Psychiatric penguins: Writing on psychiatry for Penguin Books, c.1950–c.1980. *History of the Human Sciences*, 28(4), 76–101; Hide, In plain sight.
46. Long, V. 2014. *Destigmatising Mental Illness? Professional Politics and Public Education in Britain, 1870–1970*. Manchester: Manchester University Press.
47. Toms, J. 2020. MIND, anti-psychiatry, and the case of the mental hygiene movement's 'discursive transformation'. *Social History of Medicine*, 33(2), 622–640.
48. Wall, O. 2017. *The British Anti-psychiatrists: From Institutional Psychiatry to the Counter-Culture, 1960–1971*. London: Routledge.
49. Snelson, T. 2021. From in two minds to MIND: The circulation of 'anti-psychiatry' in British film and television during the long 1960s. *History of the Human Sciences*, 34(5), 53–81.
50. Mahoney, K. 2018. The political, the emotional and the therapeutic: Narratives of consciousness-raising and authenticity in the English women's liberation movement. In Häberlen, J. C., Keck-Szajbel, M. & Mahoney, K. (eds.), *The Politics of Authenticity: Countercultures and Radical Movements Across the Iron Curtain, 1968–1989*. New York: Berghahn Books, pp. 65–88.
51. Spandler, H. 2006. *Asylum to Action: Paddington Day Hospital, Therapeutic Communities, and Beyond*. London: Jessica Kingsley; Crossley, N. 1999. Fish, field, habitus and madness: The first wave mental health users movement in Great Britain. *British Journal of Sociology*, 50, 647–670; Toms, J. 2017. Citizenship and learning disabled people: The mental health charity MIND's 1970s campaign in historical context. *Medical History*, 61(4), 481–499.
52. Thomson, Psychological Subjects.
53. Bartlett, P. & Wright, D. (eds.) 1999. *Outside the Walls of the Asylum: The History of Care in the Community, 1750–2000*. London: Athlone.
54. Taylor, B. 2011. The demise of the asylum in late twentieth-century Britain: A personal history. *Transactions of the Royal Historical Society*, 6th ser., 21, 193–215; Welshman, J. 1999. Rhetoric and reality: Community care in England and Wales, 1948–74. In Bartlett, P. & Wright, D. (eds.), *Outside the Walls of the Asylum: The History of Care in the Community, 1750–2000*. London: Athlone, pp. 204–226.
55. A values-based psychiatry is discussed in Fulford, K. W. M., Broome, M., Stanghellini, G. & Thornton, T. 2005. Looking with both eyes open: Fact and value in psychiatric diagnosis?' *World Psychiatry*, 4(2), 78–86; Richards, V. & Lloyd, K. 2017. Core Values for Psychiatrists. College Report CR204. London: Royal College of Psychiatrists. https://shorturl.at/78V2q.
56. For reflections on changes in how people narrated their own mental health across this period, see Burchell, A. & Thomson, M. 2022. Composing well-being: Mental health and the mass observation project in twentieth-century Britain. *Social History of Medicine*, 35, 444–472. For reflections on policy, see Turner, J., Angel, K., Fulford, B., Hall, J., Hayward, R., Millard, C. & Thomson, M. 2015. The history of the mental health services in modern England: Practitioner memories and the direction of future research. *Medical History*, 59, 599–624.

Chapter 4

Ailments of the Mind?

Robert B. Dudas

Introduction

Current research and clinical practice in psychiatry suffer from the lack of satisfactory theoretical foundations. Dominant models of mental illness are too narrow and reductionistic and fail to integrate the dimensions necessary to explain mental illness and recovery. An important element that is missing from these models completely or to a large degree is the role of *values*. Values are integral to the personal and the social levels, yet our current toolset for working with them in psychiatry is hugely rudimentary. This leads to a lack of real progress in research, limited treatment efficacy, and (to a certain degree) justified criticisms of psychiatry, including those by the anti-psychiatry and critical psychiatry movements. Developing better theoretical foundations in this respect will offer a chance to achieve real breakthroughs in psychiatry.

In 'Defining Mental Illness and Psychiatry', I will discuss the shortcomings of various models of mental illness in this respect ('Models of Mental Illness') and the relevance of values to some important theoretical issues in psychiatry ('Trying to Locate the Causes of Mental Disorders' and 'The Need for a Different Approach'). In 'Who Decides What Is Pathological?', I will demonstrate how values influence, often in an unacknowledged way, how various stakeholders approach mental illness on a practical level. And finally, in 'What Determines or Influences Mental Well-Being?', I will outline some potential benefits of bringing values into the picture as regards promoting mental health and treating mental illness.

Defining Mental Illness and Psychiatry

Models of Mental Illness

In psychiatry, we do not have a single, universally accepted model. The neuroscientific model currently occupies a dominant position, but there are a handful of other models that offer explanatory power. A requirement of any model is that it can successfully integrate findings from the various relevant strands of knowledge generation. This is no small challenge in psychiatry, as causal factors range widely from biological ones (e.g. genetic predisposition), through psychological influences (e.g. dysfunctional interpersonal relationships, extreme stress, and trauma), to social problems (e.g. unemployment, social isolation, deprivation, and poverty). Apart from this complexity, another major challenge is that too many pieces of the puzzle are still missing. Nevertheless, for models to provide a full explanation they are expected to take into account and relate to the symptomatology findings from (at least) four dimensions – physiological, psychological, sociocultural, and existential; the last is sometimes called reflexive. In terms of how many of these dimensions they truly integrate, it is possible to talk about one-sided, dualist, and holistic or integrative models.

Simple values are attendant on the living organism's dependence on its environment and its constant evaluation of its environment from the perspective of meeting its own needs. As humans, in addition to this, we are also able to reflect on our existence and its circumstances as well as our own actions not just in the here-and-now but also over time, which leads to the emergence of a whole world of existential values. There are two important relationships here that are relevant to our subject. *Values are closely linked to emotions*; acting in accordance with one's own values tends to be associated with positive emotions and acting against them with negative ones. *Values are also linked to actions*; they drive our actions and vice versa (Bruineberg, 2023). Values point beyond individual situations, but they are not static and can change over time. Values play a key role in mental health and illness and permeate both psychiatric concepts and clinical practice, although this is largely unacknowledged and remains unexamined in both theory and practice.

One-Sided and Dualist Models

The *neuroscientific model* is in principle a reductionistic, one-sided model. These models, even when they do consider many different aspects, trace back all relevant influences on one dimension ultimately. The neuroscientific model regards psychiatry as applied or clinical neuroscience and considers psychiatric disorders primarily to be diseases of the brain or brain circuits (Insel et al., 2010), caused by genetic or epigenetic anomalies, imbalances in neurotransmitter levels, injury, or problems with synaptic plasticity or neurogenesis. Whilst these have all been demonstrated in mental disorders, serious limitations of the neuroscientific model have been pointed out (de Haan, 2020a; Kotchoubey et al., 2016; McLaren, 1992), most importantly the lack of progress in identifying clinically relevant biomarkers and developing effective treatments for most forms of mental illness, despite the ever-increasing investment neuroscience research has received. Proponents of the neuroscientific model argue that this is largely owing to the highly complex nature of the relevant neurobiology and that progress is only a matter of time. However, critics of the model have argued that reasons for the delay in progress include the model's inability to adequately consider relevant factors at higher levels of organization (e.g. economic hardship, minority status) and its limited relevance to clinical practice in contrast to research on society, culture, and meaning (Luchins, 2010). Pertinent to our quest, it cannot adequately integrate human values, either.

Furthermore, a narrow focus on the neuroscientific model carries important risks, such as drawing away research and clinical attention from other (not directly brain-related) factors in mental illness; neglecting the treatment process; inhibiting treatment-related innovation (Deacon, 2013); reducing patients' agency in managing their illnesses (de Haan, 2020a); and increasing, rather than decreasing, the stigmatization of mental illness, contrary to expectations (Pescosolido et al., 2010). All other one-sided models, including the psychodynamic, cognitive-behavioural, systemic/family interactional, social, and conspiratorial models, can bring some specific advantages, but they all suffer from the vital weakness of not being able to take into consideration essential factors in mental illness that are not within their narrow focus.

Dualist models can go some way towards addressing the limitations of one-sided models. *Values-based practice* (VBP; Fulford, 2007; Fulford et al., 2005) itself has been described as a dualist model of mental illness that takes into consideration both scientific facts produced by evidence-based medicine and the life world and values of the patient (de Haan, 2020a). However, VBP has been criticized for not elucidating sufficiently how these two sides relate (de Haan, 2020a).

A novel theory of mental illness that acknowledges the role of values was presented by Hoyle Leigh (2010a). According to this model, early experience shapes stress responsiveness and susceptibility to certain memes (transmittable memories) via epigenetic changes. Culture is a pool of memes, and cultural memes take up residence in the brain before filtering for meme introduction develops in the child. Memes are relevant to values: they are in charge of valuations. According to Leigh (2010a), decision-making is meme processing. Some memes are conscious, some unconscious. In good mental health, toxic memes (and values) are filtered or competed out and the brain achieves a democracy of the memes within it, including those that make up personality, allowing for competition but also for compromise and tolerance. Most psychiatric conditions in this model reflect memetic conflict or turmoil, with their final common pathway including genetic, epigenetic, biochemical, and memetic elements. According to Leigh (2010b), treatment includes deconstructing or neutralizing negative, pathogenic memes and stopping their replication, using broad-spectrum solutions such as meditation, music, or dance therapy, or more specific ones such as cognitive-behavioural therapy (CBT). As an integrative attempt, Leigh's theory focusses mainly on *maladaptive (epi)genetic–memetic interaction* (Leigh, 2010a), but it also integrates to some degree the psychological dimension.

More Holistic Models

The Biopsychosocial Model

After the work of such forerunners as Zbigniew Lipowski and Roy Grinker (Van Oudenhove and Cuypers, 2014), George Engel published in 1977, in *Science*, his biopsychosocial (BPS) model, in an article entitled 'A challenge for biomedicine' and intended for the whole of medicine. He felt that in modern Western societies the status of biomedicine had changed from being a scientific model to becoming our cultural perspective about disease, too. One of the values-related consequences of this was that the expectations about the biomedical model changed; people started to expect the biomedical model to take on the functions of folk models, such as resolving crises and uncertainties around disease, which is often not possible.

Like Grinker, Engel used a *systems theory* approach, and contended that each level of organization in the hierarchical system from the atom to society implies qualities and relationships that are distinctive for that level. He argued that each level requires an investigative methodology that is appropriate for it, stating that 'in no way can the methods and rules appropriate for the study and understanding of the cell as a cell be applied to the study of the person as person or the family as family' (Engel, 1980, p. 536). In his view, whilst all the levels can contribute to our understanding about a medical condition and its treatment, for the physician the level is always the person. It could be argued that the higher levels (from family to society) are more relevant in psychiatry than in non-psychiatric specialties.

The BPS model has received a number of important criticisms, including that Engel did not make it clear enough how to integrate the three – biological, psychological, and sociocultural – dimensions (McLaren, 1998; Van Oudenhove and Cuypers, 2014) or how these causally interact (de Haan, 2021). Also, specific to our inquiry, the BPS model does not take into account the existential dimension of mental illness (de Haan, 2020a) and human values beyond what is included in the psychological dimension.

The 'Hybrid' Model

According to the 'hybrid' model of Berrios and Marková (2015), both mental symptoms and mental disorder as well as the discipline of psychiatry have a hybrid nature in that they are configured by forms and practices of both the natural and the human sciences. Berrios and Marková (2015) aver that the medicalization of psychiatry at the beginning of the nineteenth century occurred as a result not of empirical findings but of the philanthropic, social, and economic needs of the industrial revolution and was justified by philosophers as a progressive step. This had a major impact on the professionalization of alienists as medical doctors, the venues of psychiatry, and the way we think about mental illness. The result was a narrow biological understanding of mental illness that did not meet the needs of the sufferers (Berrios and Marková, 2015). According to the hybrid model, mental states and behaviours that originate from brain disease should become medical conditions; others that appear to be phenomenologically similar on a superficial level should not, but they may get misclassified as such.

To understand the formation, structure, and meaning of symptoms, the hybrid model calls on history, social psychology, anthropology, linguistics, pragmatics, philosophy, and hermeneutics. A key principle of the hybrid model is that '[i]t is only after the structure of the psychiatric object has been mapped and its components duly listed that useful empirical research can be planned and executed' (Berrios and Marková, 2015, p. 48); without this, psychiatric research can achieve little more than discovering correlations.

According to the hybrid model, mental symptoms are hybrid objects, that is, they are constituted by elements originating from admixtures of biological and sociocultural components. As regards subjective symptoms (e.g. anxiety, feelings of strangeness, or fear of being followed), there is a change in the 'normal' stream of consciousness which triggers the interpretative process to make sense of this change. This change could be caused by brain disease or by factors external to the person, for example a family conflict.

A 'brain signal' enters consciousness causing an experience of a prelinguistic, preconceptual nature. For this to be expressed in words, the sufferer needs to compare their experience with the templates available, that is, with the cognitive and emotional forms that are shared in their culture. The rate, context, and nature of the experience will influence its interpretation by the sufferer, but it will also depend on their personality traits, educational level, intelligence, past experiences, imagination, introspection, and so on. External factors such as the person's family or cultural background, that is, cultural configurators, will also shape it. In clinical practice, the clinician's input and the dialogical encounter, that is, how the clinician understands and reflects back to the patient their understanding of the patient's experience, will play a key role. Descriptions will also be translated back and forth between ordinary language and clinical terminology, which will inevitably lead to a blending of meanings.

The recognition of objective mental symptoms, that is, those observed and named by the clinician (e.g. flight of ideas, disinhibition, or incongruent affect), will depend on the knowledge, skills, and experience of the clinician. Developing operational criteria will never completely cancel out the effect of all of the above-mentioned factors, as these act at a deeper level. The core neurobiological state will be wrapped up in cultural configurators.

Judgement and interpretation will still be involved because the defining core of mental symptoms is meaning.

The hybrid model has great usefulness in providing a description of symptom formation and offering a certain form of predictive value. However, as with any trail-blazing model, important questions remain to be answered, for example regarding the role of the existential dimension, including existential values.

Enactivism

The enactivist model of mental illness is an integrative model taking into consideration four dimensions: in addition to the biological, psychological, and sociocultural, the existential dimension, too. Enactivism adopts emergence and non-linear, organizational causality to explain the relationship between them. It postulates that they are but different aspects of the same unit: the person-in-interaction-with-their-world. This is why it does not make sense to ask whether a psychological phenomenon is caused by a physiological one; they are both parts of a larger whole. Therefore, the central unit of analysis in enactivism is not the individual but *the individual in their environment* (de Haan, 2020a). This is what the word enactive refers to: meaning and experience arise from the individual's interactions with their environment. Enactivism posits part-whole or organizational bidirectional (local to global and global to local) causality which it deems better suited for multifactor diachronic explanations in complex dynamic systems.

In contrast to previous models, personal values take centre stage in Sanneke de Haan's (2020b) enactivist account. As the organism depends on its environment for survival, different aspects of the environment have a certain value or meaning for it. This value depends on the organism's current needs and concerns and is therefore dynamic. Affect is related to the value of what is encountered (de Haan, 2020b). According to de Haan (2020a, 2020b), *sense-making* refers to the evaluative interaction between the organism and its environment. She argues that our capacity to take a reflexive stance on our own self and experiences transforms the organism–environment relationship to a *person–world relationship* in humans (de Haan, 2020a, 2020b). Stance-taking involves a family of skills that people develop as they are growing up. With this comes having existential values and the desire for dignity and for living a *good* life. We take stances (the world becomes a place full of existential meaning and values) and we enact our values through our actions. In de Haan's enactivist account, values are relational realities; their emergence depends on the characteristics of both what we value and our own properties.

De Haan sees psychiatric disorders as recurrent and disordered patterns of existential sense-making in which 'evaluative interactions of the person and her world go astray' (de Haan, 2020a, p. 10). The world becomes too threatening, too meaningless or meaningful, or too chaotic for the patient. In mental illness, sense-making is not appropriate to or adequately grounded in the situation and cannot be adjusted with flexibility. For de Haan, the sense-making of the person (i.e. not of the brain or the body) is disordered for a reason; motivation is implicated. Psychiatric disorders are *enacted* and dissolve if the patient can change their interaction with the world, unlike disordered sense-making in neurological conditions. Patterns of sense-making are both real *and* socially co-constituted. In psychiatry, therapy means practising participatory sense-making. During both becoming ill and recovery, small quantitative changes can, over time, lead to qualitative changes, when the system tips into another 'stable state'.

Not inconsistent with de Haan's work, Kristopher Nielsen (2020) describes mental illness as a problem of the person acting against their own functional norms, namely, life-preserving self-maintenance and adaptivity, rather than just against a societal norm. Running counter to the values of the agent makes a cluster of phenomena amount to mental disorder (Nielsen and Ward, 2018). Placing the emphasis differently, but consistent with both de Haan and Nielsen, Michelle Maiese (2021) describes mental disorder as the person having *difficulty in meaning-making and losing their grip on their social environment* (having difficulty enacting their social roles as family member, friend, and colleague), with important consequences for their autonomous agency (Maiese, 2022). Because of their impaired adaptive sense-making (at both a biological and an existential level), the person stops being able to correctly detect their environment's affordances. Maiese points out that 'what it means for sense-making and agency to be adaptive is partly a matter of social and cultural norms' (Maiese, 2021, p. 976). The impairment of the person's ability to detect and use their environment's affordances (and thereby their agency) can be described as having three dimensions: appreciating the full scope of their affordances (options and choices), understanding what affordances are present in the here-and-now and what might be available in the future, and appraising the relevance or importance of these affordances correctly.

Although enactivist accounts attempt to include social values into their explanatory framework, it has been argued that at present it is ambiguous exactly how this should be done (Russell, 2023). Enactivism does not tell us, for example, who the legitimate stakeholders should be. This runs the risk, Russell argues, of non-epistemic (e.g. political or institutional) values having too much influence, and the value pluralism, with which enactivism is otherwise compatible, being lost.

Trying to Locate the Causes of Mental Disorders

Why Has the 'Gnomon' of Psychiatry Not Been Found?

The fact that measurement enables us to better understand phenomena and facilitates technological progress is one of the cornerstones of science. Its importance has been recognized since attempts to understand the world in a scientific way began, exemplified, for example, by the *gnomon* in mathematics. Measurement has the potential to be helpful in mental health, too, but it is more complicated than in the natural sciences or in other branches of medicine. Let us consider treatment adherence, for instance. People may not be taking their medication because of a variety of reasons: they do not believe the diagnosis, forget to take their medication, had side effects in the past and/or are afraid of getting them, and so on. Values are clearly implicated here; different people place different weight on each of these potential causes, depending on what is more important for them. Knowing the proportions in their weightings could help the person and their clinician to focus on the right things when discussing treatment. It is possible to ask people about these. However, in an area where events can, at least seemingly, have more than one co-occurring sufficient cause, that is, they are over-determined, measurements may not predict future events with the same accuracy as in the natural sciences. For example, let us suppose that we asked the person about all these things, and they believe their diagnosis, remember to take their tablets, and had no side effects in the past, but they simply really did not trust the doctor they met and their treatment recommendation. If we did not consider this, our measurement of factors of treatment adherence may have given us an incomplete (or even false) picture. To further complicate things, psychological variables have a time-varying nature, and a variable can interact with another variable within the person or in the environment (e.g. values can be context-dependent), which makes it necessary to measure all of these variables over time to get the full picture. What is clear is that, in the case of psychiatric variables, taking context and values into consideration is crucial. Unfortunately, most research looks at mental phenomena devoid of exactly these details. This is one of the reasons why progress in mental health research has been remarkably slow, despite the large amount of money that has been spent on it. In psychiatry, symptoms are determined by not just biological but also psychological and social factors (Luchins, 2010). For this reason, to investigate psychiatric phenomena we need to enlist help from the disciplines that possess the relevant methodology. To upgrade psychiatric research to meet this challenge requires careful epistemological considerations. Thorough multidisciplinary qualitative work is needed to prepare the path to developing meaningful measurements and subsequent quantitative research.

Emergent Properties and Values

The challenge of understanding and handling emergent properties in the context of mental illness has been recognized as a roadblock to the development of effective treatments (Perez et al., 2023). Still, the subject has received relatively little research attention, and little is taught about emergence in clinical or research training. Unfortunately, precious resources are used up for research that focusses on levels of organization that are too low or too disparate to be helpful in explaining and treating mental illness, at least in the absence of a precise understanding of the relationship between the levels.

The concept of emergence in psychiatry is not without antecedents. Wilhelm Wundt's principle of *creative synthesis* or *creative results* to explain mental causality, recognizing that one cannot predict the properties of the whole from the nature of its parts, foreshadowed it in psychology (Rieber, 1980). The same concept was a main part of Gestalt psychology, too, which developed in opposition to the Wundtian structuralist approach aiming to identify the elementary components of the mind.

According to the modern concept of emergentism, systems of increasing complexity begin to exhibit new properties that go beyond the properties of their component parts and behave in ways that cannot be predicted on the basis of the laws that govern less-complex systems (Kim, 1999). That is, these properties are not simply resultant. Complex neurobiological systems can give rise to properties that are radically novel and different from their physical or material properties (Van Oudenhove and Cuypers, 2014). An example could be the brain itself as an organ or human language.

Emergent properties can have certain causal influence in relation to the lower levels they emerged from. This is called 'top-down' or 'downward' causation. Upward (body-to-mind) causation can often be easier to understand. For example, a genetic mutation at the cellular level could cause an enzyme to be faulty, which could in turn lead to a metabolic disorder at the organ level. This could be associated with behavioural symptoms at the level of the person. We could propose the following as an example of downward (mind-to-body) causation. If I decide to work out more and I persevere with it over a number of weeks, I may be able to build up significant muscle bulk. The muscle bulk increase will be the result of metabolic changes in my body, but those changes will have taken place as a result of certain mental events. If I decided to work out more because my peers had made some negative comments about my body shape, then it would be reasonable to say that even the social level (my interactions with others) has contributed to my muscle bulk increase. In the context of mental illness, psychological trauma from loss events (family level) can lead to depression (person level), which in turn can be associated with certain hormonal changes (organ level) and reduced neurogenesis (tissue level). If the original loss event (e.g. losing contact with close family members owing to migration) was caused by global economic changes affecting the local labour market particularly hard and leading to an identity crisis within one's community and family (possibly combined with economic hardship), the causal chain would go from global, through regional, community, family, personal, and organ level, to cellular and molecular. The possibility of downward causation has been questioned on philosophical grounds (Kim, 1999; de Haan, 2020b) and some have felt that downward causation in the strong sense was excluded (Van Oudenhove and Cuypers, 2014), yet other researchers in psychology (Campbell, 1990) and psychiatry (Kendler, 2005) regard it as real. Enactivist conceptualizations include 'emergence as fusion' (de Haan, 2020b, p. 115), according to which higher levels are not a separate entity but consist of the lower levels, the configurations of which carve out new abilities and inabilities. De Haan argues that the relationship between physiology and culture is one of reciprocal determination (de Haan, 2020b, p. 189).

The specific sciences work reasonably well in terms of discovering the laws within their own separate realms, that is, within their own dimensions or levels of analysis. However, they are less well-equipped to study the junctions/transition points or part-whole relationships *between* levels of organization, where emergent properties arise. For example, molecular biology is good at describing biomolecules and metabolic or signal transduction pathways, but it would struggle to explain the emergent property of life. Similar explanatory gaps exist everywhere at the junctions between various levels of organization – and even more so between levels that are not immediately adjacent, for example between the biology of the brain as an organ and, say, symptom improvement at the behavioural level owing to psychotherapy. At present, it is far from clear how to integrate findings from domains of knowledge that interrogate different levels of organization. This is often the case with nascent interdisciplinary endeavours, and further philosophically informed research on this is required (Kendler, 2014).

When we talk about human values, we refer to the personal and the social levels, as human values emerge only at these levels. Human values can also be understood as emergent properties of many minds (Voneida, 1998; quoting Sperry 1972) that then determine human decisions and actions at both individual and social levels (Sperry, 1972). If we accept this, it will be easy to grasp that to understand recovery from mental illness, the effects of pharmacological interventions need to be studied at levels higher than that of the receptors and second messenger systems, as meaningful change needs to involve values.

Memes as Vehicles of Human Values

Trying to locate the causes of mental illness in faulty genes (and more recently their interaction with the environment) has been the dominant approach now for several decades, but genes are not the only units of information that can replicate themselves. Memes also do that. However, unlike in the case of genes, this information is cultural as opposed to genetic, for example it relates to a behaviour, skill, idea, or image, or their combination. There are several similarities with genetic evolution, including variation, and competition and selection between variants. Whereas genes are passed on through reproduction, memes are transferred through imitation and communication. The likelihood of a meme being perpetuated depends on the strength of the emotion it generates or how closely it links to drives (rather than whether its content is 'true'). We inherit our memes from our parents and ancestors as well as our broader cultural environment. Broadly speaking, genes determine our physical make-up and memes our behavioural make-up, with interaction between the two. Brain evolution and memetic evolution are considered to be linked processes. As we saw earlier in the description of Leigh's maladaptive gene–meme interaction model of mental illness (Leigh, 2010a), it has been conceptualized that ill-fitting or toxic memes can lead to unhelpful valuations and thereby maladaptive behaviours.

Memes existed well before the internet, although with social media use becoming more universal, memetic (and thereby also cultural) evolution has become significantly faster and more global. But can human culture and values change that fast? And if they can, is that a good thing? What is the impact of this on mental health? The fact that the message in internet memes is often accompanied by an image, reaches people repeatedly, and is usually read in a context in which we may not be exercising critical thinking to a particularly high degree makes people more likely to believe its content unquestioningly (Hyman, 2019).

Internet memes enable the people propagating them to construct their individuality and, at the same time, their affiliation with a larger community (Shifman, 2019). Internet memes spread and perpetuate values, maybe even create them (Shifman, 2019). According to Limor Shifman (2019), there are two distinct layers of values in these memes: one related to the content of the meme and another related to the conditions and norms of its communication. Memes can potentially be helpful in communicating about values. They enable the expression and negotiation of opinions and identities and provide common ground and shared cultural language for the opposing sides in a debate (Shifman, 2019), which can be particularly helpful when negotiating conflicting values.

Although internet memes have the potential to propagate misinformation and unhelpful attitudes, and despite concerns about their impact on mental health having been raised repeatedly (see, e.g., Dubicka and Theodosiou, 2020), currently there is relatively little research evidence to support this (Akram and Drabble, 2022) and research suggests that memes can also be helpful. For example, contextual humour in internet memes about mental illness may be specifically helpful for people with depression (Akram and Drabble, 2022).

Risks and Opportunities: Time to Get Our AI-related Values Right

The emergence and increasingly widespread use of artificial intelligence (AI) is an excellent example of how scientific advances increase the complexity of values, which is one of the ten principles of VBP. Various concerns have been raised about the potentially deleterious effects of AI. Psychometric profiling, for example, has the potential to be misused to influence people in unethical ways, especially when combined with insights from psychology. In the Cambridge Analytica scandal, the mining of data from the Facebook profiles of millions of people for personality profiling with the help of psychologists in order to micro target voters to steer the results of political elections led to grave concerns about the misuse of psychology (Hu, 2020; Schneble et al., 2018). Some called it psychology's 'nuclear bomb' moment owing to its potentially ruinous effect on democracy (Prichard, 2021) and warned about the moral responsibility of psychologists to educate people about relevant anti-propaganda skills.

However, AI is also an extremely promising tool for improving our understanding of how the mind works. It may also help us understand the causes of mental illness and the mechanism of improvement with treatment. Both of these are particularly difficult because there are multiple (and often very high numbers of) variables involved at different levels of organization. As described earlier, these variables interact in complex ways and often over a long time. They may exert their effects at certain key time points, only once or repeatedly, and the intensity or nature of their influence (e.g. activating/inhibitory or risk/protective) may change over time, with the order and timing of them also being relevant (Uher and Zwicker, 2017). Machines that can learn as they process data and continually adapt their hypotheses accordingly are at a clear advantage in understanding such problems compared to human researchers. Current scientific approaches with human researchers generating hypotheses and adapting them 'manually' each time on reviewing the results of the statistical tests cannot handle this level of complexity and cannot compete with appropriate AI approaches. Machine learning systems contain a network of mathematical functions that applies weights and biases to the incoming data. These are inaccurate at the beginning, but the network can train itself to learn the optimal biases. Most current systems have not just an input and output but several layers, which is called 'deep' learning. Whilst deep learning machines are superior to human capabilities in several areas, presently they also have certain limitations, for example when it comes to understanding theory of mind concepts (Langley et al., 2022).

'Narrow' or 'weak AI' is generally designed to carry out a single task, for example face recognition, and cannot cope well with abstract questions or ones that require a detailed answer. Narrow AI has been increasingly used in healthcare, for example to aid diagnosis. A review of such use in radiology to diagnose cancer highlighted specific new value-related challenges in that patients often have limited understanding of AI and this affects trust in it and also doctor–patient communication (Derevianko et al., 2023).

'Artificial general intelligence', which is AI at the next level, could edit its own programming code and potentially understand natural (human) language. This could, in theory, at some point in the future lead to the development of AI psychotherapists. An important concern with agent-like AI is intent alignment. This refers to the machine trying to fulfil only human preferences (i.e. not ones that are against human preferences, for example). There are several important questions in this context, including 'Exactly whose preferences should we have them aligned to?'.

As so often with new technology, AI is developing much faster than our ethical thinking and regulation around it. Melissa Heikkilä (2023) likened the selling of AI technology to releasing race cars without seatbelts or fully functioning brakes, and working things out as they go. Human preferences in this new context, as well as relevant ethical boundaries, need to be worked out as soon as possible. These include, in addition to the above-mentioned ones, labour displacement, inequality, and an AI race that is sacrificing safety and other values (Langley et al., 2022). It is also important to mention that running AI systems currently consumes a very considerable amount of energy. So, if we run them, we should run them for the right reasons. Furthermore, most AI is developed by private industry, not academia. The opaqueness of what is programmed into the algorithm, not having an audit trail of responsibility, the ethical agency of the AI (and any resultant moral duties we would have towards a full ethical agent AI), the anthropomorphizing of AI, and the potential to spread medical disinformation at an unprecedented scale (Monteith et al., 2024) currently remain unresolved issues. Specific concerns have been raised for the use of emotion AI for those with mental illness (Monteith et al., 2022), such as the use of AI leading to discrimination against such people due to the machine not being trained with data that includes individuals with mental illness and not being able to handle sensory impairment in the person or variables that change over time and with context, leading to a risk of increasing stigma and discrimination.

The Need for a Different Approach

My review of the history (see Chapters 1–3) and of our current models of mental illness points towards the need for a new theory of mental illness. Narrow reductionistic approaches have generally failed, and whilst the impact of person-centred ones is still with us, so far it has not led to the development of a satisfactory theory. Our best current holistic models conceive of mental illness as something that occurs in the self-reflective person in their physical, social, and cultural context. What follows is that a satisfactory theory of mental illness would need to be able to integrate, in a dynamic fashion, strands of knowledge coming from various levels of organization from genes and cells, through the person and their immediate social environment, to culture and society. It would also need to be able to handle their emergent properties, including human values, meaning, and agency, and elucidate the relevant causal relationships in illness and recovery, too.

This has some important practical consequences. Any approach based entirely (or primarily) on the natural sciences will be incapable of real progress. Psychiatry as an academic discipline and social practice should not be afraid of the humanities and social sciences; it should embrace them (once again) without reservation. That would not make it any less medical or less scientific, but it would make it more successful in helping patients.

Who Decides What Is Pathological?

When it comes to defining pathology, apart from the individual affected by the problem and their primary care doctor, psychiatrists, psychologists, the school, occupational health, the driver and vehicle licensing agency, and disability assessors may all form a view. In this section, I will study the main stakeholders in terms of their legitimacy as a stakeholder; their own interests and biases; and how they view diagnosis, psychiatric treatment and the likely efficacy of that, and the patient's agency in causation of and improvement from their illness. As we have seen, a number of different models of mental illness exist and different stakeholders, as individuals, can use different models or combinations of these (Colombo et al., 2003). Each of these models has advantages and disadvantages for their user when they are making sense of mental illness and formulating a view as to how it should be treated. The models can complement each other to some degree, but they can also radically clash. Using different models can lead to having very different values and to difficulties in communication among the various stakeholders involved in clinical decision-making. Recognizing when this is the case may help us better manage these value conflicts.

From a clinical point of view, there are two impactful distinctions:

1. Does the person suffer from a recognizable mental illness (i.e. is there a pathology) or not?
2. Is the person so ill that their mental illness renders them incapable of making decisions about major aspects of their life, including their treatment, or not? This relates to the legal concept of mental capacity.

The complexity of these questions comes not just from the fact that where there are several stakeholders there can be several legitimately different opinions; it also comes from the fact that the boundaries between health and disease are never clear because, as

George Engel (1977) put it, they are determined not just by some sort of natural scientific objective truth but also by various cultural, social, and psychological considerations. Different models of mental illness balance differently the benefits of diagnosis against the perils of pathologizing deviation from the norm, non-adherence to certain social norms, or cultural differences. Also, factors that are internal and external to the individual influence both physical and mental illness, but their relative contributions as regards pathogenesis and mechanism of improvement are perceived very differently in these two groups of conditions. Where people locate the pathology and the agency over it has a powerful effect, among others, on how people view the appropriateness, likely efficacy, and possible adverse effects of psychiatric diagnosis and treatment, and the stigma attached to the illness. All this is relevant to the solution I will propose in the summary of this section ('Guessing Evolution's Next Step: Stakeholder Tribunals?').

Stakeholders involved in this clinical decision-making process can be divided into those that will be personally involved in the case, usually meeting in person with the patient, and often also their carers – whom I will call direct deciders – and those that do not get directly involved (the patient cannot personally negotiate with them) but who will still have a significant influence on the patient's treatment and life in general (access to treatment, benefits, or other help, insurance, job prospects, etc.) through representing the values of higher levels of organization, such as professional groups, national government, or society at large – whom I will call society-level deciders.

Direct Deciders

The patient, their psychiatrist, their psychologist, their GP (general practitioner, also referred to as doctor or primary care physician), and some specific assessors are direct deciders. The *patient* is the stakeholder at the centre. Many patients are able to recognize that something is not right with their mental health, but limitations in insight into one's own mental illness can pose a particular challenge in many mental health conditions. When patients are aware of their illness, research suggests that they tend to fall into two distinct groups: those who mainly use the *medical model* of mental illness to think about diagnosis and treatment, and those who use the *psychotherapeutic [i.e., psychoanalytic] model* to explain what might have caused their problem and what might help with it (Colombo et al., 2003). The medical model posits that mental illnesses are disorders of the brain caused by gene–environment interactions. How the disorder is labelled (i.e. the diagnosis) is based on the person's symptoms. The psychotherapeutic model attempts to decode the meaning of the symptoms, rather than to use labels, and locates the causes in unusual or traumatic early experiences, loss events, and so on. The individual is seen in their social context and there is less focus on identifying the 'abnormal' or pathological. Accordingly, some patients will be expecting or asking for medication, electroconvulsive, or surgical treatment (or, at least, talk about their illness in these terms) and some will want to avoid or relegate these to the background and get help primarily through sharing their experiences with a therapist and seeking advice from them on how to lead their lives better. In the medical model the medical doctor with their expertise in physics, chemistry, biology, and medical diagnosis and treatment seems like the other natural stakeholder, whereas in the psychotherapeutic model it is the therapist with an understanding of human psychological development, life narratives, hermeneutics, and ethics.

Different models of mental illness have different conceptualizations about the rights and duties of the patient and of society. The medical model affords the sick role and a sympathetic and non-blaming attitude to the patient and expects the patient to accept and use medical terminology and to cooperate with the treatment, usually consisting of medications. According to this model, society has the right to restrain those who are at risk of harming themselves or others owing to their mental illness and society has a responsibility to provide appropriate medical facilities. The psychotherapeutic model suspends any moral judgement of the patient's behaviour and expects the patient to work with the therapist and their interpretation of the problem.

The *psychiatrist* is a professional (non-lay) direct decider. In the medical model, it is the doctor's (not the patient's) responsibility to establish the nature of the problem and to decide whether or not it is best handled within a medical framework (Engel, 1977), although in recent times this has been challenged from various directions (see Chapter 5 on psychiatry in the media and Chapter 10, 'Values Questioned and Debated').

The value context is indeed very relevant to distinguishing between mental 'disorder' (i.e. mental illness), 'disability', or 'difference', as has been demonstrated, for example, in the case of autism (Baron-Cohen, 2000). Different models of mental illness are able to take this into account in different ways and to varying degrees and offer different advantages and disadvantages. According to the research by Colombo et al. (2003), the majority of psychiatrists mainly use the medical model. However, this does not mean that individual practitioners cannot weave elements of other models into how they see certain aspects or that other models, for example the conspiratorial, cognitive-behavioural, or social models, do not feature significantly in psychiatrists' thinking as a group. A large majority of psychiatrists, for example, thought that, in addition to facilitating treatment and curing any disease (medical model), mental health hospitals also functioned to control those at risk of harming themselves or others (conspiratorial model). In similar proportions, they thought that patients had a right to the sick role and to not be blamed for their problem (medical model) and also to privacy, personal freedom, and the same civil rights as anyone (conspiratorial model). This may seem to be in apparent contradiction of what we have said about the role of the hospital, but of course it may be that what the psychiatrist regards as the appropriate response in the case of a certain patient or at a certain time may be different from what they would regard as appropriate in a different person or at a different time. This does not mean that psychiatrists' views are wishy-washy. On the contrary, it means that they need to have the ability to examine each case on its own merit and to argue their ethical stance each time.

As regards our first question – Does the person suffer from a recognizable mental illness (i.e. is there a pathology) or not? – psychiatric (medical) diagnosis has a binary nature; the patient either meets sufficient criteria for the condition or does not. This forces psychiatrists to commit themselves to a decision, although with most diagnoses it is customary to indicate the severity as well, and 'traits' can also be described in sub-threshold cases. It is almost always the psychiatrist who makes the diagnosis, and other direct deciders and society-level deciders refer to the psychiatrist for this. Assessing the patient's capacity to consent to (or to refuse) treatment for mental illness is also the prerogative of psychiatrists, although this is more complicated than diagnosis as, for detention for treatment in hospital, at least in the UK, the psychiatrist needs another doctor and an approved mental health professional to agree with him.

Clinical *psychologists* undergo thorough training in healthy psychological development and functioning as well as in abnormal psychology and psychotherapy, and treat people with a wide variety of mental health problems. However, relevant to our second question – Is the person so ill that their mental illness renders them incapable of making decisions about major aspects of their life, including their treatment, or not? – they do not usually treat patients who are deemed by them to be too unwell to have psychological therapy, for example those who are severely depressed with psychomotor retardation or agitation, people with schizophrenia who are in a catatonic state, people in acute mania, and so on.

Most clinical psychologists do distinguish between healthy and abnormal or maladaptive psychological functioning, but they use a formulation-based (rather than a binary) approach based on psychological theory to describe the person's mental health problems. Although most clinical psychologists in the UK's National Health Service (NHS) appear readily to use psychiatric diagnosis for communication, the British Psychological Society has proposed that clinical psychologists move beyond psychiatric diagnoses and develop their own ways of classifying clinical problems (Randall-James and Coles, 2018).

A significant part of the work, in the UK, of the *general practitioner* (i.e. primary care physician) is diagnosing and treating psychiatric illness (Fleury et al., 2012). They look after the brunt of mental illness in the mild-to-moderate severity bracket. However, at least in the UK, whilst they diagnose and treat depression and anxiety disorder in this category, they usually refer the patient to a psychiatrist for the diagnosis of most other forms of mental illness. For this, they need to have a good working knowledge of what counts as mental illness and the degree of that which renders the patient incapable of making a decision about their treatment.

Specific assessors, such as school, occupational health, and disability assessors, do not assume overall responsibility for the care of the person. They try to answer a specific question about ability or functioning in the context of mental illness. They can limit or facilitate participation and access (e.g. to treatment or to financial support). *Mental health tribunals* have the power to discharge patients from compulsory admission. *Hospitals and NHS trusts* act as 'quasi-society-level' deciders; they can decide about certain questions in individual cases or relating to groups of patients, such as treatments provided and referral criteria for these, in their catchment area.

Society-Level Deciders

Society-level deciders include, among others, organizations that provide healthcare (in the UK mainly the NHS), professional organizations (e.g. the Royal College of Psychiatrists), governmental and other public bodies (e.g. driver and vehicle licensing agencies, in the UK the DVLA), and parliaments. Most society-level deciders use the medical model of mental illness primarily, but elements of other models can also feature when dealing with certain specific issues. Although it does not have one unified opinion (rather it represents, to varying degrees, the value diversity in society), the media also weighs in and acts in many ways as a stakeholder on the issue of what counts as mental illness both in relation to individual cases and, sometimes, in general, which can have a significant impact on the behaviour of the other stakeholders.

Currently in the UK, the NHS provides evidence-based treatments for most conditions, but not all possible treatments are available under the NHS. How the NHS decides about what it funds is influenced by its key values: working together for patients, respect and dignity, commitment to quality of care, compassion, improving lives, and everyone counts (Department of Health and Social Care, 2023). The *National Institute for Health and Care Excellence (NICE)* is an executive non-departmental public body sponsored by the Department of Health and Social Care that assesses the scientific evidence for new health technologies with a view to getting the best care to patients and ensuring value for the taxpayer. Still, not all treatments recommended by NICE and approved by the NHS that might be beneficial are given automatically to every patient. One reason for this is having limited resources. The NHS as a whole and its organizations, such as individual NHS trusts, have their own mechanisms for making these decisions. These can include local criteria to decide whether someone will get a certain treatment or be placed on a waiting list; such criteria are usually set by making reference to the values of justice and equitability.

Professional organizations collate the views of and represent entire professional groups at the national level, including by liaising with other relevant organizations, national government, and the media. They define what is within their purview and identify the concerns, needs, and preferences of the profession, then work to resolve any conflicts with other stakeholders, often co-producing their recommendations with patients and carers. *Governmental organizations* – such as, in a British context, the Department of Health, the Department of Work and Pensions, and agencies like the DVLA – also form an opinion as to what counts as mental disorder or an incapacitating level of that which determines whether a person is eligible for financial support or can be allowed to participate in society in certain forms, for example through driving.

Two important, relevant pieces of *legislation* in UK law are the Mental Capacity Act (MCA) and the Mental Health Act (MHA). According to these, one can be deemed, respectively, to have or not to have mental capacity to make an informed decision about one's mental health treatment and to be or not to be detainable to hospital for the treatment of a mental disorder, with four possible combinations of these two binary options. A person is deemed to lack capacity only if they suffer from an impairment of the mind *and* they are not able to understand, retain, weigh up the pros and cons of, or communicate their choices about their treatment options. This could be, for example, because they have difficulty concentrating or remembering things; do not believe the information given; suffer from hallucinations or delusions, especially if those hallucinations/delusions are related to the decision in question; or have levels of psychological arousal or psychomotor retardation that are too high to allow them to engage in the process. A person is detainable to hospital for assessment under the MHA only if they are suffering from a mental disorder of a nature or degree that warrants detention, and they ought to be detained in the interests of their own health or safety, or for the protection of other persons. Although, in theory, one professional can be sufficient to assess a patient's capacity, for the purposes of the MCA the process is usually informed by other people or a multidisciplinary team (MDT). Assessments under the MHA require three professionals – an approved mental health professional and two doctors – at least one of whom will have received specific training relevant to this.

Understandably, the law cannot legislate for every situation and those using the law need to interpret the law on a case-by-case basis. This always involves relying on one's own values. Unlike other approaches, VBP can offer guidance in difficult clinical situations, for example when a cardinal feature of the illness is that the patient's value system appears to be at odds with those of the clinician and others (for a demonstration of this, see Chapter 11 on depression). Also, the law continually evolves. This is often in response to changing preferences in society, commonly represented by patient and carer groups and professional organizations. For example, the MHA definition of 'mental disorder' changed when the MHA of 1981 was amended in 2007 from 'mental illness, arrested or incomplete development of mind, psychopathic disorder and any other disorder or disability of mind' to 'any disorder or disability of the mind' (HM Government, 2007, n. 15).

Guessing Evolution's Next Step: Stakeholder Tribunals?

The existing legal framework with the MHA and the MCA leaves several important issues unresolved. The independent review that culminated in the report *Modernising the Mental Health Act* (known as the Wessely Review, see HM Government, 2018), published in 2018, was triggered by the steep increase in the number of detentions to hospital under the MHA over the preceding ten years. The Wessely Review recognizes as a major issue the need for an agreed way to resolve disputes when professionals do not agree on whether the patient has mental capacity. When the patient is felt to lack capacity or it is felt that they pose a risk to their own safety, it often has to do with their values (rather than their facts) being at odds with those of others. So how can we make sure that there is better collaboration among the stakeholders on exploring and managing this? Sometimes it requires creating a new specific formal mechanism.

Introducing a *VBP-informed stakeholder tribunal* would offer a solution to this and could also address some of the other problems identified in the Wessely Review; by doing all of this, it could significantly reduce the number of unnecessary hospital detentions. This would improve the quality of the lives of those suffering with mental illness and also lead to cost savings. Stakeholder tribunals could solve an even larger circle of difficult cases in which the MHA is not necessarily invoked but which take up an inordinate amount of time and resources in an already stretched system. In highly challenging and potentially controversial cases, having a formal mechanism for taking into consideration the values of all stakeholders – starting with the direct deciders but also including the society-level ones – would ensure that the values of freedom, dignity, and equality of all human beings are respected more fully than in the current system. There is almost always a significant element of risk in these cases – the risks of self-harm by the patient, of reputational damage for the clinicians and/or the organization, and so on. Two examples of such situations are where:

- the team/service is planning to discharge a patient who is still significantly unwell but further treatment is felt to be counterproductive or even harmful;
- the patient is capacitous and does not want to be treated and they are not detainable under the MHA but without treatment there is a high likelihood of serious deterioration in their health or death (e.g. a patient who is capacitous and not detainable intending to commit suicide by refusing treatment after a medication overdose or wanting to travel to a euthanasia clinic; see Chapter 13 on borderline personality disorder).

Deciding how to act in such cases is a very complex task; it requires careful consideration and insight from multiple domains of knowledge and skill beyond what can be expected to be ordinarily present in clinical teams or the legal system. Because the causes of and the treatment for the illness can include biological, psychological, social, and existential components, expertise in the relevant disciplines is not just helpful but necessary for optimal decision-making. Although this is recognized in the currently dominant model of multidisciplinary working in mental health, in addition to representatives of the disciplines commonly included in the MDT, *a lawyer representing the patient, a peer support worker, a philosopher*, and *a VBP-trained clinician* would also appear to be necessary stakeholders in order for the value diversity inherent to the situation to be properly recognized and considered. *Optional members* could include experts with specialist knowledge relevant to the case, for example a theologian, a sociologist, an anthropologist, or a clinical psychologist. A journalist could be instrumental in mitigating in the media any potential adverse effects of a decision. As regards the judge, a person specializing in mental health (e.g. a Court of Protection judge) would be desirable. Although, according to the partnership principle of VBP, clinical decisions should be made by those who are directly concerned, not by 'outside experts', members of the stakeholder tribunal would not be outsiders from the perspective of the larger unit within which the decision-making happens and which will be affected by the consequences of the decision, that is, the patient's community. The stakeholders would represent that community, the culture, and society. Their participation would be especially important in situations where the value conflict in the case relates to aspects of the psychiatric condition and its treatment that are influenced in an important way by factors at levels of organization above that of the individual and their immediate social environment. Although organizing such stakeholder tribunals would have significant cost implications, there are already high costs involved in handling such cases currently, and these tribunals could lead to better care.

How could stakeholder tribunals add to the existing system? There are three ways. (1) They could explore the values of all stakeholders involved in the case and provide support with the clinical decision-making process beyond what ordinary mechanisms in the NHS are generally capable of. This would be particularly relevant to the small but important minority of cases where the usual MDT has not been able to resolve a value conflict. As de Haan says, when judging the appropriateness of our sense-making, '[a]ll we can rely on is our common sense, i.e. the shared sense-making of people within their sociocultural practices' (de Haan, 2020b, p. 208). But how to harness this shared sense-making is far from obvious. As people, we all have a mixture of values: some are universal, some specific to our culture, and some idiosyncratic. Mental illness often means that the alignment of the patient's values with those of their community and/or with their own previously held values becomes temporarily or chronically absent. This may not always cause a major problem, but when it does, the solution requires expert input from professionals who are not normally available in the MDT to ensure that all avenues have been properly explored. The idea would not be to have a 'second' MHA assessment to overturn the outcome of the first one if the professionals involved are not satisfied with it but rather to bring into discussion aspects of the case previously not seen or duly recognized and to arrive at a decision that can be owned by the stakeholders – even if it is built on dissensus and not every stakeholder is satisfied with it, as expected in a proportion of the cases – because the facts and values of the case have been exhaustively identified and a good process has been followed. Importantly, this process could lead to solutions that would not have been entertained without it. (2) They could validate the clinical decision from a broader community/society perspective and thereby provide protection for those involved against a potential later challenge. This would be particularly useful in situations where the decision is very likely to be seen as controversial by the family, the local community, and/or the wider society, and is thus likely to be legally challenged and/or to generate negative media attention. (3) Last but not least, the decisions made by stakeholder tribunals could provide important feedback for reviews of mental health legislation.

What Determines or Influences Mental Well-Being?

In this section, I will first look at a number of characteristics that have been linked to subjective well-being in general and what these mean for our values in mental health. I will then look at some factors that have been found to be implicated in mental illness more specifically and the value implications of those. The focus is on illustrating the impact of relevant knowledge on our values rather than providing a comprehensive review.

The Roots of a Healthy Mental Life

Exploring what makes for a healthy mental life can help us identify and promulgate the right values to get there. Notwithstanding that subjective well-being and being free from mental illness are not the same, a number of researchers in this area have argued that the ability to be happy and contented with life is a key criterion of mental health and successful adaptation to the challenges of life (Lyubomirsky et al., 2005), including that of mental illness. Happy people are more likely to get married and stay married, have better work outcomes, and experience a state of 'flow'. They also seem to have a better functioning immune system and to live longer. Happy people tend to be more prosocial and cooperative (Lyubomirsky et al., 2005).

As to what determines subjective well-being, about half of it is estimated to be *genetic inheritance* and the rest a combination of a variety of *intentional activities* the person can effortfully participate in (e.g. leading a virtuous life, volunteering, and exercising regularly) and *circumstances* that are relatively stable and outside the person's control (e.g. age, ethnicity, gender, personal life history, occupational status, income, and physical health) but play only a relatively small part (Lyubomirsky et al., 2005). Both *temperament* in general (Cloninger et al., 2019) and having a *happy predisposition* or *better subjective well-being* in particular (Lykken and Tellegen, 1996) seem to be heritable to a significant degree, though not completely.

So, how can we improve our mental well-being? As humans, we are able to control our thinking and step outside the here-and-now to think about long-term goals. We can imagine various scenarios and discuss these with others to explore their respective pros and cons. We are capable of focussing on these pros or cons selectively and of persevering for long periods in order to attain a long-term goal. We can understand that delaying gratification is a key to success in many areas of life. All these factors make it possible for us to intentionally select and persevere with activities and behaviours that are advantageous and increase our subjective well-being in the long run, such as achieving certain personal goals or leading a virtuous life. Importantly, directing our controlled processes in this way in order to achieve things like better academic attainment or better stress tolerance is also influenced by factors that are external to us. For example, scarcity can drive people to choose short-term rather than long-term rewards (Mullainathan & Shafir, 2013). In summary, there are complex interactions between a person's genetics, their intentional activities, and their circumstances, some of which are determined at a level well above that of the person.

A relevant concept here is *affective style*. This refers to how much happiness, anxiety, shame, and so on a person experiences in their daily life. A person's affective style also determines their threshold for reacting with an emotion, how fast their emotions develop and resolve, and how strong these emotions will be. Importantly, it is possible to alter our affective style, although it requires significant effort. One way to achieve this is mindfulness meditation (see, e.g., in general Zhang et al., 2019 and specifically in relation to depressive illness Reangsing et al., 2021). Psychological treatment, for example CBT, can also eventually alter our automatic mental processes through modifying our conscious controlled processes. Taking medication such as antidepressants can alter our emotional functioning, too. Each of these options has similar efficacy but very different pros and cons. This is where VBP can be of help, in navigating the enormous value diversity in people's choices relevant to these.

The capacity to understand our own mental states and the mental states of others is very important in terms of managing and improving our own emotional life and navigating our social environment successfully. *Reflective capacities*, *mentalization*, *perspective-taking*, *empathy*, *theory of mind*, and *psychological mindedness* are terms that have been used to describe this capacity from slightly different angles. *Reflective functioning*, which is also called *mentalizing*, is the capacity to interpret both one's own self and other people in terms of internal mental states such as feelings, wishes, goals, desires, and attitudes (Fonagy et al., 2016). Having a secure attachment to one's attachment figures appears to be a necessary requirement for the healthy development of this capacity (Fonagy et al., 2007), but psychological treatment can also improve it.

'*Flow*' or 'in the zone' experiences occur when we immerse ourselves in an activity that engages our attention and tests our ability to the full (Csikszentmihalyi, 1992). This can happen during physical activity, like playing sports or driving, or during creative activities, like painting or writing, when we are getting positive feedback with every challenge successfully negotiated. Having regular flow experiences is associated with better well-being and quality of life (Csikszentmihalyi and Csikszentmihalyi, 1988; Tse et al., 2021).

Okuzono et al. (2022) found that having ikigai (a Japanese word meaning purpose in life) was associated with about a third lower risk of developing functional disability and developing dementia, in a three year follow-up study. Having ikigai was also associated with fewer depressive symptoms, less hopelessness and more happiness, better life satisfaction, and better ability to perform instrumental activities of daily living (Okuzono et al., 2022). Working in a peer-helping work role as opposed to a non-helping role was associated with finding more meaning in life and more meaning was associated with having more 'flow' experiences (Bujanover et al., 2022). All such activities represent acting in accordance with one's important personal values and devoting effort to causes that give *meaning and purpose to one's life*.

Virtues are values relating to how to live a morally good life that are shared with others within the same culture. There are six virtues that appear to be universal across all cultures: wisdom and knowledge, courage, love and humanity, justice, temperance, and spirituality and transcendence (Seligman, 2002). Various character strengths can lead to these virtues, including kindness, originality, humour, optimism, curiosity, enthusiasm, generosity, and gratitude. Gratitude strengthens social relationships and cooperation and leads to better mental health and overall quality of life (Emmons and McCullough, 2003; Mills et al., 2015; Valikhani et al., 2019). People more disposed to feelings of gratitude may also have lower levels of inflammation (Mills et al., 2015), which has been associated with certain types of mental illness (Yuan et al., 2019). Transcendence strengths seem to predict greater life satisfaction and other-directed strengths, such as kindness and teamwork, seem to be associated with less depression (Gillham et al., 2011).

Positive social relationships contribute significantly to our mental health and well-being. Married people do report, on average, greater happiness than those who were never married, or are divorced, separated, or widowed (Diener et al., 1999). This is, of course, not to say that one cannot be single and happy, and indeed the proportion of single people has been increasing steadily in recent decades in many societies (DePaulo and Morris, 2005). The association between life satisfaction and marital status is influenced by what type of society the person lives in: individualist or collectivist (Diener et al., 1999).

In addition to our family, the friends and acquaintances we have where we live and work provide us with our social support network and contribute to our well-being. Various terms have been used to describe this, including *neighbourhood social reciprocity* (Wang et al., 2019) and *neighbourhood social capital* (Aminzadeh et al., 2013; Stafford et al., 2008). It seems that people experiencing more social reciprocity exercise more often, have more interaction with their neighbours, and volunteer more often, which in turn is associated with better mental health (Wang et al., 2019). The opposite – *feelings of loneliness* (having no companion, feeling left out and isolated) – is associated with more depression and increased mortality (Luo et al., 2012).

There is evidence from scientific studies that *physical exercise* is associated with better mental health. A large study using a representative sample of 1.2 million people in the USA (Chekroud et al., 2018) found that exercise was more strongly associated with good mental health than other modifiable factors such as education and income.

Although the vast majority of these findings are from cross-sectional research looking at associations in a between-subject fashion, which does not allow for establishing cause–effect relationships, and a large proportion of the studies used small convenience samples, there is some evidence that improvement in subjective well-being linked to positive changes in intentional activities may persist longer, whilst people may adapt more quickly to positive changes in their circumstances (Lyubomirsky et al., 2005). Taken together, this suggests that building these intentional activities into our value system may be a worthwhile endeavour in order to improve our mental health.

What Are the Values That Will Get Us There?

Our values guide our actions over time and across situations. They are imbued with emotions, but cognition also plays an important role in our values: we can recognize, reason about, and change our values. In order to achieve optimal mental health (our ultimate terminal value), we need to select appropriate terminal and corresponding competence and moral instrumental values (Table 4.1).

Some of these values are primarily personal in nature and some are more social. Consequently, some can be adopted or altered at a personal level, but others will depend on other people, such as our family, our community, or our entire culture. For example, in order to have plenty of positive social relationships, one can display personal values such as being broad-minded, forgiving, loving, loyal, polite, and understanding reciprocity and boundaries, but having collectivistic as opposed to individualistic communal values in society will also facilitate this to a large degree. This is another reason why studying levels of organization higher than that of the person is also very relevant to psychiatry. Psychiatry, being a medical specialty, needs to join forces with other disciplines, such as anthropology and sociology, that have the methodology to develop a better understanding of the relationship between these values and mental health. Finally, working together with public health and social policy is helpful when advocating for and implementing changes.

Table 4.1 End-state/goal values and instrumental values to improve general mental well-being

Terminal (end-state/ goal) value	Instrumental (means-based) values
Healthy affective style	Self-control, diligence, access to mental hygiene and psychiatric care, lack of stigma around mental health problems
Optimal levels of empathy	A society supportive of childcare, women, and young families
Regular 'flow' experiences	Healthy workplaces, division of labour, distribution of wealth, and work–life balance
Finding meaning and purpose in life	Courage, imagination, solidarity
Positive social relationships	Broad-mindedness, forgiveness, love, loyalty, politeness, kindness, collectivist values
Practising virtues/leading a virtuous life	Kindness, originality, humour, optimism, curiosity, enthusiasm, generosity, gratitude
Doing enough physical exercise	Healthy work–life balance, better urban design, access to nature

Factors in Mental Illness

Most mental illnesses are believed to be the consequence of complex, multifactorial genetic and environmental causes (see, e.g., Uher and Zwicker, 2017). The part that environmental factors play is comparable to that played by genetics and is more under our control. Although a comprehensive review of these environmental factors is beyond our scope, it is relevant to examine some of their value connotations here.

Evidence suggests that *low socio-economic* status is associated with poorer mental health (Reijneveld and Schene, 1998; Stafford et al., 2008). According to research on depression (Martikainen et al., 2003, p. 718), '[t]he strong independent association between household wealth – a measure of income earned over decades and across generations – and morbidity [is] likely to be related to a set of early and current material and psychosocial benefits'. Childhood poverty has also been found to be associated with suicidal thoughts and suicide attempts later in adulthood (Lindström and Rosvall, 2018). Well-functioning welfare systems can have a powerful protective effect on population mental health (Senior et al., 2020).

During the Covid-19 pandemic, *loneliness* was the strongest predictor of mental illness in the elderly (Donizzetti and Lagacé, 2022). Loneliness can interact with poverty; in deprived households, people with less contact with local friends are more likely to suffer from common mental illness (Stafford et al., 2008). Further, people with mental illness experience more loneliness and this hinders their recovery and reduces their quality of life (Caple et al., 2023). Among those with serious mental illness, loneliness leads to depressive symptoms, which in turn leads to thoughts of self-harm (Dell et al., 2020). Improving unemployment, reducing financial strain, reducing social deprivation, improving group housing, reducing internalized stigma, and treating symptoms of mental illness, such as suspiciousness and hopelessness, as well as interventions targeting social functioning skills and social connectedness have been suggested as ways to reduce loneliness (Caple et al., 2023).

The association between *abuse and neglect* and mental ill health has been demonstrated in several conditions. These include borderline personality disorder (see, e.g., Zanarini et al., 2002), schizophrenia (see, e.g., Golay et al., 2023; Zhang et al., 2023), and neurodevelopmental disorders (see, e.g., Minnis, 2023).

Evidence from research suggests that, unfortunately, improved access to mental health care did not lead to reduced rates of mental ill health, at least not in Australia, Canada, England, or the USA (Jorm et al., 2017). This does not seem to be related to increases in risk factors or increased reporting because of greater public awareness or willingness to disclose; rather, it seems to be owing to much of the treatment being provided not meeting the minimal standards of practice guidelines and not being targeted to those in greatest need, that is, to a *lack of effectiveness in treatment delivery.*

What Are Some of the Values That Would Lead to Less Mental Illness?

Overall, the existing evidence strongly supports choosing better socio-economic status and fairer distribution of wealth, reducing loneliness and fostering positive relationships, ensuring that children grow up free from abuse and neglect, and providing effective psychiatric care as important terminal values if we want to reduce mental illness through prevention and treatment (Table 4.2). But getting society to adopt these values requires very different skills from those needed to, say, convince people about the advantages of a new medication. That said, prevention clearly plays a very important role here and we do have a relatively good understanding of what strategies might work (Hiam et al., 2024; Kirkbride et al., 2024).

Of course, one may ask, 'Is it the psychiatrists' job to fight for better-paid jobs?'. They may see doing that as something more within the remit of the trade unions and political parties, although it does seem sensible that, in the same way as those in public health and other champions of prevention fought for better sanitation to reduce infectious diseases, psychiatrists should at least research the links with mental health and bring their findings to the attention of the relevant stakeholders (e.g. governments, the media, and the public). In

Table 4.2 End-state/goal values and instrumental values to reduce mental ill health

Terminal (end-state/goal) value	Instrumental (means-based) values
Appropriate income and socio-economic status	Fair taxation and redistribution of wealth, adequate living wage, affordable and healthy housing, improving unemployment and reducing financial strain
Positive social relationships	Reducing social deprivation, improving group housing, reducing internalized stigma, reducing discrimination, building close-knit and inclusive communities
Children growing up free from sexual abuse, neglect, and discrimination	Ensuring adequate safeguarding arrangements in education, healthcare, fostering, and so on
Effective psychiatric care	Available high-quality care that meets clinical standards and is targeted to those in greatest need

the same way as psychiatry contributes to the fight against racism or prejudice and discrimination against LBGTQ+ people (Kar, 2023) or people with neurodiversity (University of Cambridge, 2017), it could be argued that it should do so against poverty and harmful levels of inequality, too. Parents who have to work long hours in exploitative jobs simply do not have the time and energy to be available for their children. Not only will they not be able to support and protect their children during unexpected or significant challenges but often they will not even be able to teach them the skills they need to cope successfully with the ordinary stresses of life. In families that are multiply disadvantaged (low income, being of migrant origin, living in areas with high crime rate, etc.), the parents may not even have these skills themselves. Trauma and other problems can then be passed on from one generation to the next. Psychiatry can no more prevent this on its own than can the healthcare system (Hiam et al., 2024), but it can helpfully point out these relationships. Psychiatry has made important forays into understanding the causes and the treatment of mental illness, but if it wants to remain relevant to its original purpose it will need to embrace the levels above the person and their immediate environment. It has been a leading light among the medical specialties, but at present the beam of its torch hardly reaches as high as the society level. These issues are sensitive, controversial, and beyond the conventional remit and expertise of clinical medicine, but it is often in connection with these issues that psychiatry has been, rightly or wrongly, chastised the most heavily by its critics, as we will discuss in Chapter 10.

References

Akram, U. & Drabble, J. 2022. Mental health memes: Beneficial or aversive in relation to psychiatric symptoms? *Humanities and Social Sciences Communications*, 9, 370.

Aminzadeh, K., Denny, S., Utter, J., Milfont, T. L., Ameratunga, S., Teevale, T. & Clark, T. 2013. Corrigendum to 'Neighbourhood social capital and adolescent self-reported wellbeing in New Zealand: A multilevel analysis' [Soc Sci Med 84 (2013) 13–21]. *Social Science and Medicine*, 91, 101.

Baron-Cohen, S. 2000. Is Asperger syndrome/high-functioning autism necessarily a disability? *Development and Psychopathology*, 12, 489–500.

Berrios, G. E. & Marková, I. S. 2015. *Toward a New Epistemology of Psychiatry*. Cambridge: Cambridge University Press.

Bruineberg, J. 2023. *Enactive Psychiatry*. New York: Springer Nature.

Bujanover, M., Mashiach-Eizenberg, M. & Moran, G. S. 2022. Meaning in life and flow experiences among people with psychiatric disabilities who are engaged in peer-helping vs. non-helping work-roles. *Journal of Vocational Rehabilitation*, 57, 275–287.

Campbell, D. T. 1990. Levels of organisation, downward causation, and the selection-theory approach to evolutionary epistemology. In Greenberg, G. & Tobach, E. (eds.), *Theories of the Evolution of Knowing*. Hillsdale, NJ: Lawrence Erlbaum Associates, pp. 1–18.

Caple, V., Maude, P., Walter, R. & Ross, A. 2023. An exploration of loneliness experienced by people living with mental illness and the impact on their recovery journey: An integrative review. *Journal of Psychiatric and Mental Health Nursing*, 30, 1170–1191.

Chekroud, S. R., Gueorguieva, R., Zheutlin, A. B., Paulus, M., Krumholz, H. M., Krystal, J. H. & Chekroud, A. M. 2018. Association between physical exercise and mental health in 1.2 million individuals in the USA between 2011 and 2015: A cross-sectional study. *Lancet Psychiatry*, 5, 739–746.

Cloninger, C. R., Cloninger, K. M., Zwir, I. & Keltikangas-Järvinen, L. 2019. The complex genetics and biology of human temperament: A review of traditional concepts in relation to new molecular findings. *Translational Psychiatry*, 9, 290.

Colombo, A., Bendelow, G., Fulford, B. & Williams, S. 2003. Evaluating the influence of implicit models of mental disorder on processes of shared decision making within community-based multi-disciplinary teams. *Social Science and Medicine*, 56, 1557–1570.

Csikszentmihalyi, I. S. & Csikszentmihalyi, M. 1988. *Optimal Experience: Psychological Studies of Flow in Consciousness*. Cambridge: Cambridge University Press.

Csikszentmihalyi, M. 1992. *Flow: The Psychology of Happiness*. London: Rider.

Deacon, B. J. 2013. The biomedical model of mental disorder: A critical analysis of its validity, utility, and effects on psychotherapy research. *Clinical Psychology Review*, 33, 846–861.

De Haan, S. 2020a. An enactive approach to psychiatry. *Philosophy, Psychiatry, and Psychology*, 27, 3–25.

De Haan, S. 2020b. *Enactive Psychiatry*. Cambridge: Cambridge University Press.

De Haan, S. 2021. Bio-psycho-social interaction: An enactive perspective. *International Review of Psychiatry*, 33, 471–477.

Dell, N. A., Huang, J., Buttafuoco, K. A., Vidovic, K. R., Murphy, A. M. & Farrar, L. A. 2020. Direct and indirect associations between loneliness and thoughts of self-harm among a clinical sample of older adults with serious mental illness. *Journal of Nervous and Mental Disease*, 208, 828–832.

Department of Health and Social Care 2023. *The NHS Constitution for England*. www.gov.uk/government/publications/the-nhs-constitution-for-england/the-nhs-constitution-for-england.

DePaulo, B. M. & Morris, W. L. 2005. Singles in society and in science. *Psychological Inquiry*, 16, 57–83.

Derevianko, A., Pizzoli, S. F. M., Pesapane, F., Rotili, A., Monzani, D., Grasso, R., Cassano, E. & Pravettoni, G. 2023. The use of artificial intelligence (AI) in the radiology field: What is the state of doctor–patient communication in cancer diagnosis? *Cancers*, 15, 470.

Diener, E., Suh, E. M., Lucas, R. E. & Smith, H. L. 1999. Subjective well-being: Three decades of progress. *Psychological Bulletin*, 125, 276–302.

Donizzetti, A. R. & Lagacé, M. 2022. Covid-19 and the elderly's mental illness: The role of risk perception, social isolation, loneliness and ageism. *International Journal of Environmental Research and Public Health*, 19, 4513.

Dubicka, B. & Theodosiou, L. 2020. *Technology Use and the Mental Health of Children and Young People*. College Report CR225. www.rcpsych.ac.uk/docs/default-source/improving-care/better-mh-policy/college-reports/college-report-cr225.pdf.

Emmons, R. A. & McCullough, M. E. 2003. Counting blessings versus burdens: An experimental investigation of gratitude and subjective well-being in daily life. *Journal of Personality and Social Psychology*, 84, 377–389.

Engel, G. L. 1977. The need for a new medical model: A challenge for biomedicine. *Science*, 196, 129–136.

Engel, G. L. 1980. The clinical application of the biopsychosocial model. *American Journal of Psychiatry*, 137, 535–544.

Fleury, M. J., Imboua, A., Aubé, D., Farand, L. & Lambert, Y. 2012. General practitioners' management of mental disorders: A rewarding practice with considerable obstacles. *BMC (BioMed Central) Family Practice*, 13, article 19.

Fonagy, P., Gergely, G. & Target, M. 2007. The parent-infant dyad and the construction of the subjective self. *Journal of Child Psychology and Psychiatry*, 48, 288–328.

Fonagy, P., Luyten, P., Moulton-Perkins, A., Lee, Y.-W., Warren, F., Howard, S., Ghinai, R., Fearon, P. & Lowyck, B. 2016. Development and validation of a self-report measure of mentalizing: The reflective functioning questionnaire. *PLoS (Public Library of Science) One*, 11, e0158678.

Fulford, B. (K. W. M.) 2007. Facts/values: Ten principles of values-based medicine. In Radden, J. (ed.), *The Philosophy of Psychiatry: A Companion*. New York: Oxford University Press, pp. 205–234.

Fulford, B. (K. W. M.), Broome, M., Stanghellini, G. & Thornton, T. 2005. Looking with both eyes open: Fact and value in psychiatric diagnosis? *World Psychiatry*, 4, 78–86.

Gillham, J., Adams-Deutsch, Z., Werner, J., Reivich, K., Coulter-Heindl, V., Linkins, M., Winder, B., Peterson, C., Park, N., Abenavoli, R., Contero, A. & Seligman, M. E. P. 2011. Character strengths predict subjective well-being during adolescence. *Journal of Positive Psychology*, 6, 31–44.

Golay, P., Abrahamyan Empson, L., Mebdouhi, N., Conus, P. & Alameda, L. 2023. A better understanding of the impact of childhood trauma on depression in early psychosis: A differential item functioning approach. *Schizophrenia Research*, 261, 18–23.

Heikkilä, M. 2023. A Cambridge Analytica-style scandal for AI is coming. *MIT Technology Review*, 25 April. www.technologyreview.com/2023/04/25/1072177/a-cambridge-analytica-style-scandal-for-ai-is-coming/.

Hiam, L., Klaber, B., Sowemimo, A. & Marmot, M. 2024. NHS and the whole of society must act on social determinants of health for a healthier future. *British Medical Journal*, 385, e078903.

HM Government 2007. *Mental Health Act 2007 Explanatory Notes.* London: National Archives. www.legislation.gov.uk/ukpga/2007/12/notes/division/6/1?view=plain.

HM Government 2018. *Modernising the Mental Health Act: Increasing Choice, Reducing Compulsion.* www.gov.uk/government/groups/independent-review-of-the-mental-health-act (specifically the report is at https://assets.publishing.service.gov.uk/media/5c6596a7ed915d045f37798c/Modernising_the_Mental_Health_Act_-_increasing_choice__reducing_compulsion.pdf).

Hu, M. 2020. Cambridge Analytica's black box. *Big Data and Society*, 7(2). https://doi.org/10.1177/2053951720938091.

Hyman, I. 2019. The menace of memes. *Psychology Today*, 31 October. https://shorturl.at/rWTPo.

Insel, T., Cuthbert, B., Garvey, M., Heinssen, R., Pine, D. S., Quinn, K., Sanislow, C. & Wang, P. 2010. Research domain criteria (RDoC): Toward a new classification framework for research on mental disorders. *American Journal of Psychiatry*, 167, 748–751.

Jorm, A. F., Patten, S. B., Brugha, T. S. & Mojtabai, R. 2017. Has increased provision of treatment reduced the prevalence of common mental disorders? Review of the evidence from four countries. *World Psychiatry*, 16, 90–99.

Kar, P. 2023. How can psychiatrists help reduce stigma surrounding LGBTQ+ mental health? Winner of Royal College of Psychiatrists Rainbow SIG Essay Prize. https://shorturl.at/sxpgg.

Kendler, K. S. 2005. Toward a philosophical structure for psychiatry. *American Journal of Psychiatry*, 162, 433–440.

Kendler, K. S. 2014. The structure of psychiatric science. *American Journal of Psychiatry*, 171, 931–938.

Kim, J. 1999. Making sense of emergence. *Philosophical Studies*, 95, 3–36.

Kirkbride, J. B., Anglin, D. M., Colman, I., Dykxhoorn, J., Jones, P. B., Patalay, P., Pitman, A., Soneson, E., Steare, T., Wright, T. & Griffiths, S. L. 2024. The social determinants of mental health and disorder: Evidence, prevention and recommendations. *World Psychiatry*, 23, 58–90.

Kotchoubey, B., Tretter, F., Braun, H. A., Buchheim, T., Draguhn, A., Fuchs, T., Hasler, F., Hastedt, H., Hinterberger, T., Northoff, G., Rentschler, I., Schleim, S., Sellmaier, S., Tebartz Van Elst, L. & Tschacher, W. 2016. Methodological problems on the way to integrative human neuroscience. *Frontiers in Integrative Neuroscience*, 10, article 41.

Langley, C., Cirstea, B. I., Cuzzolin, F. & Sahakian, B. J. 2022. Theory of mind and preference learning at the interface of cognitive science, neuroscience, and AI: A review. *Frontiers in Artificial Intelligence*, 5, 778852.

Leigh, H. 2010a. *Genes, Memes, Culture, and Mental Illness: Toward an Integrative Model.* New York: Springer.

Leigh, H. 2010b. Principles of memetic therapy. In *Genes, Memes, Culture, and Mental Illness: Toward an Integrative Model.* New York: Springer, pp. 187–194.

Lindström, M. & Rosvall, M. 2018. Economic stress in childhood and suicide thoughts and suicide attempts: A population-based study among adults. *Public Health*, 163, 42–45.

Luchins, D. J. 2010. The future of mental health care and the limits of the behavioral neurosciences. *Journal of Nervous and Mental Disease*, 198, 395–398.

Luo, Y., Hawkley, L. C., Waite, L. J. & Cacioppo, J. T. 2012. Loneliness, health, and mortality in old age: A national longitudinal study. *Social Science and Medicine*, 74, 907–914.

Lykken, D. & Tellegen, A. 1996. Happiness is a stochastic phenomenon. *Psychological Science*, 7, 186–189.

Lyubomirsky, S., Sheldon, K. M. & Schkade, D. 2005. Pursuing happiness: The architecture of sustainable change. *Review of General Psychology*, 9, 111–131.

Maiese, M. 2021. An enactivist reconceptualization of the medical model. *Philosophical Psychology*, 34, 962–988.

Maiese, M. 2022. *Autonomy, Enactivism, and Mental Disorder: A Philosophical Account*. London: Routledge.

Martikainen, P., Adda, J., Ferrie, J. E., Davey Smith, G. & Marmot, M. 2003. Effects of income and wealth on GHQ depression and poor self rated health in white collar women and men in the Whitehall II study. *Journal of Epidemiology and Community Health*, 57, 718–723.

McLaren, N. 1992. Is mental disease just brain disease: The limits to biological psychiatry. *Australian and New Zealand Journal of Psychiatry*, 26, 270–276.

McLaren, N. 1998. A critical review of the biopsychosocial model. *Australian and New Zealand Journal of Psychiatry*, 32, 86–92.

Mills, P. J., Redwine, L., Wilson, K., Pung, M. A., Chinh, K., Greenberg, B. H., Lunde, O., Maisel, A., Raisinghani, A., Wood, A. & Chopra, D. 2015. The role of gratitude in spiritual well-being in asymptomatic heart failure patients. *Spirituality in Clinical Practice*, 2, 5–17.

Minnis, H. 2023. Abuse, neglect and neurodevelopment across the life course: what can paediatricians and child psychiatrists do about this together? The Rees-Illingworth keynote lecture 2023. *Archives of Disease in Childhood*, 109, 533–535.

Monteith, S., Glenn, T., Geddes, J. R., Whybrow, P. C., Achtyes, E. & Bauer, M. 2024. Artificial intelligence and increasing misinformation. *British Journal of Psychiatry*, 224, 33–35.

Monteith, S., Glenn, T., Geddes, J. R., Whybrow, P. C. & Bauer, M. 2022. Commercial use of emotion artificial intelligence (AI): Implications for psychiatry. *Current Psychiatry Reports*, 24, 203–211.

Mullainathan, S. & Shafir, E. 2013. *Scarcity: Why Having Too Little Means So Much*. London: Allen Lane.

Nielsen, K. 2020. What is mental disorder? Developing an embodied, embedded, and enactive psychopathology. Unpublished PhD thesis, Victoria University of Wellington.

Nielsen, K. & Ward, T. 2018. Towards a new conceptual framework for psychopathology: Embodiment, enactivism, and embedment. *Theory and Psychology*, 28, 800–822.

Okuzono, S. S., Shiba, K., Kim, E. S., Shirai, K., Kondo, N., Fujiwara, T., Kondo, K., Lomas, T., Trudel-Fitzgerald, C., Kawachi, I. & Vanderweele, T. J. 2022. Ikigai and subsequent health and wellbeing among Japanese older adults: Longitudinal outcome-wide analysis. *Lancet Regional Health – Western Pacific*, 21, 100391.

Perez, A. N., Suarez, J. & Le Bars, M. 2023. *Sizing the Brain: Segmentation and Growth Factors of the Global Neuroscience Market*. Deloitte. https://shorturl.at/LszH5.

Pescosolido, B. A., Martin, J. K., Long, J. S., Medina, T. R., Phelan, J. C. & Link, B. G. 2010. 'A disease like any other'? A decade of change in public reactions to schizophrenia, depression, and alcohol dependence. *American Journal of Psychiatry*, 167, 1321–1330.

Prichard, E. C. 2021. Is the use of personality based psychometrics by Cambridge Analytical Psychological Science's 'nuclear bomb' moment? *Frontiers in Psychology*, 12, 581448.

Randall-James, J. & Coles, S. 2018. Questioning diagnoses in clinical practice: A thematic analysis of clinical psychologists' accounts of working beyond diagnosis in the United Kingdom. *Journal of Mental Health*, 27, 450–456.

Reangsing, C., Rittiwong, T. & Schneider, J. K. 2021. Effects of mindfulness meditation interventions on depression in older adults: A meta-analysis. *Aging and Mental Health*, 25, 1181–1190.

Reijneveld, S. A. & Schene, A. H. 1998. Higher prevalence of mental disorders in socioeconomically deprived urban areas in the Netherlands: Community or personal disadvantage? *Journal of Epidemiology and Community Health*, 52, 2–7.

Rieber, R. W. 1980. *Wilhelm Wundt and the Making of a Scientific Psychology*, edited by R. W. Rieber in collaboration with A. L. Blumenthal, K. Danziger & S. Diamond. New York: Plenum Press.

Russell, J. L. 2023. Problems for enactive psychiatry as a practical framework. *Philosophical Psychology*, 36, 1458–1481.

Schneble, C. O., Elger, B. S. & Shaw, D. 2018. The Cambridge Analytica affair and internet-mediated research. *European Molecular Biology Organization Reports*, 19, e46579.

Seligman, M. E. P. 2002. *Authentic Happiness: Using the New Positive Psychology to Realize Your Potential for Lasting Fulfillment*. London: Free Press.

Senior, S. L., Caan, W. & Gamsu, M. 2020. Welfare and well-being: Towards mental health-promoting welfare systems. *British Journal of Psychiatry*, 216, 4–5.

Shifman, L. 2019. Internet memes and the twofold articulation of values. In Graham, M. & Dutton, W. H. (eds.), *Society and the Internet: How Networks of Information and Communication Are Changing Our Lives*. Oxford: Oxford University Press.

Sperry, R. W. 1972. Science and the problem of values. *Perspectives in Biology and Medicine*, 16, 115–130.

Stafford, M., De Silva, M., Stansfeld, S. & Marmot, M. 2008. Neighbourhood social capital and common mental disorder: Testing the link in a general population sample. *Health Place*, 14, 394–405.

Tse, D. C. K., Nakamura, J. & Csikszentmihalyi, M. 2021. Living well by 'flowing' well: The indirect effect of autotelic personality on well-being through flow experience. *Journal of Positive Psychology*, 16, 310–321.

Uher, R. & Zwicker, A. 2017. Etiology in psychiatry: Embracing the reality of poly-gene-environmental causation of mental illness. *World Psychiatry*, 16, 121–129.

University of Cambridge 2017. *Human Rights of People with Autism Not Being Met, Leading Expert Tells United Nations*. Cambridge: Cambridge University Press. https://shorturl.at/f5Npj.

Valikhani, A., Ahmadnia, F., Karimi, A. & Mills, P. J. 2019. The relationship between dispositional gratitude and quality of life: The mediating role of perceived stress and mental health. *Personality and Individual Differences*, 141, 40–46.

Van Oudenhove, L. & Cuypers, S. 2014. The relevance of the philosophical 'mind–body problem' for the status of psychosomatic medicine: A conceptual analysis of the biopsychosocial model. *Medicine Health Care and Philosophy*, 17, 201–213.

Voneida, T. J. 1998. Sperry's concept of mind as an emergent property of brain function and its implications for the future of humankind: Paths in the brain, actions of the mind. *Neuropsychologia*, 36, 1077–1082.

Wang, R., Chen, H., Liu, Y., Lu, Y. & Yao, Y. 2019. Neighborhood social reciprocity and mental health among older adults in China: The mediating effects of physical activity, social interaction, and volunteering. *BMC (BioMed Central) Public Health*, 19, 1036.

Yuan, N., Chen, Y., Xia, Y., Dai, J. & Liu, C. 2019. Inflammation-related biomarkers in major psychiatric disorders: A cross-disorder assessment of reproducibility and specificity in 43 meta-analyses. *Translational Psychiatry*, 9, 233.

Zanarini, M. C., Yong, L., Frankenburg, F. R., Hennen, J., Reich, D. B., Marino, M. F. & Vujanovic, A. A. 2002. Severity of reported childhood sexual abuse and its relationship to severity of borderline psychopathology and psychosocial impairment among borderline inpatients. *Journal of Nervous and Mental Disease*, 190, 381–387.

Zhang, L., Zhao, N., Zhu, M., Tang, M., Liu, W. & Hong, W. 2023. Adverse childhood experiences in patients with schizophrenia: Related factors and clinical implications. *Frontiers in Psychiatry*, 14, 1247063.

Zhang, Q., Wang, Z., Wang, X., Liu, L., Zhang, J. & Zhou, R. 2019. The effects of different stages of mindfulness meditation training on emotion regulation. *Frontiers in Human Neuroscience*, 13, 208.

Chapter 5

Psychiatry from Within and in the Media

Robert B. Dudas

Introduction

In this chapter, I will describe how psychiatrists see themselves and their values as well as how they are seen from the outside. For the former, I will look at both personal and collective values. As for the latter, I will examine the portrayal of psychiatry by the media.

The Values of Psychiatry as Seen from Within

Who we think we are and what we think we do has a major impact on our professional values. The UK's National Health Service (NHS) defines psychiatry as 'a medical field concerned with the diagnosis, treatment and prevention of mental health conditions' (NHS, 2022). The Royal College of Psychiatrists uses a similar definition, stating that 'psychiatry is a branch of medicine dealing with people with a huge range of mental health conditions' (RCPsych, 2025). Although most psychiatrists have a strong medical identity, there are two, to a significant degree related, problems here. Firstly, most clinicians know that to thrive in clinical practice one needs, beyond biomedical knowledge and skills, knowledge and skills that pertain to the human disciplines. Secondly, in spite of this, in psychiatry there is an almost unbridgeable gap between clinical practice and research that is so heavily weighted towards neuroscience and epidemiology that it seems to be 'too often not continuous with the world, in general, and the clinic, in particular' (Stanghellini, 2013, p. 499). Yet, apart from their specialty training, research is one of the main sources of education for psychiatrists. These important problems have an impact on how we see ourselves both as individuals and as a profession.

Personal Values

The Origins of Our Personal Values as Psychiatrists

Where do our personal values as psychiatrists come from? Broadly speaking, we develop them throughout life. We bring many of our fundamental values from our personal history as a son or daughter, brother or sister, father or mother, friend, and member of our community. They are shaped and moulded by influences from those close to us as well as the culture (or cultures) we have lived in. Many of our personal values come from our training; some of these are rooted in current practices, and some are vestiges from the history of psychiatry (Dudas, 2022).

Although it seems intuitive, relatively little research evidence has been published about the influence of personal history on the values of clinicians in general. Autobiographical writings of prominent personalities in mental health (e.g. Clark, 1996; Gask, 2015; Sternberg et al., 2016) and biographies about them (e.g. Demorest, 2004) allow us a glimpse into how one's own life history can influence clinicians' professional practice. In *The Story of a Mental Hospital: Fulbourn 1858–1983*, David Clark (1996) gives a poignant example of how his own life experiences shaped his professional values. Clark became Medical Superintendent of Fulbourn Hospital near Cambridge when he was thirty-two and worked in that capacity from 1953 to 1971. He led a group of conscientious objectors into action during the Second World War and saw in Germany the horrors of the Nazi concentration camps. In Sumatra, he was in charge of a camp of 2,000 Dutch civilians and negotiated with them and others in order to avoid a massacre. This 'taught [him] something of the perils and responsibilities of command, . . . and left [him] with a deep distaste for locking anybody up' (Clark, 1996, p. 39). One of the reasons he took the job in Fulbourn was the wish to improve the conditions on the long-stay wards where, he describes, patients were 'left, neglected, to their hallucinatory ramblings, or worse, locked up in padded rooms, straight-jacketed or mistreated by staff because of their violence' (Clark, 1996, pp. 39–40). His experience in the Army had made him acutely aware of how people's mental health was influenced by the way in which they were led. Under Clark's leadership, the majority of the patients in Fulbourn Hospital were rehabilitated. Many of them were discharged permanently and moved back into the community.

There is a growing body of literature on illness in the clinician and the impact of that on their practice and professional values. The concept of the 'wounded healer', based on the idea that experiencing and overcoming illness personally can make one a better therapist, has a long history (Jackson, 2001). There are examples from both physical and mental health. For instance, doctors with a personal history of migraine were found to have a more somatic view of migraine (Evers et al., 2020). General practitioners' (GPs or primary care physicians) treatment choice for depression was found to be influenced by personal history of psychotherapy or antidepressant treatment, and history of depression in someone close (Dumesnil et al., 2012). Personal history has a profound effect on us as professionals. Psychiatric, psychology, pediatric, and social work professionals who had been sexually or physically abused themselves were found to be more likely to believe allegations of sexual abuse contained in sixteen case vignettes (Nuttall and Jackson, 1994). Interpretative phenomenological analysis in relation to primary care physicians revealed that experiencing disempowerment and vulnerability as a patient was particularly insightful for the physicians and helped them develop more empathy for their own patients (Fox et al., 2009).

Becoming a mental health patient as a psychiatrist is not a prerequisite, but reading about the experiences of those of us who have can certainly inform our understanding of relevant values. In *The Other Side of Silence: A Psychiatrist's Memoir of Depression*, Linda Gask (2015), an academic psychiatrist and clinician, describes how many of her values were shaped by her own illness and her interaction with psychiatry both as a psychiatrist and as a psychiatrist patient. She tells us how, when she was not well enough to treat others, she always sought help to recover first, as it would have been unethical to treat others when she was not herself. As a patient, she wanted to talk to someone who had trained as a psychotherapist: 'Even if I suspected, though with some ambivalence, that I needed first and foremost more medication, it was important for me to talk to someone who would be able to appreciate my story as well as my symptoms' (Gask, 2015, p. 175). She believes that her experience of depression has helped her become a more humane and understanding clinician, but she is aware that she still does not have all the answers.

Although Gask became clinically depressed, her description of becoming and working as a psychiatrist is also applicable to many psychiatrists who have not developed mental illness but may have shared one or two of the elements of her history. Whilst not present in every psychiatrist's upbringing, growing up in an environment where she constantly needed to use her emotional antennae to detect the 'mood' in the house (she had a brother with severe obsessive compulsive disorder) prepared her for empathizing with her patients. On the negative side, this also came with (sometimes crippling) oversensitivity to the actions of others: 'I was able to imagine myself without too much difficulty into the mental world of the people on the psychiatric unit: the anxious, the depressed and even the paranoid. I felt like I had finally reached my destination, not only because I seemed to have some kind of aptitude for psychiatry but because life on the ward resonated with something inside of me' (Gask, 2015, p. 37). She seems to have turned her history to her advantage: 'I was succeeding in my new career and I had something crucial in common with my patients: we had all been wounded by life' (Gask, 2015, p. 74).

Needs, Concerns, and Preferences Related to Working in Psychiatry

It is worth saying a few words on the specific challenges of working in psychiatry as seen by psychiatrists. In his book *The Wounded Healer*, Omar Reda (2022) says that '[e]ntering the landscape of pain . . . is a heroic act, even though caregivers do not see themselves as heroes. To console, hold, and sustain others whilst they are "falling apart" requires heroic skills. Yet that can be a heavy burden' (Reda, 2022, p. 1). Reda warns that '[b]ehind the mask also is a human, not a superhero, and not a machine, but a human who has emotions and has basic needs that deserve to be fulfilled. One way to do this is "not to take your clients home with you"' (Reda, 2022, p. 23). Psychiatrists often have a heavy caseload, work long hours, with little support, and have to drive long distances when on call, leading to fatigue (Till et al., 2018); all of this can make it difficult for them to appreciate other aspects of their lives. Tellingly, as regards the things that could tip her into despair in a matter of days, Linda Gask asks, 'Wasn't it always work? Or at least this is what I found most stressful. It was never the patients who kept me awake at night but my interactions with the system' (Gask, 2015, p. 13). As Reda explains, 'We might feel like a failure and think of quitting. We come close to walking away on multiple occasions, but the field holds a power over us every time we are about to exit its doors. That power, I believe, is love. We love what we do, and we cannot see ourselves doing anything else as rewarding' (Reda, 2022, p. 54). Talking about the needs of people in these demanding, caring roles, Reda (2022, pp. 121–123) draws attention to the importance of deep kindness and physical, sexual, psychological, social, financial, and spiritual safety.

Collective Values

But psychiatrists' values are not only shaped by individual values; they are also shaped by the norms, rules, and expectations of their profession and their regulatory bodies. Training is pivotal; therefore, I will look at the new psychiatric curricula in the UK. The curriculum of an era allows insight into the prevailing thinking around the profession's dominant values and aspirations.

The Values of Psychiatry as Reflected in the Curricula for Psychiatry Training

Values are not always immediately apparent; sometimes they are easier to notice when they are changing. This is why it may be particularly useful to look at differences in the expressed value content between the purpose statements of the old and the new curricula. The psychiatry curricula in the UK function as an educational plan tied to goals and objectives. They serve as the basis for training programmes to achieve specific knowledge, behaviour, and attitudes for future psychiatrists. They are value-laden and guide trainers in choosing educational activities preferentially. Core training is the first half of the training before trainees start off on their path of sub-specialization. The old core curriculum (RCPsych, 2013, p. 5) says: 'What is set out in this document is the generic knowledge, skills and attitudes, or more readily assessed behaviour, that we believe is common to all psychiatric specialties.' The new core curriculum (RCPsych, 2022, p. 2) emphasizes that this is a multidisciplinary activity with a variety of stakeholders: 'The purpose of the Core Psychiatry curriculum is to train medical doctors to specialise in the assessment, diagnosis, treatment and management of patients with mental disorders in a wide range of clinical settings in collaboration with the patient, other health professionals, and relevant others including families and carers of all ages.'

The new core curriculum then goes further and states that psychiatrists of the future will be well-equipped to (italics are mine):

– Maintain their key focus on *developing and achieving the necessary professional values and behaviours, professional skills, and professional knowledge to build strong therapeutic relationships with their patients, their carers and families* and to *provide safe person-centred care.*
– *Embrace continuing person-centred holistic advances* in Psychiatry, *as well as developments in technology and practice*, which are consistent with the principles of *sustainability.*
– Have the *relevant specialist knowledge and communication skills* to operate effectively in a range of service delivery landscapes. (RCPsych, 2022, p. 2)

Noticeable is the change from the old core curriculum in the order of the words '*knowledge*', '*skills*', and '*behaviour*' and the addition of '*values*' in the first position in the sentence, giving it the most weight.

In order to successfully implement the new curriculum, a document called the Silver Guide was developed. The Silver Guide was based on the Gold Guide, which is a reference guide for postgraduate medical training in the UK, maintained by the Conference of Postgraduate Medical Deans on behalf of the four UK health departments.

The Silver Guide places great importance on the person-centred holistic model of psychiatry. According to this, certain concepts are fundamental to good professional practice. These concepts include the patient as a whole person: body, mind and spirit; a compassionate clinical approach, based on both values and evidence; multidisciplinary working; shared responsibility and shared decision-making with the patient and other stakeholders; a model of the person which draws on the social sciences, neurosciences, and the humanities; and the impact of culture, religion, and social systems on individuals.

The curriculum revision working group engaged in wide-ranging discussions when considering revisions to the curriculum, highlighting the importance of reflecting the equal weighting of the psychological, biological, and social components within the curriculum and taking into consideration the cultural, religious, social, and environmental context. This should mean, at least in theory, significantly greater emphasis in training, compared to previously, on the psycho and the social aspects of the biopsychosocial (BPS) model and regarding them as of equal importance to the biological dimension. This is a very important statement and a welcome change, if successfully implemented. However, whilst the biological or neuroscience components have seen a major uplift in the UK through the Wellcome-Gatsby neuroscience project and other initiatives, there is no comparable funding initiative for the psychological and the social aspects. A similar effort would be needed to improve the social sciences and humanities content to meet the appropriately high standards of the Silver Guide.

A Closer Look at Values in the New Curricula

Fading and Emerging Values

Values feature more prominently throughout the new core curriculum. In the old core curriculum, the word values was mentioned explicitly only in the context of recognizing the value of diversity within the multidisciplinary team (MDT) and recognizing the value of reflective practice. The new core curriculum gives emphasis to the role of values in what we do by starting its purpose statement with developing our professional values. The other place where values are explicitly mentioned in the new curriculum is the section on communication, which lists as a key capability taking into consideration patients' ideas, values, concerns, and expectations as part of effective communication and shared decision-making. These are the cornerstones of values-based practice (VBP).

The new core curriculum also makes specific reference to professional documents describing these values, such as the Royal College of Psychiatrists' *Core Values for Psychiatrists* (Richards and Lloyd, 2017), which did not exist at the time the old curriculum was created, and the General Medical Council's (GMC) ethical guidance contained in *Good Medical Practice* (GMC, 2024), which describes essential values with a strong focus on communication with all important stakeholders and working in partnership with the patient, taking account of their history and their views and values. *Core Values for Psychiatrists* is a document produced by the Royal College of Psychiatrists. The fact that it was written by Veryan Richards, Patient Representative of the College, and Keith Lloyd, Chair of the Royal College of Psychiatrists in Wales, is evidence of a significant culture change within the profession. Among other sources, it draws on VBP principles. The eight values it lists as core are respect, trust, communication, dignity, empathy, fairness, honesty, and humility. One of the stated aims of this document is to '[provide] a focus for a skills-based approach to decision-making where complex and conflicting values are involved, as a reference point, and as a measuring tool for evaluating practice. It underpins the therapeutic relationship between the patient and the doctor, which in turn influences the quality of recovery' (Richards and Lloyd, 2017, p. 2).

The new core and specialist curricula and the Silver Guide keep the BPS model and emphasize and further elaborate on the holistic, person-centred approach. Although in clinical practice we refer to the BPS model every day to explain mental illness and to formulate treatment, we rarely appreciate the full capabilities of it as a scientific model, or its limitations. George Engel, who developed this model in the 1970s, realized that his was a time when many in psychiatry felt that psychiatry needed to find its way back to medicine, which was rooted in the biological sciences and had been so successful in elucidating the mechanisms of disease and in finding new treatments for (non-psychiatric) medical conditions. He felt that this was misguided and in fact that the whole of medicine was in crisis and needed to adopt a more holistic model of disease that could meet the challenge of the scientific tasks and social responsibilities of both medicine and psychiatry. This is particularly relevant because, as regards psychiatry, much of the criticisms contained in critical and anti-psychiatry relate strongly to these points. The new curriculum makes fewer explicit references to the BPS approach, especially in the context of treatment. 'Biological' and 'psychological' are mentioned particularly less often than in the old core curriculum. Contrastingly, there are significantly more mentions of *safeguarding* in the new core curriculum, suggesting a shifting emphasis in current clinical practice.

A finer-grained analysis of the content reveals some other interesting trends relating to clinical values. *Person-centred care*, referring to taking into account the whole person by going beyond a narrow focus on their condition or symptoms and also considering their preferences, well-being, and wider social and cultural background, is not mentioned explicitly in the old core curriculum but features prominently in the new. It is mentioned four times in its purpose statement alone, again under the section on professional relationships, and twice under clinical skills. *Co-production*, which means involving patients and carers as equal partners in designing the support and services they receive, appears first in the new curriculum in the context of devising a safe, systemic, effective, collaborative, and co-productive management plan. The clinical skill of understanding the inherent *power imbalance* between doctor and patient is also a new addition. *Protected characteristics*, the impact of social, cultural, spiritual, and religious factors, including the effects of deprivation, discrimination, and racism, also appear for the first time. The understanding of the relevance to our work of the *history of psychiatry*, the evolution of our current diagnostic categories and our treatments, and the historical relationships between psychiatry and society also emerge in the new curriculum. Another significant inclusion is sustainability, which has implications for prevention, patient empowerment, and efficient service delivery, apart from low carbon outcomes.

In general, more reference is made to VBP principles in the new specialist curricula too. For example, the new old age curriculum builds on from the new core curriculum as regards developing further the professional values explained in there. Under the heading of person-centred care, by the end of their training trainees are expected to demonstrate a *holistic and person-centred clinical approach* to older adults that is empathic and compassionate, and that respects their dignity whilst maintaining therapeutic optimism, thus remaining realistically optimistic and honest whilst maintaining boundaries. They should be able to conduct person-centred holistic assessments of older people, including history taking, mental state examination, and relevant psychopathology, that takes into consideration the psychological, social, cultural, spiritual, and religious aspects of ageing, activities of daily living, physical health, medication, frailty and falls, and death and dying. Similar to the new core curriculum, *co-production* appears in the new old age curriculum. Old age trainees are expected to demonstrate an *inclusive leadership style* and *awareness of the impact of hierarchy and power within relationships* with both patients and colleagues. The new old age curriculum keeps the BPS model when considering both aetiological factors and treatment. There are fewer mentions of 'medication', 'pharmacological', or 'drug', and especially of 'medical' than in the previous old age curriculum and there are more mentions of *safeguarding*.

How Could We Further Improve the Coverage of Values in the Curricula?

The new curricula include the values aspect much more prominently and describe the desired outcomes in detail in terms of clinical skills and qualities of care. What appears to be needed is bridging the gap between these ideals and their realization in actual clinical practice. Future iterations may want to include more on questions like 'How do we actually do person-centred care?'. Teaching the VBP skills of awareness, reasoning, and communication relating to values and resolving value conflicts would be relevant here. We would also need to teach trainees how to argue their point when it comes to values. If we expect psychiatrists to embrace the clinical values mentioned in the previous section, we also need to include more in the training about the evidence-base supporting the person-centred model in terms of efficacy, patient and professional satisfaction, and health economics, so as to provide arguments for its wholesale adoption beyond its intuitive usefulness. Another crucial question is how we can balance the curricula well in order to ensure that each component of the BPS model (and preferably also the existential dimension of mental illness) gets equal weight and the same high-quality coverage. And how can we ensure the same in workplace-based assessment, training courses, and exams?

It is important to mention a set of important clinical values that currently do not feature prominently and are not made explicit in the curricula but nevertheless guide current clinical training and practice. These relate to two main themes: (1) treatment of and recovery from mental illness and (2) challenges we need to negotiate in the current climate.

As regards the first of these themes, *dealing with uncertainty* is a major challenge in psychiatry that features relatively little in the curricula. It is important that we highlight possible sources of uncertainty, such as mental symptoms being *hybrid objects* (Berrios and Marková, 2015) and *overdetermined*, not having laboratory tests for most conditions, the significant unpredictability of human behaviour, and several different treatments all being potentially appropriate for a problem. Clinicians in mental health often look after or work with patients who have extraordinarily tragic life stories that most people would find difficult even to hear, or patients who display behaviours that would drive most people away, or patients who simply do not want to engage with any help. Maintaining *unconditional positive regard* in these situations is a value that is embodied by most psychiatrists but is currently only implied in the curriculum. The recovery movement in mental health has highlighted the importance of fostering healthy coping mechanisms, supportive relationships, empowerment, social inclusion, and meaning, in addition to treating symptoms. *Recovery* in this context does not always mean no longer meeting the criteria for diagnosis; it can involve recovering from the initial shock and learning to tackle mental health problems with hope and optimism, and to work towards a valued lifestyle. The patient's *personal narrative* has always been important in all branches of medicine but has never taken centre stage quite as much as in psychiatry, both in diagnosis making and in treatment. Psychiatry has a lot to offer in terms of improving our understanding of this important aspect of the healing process in the context of any illness (psychiatric or non-psychiatric) but especially in the context of long-term, chronic conditions. Psychiatrists are expert companions in a *systemic approach to help the patient explore changes in their social roles and identities.*

Regarding the second theme, dealing with the *challenges of a changing healthcare system* requires psychiatrists to think about and adopt a new set of values to manage these. The mismatch between ideal treatment and what (often shrinking) local resources allow at any given time makes it necessary to agree on framework values (e.g. minimum standards) and to negotiate these framework values with both the commissioners and the recipients of these services.

From a methodological perspective, it is important to explore the question of *how we can know that we are getting it right in terms of working with both the values of our patients individually and those of our profession.* Indications about this can come from multiple sources. In reasonably well-functioning healthcare systems, compliments usually significantly outnumber complaints, but they can both serve as validation for our chosen values:

people make compliments and complaints about things that are important to them. Patients and relatives rarely complain about lack of knowledge; they complain much more often about communication problems and about being treated rudely, insensitively, or disrespectfully (Pitarka-Carcani et al., 2000). When things have gone really well, patients and relatives praise the personal relationship much more than safety or other aspects. These all argue in favour of taking a person-centred approach (Gillespie, 2021). Job satisfaction and recruitment and retention figures are also a good measure of whether we are getting our values right at work. Last but not least, there is growing evidence that VBP principles can improve clinical outcomes (de Silva, 2011, p. 6).

Psychiatry in the Public Discourse

Why Is It Important?

Media coverage of mental illness and psychiatry serves as a barometer of public opinion (Anderson et al., 2020), shapes public attitudes and stigma (Anderson et al., 2020), and influences whether and at what point people decide to seek help for mental ill health (Nesseler, 2011). The media also provide frames for organizing information and sense-making and a forum for the active construction of everyday knowledge about health and illness by the public (Ohlsson, 2018). Another important function of the media is the examination of psychiatry as a social institution (Ohlsson, 2018). Publicity can protect people from abuse and neglect and various other wrongdoings.

What Is the Public Image of Psychiatry Like in the Media?

Although there has been increasing coverage of the subject in all types of media, most research studies focus on written and/or electronic media. There is a tendency to portray mental illness as something new and affecting increasingly large sections of the population (Nesseler, 2011; Ohlsson, 2018). On the other hand, there are also voices warning about an unhealthy societal preoccupation with health rather than serious health problems, linked to unreasonable expectations of life (Ohlsson, 2018).

Overall, the coverage of mental illness has been improving, offering a more balanced view, since around the 1990s (Gallagher et al., 2023; Grandón et al., 2022; Nesseler, 2011; Oliver et al., 2020), but mental illness still often appears in association with negative attributes, contributing to preserving unhelpful stereotypes, such as that people with mental illness are dangerous or lazy, that mental illness is a threat to public health and welfare (Ohlsson, 2018), and that treatments are cruel and ineffective (Nesseler, 2011). The portrayal of psychotic conditions has been found to be more likely to be stigmatizing (Gallagher et al., 2023; Nawková et al., 2012), whilst articles on depression have gradually become less likely to be stigmatizing (Gallagher et al., 2023). Although suicide is not a mental illness, it is often associated with it. Improvements in the way the media cover celebrity suicides have helped reduce the Werther effect, that is, spikes in the suicide rate following announcement of a celebrity suicide. The association is less clear after non-celebrity suicides, which are also frequently reported but tend to appear in local news outlets as opposed to national or global ones (Niederkrotenthaler et al., 2020). Responsible reporting guidelines recommend avoiding mention of the method used, avoiding repeatedly reporting the same suicide, and including information on treatable mental illness and where and when to seek help.

In the media, there is a tension between the need for objective portrayal and the need to attract readers, and this is reflected in the choice of words used (Nesseler, 2011). Psychiatric care is often pitched as a struggle between individual freedom and the demands of society (Nesseler, 2011). In this context, confidence in and dependence on experts is juxtaposed with (often harsh) critique and expressions of distrust (Ohlsson, 2018). The expertise of psychiatrists is questioned on grounds like psychiatry lacking scientific foundations, practice being based on obsolete ideas, and whether an objective distinction can be made between normal and pathological (Ohlsson, 2018).

The increasingly widespread use of social media has changed the media landscape profoundly: one-to-many communication has been replaced by many-to-many and many-to-one forms (Nesseler, 2011). This means that public opinion can be perceived by the stakeholders much more closely and swiftly. It has become an almost complete free-for-all. Opinion leaders without any specific training, experience, professional regulatory control, or responsibility can enter the conversation at any time. Interpreting a clinical situation is no longer done exclusively by individual professionals, professional organizations, and healthcare providers; rather, their opinion is only one of the many circulating widely within the population. There is much wider participation, but often without the support and oversight necessary for a good outcome. Some levelling out can potentially be helpful in places where there is still an unhelpful power imbalance, but it is likely ill-advised to do away completely with the fact of professionals having power over decisions that require very specific knowledge and skills: nobody would want the passengers to vote on what is wrong and what should be done next when an aeroplane is in difficulty, let alone allow the one with the loudest voice to decide. Research (Ohlsson, 2018) has found that some in the media have expressed that the intermingling of views from experts and those without proper knowledge on the subject may even contribute to the stigmatization of mental illness. It is important to note that this is different from including in the debate the voices of patients and carers who are experts by lived experience, which is of course vital.

Nowadays, patients and carers often look up information on the internet on diagnosis, treatment, and/or likely outcomes. Depending on the quality of the source and the reader's ability to engage with the information in the absence of expert help, this can be very helpful but can also bring a whole raft of potential problems: a totally different range of expectations, incorrect understanding of what one needs in order to get better, and sometimes significant concerns without a good reason. Some patients and carers will just bring the information they collected into the discussion, whilst others will go further and make their own self-diagnosis or demand certain treatments on the basis of that. It has been highlighted that the rapid and widespread appearance of synthetic media (material created by artificial intelligence) poses a new threat by spreading misinformation (Monteith et al., 2024).

Old stereotypes about mental illness and psychiatry are still very much present in the public mind and the media (Nesseler, 2011); there is a significant lag between the public image and current clinical practice (Dudas, 2020). There are, however, some specific positive new developments, too, including self-help chat forums and high-quality documentaries allowing a glimpse into the lives of people with mental illness and into what stigma feels like for those on the suffering end.

Suggestions for the Future

Similar to the guidelines for responsible reporting on suicide, guidelines for portraying patients with mental illness and their care have been called for. In order to make a positive change in public attitudes, mental health stories would need to be consistently contextualized and use inclusive language (Oliver et al., 2020). Stories illustrating successful interventions should also see the light of day (Oliver et al., 2020). This is particularly important in light of research showing that mental health services and mental health professionals were seen as poorly represented by the news media, which was thought to deter help-seeking and hinder trust (Oliver et al., 2020).

References

Anderson, C., Henderson, C., Hildersley, R. & Potts, L. 2020. Improvement for most, but not all: Changes in newspaper coverage of mental illness from 2008 to 2019 in England. *Epidemiology and Psychiatric Sciences*, 29, e177.

Berrios, G. E. & Marková, I. S. 2015. Toward a new epistemology of psychiatry. In Kirmayer, L. J., Lemelson, R. & Cummings, C. A. (eds.), *Re-visioning Psychiatry: Cultural Phenomenology, Critical Neuroscience, and Global Mental Health*. Cambridge: Cambridge University Press, pp. 41–64.

Clark, D. H. 1996. *The Story of a Mental Hospital: Fulbourn 1858–1983*. London: Process Press.

Demorest, A. P. 2004. *Psychology's Grand Theorists: How Personal Experiences Shaped Professional Ideas*. Mahwah, NJ: Lawrence Erlbaum Associates.

De Silva, D. 2011. *Helping People Help Themselves: A Review of the Evidence Considering Whether It Is Worthwhile to Support Self-Management*. London: Health Foundation.

Dudas, R. 2020. The discontents of psychiatry: What can the history of psychiatry and values-based medicine contribute to resolving them? In Marková, I. S. & Chen, E. (eds.), *Rethinking Psychopathology: Theory and History in the Human and Social Sciences*. Cham: Springer, pp. 145–152.

Dudas, R. B. 2022. Values-based practice: How can history taking help psychiatrists explore the values involved in clinical decision-making? *British Journal of Psychiatry Advances*, 28, 153–162.

Dumesnil, H., Cortaredona, S., Verdoux, H., Sebbah, R., Paraponaris, A. & Verger, P. 2012. General practitioners' choices and their determinants when starting treatment for major depression: A cross sectional, randomized case-vignette survey. *PLoS (Public Library of Science) One*, 7, e52429.

Evers, S., Brockmann, N., Summ, O., Husstedt, I. W. & Frese, A. 2020. Primary headache and migraine in headache specialists: Does personal history of doctors matter? *Cephalalgia*, 40, 96–106.

Fox, F. E., Rodham, K. J., Harris, M. F., Taylor, G. J., Sutton, J., Scott, J. & Robinson, B. 2009. Experiencing 'the other side': A study of empathy and empowerment in general practitioners who have been patients. *Qualitative Health Research*, 19, 1580–1588.

Gallagher, M., O'Leary, C., McGreal-Ballone, A. & Duffy, R. 2023. The portrayal of mental health in Irish mainstream news media. *International Journal of Social Psychiatry*, 69, 467–475.

Gask, L. 2015. *The Other Side of Silence: A Psychiatrist's Memoir of Depression*. Chichester: Vie Books.

General Medical Council (GMC) 2024. *Good Medical Practice*. www.gmc-uk.org/-/media/documents/good-medical-practice-2024—english-102607294.pdf.

Gillespie, A. & Reader, T. W. 2021. Identifying and encouraging high-quality healthcare: An analysis of the content and aims of patient letters of compliment. *BMJ (British Medical Journal) Quality and Safety*, 30, 484–492.

Grandón, P., Fernández Vega, D., Sánchez Oñate, A. A., Vielma Aguilera, A. V., Villagrán Valenzuela, L., Vidal Gutiérrez, D., Inostroza Rovengno, C. & Whitley, R. 2022. Mental disorders in the media: A retrospective study of newspaper coverage in the Chilean press. *International Journal of Social Psychiatry*, 68, 1351–1362.

Jackson, S. W. 2001. The wounded healer. *Bulletin of the History of Medicine*, 75, 1–36.

Monteith, S., Glenn, T., Geddes, J. R., Whybrow, P. C., Achtyes, E. & Bauer, M. 2024.

Artificial intelligence and increasing misinformation. *British Journal of Psychiatry*, 224, 33–35.

National Health Service (NHS) 2022. Psychiatry. www.nhs.uk/mental-health/talking-therapies-medicine-treatments/medicines-and-psychiatry/psychiatry.

Nawková, L., Nawka, A., Adámková, T., Rukavina, T. V., Holcnerová, P., Kuzman, M. R., Jovanović, N., Brborović, O., Bednárová, B., Žuchová, S., Miovský, M. & Raboch, J. 2012. The picture of mental health/illness in the printed media in three central European countries. *Journal of Health Communication*, 17, 22–40.

Nesseler, T. 2011. Narrated truths: The image of psychiatry in the media. *European Archives of Psychiatry and Clinical Neuroscience*, 261, S124–S128.

Niederkrotenthaler, T., Braun, M., Pirkis, J., Till, B., Stack, S., Sinyor, M., Tran, U. S., Voracek, M., Cheng, Q., Arendt, F., Scherr, S., Yip, P. S. F. & Spittal, M. J. 2020. Association between suicide reporting in the media and suicide: Systematic review and meta-analysis. *British Medical Journal*, 368, m575.

Nuttall, R. & Jackson, H. 1994. Personal history of childhood abuse among clinicians. *Child Abuse and Neglect*, 18, 455–472.

Ohlsson, R. 2018. Public discourse on mental health and psychiatry: Representations in Swedish newspapers. *Health*, 22, 298–314.

Oliver, N., Beddoe, L. & Adamson, C. 2020. Mental health and the news media in Aotearoa New Zealand: Key informant perspectives. *Aotearoa New Zealand Social Work*, 32, 158–171.

Pitarka-Carcani, I., Szmukler, G. & Henderson, C. 2000. Complaints about care in a mental health trust. *Psychiatric Bulletin of the Royal College of Psychiatrists*, 24, 372–376.

Reda, O. 2022. *The Wounded Healer: The Pain and Joy of Caregiving*. New York: W. W. Norton and Company.

Richards, V. & Lloyd, K. 2017. *Core Values for Psychiatrists*. College Report CR204. London: Royal College of Psychiatrists. www.rcpsych.ac.uk/docs/default-source/improving-care/better-mh-policy/college-reports/college-report-cr204.pdf?sfvrsn=5e4ff507_4.

Royal College of Psychiatrists (RCPsych) 2013. *Core Training in Psychiatry CT1–CT3: A Competency Based Curriculum for Specialist Core Training in Psychiatry*. www.rcpsych.ac.uk/docs/default-source/training/curricula-and-guidance/curricula-core-psychiatry-curriculum-april-2018.pdf?sfvrsn=881b63ca_2.

Royal College of Psychiatrists (RCPsych) 2022. *Core Psychiatry: Royal College of Psychiatrists Core Training Curriculum (CT1–CT3)*. Version 1.0. www.rcpsych.ac.uk/docs/default-source/training/curricula-and-guidance/2022-curricula/core-psychiatry-curriculum-final-17-august-2022.pdf?sfvrsn=36b5ba25_10.

Royal College of Psychiatrists (RCPsych) 2025. What is psychiatry? www.rcpsych.ac.uk/become-a-psychiatrist/choose-psychiatry/what-is-psychiatry.

Stanghellini, G. 2013. The portrait of the psychiatrist as a globally minded citizen. *Current Opinion in Psychiatry*, 26, 498–501.

Sternberg, R. J., Fiske, S. T. & Foss, D. J. (eds.) 2016. *Scientists Making a Difference: One Hundred Eminent Behavioral and Brain Scientists Talk About Their Most Important Contributions*. Cambridge: Cambridge University Press.

Till, A., Walker, T., Kansagra, A., Bailey, A., Blewett, C. & Milward, K. 2018. *Supported and Valued? Staying Safe – A Trainee Led Review into Fatigue within Psychiatry*. London: Psychiatric Trainees' Committee, Royal College of Psychiatrists. www.rcpsych.ac.uk/docs/default-source/training/training/ptc/supported-and-valued-staying-safe.pdf?sfvrsn=5cbebec6_2.

Chapter 6

The Image of Psychiatry and the Figure of the Psychiatrist in Literature

Femi Oyebode

Introduction

Literature focusses on the use of language to explore and describe the subjective experiences of people, whether this be in the form of fiction, poetry, memoirs, biography, or essays. This valuation of the subjective privileges what it is like to be human, in context, whilst at the same time underscoring how the trivial or mundane, as well as the portentous or grave, influences mood, emotions, cognitions, and inner life. It is apparent that psychiatry also treads the same ground, emphasizing what is personal and intimate, and exploring the determinants and mediating factors that colour, shape, and give meaning to existence. But psychiatry is more than this; it also embraces the social and the natural sciences and, in these, balances the objective, the purely scientific, against the narrative tendency, the human desire for storytelling, the impetus to ascribe meaning to human interactions and to symbolize and use metaphors in communication.

In this, psychiatry, unlike other medical specialties, operates in a contested zone. Where it is undeniable that human beings are material beings and that without the materiality of embodiment no psychology or social life is possible, there is a sense in which the complexity of the material, especially of neural systems and the unfathomable transformation of material processes into subjective experience, makes the territory that psychiatry traverses even more problematic. It is relatively easy to accept that external visual objects are represented in the occipital cortex and then projected outwards to be perceived in the external world. In other words, the processes that deal with the transformation of sensory data into perceptions are uncontested. On the other hand, any suggestion that human feelings and subjective experiences – such as hope, love, jealousy, envy, and sadness – are fundamentally and ultimately material in nature is disquieting and the biological basis of these feelings and experiences arouses suspicion and resistance. The impossibly hard conceptualization of how the neurotransmitters serotonin and dopamine could ever code for emotions and the implausibility of how neurological structures such as the nucleus accumbens and the midline raphe nuclei can process and determine feelings, motivations, and actions are just two examples of the gap between scientific explanation and psychological understanding.

There is also the further compounding and confounding feature of conscious life, the belief that the first-person perspective is both privileged and immune from error. To emphasize this point: most people are prepared to accept that their knowledge of the nature and composition of bones, muscles, livers, and spleens is fairly rudimentary; hence, there is little or no contestation of expert knowledge in these domains. This contrasts with the degree of certainty we all possess about our self-knowledge and self-understanding and our ability to judge and predict other people's behaviours. This fact of being intuitive psychologists and sociologists has implications for the patient–doctor relationship in psychiatry, and for the status of knowledge and the hierarchies of power in psychiatry within the clinical encounter.

In this chapter, I will explore the image and representation of psychiatry in literature. Furthermore, I will examine the figure of the psychiatrist in literature, setting this in the context of the value systems extant in society and drawing attention to the role of literature both in shaping and in sustaining how society responds to psychiatry and psychiatrists. I will also underline the distinctions between psychiatry and other medical specialities, and how these differences influence literature. My exploration will rely on the full range of literature, taking in drama, fiction, poetry, and memoirs. This is to ensure that the multifaceted dimensions of human experiences and perspectives are taken into account and that psychiatry, the clinical subject that is most embedded in language and most truly human in its extent, is fully examined.

Literature and Psychiatry

One of the most directly relevant aspects of literature for medicine and psychiatry is the portrayal of the life of patients. It is obvious that illnesses occur within a life and to a person, and this is even more pertinent and true in psychiatry. Where in general medicine and surgery diseases can be envisaged as diseases of organs, in psychiatry, no matter how conceptualized, psychiatric disorders manifest as afflictions of the person, expressed and presented within the manifold guises of lives. This simple fact can easily be lost to our apprehension in the business of clinical medicine. Our preoccupation can narrowly focus on the matter of history-taking, examinations, diagnosis, and treatment to the exclusion of a full understanding of the impact of disease on a life. Here, literature can and does help to illustrate what it is like to live with disease by extending our appreciation well beyond the mere recounting of symptoms and the obvious disabilities associated with medical diagnoses.

To illustrate this point, first, I turn to Jean-Dominique Bauby's (1997) account of 'locked-in' syndrome, *The Diving Bell and the Butterfly*. His account is impressive and important for many reasons, not least because it gives an insight into the first-person perspective of a person who is unable to communicate verbally yet whose inner life is rich and immensely vital. Bauby (1997, pp. 61–62) wrote:

> I have known gentler awakenings. When I came to that late January morning the hospital ophthalmologist was leaning over me and sewing my right eyelid shut with a needle and thread, just as if he were darning a sock. Irrational terror swept over me. What if this man got carried away and sewed up my left eye as well, my only link to the outside world, the only window to my cell, the one tiny opening of my cocoon? Luckily as it turned out, I wasn't plunged into darkness. He carefully packed away his sewing kit in padded tin boxes. Then in the tones of the prosecutor demanding a maximum sentence for a repeat offender, he barked out: Six months. I fired out a series of questioning signals with my working eye, but this man – who spent his days peering into people's pupils – was apparently unable to interpret a simple look. He was the very model of the couldn't-care-less-doctor, arrogant, brusque, sarcastic, the kind who summons his patients for 8.00 a.m., arrives at 9.00, and departs at 9.05 after giving each of them forty-five seconds of his precious time.

This passage illustrates the triumph of literature, of words in the clinical arena. It shows how words can reinstate the human or the humane in a space that in many regards is impoverished and that, even if technically correct, is lacking what matters most, empathy. Bauby (1997) compels us to take account of his perspective by introducing moral virtue into the discourse. What is it that makes a good doctor? Is it technical adroitness or something more personal, some attitudinal orientation towards the human needs of patients?

The concerns of patients do not necessarily coincide with those of their doctors. The effects of disease on the wider network of family, friends, and colleagues and the impact on self-esteem, on intimacy, on hidden fears, and on dreams and goals are not, but ought to be, matters of priorities for doctors, too. Ulla-Carin Lindquist (2004, p. 116), in her account of living with motor neurone disease, *Rowing Without Oars*, voices her fear as follows: 'How does a woman who still wants to be attractive to her husband learn to accept that in all probability she no longer is?' Similar, in the account of Ruth Picardie's (1998) fight against breast cancer, her husband (Matt Seaton) writes this in the wake of her mastectomy:

> If I close my eyes, and travel in time, I can still feel the delicious weight of Ruth's left breast in my right hand. Eros and, as it turned out, Thanatos gorgeously cupped in my palm. That was before we knew about her cancer. Once we knew, I found it unbearable to touch her there. She never seemed to blame my squeamishness, but in retrospect the lump not only grew within her, but between us, spreading, as inexorably as the cancer itself did.
>
> (Picardie, 1998, pp. 102–103)

I have paid particular attention to the role of the personal account in medicine and surgery, to make the point that if these human voices, these intimate details of the way illnesses prosecute life, can charge the most ordinary things with exquisite pain and distress in the domain of the physical, how much more pressing and relevant will literature be to psychiatry. Here, I am referring not merely to the depth of meaning and the profound examination of how depression or mania can interfere with mood and then with life but also to how to imagine the unimaginable or give words to the unspeakable. One of the problems that patients face in psychiatry is that the subjective experience of mental illness is often outside the realm of the commonplace, so that patients are stranded, set apart from others, and do not have the language to seek or sustain affiliation. Poetry is, perhaps, the literary mode that, by use of images, metaphors, and other devices, most ably builds a bridge to link the distressed and the disturbed to others, making possible some connection and a degree of mutual understanding between what stands for the normal and what is disfiguring and unwholesome. For instance, in his poem 'To God', Ivor Gurney (1890–1937) wrote:

> Why have you made life so intolerable
> And set me between four walls, where I am able
> Not to escape meals without prayer, for that is possible
> Only by annoying an attendant. And tonight a sensual
> Hell has been put on me, so that all has deserted me
> And I am merely crying and trembling in heart
> For Death, and cannot get it. And gone out is part
> of sanity. And there is dreadful hell within me.
> And nothing helps, ...
>
> *(Gurney, 1982, ll. 1–9)*

In this poem, we can see how alienating melancholia is, how the internal feeling is no ordinary sadness but an intolerable and sensual or physical anguish. Gurney (1982), in reaching out to us through his poetry, is also expressing what William Styron (1990, p. 7) has described as 'a disorder of mood, so mysteriously painful and elusive in the way it becomes known to the self – to the mediating intellect – as to verge close to being beyond description'.

Literary accounts give depth to descriptions of anguish and despair, as just described. But the metaphors that authors use also point towards the predominant motifs or at least borrow from motifs that are comprehensible to the reader. This is another way of saying that culture and language provide the framework and the images that make comprehensible experiences that are outwith the normal ken. Styron (1990) compares his experience of mood disturbance to an outmoded small-town telephone exchange 'being inundated by flood waters. One by one, the normal circuits began to drain, causing some of the functions of the body and nearly all those of the instinct and intellect to slowly disconnect' (Styron, 1990, p. 47). What Styron does here is to appropriate the image of a telephone exchange to exemplify what a breakdown of mental functions can be like. This appropriation works precisely because it relies on a shared experience, even if it is historically constrained to those of a certain age and culturally shared experience. Chigozie Obioma (2015), in his novel *The Fishermen*, uses a different metaphor altogether:

> I saw her eyes fill up with tears. I have come to believe that the confrontation was the needle that poked her psychic wound and it started bleeding from that day. She stopped talking, and the silence that would numb her entire world began. From then on, she sat in the house, silently staring wildly at nothing in particular. Most times when Father spoke to her, she stared merely at him as if she heard nothing at all. This tongue, which was frozen, used to produce words as fungi produced spores. When agitated, words often sprang from her mouth, and poured like leaks from a broken pipe when sober. But, from that night onwards, words pooled in her brain but only very little leaked out; they congealed in her mind.
>
> (Obioma, 2015, pp. 184–185)

The reach of literature is profound; it draws attention to the variety and richness of the metaphors that are available to people to use when in that alien territory, the strange country that is mental illness. Literature can prepare the clinician for the wondrous nature of language, the subtle and the grossly obvious methods by which words engage us, influence us, shock us into action, or simply alert us to the inner mechanisms of abject despair, frustrated hope, or unfathomable inner attrition. Reading requires an attunement to the purposes of the writer in much the same way as the clinical encounter demands an attunement to the language of the patient, the purposes and goals that the patient is aiming for.

There is more than the patient involved in the maelstrom that severe mental illness causes. There are parents and siblings, friends and partners, colleagues at work and neighbours. The perspectives of these people, the ways in which they are affected, and the impact of their observations and the traumatic encounters with severe illness are often relegated to the periphery of our concern. Literature that deals with the effects of mental illness on these secondary victims is important because it emphasizes what is too often ignored.

In the preface to the book *Henry's Demons* (Cockburn and Cockburn, 2011), which he co-wrote with his son Henry, Patrick Cockburn writes:

> This book is about how my son Henry was diagnosed with schizophrenia in 2002 and how this affected him and our family. As he started to recover – and this recovery is by no means

> complete – about three years ago, I began to think that he and I should write about our experiences. I felt that we might turn everything he had suffered into an asset. He was ideally placed to write from the *inside* about what it was like to have an acute mental illness in which trees and bushes spoke and voices called him to flee into the night or plunge into icy water where he might drown. He knew what it was like to live in mental hospitals, places that most people regard with ignorance and dread. I believed that Henry and I could serve a broader public purpose by making schizophrenia and mental illness in general less of a mystery which people are embarrassed to discuss. I began to think with growing enthusiasm about writing a book with Henry about what he, along with the rest of his family, had been through. (Cockburn and Cockburn, 2011, p. xiii)

As psychiatrists, we must accept that the behaviours of patients and the consequences of those behaviours for the wider network of their families and others, which we come to recognize or be aware of, are but a fraction of what goes on. This is where literature can shed some light on the degree to which mental illness impairs family function as much as it limits the life of the patient. Patrick Cockburn (Cockburn and Cockburn, 2011) talks of his sense of personal guilt, of the poor continuity of care that the services provided; he refers to the mutual distrust between his son and the nurses, of the family's recourse to prayer, of his appreciation for the comfort of strangers, and so on. These subjective experiences enrich our understanding of how pervasive and pernicious are the effects of mental illness. Attempts to use euphemisms such as 'mental health' to denote a devastating irruption, a potentially fatal disease, altogether miss the point. They merely serve to entrench the belief that these conditions are minor afflictions, if afflictions at all.

What Can Psychiatrists Learn from Literature?

Literature affords clinicians the opportunity to understand how they are perceived by patients. It is far too easy to think that the clinical encounter is structured as an evaluative system in which the clinician is judging the patient; in fact, the encounter is bidirectional – the patient is always making judgements about the clinician, too. The humanity of the clinician is under scrutiny, as well as the degree to which the clinician can inspire confidence, the clinician's apparent knowledge, their ability to communicate explicitly and truthfully – all these aspects are being judged and determined by the patient. These matters are often the subject of autobiographical narratives of illness and indeed also of fictional narratives.

Writing about why she penned *The Yellow Wallpaper*, Charlotte Perkins Gilman (1899/1998) said:

> For many years I suffered from a severe and continuous nervous breakdown tending to melancholia – and beyond. During about the third year of this trouble I went, in devout faith and some faint stir of hope, to a noted specialist in nervous diseases, the best known in the country. This wise man put me to bed and applied the rest cure, to which a still good physique responded so promptly that he concluded there was nothing much the matter with me, and sent me home with solemn advice to "live as domestic a life as possible," to "have but two hours' intellectual life a day," and "never to touch pen, brush or pencil again as long as I lived." This was in 1887. I went home and obeyed those directions for some three months, and came so near the border of utter mental ruin that I could see over. Then, using the remnants of intelligence that remained, and helped by a wise friend, I cast the noted specialist's advice to the winds and went to work again – work, the normal life of every

> human being; work, in which is joy and growth and service, without which one is a pauper and a parasite; ultimately recovering some measure of power . . . Many years later I was told that the great specialist had admitted to friends of his that he had altered his treatment for neurasthenia since reading *The Yellow Wallpaper*. (Gilman, 1899/1998, pp. 348–349)

This is feedback at its best. Gilman acted contrary to the instructions of her psychiatrist and benefited from this decision. Even more remarkably, Dr S. Weir Mitchell, her psychiatrist, changed his practice in response to her criticism. Portrayals of psychiatrists and psychiatric treatment abound in literature. These representations are not all negative, but many are. The portrayal of doctors in general or doctors who specialize in treating mental illness goes back at least to the Greco-Roman period as exemplified in plays such as *The Wasp*, written in 422 BC by Aristophanes, and Plautus's *The Brothers Menaechmus*, written around the beginning of the second century BC. In *The Wasp*, Asclepius, the God of Healing, fails in treating a curious addiction to attending the courts and acting as a judge, and in *The Brothers Menaechmus*, the doctor makes an erroneous diagnosis of mental illness in someone who is obviously dissimulating. In both comedies, the failure of medicine is for comic effect, but it also reveals the public ambivalence towards the role of doctors within the domain of mental illness.

More recently we have the fictional but autobiographical writings of Janet Frame to draw from. In *Faces in the Water*, Frame (1961/1980) used her experience of having spent time in asylums in her native country, New Zealand, to describe in some detail what life was like in asylums, including what role the doctors played and the power they wielded. She wrote:

> Always when I saw the doctor my heart contracted with suspense, for in spite of the influence of Matron Glass and Sister Bridge it was the doctor's decision which mattered – yet how could he decide if he didn't know you, didn't really know you except to say in Ward Four "Good Morning," and in Ward Two, nothing, and to listen only to Sister Bridge asserting that what you needed was a lesson to teach you how to behave and pull yourself together, a girl with your education. So when I was whirled in a waltz past the royal dais I would tremble with apprehension and try to dance well, and think "There's Dr. Steward, he's watching me, he's seeing that someone has asked me to dance, that I'm not a wallflower, he's seeing that I am well, that I needn't be in Ward Two spending all my day shut in the dayroom or the yard or the park; he's deciding about me. Deciding now." But when I came closer to him and dared to sneak a glance at him sitting in royalty there, it appeared that he wasn't thinking about me at all, that he hadn't even noticed me, he was talking to someone, saying "Yes, I . . . I . . . I . . ."
>
> Of course. Like me, like all of us, he was thinking and talking about himself.
>
> (Frame, 1961/1980, pp. 190–191)

Here we see the power of the doctor, his reification into almost a godlike figure, and the disappointment of the patient in coming to the realization of how ordinary and human the doctor was and how self-obsessed, too. There is also the invisibility of the patient, their anonymity and the rigid social distance within the asylum hierarchy that maintained this unhealthy situation. Whilst it could be argued that modern psychiatry has done away with the worst excesses of the asylum, the perception of the psychiatrist as a distant person who rarely visits the wards, whose attendance and interactions are regulated and minimal, and whose care and concern are administered at arm's length remains extant.

And in her *Autobiography* Frame (1983–1985/1990) wrote of her relationship with Dr Cawley at the Maudsley Hospital in London, emphasizing what it was about him that made her take to him readily:

> I think I was able to accept Dr Cawley because I was aware that his view was wider, over a range of studies and disciplines and personal experience, just as I had readily accepted Dr Miller because he was interested in music and art. The qualifications of medicine and psychiatry were extensions of these men, not starting and ending points.
>
> (Frame, 1983–1985/1990, p. 383)

This statement goes to the heart of my earlier point that in the clinical encounter there is a reciprocity of evaluative attention, a bidirectionality of interest and judgement that is fundamental to the quality of the patient–doctor relationship. This aspect of the clinical encounter is most transparent in the writings of people who are not merely imagining the nature of clinical situations but who have themselves experienced what it is like to be exposed to scrutiny, to be examined and inspected for signs of anomaly whilst at the same time having little overt power in the situation. What is inescapable is that even in the context of severe emotional disturbance there is always an aspect of the self that views and monitors the experience, making value judgements and assigning moral significance to the whole situation as well as determining the moral contours and disposition of the individuals who carry power and authority within the situation. For instance, Frame makes this further point about Dr Cawley: 'I had observed his development as an assured psychiatrist who, I felt, would always respect the human spirit before the practice, the fashions and demands of psychiatry. I was influenced also by the persistence of Dr Cawley in being "himself" and not some "image" of a psychiatrist: he did not patronise or pretend' (Frame, 1983–1985/1990, p. 385).

What literature is doing here is allowing the clinician a window into the private and the hidden, the unspoken inner commentary of the patient both on how the clinical encounter is enacted and on the mutuality of the alliance that makes the clinical encounter a privileged situation, one that promises the possibility of growth for both parties, not only the patient. Elizabeth Jennings (1926–2001) in her poem 'Night Sister' expresses her admiration for the care that the night nurse gives and also for the compassion that makes it possible:

> How is it possible not to grow hard,
> To build a shell around yourself when you
> Have to watch so much pain, and hear it too?
> Many you see are puzzled, wounded; few
> Are cheerful long. How can you not be scarred?
>
> To view a birth or death seems natural,
> But these locked doors, these sudden shouts and tears
> Graze all the peaceful skies. A world of fears
> Like the ghost-haunting of the owl appears.
> And yet you love that stillness and that call.
>
> . . . *(ll. 1–10, Jennings, 2002, p. 74)*

This poem emphasizes the degree to which the patient too has both compassion for the nurse's feelings and admiration for the nurse's calling to do good. It also shows an awareness of the mood, the atmosphere of psychiatric wards, and the anguish that other patients suffer quite aside from their own. But this sits side by side with an appreciation, too, of arrogance, the overly confident clinician. In her poem 'The Interrogator', Elizabeth Jennings writes:

> He is always right.
> However you prevaricate or question his motive,
> Whatever you say to excuse yourself
> He is always right.
>
> He always has an answer;
> It may be a question that hurts to hear.
> It may be a sentence that makes you flinch.
> He always has an answer.
>
> He always knows best.
> He can tell you why you disliked your father,
> He can make your purest motive seem aggressive.
> He always knows best.
>
> . . . *(ll. 1–12, Jennings, 2002, pp. 73–74)*

The professional stance includes the need to project confidence and certainty; it valorizes calmness and imperturbability, and the distinction between being authoritative and authoritarian can become blurred. Jennings (2002) is here addressing this tension between formality and humanity, between the informal and the scrupulously objective. This is not to argue that arcane knowledge that sets clinicians apart from their patients does not exist, but it is to say that the distance between the hieratic and the demotic must somehow be bridged, that language and attitudes must or ought to recognize this disparity and aim to reduce the gap. Then, there's the view of a detached observer of the mundane goings-on in hospital. The things that we take for granted, the culture of hospitals, the impact of these on patients and perhaps on clinicians, too. How ward rounds serve the purposes of doctors, what it is like to be at the end of questionnaires and forms that are administered prior to assessments and treatments, and the degree to which members of staff can seem to be idle and unhelpful to patients and their relatives. Poet U. A. Fanthorpe, who had worked as a hospital receptionist, is the master of the observed life, the small but important behaviours and the preoccupations of patients, relatives, nurses, doctors, and managers. She is all the time revealing us to ourselves, with wit and compassion, and sometimes with the necessary criticism. But always in a voice that is recognizable, that is inflected with the breath and stride of people whom we meet daily but whom we sometimes fail to see properly, that is, who remain invisible until Fanthorpe shapes their outline and crystallizes their form, clarifying and giving them density and materiality.

In 'Patients', Fanthorpe writes:

> Not the official ones, who have been
> Diagnosed and made tidy. They are
> The better sort of patient.
>
> They know the answers to the difficult
> Questions on the admission sheet
> About religion, next of kin, sex.
>
> They know the rules. The printed ones
> In the *Guide for Patients*, about why we prefer
> No smoking, the correct postal address;

Also the real ones, like the precise quota
Of servility each doctor expects,
When to have fits, and where to die.

These are not true patients. They know
Their way around, they present the right
Symptoms. . . .
(ll. 1–15, Fanthorpe, 2005, p. 143)

In 'Lament for the Patients', Fanthorpe deals with patients as people, showing the tragedy of diseased and afflicted lives but also of the failures of medicine. For her, these are the patients on whom

. . . specialists had practised specialities;
Had weighed and measured; had taken samples
Of blood and urine; had tested IQs,
Reflexes, patience; had applied
Shock treatment, drugs and nice hot cups of tea.
Of these specialists had washed their hands,
Having failed to arrive at a satisfactory
Diagnosis . . .
. . .. Therefore they died.
(ll. 10–17, 18, Fanthorpe, 2005, pp. 86–87)

And, in the same poem, Fanthorpe memorializes some of these patients thus:

These I remember:
Sonia, David, Penny, who chose death.
Lynn and Gillian, who died undiagnosed.
Peter, whose death was enigmatic.
Simple Betty, who suddenly stopped living.
Lionhearted Gertrude, who persevered to the end.
Patricia, so sorry for herself,
For whom I was not sufficiently sorry.
Julian, the interesting case. Alan,
Broken by a lorry, resurrected by surgeons,
Who nevertheless contrived at length to die.
. . . *(ll. 33–43, Fanthorpe, 2005, p. 87)*

I always think of this poem as an explicit expression of the many unsaid and unreported thoughts that psychiatrists have daily. The 'unprofessional' thoughts that 'professionalism' keeps at bay. How the mundane but perfectly normal response to another human being is kept on a tight rein. There is work to do to understand how far these unexpressed and unacceptable thoughts influence clinical practice in the long run; whether compassion fatigue is more likely because these thoughts lurk in the wilderness of inner life rather than being discussed and recognized as normal; whether shame at being found vulnerable to unacceptable thoughts complicates the capacity for enduring compassion. What is important is to state clearly that literature makes it possible to encounter these unruly thoughts and therefore to examine them, to comprehend them, and to come to terms with our own fragility as clinicians.

Literature and Values

Clinical medicine, including psychiatry, is practised within a cultural context. This context determines the moral values that guide practice. The pre-eminent values include those that derive from autonomy, the overriding desire for self-governance, the wish to have one's own projects and goals, and the compelling requirement to be treated as an agent in one's own affairs rather than as a passive recipient of care and attention. Respect for life, for the dignity of an individual, for establishing consent to treatment, truth-telling, and promise-keeping are some of the values that flow directly from the priority that is given to autonomy in clinical practice.

Mental illness can sometimes compromise an individual's ability to act autonomously. This fact has implications for care and treatment, for decision-making in the context of impaired judgement. A critique of the grounds for coercive treatments is outside the scope of this chapter. However, subjective accounts of the experience of incarceration and of enforced treatment are valuable insofar as they point to the effects of compulsion and coercion on the self-esteem of patients, as well as the repugnance they feel towards a system that deprives them of their liberty and that too often treats them without dignity or respect. John Perceval was the fifth son among the twelve children of Spencer Perceval, a former prime minister of the United Kingdom (from 1809 until his assassination in 1812). John Perceval's memoirs of his mental illness spanning 1830–1832 give an account of aspects of asylum care, the subjective experience of mental illness, and the impacts of it on family life and relationships. He wrote:

> The gross want of respect to situation, rank, character, or profession, manifested by these men on all occasions, is shocking to the imagination, and revolting to reflection; and also, that whilst a lunatic is exposed to immediate and unsparing chastisement from them, from any ebullition of frenzy; he may be tempted to acts of violence repeatedly, both in self-defence, and in common justice to others; which nevertheless, by the ignorant and shuffling magistrates who visit him, would be infallibly perverted into proof of his continued insanity, upon the report of those who are most interested to distort facts to detain him, and to revenge themselves upon him for his noble and spirited resistance, and uncompromising representations. The very acts of impatience and impetuosity which gave me self-confidence and hope that I was returning to my sound senses, too sound to be liked by those feeding on my supineness and imbecility; the very acts which I hailed in my fellow prisoners as symptoms of restored life, and of gallant, though God knows, imprudent resentment of galling mockery, insult, and oppression, were looked upon, and held up by my doctor to the keepers as the signs of mania; the very disorder for which I was to be detained.(Perceval, 1838/1962, p. 158)

Here we see an account of the way in which deprivation of liberty in consonance with loss of standing and influence further aggravates whatever dignity was left. The paradox of the disruptive behaviour that results from poor care being used to justify continuing detention is a sore point for Perceval. And the failure to adjust care to take account of the individual characteristics of the patients undermines whatever residue of self-respect is left. Perceval makes this further point:

> Tie an active limbed, active minded, actively imagining young man in bed, hand and foot, for a fortnight, drench him with medicines, slops, clysters; when reduced to the extreme of nervous debility, and his derangement is successfully confirmed, manacle him down for twenty-four hours in the cabin of a ship; then for a year shut him up from six A.M. to eight P.

> M. regardless of his former habits, in a room full of strangers, ranting, noisy, quarrelsome, revolting, madmen; give him no tonic medicines, no peculiar treatment or attention, leave him to a nondescript domestic, now brushing his clothes, sweeping the floors, serving at table, now his companion out of doors, now his bed-room companion; now throwing him on the floor, kneeling on him, striking him under all these distressing and perplexing circumstances; debar him from conversation with his superiors, all communication with his friends, all insight into their motives, every impression of sane and well-behaved society! [S]urprise him on all occasions, never leave harassing him night or day, or at meals; whether you bleed him to death, or cut his hair, show the same utter contempt for his will or inclination; do all in your power to crush every germ of self-respect that may yet remain, or rise up in his bosom; manacle him as you would a felon; expose him to ridicule, and give him no opportunity of retirement or self-reflection; and what are you to expect. And whose agents are you; those of God or Satan? And what good can you reasonably dare to expect? [A]nd whose profit is really intended? (Perceval, 1838/1962, pp. 136–137)

We might reasonably argue that the details of Perceval's experiences in the 1830s are not true for today, but it is inescapable that there is an enduring truth in his contentions that is attendant on the position of the mentally ill within the social structure of the asylum. Underpinning his descriptions are pervasive and systematic attacks on self-esteem and the absence of respect for the person. Whatever the mechanisms, the opposition of autonomy and paternalism within the hospital system is still present and there is yet to be a true appreciation of the effects of these dehumanizing attitudes on patients.

I want now to turn to Daniel Schreber (1842–1911), whose *Memoirs of My Nervous Illness* (Schreber, 1903/1955) have been described as the greatest single contribution to the phenomenology of the psychoses and whose writings are usually mined for the descriptions of abnormal phenomena. My intention is to emphasize his views on the legal grounds for detention. Schreber was a lawyer by background and rose to the position of Senatspräsident (president of a panel of judges) at the Court of Appeal at Dresden. Schreber was first admitted to hospital in December 1884 then discharged in June 1885 and fully recovered by December 1885. He suffered his second episode in October 1893 and remained in hospital until 1903 when he succeeded in his appeal against his detention. This second episode of illness is the subject of his *Memoirs*. Schreber gave a detailed response to the medical report to the court of his psychiatrist Dr Weber. This response was thorough and well argued. In essence, first, Schreber disagreed with his psychiatrist's contention that he was mentally ill. He was keen to make a distinction between mental illness and nervous illness, preferring nervous illness because it did not imply that his intellect was in any way impaired. Second, he disagreed that his abnormal experiences, which included hallucinatory experiences and delusional beliefs, were features of mental illness, instead attributing them to spiritual origin. Third, and crucially, he argued that even if he was mentally ill, he did not pose a risk to anyone, most especially not to his wife, and furthermore he did not pose any risk to his own social reputation. The Royal Superior Court of Dresden gave its judgment on 14 July 1902, stating:

> The Court is in no doubt that the appellant is insane. One would not wish to argue with him whether in fact he suffers from a mental illness known as paranoia. He lacks insight into the pathological nature of the inspirations and ideas which move him. What to objective observation is hallucination and delusion is for him irrefutable certainty. Even now he holds fast to the conviction that God manifests Himself to him directly and continuously

performs His miracles on him. This conviction, as he says himself, towers high above all human insight and science. (Schreber, 1903/1955, p. 342)

Although the court came down firmly on the side of the doctor's affirmation that Schreber was mentally ill, it found that mere presence of mental illness, no matter how severe, does not necessarily impair the ability to manage one's own affairs and was not in itself good enough reason for continuing detention. The court concluded that '[the] plaintiff [Daniel Schreber] is capable of dealing with the demands of life in all its spheres ... the orderly regulation of which is the object of the Law. There is no evidence and it cannot be regarded as ascertained that he is incapable of managing his affairs owing to his delusional ideas' (Schreber, 1903/1955, p. 355).

This case, which is reported in full as an appendix to Schreber's *Memoirs*, is important for several reasons. It reveals the value system under which psychiatry is practised, indicating the approach that we take to determine what is normal experience and what counts as normal beliefs. It also shows what the possible grounds are for depriving an individual of their liberty, namely the risk to self or others, including the risk to social reputation. Finally, it makes clear that safe and proper management of one's affairs, particularly of financial dealings, is separate from risk to self and others, and in some respects more important. Decorum, behaviour that is becoming in outward appearance and that evinces due propriety, is important in determining whether an individual has recovered or not. Schreber (1903/1955) was aware of this and mustered it as ammunition to convince the court that he was well, and certainly well enough to be released from hospital. He argued:

On the whole I believe I am justified in asserting that the medical expert has only come to know me really well in the last year, that is to say since I have taken my meals regularly at his family table; his opinion about me after another six months of such contact would probably again be much more favourable than at the time of writing the last report ... It is impossible in a large asylum to devote uninterrupted and detailed observation to every single patient; in view of the intransigence I showed in the first years in this Asylum it was in fact difficult to get any correct impression of my mental life ... In any case even the medical specialist himself, according to his report, is now convinced that one need not worry about letting me take part in social intercourse, as well as in occasions where a great number of persons are gathered together, as at theatre, Church, etc. The pathological events (grimacing, clearing my throat and suchlike), which at times are noticeable even on such occasions, are as experience shows, not of such severity as to be very disturbing to other people. (Schreber, 1903/1955, pp. 297–298)

What is revelatory in Schreber's rebuttal of his psychiatrist's contention is how much emphasis there is on predictable social intercourse and microscopic behaviours such as throat clearing or grimacing to determine not simply whether a person has recovered but whether they are ready to be discharged. The underlying value appears to be a need to ensure that individual behaviours are not disturbing to others. In other words, there is an impetus to ensure social harmony and an implicit threshold of aberrant behaviours that do not breach this (often unexpressed) yardstick which the psychiatrist uses in determining clinical recovery.

I have been arguing that literature is capable of exposing aspects of the cultural and moral context of practice, even though often these are areas of existence that we are unintentionally silent about. Sartre (1948/1993, p. 51) put it this way: '[P]eople of the same period and community, who have lived through the same events, who have raised or avoided the same questions, have the same taste in their mouth; they have the same complicity, and there are the same corpses among them. That is why it is not necessary to write so much; there are key-words.'

Schreber (1903/1955), in his forceful account, compels us to take him seriously, to listen carefully to his arguments, to engage with his rhetoric, and thereby to reflect upon our position. There is a compact between society and psychiatrists, mores and values that permeate our interactions with patients and influence our decisions and actions. What writings such as those by Perceval and Schreber do is to show us our

> implicit recourse to institutions, customs, certain forms of oppression and conflict, to the wisdom and folly of the day, to lasting passions and passing stubbornness, to superstitions and recent victories of common sense, to evidence and ignorance, to particular modes of reasoning which the sciences have made fashionable and which are applied to all domains, to hopes, to fears, to habits of sensibility, imagination, and even perception, and finally to customs and values which have been handed down. (Sartre, 1993, pp. 52–53)

Conclusions

Literature relies on language, as does psychiatry. Words, these precious utterances, are the tools, the currency of exchange, by which we communicate with others. In psychiatry, they are the most important means of interacting with people who are in distress or who are disturbed. Words are fundamental to the practice of psychiatry just as they are in literature. If only for this reason, literature and psychiatry have an inseparable link.

References

Bauby, J. 1997. *The Diving-Bell and the Butterfly*, translated by J. Leggat. London: Harper Perennial.

Cockburn, P. & Cockburn, H. 2011. *Henry's Demons: A Father and Son's Journey out of Madness*. London: Simon and Schuster.

Fanthorpe, U. A. 2005. *Collected Poems*. Calstock: Peterloo Poets.

Frame, J. 1961/1980. *Faces in the Water*. London: Women's Press.

Frame, J. 1983–1985/1990. *An Autobiography: Vol. 1: To the Is-Land; Vol. 2: An Angel at My Table; Vol. 3: The Envoy from the Mirror City*. London: Women's Press.

Gilman, C.P. 1899/1998. *The Yellow Wallpaper*, edited by D. M. Bauer. Boston, MA: Bedford Cultural Editions.

Gurney, I. 1982. *Collected Poems*, edited by P. J. Kavanagh. London: Carcanet Press.

Jennings, E. 2002. *New Collected Poems*. London: Carcanet Press.

Lindquist, U. 2004. *Rowing Without Oars*, translated by M. Myers. London: John Murray.

Obioma, C. 2015. *The Fishermen*. London: Pushkin Press.

Perceval, J 1838/1962. *A Narrative of the Experience of a Gentleman during a State of Mental Derangement to Explain the Causes and the Nature of Insanity, and to Expose the Injudicious Conduct Pursued towards Many Sufferers Under Calamity*. Reprinted in 1962 as *Perceval's Narrative*, edited by G. Bateson. London: Hogarth Press.

Picardie, R. 1998. *Before I Say Goodbye*. London: Penguin Books.

Sartre, J. P. 1948/1993. *What Is Literature?*, translated by B. Fechtman. London: Routledge.

Schreber, D. P. 1903/1955. *Memoirs of My Nervous Illness*, translated by I. Macalpine & R. A. Hunter. London: William Dawson & Sons.

Styron, W. 1990. *Darkness Visible: A Memoir of Madness*. London: Cape.

Chapter 7

Multidisciplinarity in Psychiatry

Robert B. Dudas, Elizabeth Fistein, and Toby Williamson

Introduction

Much of psychiatric care nowadays takes place in a multidisciplinary context that is considered to be more effective in providing holistic care and reaching goals that would not be possible for individual disciplines working in isolation (McAllister et al., 2011). A major tenet of values-based practice (VBP) is that the different values perspectives that the various professions of the multidisciplinary team (MDT) bring to the table, rather than being a hindrance, are an asset, as the more diverse these value perspectives are, the more likely it is that they will be able to cater for the equally diverse needs and value perspectives of patients and carers. If this is true in general, it is likely to be even more true in populations that are ethnically and socio-economically increasingly diverse.

In this chapter, three authors from a multidisciplinary background have joined to examine how the professions typically present this, in an MDT approach, in their own way, where potential gains lie, and what the challenges in training in and applying good MDT working are. Robert B. Dudas begins to explore in this chapter the impact on psychiatry of its medical roots, the great opportunities that lie in broadening neuroscience research to include the existential and social factors in mental illness, and psychiatry's relationship with neurology. Elizabeth Fistein further explores the ramifications of the medical model from a VBP perspective and then examines the value perspectives and important contributions to psychiatry of some of the other disciplines within the MDT, namely psychology, anthropology, social work, and law. Finally, Toby Williamson demonstrates how VBP can ease some of the tensions that can arise during working together between nursing and social work and the other disciplines within the MDT.

Medicine, Neuroscience, and Neurology

Robert B. Dudas

Medicine

Psychiatry is a medical specialty. Its practitioners go to medical school before specializing in psychiatry where they are taught natural sciences with the expectation that they will use this knowledge to diagnose and treat patients (Novick and Ross, 2020). They first become a doctor, then a psychiatrist, which influences how they see mental distress or illness, and help seeking. Medical students do have a relatively small amount of psychiatry training and, as a result, at the beginning of their specialty training, psychiatric trainees know far more about medicine in general than about psychiatry. In most medical schools, preclinical studies predominantly include natural sciences and a smaller amount on other subjects like medical ethics, psychology, anthropology, sociology, and other related disciplines. This is generally sufficient for most specialties, but those preparing to become psychiatrists will need to acquire significantly more – mainly psychological and legal, but also other social scientific – knowledge and skills if they are to be successful at negotiating the challenges of working in psychiatry.

Medicine has its own model of illness and recovery and deploys concepts such as diagnosis and (medical) treatment. There are also certain expectations about the rights and responsibilities of people within this model, with specific roles, such as doctor, patient, and carer. The same is true about how research should be done, what research questions and corresponding methodologies are seen as relevant and appropriate, and so on. Importantly, all these have aspects that are different in psychiatry compared to non-psychiatric medical specialties. For example, in psychiatry there are currently no laboratory tests to rule in or out a specific mental health diagnosis. These differences are even more pronounced between psychiatry and the non-medical disciplines within the MDT, such as psychology or social work. Individual medical practitioners in psychiatry each have a slightly different way of defining and retaining their professional identity in the multidisciplinary environment within which they train and operate.

Practitioners in different professions of the MDT often identify the needs of both the patient and themselves somewhat differently, and have a different pattern of concerns and preferences, at times leading to a sense of need for demarcation from other disciplines. Collaboration may, at first sight, seem like a major source of conflict and the advantages may appear far from obvious. Training in and positive experiences of good MDT working do, however, have the potential to change this (McAllister et al., 2011).

In medicine, treatment typically involves medication or a physical procedure, for example surgery. In a psychiatry MDT, similar expectations often operate towards the psychiatrist member. Even though psychiatry embraces a biopsychosocial approach, what is considered 'medical' within psychiatric treatment is typically biochemical (medication) or physical (electroconvulsive therapy (ECT), magnetic stimulation). In medicine, there is a preference for interventions that are more measurable (e.g. they can be 'dosed' and a dose–response relationship can be assumed) and can be given as a well-defined course of treatment, for example cognitive-behavioural therapy (CBT). The venues are also important: although home visits are part of everyday practice, especially in old age psychiatry or crisis resolution and home treatment teams, psychiatry mainly happens in the general practitioner's (primary care physician's) surgery, in psychiatric clinics, or on the hospital ward. An important recent development is the huge expansion of liaison psychiatry services where psychiatrists work together, in most services in a consultative model, with non-psychiatric specialists to look after the mental health needs of patients who are in hospital for a physical health condition.

An important challenge for good MDT working is the *relative scarcity of relevant training* on it in most professional curricula. Successful MDT working requires at least some understanding of each profession's contribution to the care of the patient and their value systems. This facilitates effective communication and problem-solving whilst working collaboratively towards a shared goal. Good MDT working can come from being courageous, realizing one's own professional limitations in meeting the complex needs of patients, and fostering one's own openness to and care for the values and contributions of MDT colleagues from other professions. Another major challenge is when *professionals feel that members of other professions are impinging on their role or they are expected to take on others' roles* for reasons other than legitimate professional considerations, not infrequently as a result of top-down intervention to make savings. Finally, although psychiatrists have been relieved of some of their former responsibilities (in the UK this was one of the declared objectives of the Department of Health's best practice implementation guide 'New Ways of Working' (CSIP and NIMHE, 2007), they are now often expected to supervise (or advise, as they have no line management relationship with them) other members of the MDT who are now carrying out much of the assessments and treatments that psychiatrists used to do themselves. Consistent with the 'squeaky wheel' principle of VBP, the needs and expectations of team members towards other MDT members become fully explicit only when a conflict or problem arises. One of the consequences of the above-described structural changes in the healthcare system, for example, is that psychiatrists are now allocated *less time to see their patients whilst remaining responsible for their overall care*, which can lead to intense emotions as well as logistical challenges in situations in which medical input is essential but hard to provide now.

Neuroscience

There seems to be a widely shared tacit understanding among many stakeholders in psychiatry that neuroscience or neurobiology is the cornerstone of clinical psychiatry (Burn, 2019; Muzyk et al., 2017). Although neuroscience is the study of the nervous system and the brain, and the brain is always involved in mental phenomena, the above proposition does not automatically follow without further qualification. The reason we need to state this here is that it has been asserted that psychiatrists need more neuroscience knowledge (Cuttle and Burn, 2020) and its coverage in psychiatry curricula has been strengthened (Roffman et al., 2006; Strege et al., 2021), whilst other relevant disciplines focussing on the relational, social, or existential dimensions or the more directly clinical aspects of psychiatry (e.g. descriptive psychopathology) seem to have been receiving much less attention and investment. Although there have been major advances in neuroscience, for example as regards our understanding about cognition, emotion, or decision-making, so far, their impact on everyday clinical practice in psychiatry has been relatively small. Contrary to expectations (Burn, 2019; Cuttle and Burn, 2020; Novick and Ross, 2020; Schildkrout et al., 2016), and despite the enormous research investment over recent decades, neuroscience has not yet yielded important new tools for diagnostic classification or diagnosis making, treatment, or prognosis (Paulus et al., 2016; Stein et al., 2022) in an obvious way. This begs the question why. Is it because the subject matter of neuroscience and the translation of its findings are immensely complex and we need more time, or perhaps because the relevance of neuroscience to clinical care is much less direct than it has been thought, or both?

Teaching more neuroscience to trainees tends to generate more interest in the subject, which is expected. This, however, takes away the time and attention from other subjects that may be just as relevant to clinical work. When there are problems in the therapeutic relationship, patients and relatives rarely complain about a lack of neuroscientific knowledge; they are much more likely to complain about the relationship with the clinician (Pitarka-Carcani et al., 2000). A noteworthy argument in favour of integrating neuroscience into psychiatry more is that it could enhance empathy, for example when negative behavioural aspects of the patient's presentation are perceived as being separate from the disease (Novick and Ross, 2020). Research on the impact on stigma of emphasizing a biological understanding of mental illness has, however, revealed a more complex relationship with an increase or no change in stigma as a result (Pescosolido et al., 2010; Strege et al., 2021).

After decades of the dominance of biological psychiatry, computational psychiatry is the new kid on the block. *Computational psychiatry* is interested in using mathematical models, representing a perhaps even greater departure from studying mental phenomena at the person level and a higher degree of abstraction. Initially, it focussed primarily on modelling and linking to neural measures decision-making choice data, but more recently it has expanded to include a wide array of non-choice type data, such as reaction time, eye-tracking, and facial, voice, or movement data; naturalistic paradigms and real-world data; and even subjective data, such as self-report.

Does all this mean that neuroscience is irrelevant to clinical psychiatry? Certainly not, but it forces us to consider the currently rather large gap between research and clinical practice in psychiatry. Owing to the very nature of mental illness, real breakthroughs in diagnosis and treatment are likely to occur only if *research questions genuinely include, alongside the neurobiological dimension, at least one (and preferably all) of the other dimensions (i.e. experiential, existential, and social) of mental illness and if their methodology suits the needs of this type of research.* This is challenging for a variety of reasons. The disciplines interrogating these started out using very different languages, but these differences could be reduced to improve their complementarity (Strege et al., 2021). This would have a direct, beneficial impact on multidisciplinarity both in research and in clinical psychiatry, and it would help us close the gap between research and clinical practice. Coming back to our earlier example, incorporating neuroscientific content into doctor–patient communication can be beneficial but for optimal results (and to avoid the whole thing backfiring) neuroscientists could work out the best ways of doing this with psychologists, medical anthropologists, and sociologists. Encouragingly, the impact of social factors in psychiatry is beginning to be understood (Bhugra et al., 2017), and if multidisciplinary research gets comparable levels of funding, the import of neuroscience research can begin to percolate through in earnest into clinical training and everyday clinical work.

Neurology

Finally, mention must be made of the other medical specialty concentrating on the functioning of the brain: neurology. Although some conditions are within the remit of both specialties, their focus and clinical approach are rather different. Neurology focusses on so-called organic conditions in which a biological cause at cell, tissue, or organ level (e.g. genetic or developmental anomaly, infection, neoplasm, vascular disease) can be identified, and relegates problems without these to the category of so-called functional conditions (e.g. non-epileptic seizures). In contrast, in most psychiatric conditions it has proven difficult to demonstrate a pathomechanism at these levels and they are believed to be caused by a combination of genetic predisposition and environmental influences in more or less equal measures. As a result, the two specialties have different needs, concerns, and preferences; although knowledge about the other specialty and collaborative working, especially in specific cases, are certainly helpful, full integration between them seems unlikely, even though calls for integration have been made repeatedly (Keshavan et al., 2020).

Psychology, Anthropology, Sociology, and Law

Elizabeth Fistein

Medical practice is sometimes criticized for having a tendency to focus on the physical, biological aspects of the human condition, reducing human beings to a diagnosis, a collection of symptoms, or a set of investigation results. The biomedical approach, coupled with scientific and technological advances, has enabled the development of effective medical practice that has brought about increased life expectancy and the elimination of some diseases. Viewed from a perspective that values these endpoints, the biomedical approach looks like an enormous success. However, a focus on the elimination of experiences labelled as symptoms or on maximizing quantity of life at the expense of its quality can also be viewed (in the language of VBP) as an example of 'values myopia': an assumption that the values of biomedicine are universal and that the extension of life and elimination of symptoms are ends that should always be pursued. The risks of such an assumption include the development of practices that, for at least some patients, have an adverse impact on overall well-being. Sometimes, the cure is worse than the disease. As the 'science-driven' principle of VBM notes, progress enables us to do much more for our patients, and this brings the full diversity of values into play. Now that we can do so much, the question becomes whether we should do it.

This can be particularly evident in psychiatric practice, where experiences and behaviours that fall beyond a certain point on a spectrum are defined as psychopathological symptoms and signs. The selection of a cut-off point is subjective and therefore inherently value-laden. Perhaps because of this distinctive feature of psychiatry, or in response to the anti-psychiatry movement's critique of the practice of psychiatric diagnosis (Szasz, 1974), modern psychiatry typically takes a multidisciplinary approach. This can be viewed as a means of embedding VBP's 'space of values' and 'multi-perspective' principles within psychiatric practice: enabling different perspectives to emerge and seeking to achieve a balance between them.

Having considered some of the ends that are traditionally valued in medical practice (eliminating symptoms and saving lives), and the advantages and disadvantages of making these the main goals of work with patients, the question arises: how do the values of other disciplines differ from the values of medicine, and how does incorporation of these values influence psychiatric practice?

Psychology can be defined as the scientific study of the mind, and how it dictates and influences our behaviour. The discipline focusses on understanding human behaviours in relation to cognitive processes and emotional responses to environmental triggers, mediated by associations and learning accrued through experience. The focus is on understanding human beings not as biological, embodied entities but as psychological selves. Viewed from this perspective, different ways of understanding and responding to mental distress emerge.

In contrast with the categorical approach of medical diagnosis, the psychological approach is dimensional and descriptive, arriving at a formulation. A psychological formulation includes a summary of the current difficulties, as experienced by the individual, alongside the psychological vulnerabilities that may have predisposed this person to experience these difficulties, the triggers that may have precipitated a crisis, the factors such as 'secondary gain' that may impair recovery, and the psychological strengths that bolster resilience. A bespoke formulation is, in contrast with an 'off-the-peg' categorical diagnosis, not so easily matched to evidence-based treatment guidelines, which rely on accurate diagnosis to direct people into effective treatment pathways. However, formulation enables a richer understanding of an individual's mental distress, in the context of their own lived experience. This dimensional approach is increasingly being incorporated into the diagnostic processes of psychiatry, with the development of the latest version of the Diagnostic and Statistical Manual of Mental Disorders (DSM-5; APA, 2013), which still includes diagnostic categories but also incorporates dimensional measures of severity.

Viewing mental illness as the product of psychological processes, rather than (or as well as) neurochemical changes, widens the scope for developing effective interventions. Medical practice traditionally uses pharmacological and physical interventions to control symptoms. Incorporating the perspective of psychology has enabled psychiatric practice to broaden its therapeutic repertoire and offer a wide range of psychological therapies, perhaps the best known being the CBTs. This psychological turn in psychiatry has, in turn, been adopted by other medical specialties, where the importance of understanding the meaning given by the patient to their symptoms has been recognized in recent decades (Kleinman, 1988). Increasingly, psychological approaches such as CBT are being used in the management of chronic physical conditions (NICE, 2020). However, psychological therapies, like pharmacotherapies, are associated with both costs and benefits. As the science-driven principle of VBP predicts, the fact that we are now able to do more (or achieve the same ends using different means) brings diversity of values into play. Decisions about which treatment option to pursue become more complex and may be finely balanced, and patients will need time and support in order to engage in effective shared decision-making.

Anthropology is the study of the human race, its culture and society, and its physical development, and *sociology* is the study of social life, social change, and the social causes and consequences of human behaviour. These disciplines understand human beings as social persons and human behaviour as being driven by inter-subjectivity and social context.

The culture-bound aspects of human behaviour are well-recognized in psychiatry, with the psychiatric symptom of delusional belief being defined as a fixed belief that is not based upon evidence and is not explained by a person's usual cultural or religious concepts. When psychiatrist and patient come from different cultures, sensitivity and a willingness to learn about other cultural contexts are important factors in the development of a therapeutic relationship. Following the 'how it's done' principle of values-based medicine (VBM), listening to and exploring the values of the patient's culture is a necessary step to understanding the meaning of their experiences and whether they are, or are not, an appropriate focus for psychiatric treatment.

Even within a shared culture, understanding social context is essential if we are to effectively address mental distress and recovery. The contribution of researchers in *sociology* transformed the practice of psychiatry in the second half of the twentieth century, recognizing the effects of stigma and institutionalization, as opposed to any underlying illness, in contributing to disability (Goffman, 1961). Incorporating this perspective led to the practice of de-institutionalization, the development of rehabilitation and social psychiatry, and the recovery movement (which focusses on working with patients to maximize functional ability and quality of life, rather than concentrating exclusively on symptom management). The social model of disability and the imperative to tackle structural inequalities that prevent equality of access to society for people with all forms of disabilities (mobility or sensory impairment as well as neurodiversity) have grown from the insights of sociologists' engagement with psychiatric practice.

These examples demonstrate how psychiatry has pioneered the biopsychosocial approach to medicine, perhaps assisted by the way in which diversity of values can be more evident in psychiatry than in physical medicine, which, in turn, triggers the search for different perspectives. Indeed, engagement with the discipline of *philosophy*, especially careful analysis of the concepts of health and illness and recognition of the fact/value distinction (Fulford, 2007), has placed psychiatry at the forefront of VBP. Psychiatry is sometimes compared unfavourably to other medical specialties with regard to the scientific evidence-base for its practices (Read et al., 2016), and as a specialty it does face particular challenges in the adoption of evidence-based medicine (EBM), stemming from the subjective nature of most psychiatric diagnoses. However, compared with other specialties, the practice of VBP is perhaps more advanced in and embedded within psychiatry.

Law, both as academic discipline and as professional practice, is an approach primarily concerned with justice, the principle that people should be treated fairly and with respect. From the latter half of the twentieth century, a rights-based approach, with a focus on ensuring that individuals are not arbitrarily deprived of civil-political rights, such as the right to liberty, has predominated. When working with someone who appears to be mentally ill but who declines psychiatric treatment (potentially as a result of a lack of insight caused by the underlying illness), a tension arises between the core values of medicine, which emphasize restoration of health, and those of law, which emphasize the right to liberty and personal autonomy.

In English law, this tension is illustrated by a shift in focus from the paternalistic approaches of the 1959 Mental Health Act to the more rights-based 1983 Mental Health Act (Hoggett, 1996), driven by the work of human rights lawyer Lawrence Gostin (1975). In 2007, the 1983 Act was amended and the pendulum swung away from the rights-based approach in favour of public protection, driven perhaps by the values of wider society concerning the appropriate balance between individual liberty and risk, most likely influenced by a series of high-profile cases where members of the public were harmed by people with a diagnosis of mental disorder (Joint Committee on the Draft Mental Health Bill, 2004).

Internationally, the UN Convention on the Rights of Persons with Disabilities (United Nations General Assembly, 2007) requires equality before the law for all people with disabilities, including long-term or recurrent mental health conditions. Legal scholars argue that English mental capacity and mental health legislation, both of which include a diagnostic criterion in their tests for legally justifiable non-consensual treatment, are at odds with the Convention's requirements (Martin et al., 2014). Arguably, compliance with international conventions demands a move away from acting in patients' 'best interests' or the interests of their 'own health or safety, or for the protection of others' and towards acting only in accordance with their rights, will, and preferences (Donnelly, 2016). This would represent a significant shift in practice, but the framework of VBP, with its attention to the 'patient perspective' principle, may provide useful support for this change.

Mental Health Nursing and Social Work

Toby Williamson

Introduction

For many years, a multidisciplinary approach, involving practitioners from a range of different professional and expert backgrounds, has been an accepted mainstay of mental health services. This reflects the widely accepted biopsychosocial model of mental health problems and the need to respond in multidimensional ways to people experiencing those problems. Mental health nursing and social work are two key elements of a multidisciplinary approach. Using England as an example, this section explores the values that underpin the two disciplines, some of the key challenges that can arise when nurses and social workers work together to contribute to multidisciplinary working, and how those challenges may be overcome. It considers the part that VBP and a rights-based approach can play in supporting effective multidisciplinary working.

Background: Multidisciplinarity

Multidisciplinary mental health teams (MDTs) have been a key element of psychiatric services in the UK and many other countries for several decades. This has usually been based on a biopsychosocial model of mental health problems that recognizes the multidimensional nature of mental health, including genetic and biological factors, psychological, cognitive, emotional, and behavioural elements, and the part played by social and environmental factors. Such MDTs have the involvement of medicine, nursing, social work, psychology, and occupational therapy, and reflect the need to have a range of responses to those multidimensional factors. The benefits of MDTs include better access, management, and continuity of care and treatment, collaborative working, and the ability to draw upon a wide range of expertise and specialisms.

Published in 2001, the Mental Health Policy Implementation Guide (MHPIG) for England is a clear expression of multidisciplinarity in policy and service delivery terms. It describes the service models within the National Service Framework for Mental Health (Department of Health, 1999, 2001). The MHPIG outlines a range of different MDTs that should exist within psychiatric services, including community mental health teams, early intervention teams, home treatment and crisis resolution teams, and assertive outreach teams. To a lesser or greater extent, all these teams have an evidence-base for their effectiveness; the work of Steve Onyett (2003) describes in detail the research that provided that evidence-base.

Team composition; client groups; systems of care, management, and leadership; service availability; integration with other services and agencies; and other factors have varied over time and place and Onyett (2003) identifies the features which contribute to more or less effective team working. However, MDTs remain a central part and are the workhorses of mental health services. The National Health Service (NHS) plan published in 2019 stated that 'local areas will be supported to redesign and reorganise core community mental health teams to move towards a new place-based, multidisciplinary service across health and social care aligned with primary [health]care networks' (DHSC, 2019a, p. 69). And the NHS Mental Health Implementation Plan for 2019/20–2023/24, published in the same year, said that by 'increasing access to multi-disciplinary staff groups such as peer support workers, psychologists, occupational therapists and other Allied Healthcare Professionals throughout an inpatient admission, it is expected that both the effectiveness and experience of care will be improved' (DHSC, 2019b, p. 34).

Multidisciplinarity has been supported by a wider policy objective of integrating health and social care with the aim of making a more seamless service. To achieve this, the NHS Plan outlines the objective of moving to 'integrated care systems' (ICS) across all parts of the NHS. It defines ICS as bringing together 'local organisations in a pragmatic and practical way to deliver the "triple integration" of primary and specialist care, physical and mental health services, and health with social care' (DHSC, 2019a, p. 10).

However, it should be noted that both the concept and the application of multidisciplinarity and integration in mental health services have been led by and based in healthcare policy and practice, rather than social care. Values associated with healthcare conceptualizations of disease, especially a biomedical, disease model of mental health conditions, supplemented by social care interventions, have therefore tended to be dominant in MDTs. Values associated with social justice and social inclusion approaches to understanding mental health problems, exemplified by the social model of disability, have had to play second fiddle.

The dominance of healthcare models and values is reflected in the staffing composition of psychiatric services and MDTs. In 2020, there were 6,249 mental health social workers working in England (HEE, 2020). This number is small in comparison to psychiatric nurses; in 2016 the Health Minister for England stated that there were 38,774 mental health nurses working in England, including those working in inpatient settings (a 15% drop in numbers since 2010), but since then it appears that numbers have risen again to around 42,000 in 2020 (Campbell, 2016; NHS Digital, 2020). Both Onyett (2003) and Evans et al. (2012) cite evidence to indicate that whereas nurses have made up roughly a third of community mental health teams over the last thirty years, social workers have accounted for less than 20% of staff in teams, although the latter figure has increased since the 1990s, as has the number of social care support workers (non-qualified social workers) in teams.

Furthermore, experts in the field have pointed out that progress on integration, despite being 'a policy goal of successive UK governments for over 40 years . . .[,] has been patchy and limited' (Humphries, 2015). This is reflected in the data: although 78% of local authorities reported full or partial integration of health and social care in mental health services, 22% stated that their services were not integrated, equating to 30 out 152 authorities in England (NHS Benchmarking Network and ADASS, 2018). In other words, MDTs in those areas contained no mental health social workers employed by social care organizations. The supposed benefits of multidisciplinarity and integration appear to be not as realizable in practice as they are in theory.

Roles and Functions of Mental Health Nursing and Social Work

If MDTs are the mainstay of psychiatric services, mental health nursing and social work are two of the key professional disciplines considered essential to have in those teams. The roles and functions of both disciplines are well understood, but, put briefly, the input of nursing includes assessment of psychiatric symptoms and other health issues, treatment, and provision of a range of other therapeutic interventions. Social work focusses on the assessment, provision, and management of personal care and wider social needs, including accommodation, personal finances, social supports, and activities (many of which are statutory duties under the Care Act 2014 (HM Government, 2014)). Some social workers may also provide therapeutic interventions. Both disciplines will often also work with a service user's family carers and support networks. The duties of nurses and social workers are also defined by their professional bodies and the organizations that regulate them. Historically, social workers, together with doctors, were the only profession with powers to detain service users in hospital and require them to accept treatment under mental health legislation, but, since the Mental Health Act in England and Wales was reformed in 2007, this role has been opened up to other professions (although the majority of staff with these statutory powers have remained social workers).

The different roles and functions of nursing and social work indicate that the values and models which underpin the two professions will differ as well. But it is also important to note that in the UK the two disciplines represent two different systems and structures, even when they are part of the same MDT. Mental health nursing is generally seen to be part of the UK's NHS, which provides free healthcare to any citizen of the UK at the point of need. Mental health social workers, on the other hand, are usually considered to be part of the system of social care services provided by local government ('local authorities'). Adult social (care) services are provided on the basis of severity of need and financial eligibility, although there are some universal statutory responsibilities for assessment, care, and treatment of people with mental health conditions under mental health, mental capacity, and care legislation.[1] However, it may come as some surprise that around a third of all mental health social workers in England are employed directly by NHS organizations, so many will have a more hybrid role involving both health and social care functions (HEE, 2020).

Values in Mental Health Nursing and Social Work

Given that the roles, functions, and systems of the two professions differ, it is not surprising to find that there are differences in the values underpinning them as well. Values partly reflect history and context and in the case of nursing and social work there are two quite separate traditions in the UK.

The origins of modern nursing are commonly linked with the work of Florence Nightingale and Mary Seacole during the Crimean War in the nineteenth century. However, modern nursing has also been shaped by the creation of the NHS in 1948, which introduced free universal healthcare, although psychiatric services were initially limited largely to the traditional asylums. To some extent, healthcare has always reflected aspects of a military organization with a hierarchy of roles (nurses being subordinate to doctors) and centralized command with very limited local democratic accountability. Power was largely in the hands of the doctors in the old asylum system (though on a day-to-day basis many patients may have felt it exercised more by nurses). The shift to more community-based services towards the end of the twentieth century has enabled nurses to expand their role, although formal medical responsibility for a service user remains with a doctor. So, whilst mental health nursing values can be seen in broad terms as being based in processes of healing and caring for all, there can be more negative elements associated with the exercise of medical power harking back to institutional models of care.

Yet values also reflect education and practice and, in this sense, as Norman and Ryrie (2018) point out, the two concepts of therapeutic engagement and evidence-based healthcare are fundamental to mental health nursing. As the development of pharmacological, evidence-based interventions for mental disorders has slowed down over the last twenty years (especially in the case of dementia), and healthcare interventions have met with some resistance or avoidance by service users, nursing practice has had to draw upon other values to enable therapeutic engagement to continue. This has involved a greater focus on concepts of recovery (meaning regaining control as defined by the service user, rather than a more traditional notion of 'getting better'), social inclusion, and the rights of service users (McIntosh and McCraig, 2018).

Although social work as a profession in the UK emerged between the two world wars, its roots in social care mean that its values partly go back to nineteenth-century concepts of 'deserving' and 'undeserving poor'. Yet, even if those nineteenth-century concepts have to some extent affected who social workers have provided services to, social workers have always had more autonomy in their practice than nurses and have been largely based in a system of social care that was democratically accountable at a local level. And from the middle of the twentieth century onwards, an explicit values-base of mental health social work (and social work in general) has gradually emerged, focussing more and more on citizenship, rights, social justice, anti-discriminatory practice, recovery, strengths-based practice, supporting the empowerment of service users, working with communities, professionalism, and leadership (Bogg, 2010; NHS Benchmarking Network and ADASS, 2018). Many mental health social workers have also drawn upon psychotherapeutic values and approaches to enhance their practice. But lurking behind these more progressive and positive values have been more negative ones associated with the statutory powers that many mental health social workers can wield as gatekeepers of social care services, and to authorize the detention in hospitals and care homes for care and treatment of service users with mental disorders or who lack mental capacity. The debate about values involving choice or those underpinning control goes back many years in mental health practice (Perkins and Repper, 1998; Williamson and Daw, 2013). Whilst it is important to note that statutory powers of detention and treatment also come with legal safeguards for service users (e.g. rights to representation, review and appeal), people's experience of involuntary inpatient care is often frightening and distressing and dependent more on how values are expressed in practice than in principle (Akther et al., 2019).

Although there are clear differences in values, as well as practice, between nursing and social work, there are also commonalities and some convergence. The shift in mental health nursing values to reflect more closely some of the values of social work echoes a move in MDTs to more generic ways of working where different professional disciplines undertake shared roles such as coordinating the care of service users. Perhaps the starkest indicator of this is that mental health nurses (and other professionals) can now be qualified to exercise statutory powers under mental health law, a role which previously only social workers were allowed to undertake.

Challenges to Multidisciplinarity

There is, however, evidence of problems with multidisciplinarity, particularly for mental health social work. Social work often struggles to articulate its particular contribution in the context of MDTs, and there are few differences evident between service users' experiences of mental health social workers compared with other mental health staff (Boland et al., 2021). In a study of community mental health teams for older adults, only two-thirds of the 376 teams surveyed reported having social workers, and those teams that did reported an average of 1.8 social workers compared to 5.5 nurses; 73% of teams were also managed by a nurse (Verbeek et al., 2018). Using data from the same survey, another study reported that only modest progress was found in the integration of social workers within the teams and one respondent reported that 'social workers had recently left their team, and that the team had "gone back to doing what we know best"' (Wilberforce et al., 2013, p. 1489). Yet problems were also identified in the opposite direction: most teams surveyed could not access local authority service user records, nor were health staff within most teams able to commission social care services (Verbeek et al., 2018; Wilberforce et al., 2013).

It has been argued that the difficulties described mean that it is difficult for social workers to bring social perspectives, skills, or interventions to people with mental health problems using MDTs and social workers can be 'subsumed into the health and managerial culture of the NHS' (Woodbridge-Dodds, 2018, p. 3). There has certainly been a re-evaluation of integrated MDTs in some areas, especially from the perspective of local authorities:

> In Adult Social Care, models of delivery have in recent years moved towards greater integration with health. In contrast, in Mental Health, AMHPs [approved mental health professionals, i.e., social workers] and other council resources previously seconded to provide services within Mental Health Trusts [NHS organizations], have in some areas been brought back under direct council control.
>
> (NHS Benchmarking Network and ADASS, 2018, p. 8)

In other words, 'de-integration' has occurred and multidisciplinarity has been diluted. This seems to have occurred because some MDTs exclude a significant number of people who have social care needs but whose mental health needs or diagnoses do not meet the entry criteria for the team. Evidence is limited on how far this affects the day-to-day application of multidisciplinarity and whether it results in the service users of some MDTs not benefiting from the input of mental health social workers and social care services. Some MDTs are clinic-based, so they are not able to get a clear picture of what is going on in the person's home environment. Yet 'de-integration' doesn't automatically mean a poorer service; service users still have the same entitlement to mental health social work and the separation of services may mean greater clarity in roles and responsibilities.

Practice Examples

So, what does this all mean on the ground for mental health services and their clients? In an MDT, access to a nurse or a mental health social worker (and the services they provide) can be represented in a Venn diagram, where the two overlapping circles represent social work and nursing within an MDT:

Considering these three clients, multidisciplinarity is somewhat of a chimera. Of course, it does not necessarily mean that nurses and social workers don't want to provide a service

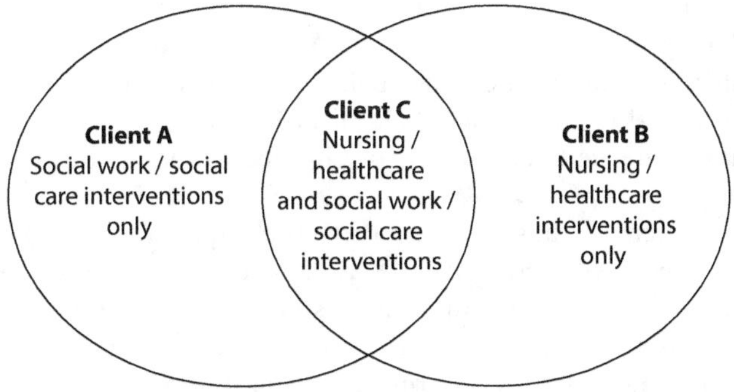

Box 7.1 Systemic tensions between social care and health care

Client A has significant social care needs associated with what appears to be a mental health problem: excessive hoarding, very poor self-care that constitutes a risk to himself and others, and unpredictable, antisocial behaviour towards neighbours. Yet when he is assessed by a psychiatrist, the conclusion is that he has no mental disorder and is therefore not treatable. There is no suitable nursing intervention for Client A, but the social workers consider him to have significant social care needs and there is no other social care service he can be referred to (local generic social care services may refuse to take on a client like this because they perceive it as a mental health issue that they do not have the expertise for). A disagreement arises between the social workers and the nurses about whether the team should take him on as a client.

Client B has been diagnosed with clinical depression and is seen regularly by the nurses. Although lonely and isolated, she lives independently in a house she owns, has significant financial savings and is just about able to care for herself, with support from a sister. The nurses want the social workers to offer her social support but she is not assessed as having severe social care needs, nor is she financially eligible for publicly funded social care, so the social workers cannot offer her a service apart from information about where she might get help from. Again, there is potential for a disagreement about what support the MDT can offer her.

Only Client C benefits from the full multidisciplinarity of the MDT. Client C has been diagnosed with a psychotic illness and early-onset dementia, has been detained and treated in hospital, is reliant on welfare benefits, and requires accommodation. The nurses need to monitor their mental health and ensure that they receive therapeutic input, whilst the social workers, who authorized their detention in hospital, need to arrange suitable post-discharge accommodation.

for Clients A and B, but the structure and the values of the systems they work for prevent them from doing so. Systemic tensions are then played out in arguments between professionals, schisms in MDTs, and flaws in multidisciplinarity.

The Contribution of VBP

Differences in values and practice between mental health nurses and social workers are a reflection of both the benefits and the challenges of multidisciplinarity. As a way to resolve this, VBP provides a framework and a process for working with diverse sets of values, including situations where these may be the cause of professional conflicts, or disagreements involving service users and family carers (Fulford et al., 2012; Woodbridge and Fulford, 2004). The premise of VBP, a mutual respect for differences of values, together with its ten pointers to a 'good process' for balanced decision-making involving values, can be usefully applied in these situations. Whilst VBP works in partnership with evidence-based practice, the evidence tends to be more limited in mental health care compared to physical healthcare.

More recently, attention has been drawn to the importance of VBP also working in partnership with a rights-based approach that takes into account human rights and other legal frameworks (Hughes and Williamson, 2019). A rights-based approach can potentially help overcome some of the differences in values and practice, providing that there is a shared understanding of the relevant legal frameworks, as values expressed in law and legal processes are universal in their application, irrespective of discipline. A rights-based approach can also act as a reminder that the right to healthcare may not be the same as the right to social care; the two systems are underpinned by different values. Although at times this is frustrating, especially for service users, it is beyond the power of a social worker or nurse to change this, so understanding the differences is a better approach when disagreements arise than expecting one system to operate according to the values of the other.

As already described, there has been a convergence in the values and the practice of nurses and social workers which in many places will have assisted multidisciplinarity. Although a biopsychosocial model of mental health problems is common in the approach of many MDTs, difficulties can still persist because of the greater numbers of healthcare professionals, and issues such as role clarity and access to the different professions and services they provide. Furthermore, in some places 'de-integration' of MDTs has led to a reduction in multidisciplinarity and a separation of nurses and social workers.

Yet these difficulties may not need to be a problem if VBP's principles and process are used effectively to understand the values of the two professions and respect their differences, whether nurses and social workers are working in the same team or not (Fulford et al., 2012). Separate services may provide greater clarity of role and function. Conversely, where integrated MDTs are working with service users with complex needs who show little interest in a 'therapeutic relationship', values and practice based on engagement, even when described for nurses, can be shared and applied by any discipline (Thurgood, 2009).[2] Drawing on VBP's premise of mutual respect for differences in (professional) values, being person-centred, and using balanced decision-making based on shared values and practice skills, multidisciplinarity and engagement may help to resolve situations where values appear to be in conflict. For example, Client A and Client B in Box 7.1 clearly have some psychological and social needs, respectively, and it may be that organizational values could play a role as well. If the MDT is able to do short-term interventions, perhaps social work staff could support Client A whilst the nursing staff (or psychologists) could advise generic social care services on how to work with the client so they could be handed over. Similarly, nursing staff could support Client B until social work staff have referred her over to a local voluntary-sector befriending service.

Concluding Remarks

Although this section has focussed on the role of mental health nurses and social workers in MDTs in England, many of the underlying issues will be similar in other countries with comparable services. Contained within the benefits of multidisciplinarity are also some of its problems, in terms of differences in values, practices, and systems of care, particularly if a biomedical model (as opposed to a biopsychosocial model) does not sufficiently take into account service users' social care needs. These tensions are not something to try to avoid or smooth over, as they reflect contradictory aspects of the human condition: one only needs to think of the need and desire for social contact versus the fear of infection that millions of people will have felt under the Covid-19 pandemic to see this. Additionally, VBP prepares the ground and raises awareness of values diversity, including how different professional values in MDTs are there precisely so that the service can respond effectively to the values that may be important to different service users, whether these are focussed on treatment or social care needs, or the need for other interventions. But to ensure that tensions about values are eased, values need to be made explicit and made amenable to working with, rather than worked against. Values-based practice can make a real contribution in achieving this for nurses and social workers, to greatly enhance multidisciplinarity in mental health services.

Conclusion

The different needs, concerns, and preferences of the professions constituting the MDT reflect the hybrid nature of the subject matter of psychiatry. Although training can improve MDT working, currently, professionals receive relatively little specific training on this. Most of them develop their relevant skills on the job, working closely with the other professions. Neuroscience fits well with other medical preclinical disciplines, but its findings have rarely been easily translatable into clinical classification or treatment directly. Further research is needed on how to integrate neuroscience research with research on the other dimensions of mental illness. Improving understanding of the psychological dimension of mental illness has led to new treatments that have similar efficacy to medications. Our current approach to treating mental illness has also benefited greatly from insight from sociology and anthropology. Traditionally, medicine sat at the top of the hierarchy in the professions of the MDT. This hierarchy has become more horizontal in recent decades, but MDTs are still situated primarily within healthcare. The integration of health and social care has been attempted continually over the last forty years with more or less success. Although close working together is clearly beneficial, advantages and disadvantages have been described for both integrated and separate services. Values-based practice principles can provide a good process for care decisions in both.

Notes

1. It should be noted that devolving powers in the UK to Scotland, Wales, and Northern Ireland has meant that whilst similar principles of health and social care exist across the UK, policies, systems, and legislation differ.
2. It is worth noting that Thurgood's chapter, in subsequent editions of this textbook for mental health nurses, was replaced by a chapter written by different authors with the same title but preceded by the words 'The Therapeutic Relationship'.

References

Akther, S. F., Molyneaux, E., Stuart, R., Johnson, S., Simpson, A. & Oram, S. 2019. Patients' experiences of assessment and detention under mental health legislation: Systematic review and qualitative meta-synthesis. *British Journal of Psychiatry Open*, 5(3), e37.

American Psychiatric Association (APA) 2013. *Diagnostic and Statistical Manual of Mental Disorders: DSM-5*, 5th ed. Arlington, VA: APA.

Bhugra, D., Tasman, A., Pathare, S., Priebe, S., Smith, S., Torous, J., Arbuckle, M. R., Langford, A., D'Alarcón, R., Chiu, H. F. K., First, M. B., Kay, J., Sunkel, C., Thapar, A., Udomratn, P., Baingana, F. K., Kestel, D., Ng, R. M. K., Patel, A., De Picker, L., McKenzie, K. J., Moussaoui, D., Muijen, M., Bartlett, P., Davison, S., Exworthy, T., Loza, N., Rose, D., Torales, J., Brown, M., Christensen, H., Firth, J., Keshavan, M., Li, A., Onnela, J.-P., Wykes, T., Elkholy, H., Kalra, G., Lovett, K. F., Travis, M. J. & Ventriglio, A. 2017. The WPA-Lancet Psychiatry Commission on the future of psychiatry. *Lancet Psychiatry*, 4(10), 775–818.

Bogg, D. 2010. *Values and Ethics in Mental Health Practice*. Exeter: Learning Matters.

Boland, J., Abendstern, M., Wilberforce, M., Pitts, R., Hughes, J. & Challis, D. 2021. Mental health social work in multidisciplinary community teams: An analysis of a national service user survey. *Journal of Social Work*, 21, 3–25.

Burn, W. 2019. Integrating neuroscience into psychiatric training in the United Kingdom: The Royal College of Psychiatrists Gatsby/Wellcome Neuroscience Project. *European Neuropsychopharmacology*, *29*, S1062.

Campbell, D. 2016. Number of NHS mental health nurses has fallen by 15% under Tories. *Guardian*, 1 November. www.theguardian.com/society/2016/nov/01/number-mental-health-nurses-nhs-drops-sixth-tories.

Care Services Improvement Partnership (CSIP) & National Institute for Mental Health in England (NIMHE) 2007. *New Ways of Working for Everyone: A Best Practice Implementation Guide*. https://shorturl.at/IM3D1.

Cuttle, G. & Burn, W. 2020. Neuroscience: The way forward. *British Journal of Psychiatry Advances*, 26(6), 318–319.

Department of Health 1999. *National Service Framework for Mental Health*. London: Department of Health. https://shorturl.at/0XiKq.

Department of Health 2001. *The Mental Health Policy Implementation Guide*. London: Department of Health. https://shorturl.at/WcTGm.

Department of Health and Social Care (DHSC) 2019a. *NHS Long Term Plan*. London: DHSC. www.longtermplan.nhs.uk/.

Department of Health and Social Care (DHSC) 2019b. *NHS Mental Health Implementation Plan 2019/20–2023/24*. London: DHSC. www.longtermplan.nhs.uk/publication/nhs-mental-health-implementation-plan-2019-20-2023-24/.

Donnelly, M. 2016. Best interests in the Mental Capacity Act: Time to say goodbye? *Medical Law Review*, 24(3), 318–332.

Evans, S., Huxley, P., Baker, C., White, J., Madge, S., Onyett, S. & Gould, N. 2012. The social care component of multidisciplinary mental health teams: A review and national survey. *Journal of Health Services Research and Policy*, 17(Suppl. 2), 23–29.

Fulford, B. (K. W. M.) 2007. Facts/values: Ten principles of values-based medicine. In Radden, J. (ed.), *The Philosophy of Psychiatry: A Companion*. New York: Oxford University Press, pp. 205–234.

Fulford, B. (K. W. M.), Peile, E. & Carroll, H. 2012. *Essential Values-Based Practice: Clinical Stories Linking Science with People*. Cambridge: Cambridge University Press.

Goffman, E. 1961. *Asylums: Essays on the Social Situation of Mental Patients and Other Inmates*. Garden City, NY: Anchor Books.

Gostin, L. 1975. *A Human Condition: Vol 1: Mental Health Act from 1959 to 1975 – Observations, Analysis and Proposals for Reform*. London: MIND.

Health Education England (HEE) 2020. *National Workforce Stocktake of Mental Health Social Workers in NHS Trusts*. Report V1.2. www.hee.nhs.uk/sites/default/files/documents/NHSBN%20NHS%20Social%20Worker%20Findings%20for%20HEE.pdf.

HM Government 2014. Care Act 2014, c. 23. London: National Archives. www.legislation.gov.uk/ukpga/2014/23/contents.

Hoggett, B. 1996. *Mental Health Law*, 4th ed. London: Sweet & Maxwell.

Hughes, J. C. & Williamson, T. 2019. *The Dementia Manifesto: Putting Values-Based Practice to Work*. Cambridge: Cambridge University Press.

Humphries, R. 2015. Integrated health and social care in England: Progress and prospects. *Health Policy*, 119(7), 856–859.

Joint Committee on the Draft Mental Health Bill 2004. Minutes of evidence: Wednesday 8 December 2004, examination of witnesses (questions 497–499). https://publications.parliament.uk/pa/jt200405/jtselect/jtment/79/4120810.htm.

Keshavan, M. S., Price, B. H. & Martin, J. B. 2020. The convergence of neurology and psychiatry: The importance of cross-disciplinary education. *Journal of the American Medical Association*, 324, 554–555.

Kleinman, A. 1988. *The Illness Narratives: Suffering, Healing and the Human Condition*. New York: Basic Books.

Martin, W., Michalowski, S., Jutten, T. & Burch, M. 2014. *Achieving CRPD Compliance: Is the Mental Capacity Act of England and Wales Compatible with the UN Convention on the Rights of Persons with Disabilities? If Not, What Next?* Colchester: Essex Autonomy Project. https://autonomy.essex.ac.uk/wp-content/uploads/2017/01/EAP-Position-Paper-FINAL.pdf.

McAllister, M., Morrissey, S., McAuliffe, D., Davidson, G., McConnell, H. & Reddy, P. 2011. Teaching ideas for generating critical and constructive insights into well-functioning multidisciplinary mental health teams. *Journal of Mental Health Training, Education, and Practice*, 6(3), 117–127.

McIntosh, G. & McCraig, M. 2018. Recovery, rights and social inclusion. In Norman, I. & Ryrie, I. (eds.), *The Art and Science of Mental Health Nursing: Principles and Practice*, 4th ed. Milton Keynes: Open University Press, pp. 49–64.

Muzyk, A. J., Gagliardi, J. P., Rakesh, G., Jiroutek, M. R., Radhakrishnan, R., Pae, C.-U., Masand, P. S. & Szabo, S. T. 2017. Development of a diverse learning experience for diverse psychiatry resident needs: A four-year biological psychiatry curriculum incorporating principles of neurobiology, psychopharmacology, and evidence-based practice. *Psychiatry Investigation*, 14(3), 289–297.

NHS (National Health Service) Benchmarking Network & Association of Directors of Adult Social Services (ADASS) 2018. *AMHPs, Mental Health Act Assessments and the Mental Health Social Care Workforce*. London: ADASS.

NHS (National Health Service) Digital 2020. NHS workforce statistics. https://digital.nhs.uk/data-and-information/publications/statistical/nhs-workforce-statistics.

National Institute for Health and Care Excellence (NICE) 2020. *Chronic Pain in Over 16s: Assessment and Management.* Draft for consultation. www.nice.org.uk/guidance/ng193/documents/draft-guideline.

Norman, I. & Ryrie, I. eds. 2018. *The Art and Science of Mental Health Nursing: Principles and Practice*, 4th ed. Milton Keynes: Open University Press.

Novick, A. M. & Ross, D. A. 2020. Dualism and the 'difficult patient': Why integrating neuroscience matters. *British Journal of Psychiatry Advances*, 26(6), 327–330.

Onyett, S. 2003. *Teamworking in Mental Health.* London: Palgrave Macmillan.

Paulus, M. P., Huys, Q. J. M. & Maia, T. V. 2016. A roadmap for the development of applied computational psychiatry. *Biological Psychiatry: Cognitive Neuroscience and Neuroimaging*, 1(5), 386–392.

Perkins, R. & Repper, J. 1998. *Dilemmas in Community Mental Health Practice: Choice or Control.* Abingdon: Radcliffe Medical Press.

Pescosolido, B. A., Martin, J. K., Long, J. S., Medina, T. R., Phelan, J. C. & Link, B. G. 2010. 'A disease like any other'? A decade of change in public reactions to schizophrenia, depression, and alcohol dependence. *American Journal of Psychiatry*, 167(11), 1321–1330.

Pitarka-Carcani, I., Szmukler, G. & Henderson, C. 2000. Complaints about care in a mental health trust. *Psychiatric Bulletin of the Royal College of Psychiatrists*, 24, 372–376.

Read, J., Runciman, O. & Dillon, J. 2016. In search of an evidence-based role for psychiatry. *Future Science OA*, 2(1), FSO101.

Roffman, J. L., Simon, A. B., Prasad, K. M., Truman, C. J., Morrison, J. & Ernst, C. L. 2006. Neuroscience in psychiatry training: How much do residents need to know? *American Journal of Psychiatry*, 163(5), 919–926.

Schildkrout, B., Benjamin, S. & Lauterbach, M. D. 2016. Integrating neuroscience knowledge and neuropsychiatric skills into psychiatry: The way forward. *Academic Medicine*, 91(5), 650–656.

Stein, D. J., Shoptaw, S. J., Vigo, D. V., Lund, C., Cuijpers, P., Bantjes, J., Sartorius, N. & Maj, M. 2022. Psychiatric diagnosis and treatment in the 21st century: Paradigm shifts versus incremental integration. *World Psychiatry*, 21(3), 393–414.

Strege, M. V., Persons, J. B., Ressler, K. J., Krawczak, R. A., Fang, A., Goldin, P. & Siegle, G. J. 2021. Integrating neuroscience into clinical practice: Current opinions and dialogue between Drs. Jacqueline Persons and Kerry Ressler. *Behavior Therapist*, 44(7), 326–334.

Szasz, T. S. 1974. *The Myth of Mental Illness: Foundations of a Theory of Personal Conduct*, rev. ed. New York: Harper & Row.

Thurgood, M. 2009. Engaging clients in their care and treatment. In Norman, I. & Ryrie, I. (eds.), *The Art and Science of Mental Health Nursing: A Textbook of Principles and Practice*, 2nd ed. Milton Keynes: Open University Press, pp. 621–636.

United Nations General Assembly 2007. *Convention on the Rights of Persons with Disabilities: Resolution Adopted by the General Assembly*. A/RES/61/106, 24 January. www.refworld.org/legal/resolution/unga/2007/en/49751.

Verbeek, H., Worden, A., Wilberforce, M., Brand, C., Tucker, S., Abendstern, M. & Challis, D. 2018. Community mental health teams for older people in England: Variations in ways of working. *International Journal of Geriatric Psychiatry*, 33(3), 475–481.

Wilberforce, M., Tucker, S., Abendstern, M., Brand, C., Giebel, C. M. & Challis, D. 2013. Membership and management: Structures of inter-professional working in community mental health teams for older people in England. *International Psychogeriatrics*, 25(9), 1485–1492.

Williamson, T. & Daw, R. 2013. *Law, Values and Practice in Mental Health Nursing: A Handbook*. Milton Keynes: Open University Press.

Woodbridge, K. & Fulford, B. (K. W. M.) 2004. *Whose Values? A Workbook for Values-Based Practice in Mental Health Care*. London: Sainsbury Centre for Mental Health. https://valuesbasedpractice.org/wp-content/uploads/2015/04/Whose-Values-A-Workbook.pdf.

Woodbridge-Dodds, K. 2018. *Integrating Mental Health and Social Care: Does It Work in Practice?* London: Centre for Mental Health.

Chapter 8

Progressive Developments in Psychiatry

Robert B. Dudas and David Crepaz-Keay

Introduction

Psychiatry is a unique medical speciality in the sense that its treatments tend to fall into two very different groups in terms of the level of organization they target: biomolecules and minds, or the cellular and the organismic levels. Understandably, from a values perspective, they each have their own attendant needs, concerns, and preferences. Historically being associated with dramatic improvement in mental illness, pharmacological therapies in psychiatry have experienced a several-decades-long stagnation and, more recently, received a lot of constructive criticism about their efficacy and safety, especially in the long term. Problems have been increasingly recognized, such as the epidemic proportions of antidepressant and benzodiazepine prescribing, which stands in stark contrast to the lack of corresponding improvement in mental health at population level, the so-called *treatment–prevalence paradox* (Jorm et al., 2017; Ormel and Emmelkamp, 2023). One of the main challenges is that drug development and pharmacotherapy have traditionally relied on the biomedical model and randomized controlled trials (RCTs), but these can only go so far when it comes to personalized medicine and a more transparent, more effective, and truly therapeutic use of this still very important arm of treatments. What is currently under-recognized is that if we want to solve the above-mentioned problems and to avoid them in the future, we need a great deal of input from other relevant disciplines, such as public health, psychology, anthropology, sociology, politics, and law, and a progressive approach that is capable of integrating all relevant levels from molecular to social.

This chapter will show examples of how thinking at higher levels of organization, namely, relative to the person in their social world, can open new avenues in research and treatment, and how it has already helped psychiatry transform itself, to some degree, from an earlier, now outdated version in which treatment was done *to* patients to a more modern version in which treatment is done *with* patients and their social environment. The first section by Robert Dudas describes how psychopathological phenomenology (PP) and existential psychotherapy (EP) can meet and help us improve our understanding of our situatedness in the world and our stance-taking, and the potential benefits of this for research and treatment. He will also highlight some opportunities for synergism between motivational interviewing (MI) and values-based practice (VBP). The second section by David Crepaz-Keay describes two notable progressive developments in psychiatry: recovery and co-production.

Promising New Developments in Treatment

Robert B. Dudas

Revival of Old Approaches with Great Potential: Phenomenology and Existential Psychotherapy

Since the beginning of psychiatry as a medical specialty, there has been a constant change in terms of its dominant paradigm. Some approaches disappeared almost completely, whilst others fell into disuse before making a return. In this section, I will review two such approaches that also share as their key features working with values and using empathy as a major methodological tool for that: EP and MI. The former has strong links with phenomenology and the latter with the Rogerian non-directive or humanistic approach.

Both PP and EP are in themselves of interest from a values point of view. Phenomenology aims at studying all aspects of lived experience and the meaning structures of that. Values are very much within its purview. Specifically, EP deals with one's stance towards their situatedness in their body and their world, paying special attention to a number of key themes such as isolation (being alone in the world), individual freedom and responsibility, the finitude of life, and meaninglessness (Yalom, 1980). These themes permeate everyday life and frequently appear in mental illness in various disguises. Some are obvious, others less so: for example loneliness, indecision, and the impression of no change being possible in depression; or one's body being changed or interfered with, shrinking, or disappearing in schizophrenia (Röhricht and Priebe, 2006; Stanghellini, 2009). In recent decades, PP and EP have made great strides in advancing our understanding of mental illness; they offer great potential for resolving the problem of integration in psychiatry, especially as regards integrating the existential dimension with the biological, experiential, and social dimensions of mental illness.

In a thought-provoking paper, Ernesto Spinelli (2006) asserts that EP is an expression of phenomenological research. In his view, phenomenology and EP have similar aims and methodology as well as similar values and they both regard interrelatedness as important. He asserts that in EP symptomatic disorders are considered to be direct expressions or consequences of the patient's stance towards being, that is, their world view. One's world view in this context includes one's beliefs and values. Spinelli (2006) makes the argument that choice, responsibility, and freedom cannot be isolated within a separate being (i.e. self or other) as they always have an interpersonal or interrelational dimension. He goes further to say that fundamentally all subjective experience is interrelational. Taking this theoretical assertion seriously has implications for both clinical practice and research. Spinelli talks about *I-*, *you-*, *we-*, *and they-focussed realms of encounter*. These relate to my experience of being myself in a relationship, my experience of your experience of me, our individual experiences of us being in a relationship, and my experience of how other people in my world experience their own interrelational realms in response to my current way of being, respectively. The realms focussing on other than my experience of myself are particularly relevant to changes the patient makes in the context of psychotherapy. These are never changes without impact on the patient's experience of how others in their world experience their relationships with the patient. Spinelli (2006) uses the example of the therapist inviting the client who is considering leaving his wife for another woman to consider the meaning and impact of his decision on his wife's relationship with their children and their friends, and so on. Spinelli argues that it would be 'interrelationally irresponsible' not to examine the impact on at least those relations of the client that they indicated as important to them. Carrying out this work with the client can stop them from construing a world in their mind that will not fit with their actual lived experience. The nature of this work is, to a large extent, that of an ethical-moral dialogue and it often receives less attention than other elements of the dominant modalities, despite the fact that patients almost always regard it as important.

For research, these approaches open exciting new avenues of inquiry. For example, neuroscience research could study choice in this new, interrelational context, as, again, the person never makes their choices in isolation from others. Although demand characteristics, a related but much narrower concept, has been described as an important factor in psychological experimentation, information that would enable the reader to gauge the impact of these on the results of a given experiment is increasingly absent from scientific papers (Klein et al., 2012). This sort of existential phenomenological inquiry and bidirectional input with descriptive psychopathology could contribute to capturing symptoms more precisely and more meaningfully at the level of the person. For example, in a research study linking experiential (psychological) variables (e.g. self-report answers on a rating scale) to functional brain imaging variables, 58 out of 250 participants may indicate 'strongly agree' on an item and this may show relatively weak correlation with a certain activation pattern. However, the fifty-eight participants who endorsed 'strongly agree' may have done so for a variety of reasons in terms of their existential stance regarding that rating scale item and this may explain some of the 'noise' in the data. Examining the correlation in those with a similar existential stance may improve the precision of the measurement and the replicability.

A key understanding from this line of inquiry is that it is not possible to examine our thinking in isolation from the influences of our position in the world, in society, and in history (Smith et al., 2022, pp. 7–33). When studying the objects of psychiatry, making the effort to first describe all the relevant particulars before progressing to analysis and classification pays dividends. This more-precise approach may reduce the noise in the data and may help us progress beyond simply identifying associations between relatively crude and imprecise variables from very different levels of measurement and, ultimately, develop a better understanding of psychiatric symptom formation and better treatments.

A Treatment Modality Working with Values: Motivational Interviewing

All treatments work with values to some degree, but for some the values are the primary or main focus. Motivational interviewing is a style of communication that focusses on the language of change (Miller and Rollnick, 2013). Its aim is to enhance the patient's motivation and commitment to a specific goal by exploring the patient's reasons for change. These reasons almost always relate, in some way, to needs, concerns, and preferences, that is, to the patient's values. Therefore, MI provides an example of working with values therapeutically.

There is a significant evidence base for MI as regards its efficacy for a variety of psychiatric problems (Arkowitz et al., 2015, p. 18; Rubak et al., 2005). As to how it works, empathy, collaboration, and enhancing the patient's autonomy were found to be important factors in achieving positive change in the patient's behaviour (Zuckoff et al., 2015, p. 254). It is designed to increase the person's agency by enabling them to draw out the personal meaning and importance of change.

Further, MI is compatible with a variety of models of mental illness and treatment modalities that include working with the patient's values as an important element. Helping people examine their situation and options, in other words, their affordances, for example, makes sense from the perspective of the *enactive model* of psychiatry. From a practical point of view, there are many similarities between core elements of MI and VBP. For one thing, MI's starting points are similar to those of *VBP*: *respect* and providing a *good process* for curious exploration through reflective listening and empathy as opposed to providing off-the-shelf solutions, instructing, or directing. Non-judgemental acceptance and engaging with the patient as an equal partner are also shared principles. Recognizing the importance of values and identifying value conflicts at the root of the patient's inability to move towards recovery are further similarities, as is their methods being compatible with many different treatment modalities. Thus, MI can be considered, in many respects, a practical application of VBP principles in psychotherapy. There are also similarities with other treatment frameworks. Moreover, MI's exploratory approach is not dissimilar to the 'not knowing stance' of *mentalization-based treatment* (MBT; Bateman and Fonagy, 2004). Assuming that positive change would naturally occur through following a good process is also a key principle of *good psychiatric management* (GPM; Gunderson and Links, 2014).

An important aspect of MI is its focus on *ambivalence* (Arkowitz et al., 2015, p. 5), that is, when the person has mixed feelings about change. This is very pertinent to value conflicts, which are often implicated as psychological precipitating and/or maintaining factors of mental illness and as a stumbling block on the road to recovery. For example, patients can be ambivalent about whether to leave an unhappy relationship. This could be linked to a variety of conflicting values; for example, they may struggle to resolve the conflict between their need for self-esteem, which cannot be met with an abusive and controlling partner, and their preference for stability or having a comfortable life. Not uncommonly, patients with severe illness may even feel conflicted about whether they want to carry on living. Similarly, they may have ambivalence about seeking psychiatric help, taking medication, or making adaptive changes in their lives in the context of psychotherapy.

Allan Zuckoff and colleagues, in their book *Finding Your Way to Change: How the Power of Motivational Interviewing Can Reveal What You Want and Help You Get There* (Zuckoff et al., 2015, p. 140), describe how values, that is, our beliefs about how we should live our lives and our aspirations, are the engine of change. They shape our attitudes and how we see our own behaviour and that of others. Zuckoff et al. (2015) note that our values come from our family, culture, and religious traditions, but they also point out that whilst some people continue to live by these values passed down to them, others intentionally replace them with values of their own choosing, that is, personal values that are amenable to adaptive modification. Relevant to resolving value conflicts, they describe how identifying a person's core values, that is, their values about what it means to be a good person and to live a good life, can change how that person sees a situation and help them resolve ambivalence about change. We can see how this is similar to awareness, knowledge, and reasoning about values in VBP. This is also similar to how improvement with treatment can be conceptualized in the enactive model of psychiatry as improving a person's ability to take a reflexive stance and to notice all their affordances – processes that have been impaired by illness. Zuckoff et al. (2015) acutely observe that a person may not know exactly what their values are until they have put them into words and heard themselves speak. This is one of the reasons why talking about one's values is important. Accurately mapping one's relevant values in order to make adaptive change possible is an essential part of psychiatric treatment, and we will explore this more in Chapters 11 and 13.

As we said, conflicting values can be precipitating and maintaining factors in psychiatric illness. These value conflicts can also be a major obstacle to clinical improvement, which can lead to prolonged suffering and an inability to move on. The most crippling value conflicts often include the *core values of the person*. When one's core values cannot be lived out because they are conflicting with each other, the ensuing dissonance and suffering act as a powerful force that has the potential to destabilize mental health. What may help with reducing the conflict is finding new ways to live out the conflicting values that do not involve going against any of the other core values. Zuckoff et al. (2015, p. 143) provide the example of a man who was unable to give up smoking, as smoking represented living out one of his core values: *excitement* (thrill seeking, living life to the full, and achieving a sense of doing something risky). This was in conflict with *being healthy* and viewing his body as a temple, which was another of his core values. The conflict led to 'self-dissatisfaction'. Whilst in the past he was able to live out his core value of excitement through partaking in extreme sports, in his current life situation smoking was the only activity representing it within his otherwise well-ordered and responsible existence. For him, the only way to be successful in giving up smoking was to find a way to honour both of these values, instead of having to choose between them. Core values are associated with a complex web of cognitions, emotions, and behaviours, and much of therapy is focussed on improving the person's awareness of these. This is worthwhile investment because this knowledge can be helpful for *improving the person's ability to utilize their environment's affordances to live out their core values*. Another way to reduce value conflicts is *changing one's values*. This would mean that a core value becomes no longer as core as it once has been. There are at least two avenues that can lead to success with this. The first one follows from the fact that one's values (or their perceived relevance and importance) can change as a result of changes in how one perceives themselves, the world, and themselves in their world (e.g. via improved sense-making). This can be achieved via cognitive intervention, such as conscious exploration and reasoning about their values and the cognitions, emotions, and behaviours associated with them, in either a one-to-one or a group setting, the latter offering more opportunity to learn from other people's examples. The other avenue, though generally less useful for treatment, is through the gradual change that occurs naturally, without intervention, in one's values over time. This happens at a slower pace, with occasional, more-sudden shifts in the context of major life events (e.g. losses and other role transitions). These ways of reducing value conflict are also germane to *improving dissensus tolerance*, another key concept in VBP. When there is dissensus, stakeholders have irreconcilable views about what should be done in a clinical situation. Similar to value conflicts within the person, conflicts between the values of two or more people can lead to intense dissatisfaction, mental illness, and non-adherence to or dropping out of treatment. The impact of dissensus is not always entirely negative, though; it can also lead to positive changes, for example through broadening the stakeholders' horizons in terms of their options. Adapting one's personal values (i.e. transforming their meanings or the hierarchy between them) or finding alternative ways to live them out can be helpful here, too. Either of these can significantly reduce or fully remove the value conflict and help the patient grow and move on.

Zuckoff et al. (2015, p. 155) invite us to examine how others around us would know what our core values are from the way we go about our lives. They do this in the context of exploring which values we are living out more or less fully, but this question also draws attention to the social aspect of our values, that is, the fact that I experience living out my own values in the context of other people living out their own values (proximity of values). Others may help or hinder me in living out my values. They may show appreciation, indifference, or condemnation of my actions, to which I may respond with pride or satisfaction; a sense of being accepted, ignored, or rejected; or shame. I may be able to cope with this to varying degrees, which will have an impact on how much I will be motivated to change. Also, I can experience my living out my values as being in contrast with others living out theirs. Not being able to live out one of my core values may lead to less self-dissatisfaction if none of my peers is able to live out theirs, and so on.

In summary, MI skills are highly relevant to VBP. They relate to the VBP skills of awareness, reasoning, knowledge, and communication about values, as well as to other key pointers of good process such as person-centredness and partnership. Further research could fruitfully explore how MI skills and techniques could specifically help us resolve ambivalence in the context of conflicting values in clinical decision-making. The technique of MI is teachable, learnable, and measurable (Hettema et al., 2005) and studies could look at how MI could be adapted to further develop and enrich the methodology of VBP. This is a promising area with significant potential for cross-fertilization.

Recovery and Co-production

David Crepaz-Keay

Recovery

In traditional medicine, recovery typically means being illness free or unaffected by symptoms of an illness. The term has also been used in the addiction field where it is more often used in the context of an individual being in control rather than being 'cured'. In mental health, the word recovery has been used in a variety of ways by people who have received a psychiatric diagnosis, though this would rarely be considered 'cured' in the traditional medical sense. 'Recovery has been defined as "a deeply personal, unique process of changing one's attitudes, values, feelings, goals, skills, and/or roles" and "a way of living a satisfying, hopeful, and contributing life even within the limitations caused by illness"' (Slade et al., 2014, p. 12).

Recovery was initially regarded as a progressive alternative to the narrow diagnosis, treatment, and control of symptoms approach that characterized the community-based approach the UK adopted following its closure of the long-stay Victorian asylums in the 1990s. The language of recovery has since become widespread in UK mental health services, and it is almost impossible to find a service that is not recovery-orientated. There has also been a corresponding growth in recovery colleges, with a 2017 survey identifying eighty-five in the UK; thus, there is little doubt that recovery is big business and a strong brand.

The concept of recovery historically lived firmly in the medical domain in the sense of recovering from illness. As recovery has become more common in progressive policy and practice developments in mental health services, it has taken on a range of interpretations which could be categorized as (1) recovery from illness, that is, an outcome of successful treatment; (2) recovery from impairment, that is, an outcome of successful rehabilitation; or (3) recovery from invalidation, that is, an outcome of successful survival (Pilgrim, 2008). One of the most important effects of the concept of recovery as adopted into mental health policy is the notion that people *can* recover. Particularly in the case of psychosis diagnoses, the historical assumption was that such a diagnosis was for life, but professional acceptance of the concept of recovery has underlined that people do not need to be treated for life, with at least one major cohort study demonstrating that long-term recovery for first episode psychosis is best served by reducing or ceasing medication rather than following the traditional orthodoxy of medication maintenance for life (Wunderink et al., 2013). Whilst the concept has been received with both enthusiasm and scepticism (see, for example, Bonney and Stickley, 2008; Crane-Ross et al., 2006; Drake and Whitley, 2014; Harper and Speed, 2012), there is at least consensus that using the word is not sufficient; to give the concept meaning, that is, for the notion of recovery to be valuable, certain principles or approaches are necessary (Slade et al., 2014). This should provide significant support for progressive clinicians to enable them to approach recovery-orientated practices in a manner that is both evidence-based and effective in bringing professionals and patients together.

Co-production

Co-production as a term is much newer; it was almost unheard of ten years ago, but has seen a meteoric rise since. In mental health terms, co-production has at least some of its roots in service user involvement, an approach that was born, in the UK at least, from the somewhat diverse parents of civil/disability rights on one side and consumerism on the other.

> Co-production means delivering public services in an equal and reciprocal relationship between professionals, people using services, their families, and their neighbours. Where activities are co-produced in this way, both services and neighbourhoods become far more effective agents of change. (Boyle and Harris, 2009, p. 11)

Whereas service user involvement was generally predicated on an agreed service need, a group of people currently using those services and a desire to develop and improve the services so that they serve more effectively, co-production should be about a diverse team bringing together a range of valuable skills and experience to create something new. Though the language of co-production is much newer than that of recovery, it seems to be vulnerable to the same risk of co-option, expansion, and dilution which many are concerned has taken a progressive concept and transformed it into another logo for the corporate website.

So Why Now, and Why Recovery and Co-production?

No advances in psychiatry have managed to reduce the prevalence or incidence of mental illness, nor are our mental health services proving to be particularly effective at mitigating the impact of poor mental health or improving well-being.

It is also impossible to ignore the impact of the coronavirus pandemic on mental health, mental health services, and the profile of mental health policy. This is the first global health event where the psychological effects have been identified and reported alongside the purely physical health impact. This has led to both an increase in poor mental health and an additional strain on the health and mental health resources that are available to meet this elevated demand.

In short, psychiatry needs all the help it can get, and both the focus that recovery provides and the additional resources offered by co-production should be welcomed by all – provided it is done with skill, sensitivity, and authenticity.

Recovery as a Progressive Tool

Recovery highlights both the potential and the problems faced by progressive psychiatry. The role of psychiatrists has been to identify and treat the symptoms of mental illness. But even identifying mental illness is not a purely objective endeavour. There are no blood tests, brain scans, or biopsies that identify psychiatric conditions, nor are there any physical markers like rashes or hair loss. Diagnoses are made on the basis of observations of behaviour and analysis of reported feelings and experiences. A traditional medical approach would be left with the question 'What is someone recovering from?'. The mental health context of recovery can be helpful here, provided we think of recovery as a move towards the life someone wants in the context of their perceived mental ill-health – not as a move towards being free of illness. This distinction is important because many of us who have been diagnosed and treated, often against our expressed choices, do not always see what may be described as symptoms in a clinical, or even necessarily a negative, way.

One way to illustrate this difference is to consider hallucinations versus hearing voices. Historically, the individual experience of hearing or seeing things that others do not has been considered to be hallucinations – a symptom of psychosis. A progressive recovery approach would identify whether voices are causing any problems to someone's day-to-day living. It may be that the only problem is the fear that hearing voices is indicative of going mad; this is not unusual and in this case the mental health impact is fear of madness rather than the voices per se. With this in mind, the recovery is understanding that hearing voices is a widespread human experience shared by many.

For many people, voices can feel like anything from an occasional irritant to a non-stop disabling assault. Where voices are disruptive or disabling, recovery may mean learning to live with or manage the voices, or it may mean finding ways to get rid of them altogether. Significant work has been done on helping people to manage and live with voices, ranging from self-help and peer support to psychological interventions.

In some cases, the chosen intervention – anti-psychotic medication – may well be the same as indicated by a standard psychiatric approach, but the narrative that gets the person and their psychiatrist there is a different one – a shared understanding of the experience, the desired outcome, and the means to achieve it. This should have a number of benefits including a more empowering feel, a more constructive therapeutic relationship, agreement on treatment, and agreed criteria by which to judge whether the treatment has succeeded or needs to be reappraised.

Co-production in Progressive Psychiatry

It should be clear from the developing narrative that one key to progressive psychiatry is changing the nature of the relationship between doctor and patient. I have chosen to use the titles 'doctor' and 'patient' here to describe the people in each role to reflect the differences in power and status attached to them, noting that these differences do not simply vanish when we change the words. Traditionally, the doctor's job was to identify and treat illness; the patient's role was one of passive recipient. This has certainly changed with both General Medical Council guidance and legal rulings (particularly the Montgomery ruling on shared decision-making – see Hughes et al., 2018), all of which will support progressive thinking in psychiatry.

The doctor–patient relationship needs to be complemented by a change in the relationship that communities and countries have with individuals considered outsiders and the readiness to apply a diagnosis of mental illness to reinforce what society considers to be abnormal behaviour (though it may be nearly fifty years since homosexuality left America's diagnostic handbook – Drescher, 2015). The World Health Organization guide to diagnosis still requires a judgement of whether a delusion is 'culturally inappropriate' when making a diagnosis of schizophrenia (Drescher, 2015).

Co-production is an important tool for facilitating this. Whilst there are more sophisticated definitions of co-production, there are two simple components that form its essence. These are the bringing together of a group of people (the 'co' bit) for the purpose of creating something (the 'production' bit). In the case of progressive psychiatry, this means at the very least bringing together the psychiatrist and their patient to develop something that will improve the life of the latter.

In its most basic implementation, then, co-production encourages a jointly developed picture of what recovery looks like. This offers two benefits: it places recovery in the heart of the mental health service interaction and it ensures that recovery is not just a doctor treating symptoms of illness (unless, of course, that is the mutually agreed definition).

In practice, for co-production to make sense in making psychiatry more progressive, it needs to start beyond the consulting room. It needs to start with a change in the way societies see mental illness. Though we would rightly scorn society considering to be psychiatric conditions the state of having children outside marriage or having a partner of the same gender, we would be guilty of historic arrogance if we assumed that what we currently see as mental illness would be uncritically regarded as such by our successors in fifty years' time.

A co-produced understanding of mental health, poor mental health, and mental illness could be a strong starting point. What is currently understood primarily as disorders of individuals, building on collections of symptoms, identified through observed behaviours, could be complemented with, and in some cases avoided by, a co-produced outline of the psychosocial determinants of poor mental health/mental illness and community-level interventions that prevent its development. The evidence for the role of social determinants of mental health and mental ill-health is compelling (Kirkbride et al., 2024) and academic psychiatrists can help with this by highlighting the causal link between certain psychosocial factors and poor mental health. Implementing community-level interventions is not possible without attention from and action by the political parties, Parliament, that is, governments. Professional organizations that represent psychiatry at national level, such as the Royal College of Psychiatrists, contribute to this work by participating in policy development, following similar work done by the American Psychiatric Association's (APA) Presidential Task Force on Social Determinants of Mental Health (APA, 2022).

Given the opportunity, people who have lived with psychiatric diagnoses are well placed to contribute to the process of developing a deeper understanding both of the social determinants and of interventions that have been found to mitigate their impact – and psychiatrists and other mental health professionals are well placed to help them articulate this. Though this often happens within a therapeutic environment, and sometimes in the co-production of mental health services, it rarely forms a constructive part of broader community development. It is difficult for people with a psychiatric diagnosis to achieve this change alone, but a collaborative effort that draws on progressive psychiatric practice and applies learning from analogous public health practice could help create a significant shift in community attitudes and behaviours.

There are historical precedents for this. Franco Basaglia, a radical psychiatrist who worked in post-war Italy, helped transform mental health services firstly in Gorizia and subsequently in Trieste long before the UK (throughout the 1960s and 1970s – see Basaglia, 1987; Crepaz-Keay et al., 2015). Basaglia understood that building communities that supported people who were previously diagnosed, treated, and kept in institutions was much more complicated than closing institutions and expecting communities to embrace and care for former inpatients. Basaglia's lasting legacy was to build inclusive communities with the drive being art and culture rather than disorder and treatment.

This could be described as co-production of public mental health. If this were to work in harness with the co-production approach to recovery described earlier, it is plausible that we would see a more coherent and holistic approach to mental health in which people could apply their expertise, whether that arises from experience of poor mental health, from professional experience of delivering good public health, or from learning of professional psychiatry. For this to work, all partners would need to respect and value the knowledge, expertise, and experience that everyone brings.

Progressive psychiatrists will already be good at helping their patients articulate their needs more effectively and this expertise needs to be recognized, applauded, and replicated. Psychiatrists also need to know when to stand back and let others lead. This may be more difficult, particularly if psychiatrists see this as putting their patients at risk. Further, UK services have been known to develop an unhelpful blame culture that can easily encourage a defensive approach to practice where constructive risk-taking is discouraged. For co-production to fulfil its potential, we need systems of accountability that protect everyone from poor practice but do not stifle innovation or leave psychiatrists as the scapegoats for society's failings.

But psychiatry should also recognize its limits. Whilst we welcome the broad acknowledgement that there is a mental health component to everything from education to socio-economic circumstances, and even to global pandemics, this should not be seen as a green light to expand psychiatry into every aspect of our lives. There is a difference in both attitude on consequences of between understanding the psychological impact and pathologizing every aspect of human life.

In summary, progressive psychiatry is not only possible, it can be an important driver of a progressive society. In order to fulfil this potential, psychiatry needs to eliminate the structural discrimination within and to contribute to dismantling the discrimination that exists in the wider world. Psychiatrists need to articulate the importance of mental health in all things whilst resisting the temptation to stick a diagnosis on everything. Psychiatrists need to be good team players, sometimes leading, sometimes standing back to let others lead. Done well, this can support recovery not just for individuals but for whole communities – provided that this is genuinely co-produced.

Conclusion

After years of stagnation, opportunities are arising for psychiatry to make significant achievements in integrating the biological, experiential, social, and existential dimensions of mental illness in the form of new developments in PP and EP, enrichment of VBP through MI, new conceptualizations of recovery, and co-production. Progressive psychiatry is possible and, if realized, it could be an important driver of a progressive society.

References

American Psychiatric Association (APA) 2022. *Report of the Presidential Task Force on the Social Determinants of Mental Health.* Washington, DC: APA. https://shorturl.at/wqpDC.

Arkowitz, H., Miller, W. R. & Rollnick, S. (eds.) 2015. *Motivational Interviewing in the Treatment of Psychological Problems.* New York: Guilford Press.

Basaglia, F. 1987. *Psychiatry Inside Out: Selected Writings of Franco Basaglia.* New York: Columbia University Press.

Bateman, A. & Fonagy, P. 2004. *Psychotherapy for Borderline Personality Disorder: Mentalization-Based Treatment.* Oxford: Oxford University Press.

Bonney, S. & Stickley, T. 2008. Recovery and mental health: A review of the British literature. *Journal of Psychiatric and Mental Health Nursing*, 15, 140–153.

Boyle, D. & Harris, M. 2009. *The Challenge of Co-production: How Equal Partnerships between Professionals and the Public Are Crucial to Improving Public Services.* London: NESTA. https://media.nesta.org.uk/documents/the_challenge_of_co-production.pdf.

Crane-Ross, D., Lutz, W. J. & Roth, D. 2006. Consumer and case manager perspectives of service empowerment: Relationship to mental health recovery. *Journal of Behavioral Health Services and Research*, 33, 142–155.

Crepaz-Keay, D., Cyhlarova, E., Daumerie, N. & Marsili, M. 2015. Lessons from Lille. In Crepaz-Keay, D. (ed.), *Mental Health Today and Tomorrow.* Brighton: Pavilion.

Drake, R. E. & Whitley, R. 2014. Recovery and severe mental illness: Description and analysis. *Canadian Journal of Psychiatry*, 59, 236–242.

Drescher, J. 2015. Out of DSM: Depathologizing homosexuality. *Behavioral Sciences*, 5, 565–575.

Gunderson, J. G. & Links, P. S. 2014. *Handbook of Good Psychiatric Management for Borderline Personality Disorder.* Washington, DC: American Psychiatric Publishing.

Harper, D. & Speed, E. 2012. Uncovering recovery: The resistible rise of recovery and resilience. *Studies in Social Justice*, 6, 9–26.

Hettema, J., Steele, J. & Miller, W. R. 2005. Motivational interviewing. *Annual Review of Clinical Psychology*, 1, 91–111.

Hughes, J. C., Crepaz-Keay, D., Emmett, C. & Fulford, K. W. M. 2018. The Montgomery ruling, individual values and shared decision-making in psychiatry. *British Journal of Psychiatry Advances*, 24, 93–100.

Jorm, A. F., Patten, S. B., Brugha, T. S. & Mojtabai, R. 2017. Has increased provision of treatment reduced the prevalence of common mental disorders? Review of the evidence from four countries. *World Psychiatry*, 16, 90–99.

Kirkbride, J. B., Anglin, D. M., Colman, I., Dykxhoorn, J., Jones, P. B., Patalay, P., Pitman, A., Soneson, E., Steare, T., Wright, T. & Griffiths, S. L. 2024. The social determinants of mental health and disorder: Evidence, prevention and recommendations. *World Psychiatry*, 23, 58–90.

Klein, O., Doyen, S., Leys, C., De Saldanha da Gama, P. A. M., Miller, S., Questienne, L. & Cleeremans, A. 2012. Low hopes, high expectations: Expectancy effects and the replicability of behavioral experiments. *Perspectives on Psychological Science*, 7, 572–584.

Miller, W. R. & Rollnick, S. 2013. *Motivational Interviewing: Helping People Change.* New York: Guilford Press.

Ormel, J. & Emmelkamp, P. M. G. 2023. More treatment, but not less anxiety and mood disorders: Why? Seven hypotheses and their evaluation. *Psychotherapy and Psychosomatics*, 92, 73–80.

Pilgrim, D. 2008. 'Recovery' and current mental health policy. *Chronic Illness*, 4, 295–304.

Röhricht, F. & Priebe, S. 2006. Effect of body-oriented psychological therapy on negative symptoms in schizophrenia: A randomized controlled trial. *Psychological Medicine*, 36, 669–678.

Rubak, S., Sandbaek, A., Lauritzen, T. & Christensen, B. 2005. Motivational interviewing: A systematic review and meta-analysis. *British Journal of General Practice*, 55, 305–312.

Slade, M., Amering, M., Farkas, M., Hamilton, B., O'Hagan, M., Panther, G., Perkins, R., Shepherd, G., Tse, S. & Whitley, R. 2014. Uses and abuses of recovery:

Implementing recovery-oriented practices in mental health systems. *World Psychiatry*, 13, 12–20.

Smith, J. A., Flowers, P. & Larkin, M. 2022. *Interpretative Phenomenological Analysis: Theory, Method and Research*. Thousand Oaks, CA: SAGE.

Spinelli, E. 2006. The value of relatedness in existential psychotherapy and phenomenological enquiry. *Indo-Pacific Journal of Phenomenology*, 6, 1–8.

Stanghellini, G. 2009. Embodiment and schizophrenia. *World Psychiatry*, 8, 56–59.

Wunderink, L., Nieboer, R. M., Wiersma, D., Sytema, S. & Nienhuis, F. J. 2013. Recovery in remitted first-episode psychosis at 7 years of follow-up of an early dose reduction/discontinuation or maintenance treatment strategy: Long-term follow-up of a 2-year randomized clinical trial. *Journal of the American Medical Association Psychiatry*, 70, 913–920.

Yalom, I. D. 1980. *Existential Psychotherapy*. New York: Basic Books.

Zuckoff, A., Gorscak, B., Miller, W. R. & Rollnick, S. 2015. *Finding Your Way to Change: How the Power of Motivational Interviewing Can Reveal What You Want and Help You Get There*. New York: Guilford Press.

Chapter 9

Using Values-Based Medicine at Scale to Provide Holistic Care for the Frail Elderly

Benjamin R. Underwood and John Martin

Introduction

Values-based medicine (VBM) provides a way of thinking about the patient's perspective on the value of treatment and using that knowledge to deploy available resources most effectively (Bae, 2015). This approach can be applied at the level of individual clinicians and patients making decisions together. Can it also be applied at a larger scale? Here we present our experience of integrating mental and physical healthcare for the elderly population of Cambridgeshire.

Background

Cambridgeshire is a county in England, UK. It has a total population of around 1 million people including 165,000 people over the age of 65 (Cambridgeshire and Peterborough Insight, 2011). In common with many parts of the UK, the proportion of people in later life is growing. This means that conditions that are common in later life are set to increase; for example, the number of people with dementia is predicted to nearly double in Cambridgeshire in the next fifteen years (Wittenberg et al., 2020). Cambridgeshire is also a health economy that, historically, has struggled financially. In 2012 the funding shortfall was predicted to rise to some £250 million by 2018 (Comptroller and Auditor General, 2016). As a result of these financial and demographic pressures, a decision was taken by the Cambridgeshire clinical commissioning group to radically redesign services, focussing on a top priority of out-of-hospital care for older people. This priority had been identified following extensive consultation with the public, the third sector (i.e. a range of organizations that are neither public sector nor private sector), and professional stakeholders. Interestingly, this produced a remarkable unanimity of view, including that services were too 'fragmented' and that people would prefer to be cared for at home if possible, a strong signal that later informed the top priority – 'At Home Is Best' – of the Cambridgeshire Sustainability and Transformation Partnership (Health Scrutiny Committee, 2017). This reflects a crucial aspect of VBM; building new hospitals may seem an obvious way to invest visibly in health services, but, whilst high-quality hospital care is essential, people only want to go to hospital if it is really necessary, and this is particularly the view of older people. That this approach was also supported almost uniformly by other stakeholders provided a strong impetus for change.

Whilst the total aspirations for this service were not fully realized, in April 2016 all community services for older people's health came under one organization, Cambridgeshire and Peterborough National Health Service (NHS) Foundation Trust. This included district nursing, occupational therapy, physiotherapy, old age psychiatry, community geriatrics, 102 inpatient rehabilitation beds, 52 inpatient psychiatric beds for older people, 3 minor injury units, and a plethora of specialist teams for areas including diabetes, Parkinson's, respiratory conditions, cardiac conditions, speech and language therapy, neurological conditions, and dietetics. This encompassed nearly 2,000 staff in more than 50 teams working from as many locations to deliver nearly 1 million patient contacts per year. This presented a unique opportunity both to integrate physical and mental healthcare and to use VBM to inform our new service.

Operationalizing a Service at Scale Using VBM

Owing to the extensive public and stakeholder engagement prior to starting the service, we felt that we had a strong mandate to deliver care that was based in people's homes and that was integrated. People did not want to continually retell their stories to different healthcare professionals; they wanted all professionals to be working together as a team. This was felt to be particularly important for the frail elderly, where many different team members are often involved. Integrating mental and physical healthcare was seen as important. One person who suffered from mental and physical health problems told us: 'You're not just ill in your mind, you are physically ill as well; the two go together and are connected; you are a person and one entity.' On being treated at home, they said: 'In the past I would have been whipped into hospital, but the adjustment to coming home is difficult. Being treated at home, I've been able to see my relatives and friends and I've been able to keep in touch with life. Being treated at home means I have been able to get better quicker, so all praise to the service.' In a further attempt to embed a values-based approach, the service has promoted health coaching, where the starting point is what is important to the patient, and then the role of the healthcare professional is in how they might help the patient achieve those goals.

The next step was to see how we could use these principles to enhance services further. We were mindful of the need to keep in mind the VBM principle of efficient use of resources. In England the dominant provider of healthcare is the NHS, which is funded from central taxation, so for us our patients were also the people who funded the service. As a result, we collaborated as a system to provide a transformational fund which paid for a number of evidence-based schemes, all aimed at maintaining older patients at home and preventing illness and disability. To be approved, each scheme had to show savings to other parts of the system in excess of the cost of the scheme (i.e. a greater than one:one return on investment).

One example of these schemes was the expansion of a community specialist heart failure service. At its inception, fewer than 5% of patients with heart failure were reviewed within two weeks of leaving hospital. Heart failure admissions have increased nationally by a third in the last five years, increasing pressure on the acute hospitals (Gallagher, 2019). It is also a serious life-limiting condition with significant morbidity – asking patients to come to the hospital for review would be to significantly challenge many of them. Within eight months of the community service starting, 95% of patients were being seen within two weeks of discharge and emergency admissions for heart failure in Cambridgeshire had declined to the lowest they had been for four years (unpublished data). A second example was the creation of the JET (Joint Emergency Team) which provided a sub-acute (within four hours) response at home for the elderly or those with long-term conditions from a paramedic or senior nurse with a view to managing them at home and avoiding a hospital admission. This service was evaluated seven times in the first two years of operation. It sees around 10,000 referrals a year and overwhelmingly manages to maintain people at home. Only 17.5% of patients required admission within thirty days of being seen by JET (Underwood et al.,

2018). These services have been popular with patients, with much feedback focussing on the benefits of being able to be treated at home.

Of course, services and populations evolve over time. How can one make sure that the patients' voices continue to be heard? The organization has a number of ways of collecting feedback, including the NHS 'friends and family test' (FFT) where patients are simply asked how likely they would be to recommend this service for their friends and family, as well as to give more detailed feedback. The service receives nearly 10,000 patient responses and 1,000 carer responses annually. This includes free text boxes, the contents of which are shared each month with the directorate and the trust senior team. It is also important to refresh our understanding of the broader context of the community so we are part of a 'big conversation' with the community, which includes how we measure performance of our services and also the priorities of the community as to where financial resource should be targeted (Gardner, 2019).

Outcomes

Were there any benefits to adopting this approach and has it contributed to improved outcomes or patient satisfaction? Patient feedback found that 95% of our patients are likely or very likely to recommend the service to their friends and family. In 2018, we had one complaint for every 12,000 patient contacts (but 62 compliments for every complaint) and one serious incident for every 37,000 contacts. There remains strong support from staff for the principles underpinning the service, and staff sickness is at the lowest rate it has been in the last four years.

Many of the outcomes described so far have been achieved in a consensual way without explicitly referring to, or necessarily being aware of, VBM. However, the principles underpinning the change and the positive outcome suggest that VBM could be employed to integrate services in a way asked for by the people that use them, and that this could inform services at scale, including the prioritization of resources.

References

Bae, J. M. 2015. Value-based medicine: Concepts and application. *Epidemiology and Health*, 37, e2015014.

Cambridgeshire and Peterborough Insight 2011. Census 2011. https://cambridgeshireinsight.org.uk/population/census-2011/.

Comptroller and Auditor General 2016. *Investigation into the Collapse of the Uniting Care Partnership Contract in Cambridgeshire and Peterborough*. London: National Audit Office.

Gallagher, P. 2019. Heart failure hospital admissions rise by a third in five years putting 'immense pressure' on the NHS. iNews, 4 November. https://inews.co.uk/news/health/heart-failure-nhs-hospital-admissions-rise-358385?srsltid=AfmBOorVtDjTAt66KuUZTiETZVrSYDR1V8Q8HOx_QnxSD2lqPeviXIAF.

Gardner, G. 2019. Why Cambridgeshire's £1.3bn healthcare service needs public's help. Cambridge Independent, 5 October. www.cambridgeindependent.co.uk/news/why-1-3bn-healthcare-service-needs-public-s-help-9085166/.

Health Scrutiny Committee 2017. *Report of the Cambridgeshire and Peterborough Sustainability and Transformation Plan (STP)*. https://democracy.peterborough.gov.uk/documents/s29819/6.%20Sustainability%20and%20Transformation%20Plan.pdf.

Underwood, B., Rowland, P., Slann, M. & Cooke, M. 2018. A joint emergency response for those at risk of acute hospital admission in Cambridgeshire. *International Journal of Integrated Care*, 18, article 180.

Wittenberg, R., Hu, B., Jagger, C., Kingston, A., Knapp, M., Comas-Herrera, A., King, D., Rehill, A. & Banerjee, S. 2020. Projections of care for older people with dementia in England: 2015 to 2040. *Age and Ageing*, 49(2), 264–269.

Chapter 10

More on the Current Climate in Psychiatry

Robert B. Dudas and Elizabeth Fistein

Introduction

In each era, there are a number of contentious issues or crises that plague the profession. In recent times, these included the related issues of changing ways of working in psychiatry and difficulty recruiting and retaining professionals in psychiatry, the extreme focus on eliminating suicide, and psychiatry's critical voices calling for either the complete abolition or the major transformation of psychiatry. In the first section of this chapter, Robert Dudas will describe the changes in the value context of specializing and working in psychiatry. This is followed by Elizabeth Fistein's analysis of the zero suicide ambition from a values-based practice (VBP) perspective. Finally, Robert Dudas looks at some of the values of anti-psychiatry and critical psychiatry.

Specializing and Working in Psychiatry

Robert B. Dudas

Medicine has traditionally been a profession of high prestige. In most societies, becoming a doctor was a popular career choice. The number of applicants generally tended to outnumber the available university places and, in most specialties, the training places for specialty training. This has changed over recent decades. Other, non-medical career opportunities have become more popular and newer, more attractive ones have appeared. Medicine has lost some of its appeal as a career choice. Changing values, such as health increasingly becoming a commodity in many societies and the declining prestige of the medical profession, may play a role in this.

Psychiatry is one of the specialties that has experienced a significant shortage of trainees in the last decade in the UK (CFWI, 2014). It is hard to be precise about the exact cause of this, but Table 10.1 lists some factors that might have played a role. Although some of the changes listed may not be entirely negative, and paradoxically may even be positive developments from a different point of view, all these changes affect the preferences and expectations of final year medical students and doctors already in training.

Factors influencing career choice, working conditions, and retention are closely linked. This section will examine some of the recent positive as well as negative developments and their value associations.

Choose Psychiatry

In the UK in recent years, the Royal College of Psychiatrists (2023) launched its 'Choose Psychiatry' campaign to improve recruitment into psychiatry. Its answer as to why students

Table 10.1 Factors influencing career choice and retention in psychiatry

	Influencing factor
Changing values and attitudes towards medicine and psychiatry	Changing prestige of the medical profession (Pescosolido et al., 2001) Commercialization of healthcare; health becoming a commodity, consumerism (Timmermans and Oh, 2010) Public attitudes towards psychiatry: • Attitudes towards mental illness (Mehta et al., 2009) • Increasing explicit or implicit expectations from society • Expectation to prevent patient suicide (Gibbons et al., 2019) • Expectation to prevent harm to others (Buchanan and Grounds, 2011) Attitudes of cognate specialisms towards psychiatry (Oliveira et al., 2020; Sebbane, 2014):
Changes in training	• Medical students' experience of psychiatry during their undergraduate years (Kerebih et al., 2019; Khajeddin et al., 2012) • Junior doctors' experience of psychiatry (Holdsworth et al., 2023; Paris, 2005) • Changes to the degree to which learning psychotherapy is considered part of psychiatry training (Paris, 2005) • Strong emphasis on neuroscience (Insel and Quirion, 2005; Schildkrout et al., 2023) • Creation of a separate academic training path (Beattie et al., 2017; HEE, 2020) • Recent changes around core and higher specialty training (uncoupled/run-through)
Changes in ways of working	At individual or team level: • Excessive demands on doctor's role (GMC, 2019) • Increasing workload pressure (GMC, 2019) • Increasing pressure to see patients only once or infrequently owing to supply–demand mismatch • Changing role: less psycho-education or psychotherapy (delegating these to other multidisciplinary team (MDT) members) and more consulting and management of acute and emergency care (Paris, 2005) • More horizontal team structure but unchanged level of personal responsibility of psychiatrist • Less time and opportunity to get support from peers, senior colleagues, and other colleagues; 'the erosion of many informal structures' (Elton, 2019, p. 3) At the level of the healthcare system at large: • The system presenting too many barriers to patient care (GMC, 2019)

Table 10.1 (cont.)

	Influencing factor
	• Changes in the way psychiatrists are supported as employees (e.g. secretaries, IT, etc.) (Deahl, 2023) • Employers looking after psychiatrists' well-being (GMC, 2019) (e.g. treated them as unique human beings with individual and legitimate choices and preferences in the same way that psychiatrists are expected to treat their patients in a person-centred system); '[g]ood patient care is predicated on good care of the carer' (Elton, 2019, p. 2) • Clinician burnout seen as the responsibility of the clinician instead of as a problem needing to be addressed at organization level (Shanafelt and Noseworthy, 2017) • Blurring of professional line management

should consider psychiatry included having a huge impact on lives, working through new challenges every day as a team, working in a range of settings, having the ability to do part-time working, participating in growing scientific knowledge, and enjoying the high prestige associated with the profession.

In the last few decades, there has been a strong push to portray psychiatry as applied cutting-edge neuroscience (Insel and Quirion, 2005; Schildkrout et al., 2023), often in the context of trying to improve recruitment and retention. In that vein, in the UK the Royal College of Psychiatrists' Gatsby/Wellcome Neuroscience Project has been set up to carry out much-needed modernization and improvement of the neuroscience curriculum and to connect trainers with neuroscientists and the most recent developments in the field. Although this coincided with improved recruitment figures, it is hard to be certain as to what caused this. There were a number of other initiatives at the same time; for example, medical student psychiatry societies have sprung up in many medical schools (e.g. Pandian et al., 2020). Regrettably, and in line with the general trend for decline of investment in the humanities and other non-STEM (science, technology, engineering, and mathematics) subjects worldwide (Goldstein, 2021), we have seen much less of a similar, well-funded and centrally coordinated effort to improve the coverage of any of the other constituting elements of psychiatry, such as psychotherapy, social psychiatry, or the medical humanities, to name but a few. The social sciences, with their emphasis on phenomena above the individual level, help to anchor psychiatry in the right place in terms of its focus and prevent it from moving too far in the direction of neuroscience (especially parts that are irrelevant to psychiatry's subject matter). The natural sciences, although clearly important, are but one pillar on which the clinical and academic branches of psychiatry rest. It is important to note that not everyone who is drawn to psychiatry is interested in genetics, molecular psychiatry, brain imaging, or computational psychiatry. Also, if we as a profession focus on attracting only those who are, we are inevitably going to steer the specialty into one arguably very narrow direction. This may risk not only seriously limiting the potential of our profession to advance our understanding of mental illness and developing treatments for it but also, crucially, losing our identity. Cogent criticism of overreliance on biomedicine and psychopharmacology in psychiatric training has been articulated, highlighting that 'there is a real danger that psychiatric residents are being trained to become psychopharmacological technicians rather than humanistic physicians' (Paris, 2005, pp. 113–114).

Psychiatry – lying at the intersections of neuroscience, psychology, social care, sociology, anthropology, philosophy, and law – occupies a unique position in that it behaves in some respects as an exact science but in other respects as a so-called inexact science. Whilst in the exact sciences there is an expectation that a problem has one correct explanation or solution, in the inexact sciences this is not so, and multiple perspectives or interpretations are not just possible but often desirable or essential. In psychiatry, perhaps even more so than in other specialties, it is often the case that one can choose from a variety of clinical approaches which may all lead to the same outcome and it is difficult to say that one approach is better than the other. The preclinical science subjects, mainly including natural sciences as opposed to social science and humanities subjects, prepare medical students more for the 'only one solution can be correct' type of thinking. Clinical training primes students for some of the skills required for handling uncertainty and unpredictability, which is inherent in medicine, but these skills would be much less honed at that stage. This makes it less likely for students to choose psychiatry.

In the current climate, psychiatrists are increasingly under pressure to see patients only once (typically for an initial assessment) or infrequently (e.g. specifically for a medication review) and to adopt a multidisciplinary approach whereby much (if not most) of the contact is delegated to other professionals, most often psychiatric nurses or psychologists. This creates a problem for psychiatrists as seeing the patient only once or for a limited number of times offers only a cross-sectional view, a snapshot; at best they have a limited opportunity to get to know their patients as people, which was often why they came into this profession. It is also hard to remain part of the therapeutic dialogue with the patient this way. If this is the working mode that medical students and psychiatric trainees see, it can discourage them from choosing psychiatry, especially if developing a deeper understanding and building a therapeutic relationship with the patient was an important motivation for them to come into psychiatry.

Importantly, both recruitment and later retention can be affected by what psychiatrists feel they are expected to manage. Most psychiatrists, for example, feel that it is their responsibility to prevent highly unpredictable events such as patient suicide and also feel pressured by others to do so whilst knowing that suicide is only preventable to some degree (Gibbons et al., 2019).

But it seems that, at least for now, all is not lost. In the UK, it has been recognized at the highest levels that meeting future patient demand will require more psychiatrists (GMC, 2019) and that freshly graduated doctors need to have more exposure to the specialty at foundation year level if shortages are to be reduced (HEE, 2020). There are some positive signs that interest in psychiatry among medical graduates may be improving. The GMC Workforce Report described, 'after years of stagnation and decline' (GMC, 2019, p. 4), a small increase (2%) in the number of doctors in psychiatry training, and according to the Royal College of Psychiatrists (2019, n.p.), in 2019 the number of junior doctors choosing psychiatry was 'at an all-time high', with 92% of the training places filled, which they associated with an increase in public awareness owing to more investment into mental health services by the government and the College's 'Choose Psychiatry' campaign.

Working in Psychiatry

The change over recent decades in how clinical psychiatry is done has been tremendous. In his editorial in the *British Journal of Psychiatry*, Martin Deahl laments the pressure from managers and the 'veneer of quality improvement while at the same time witnessing services unravelling' (Deahl, 2023, p. 2). Indeed, funding for core services becoming increasingly insufficient is a major obstacle to providing person-centred care. Today's psychiatric trainees socialize into a profession struggling with underfunding and resultant supply–demand mismatch characterized by chronic staff shortages and long waiting lists (Punton et al., 2022). With the reduction of inpatient bed numbers, it is now only the sickest who get admitted, if at all. Admitting patients for longitudinal assessment or for a change of environment has become a luxury hardly seen anymore. Patients nowadays can only spend a very short spell on the ward, sometimes as brief as a few days, before they are back in the community, often under the care of an extremely overstretched crisis resolution and home treatment team. Care is spread very thinly, allowing little time to really get to know the patient.

The way consultant psychiatrists work has changed tremendously too. Joel Paris (2005, p. 112) describes how Heinz Lehmann, whilst addressing the Canadian Psychiatric Association in a lecture in 1985, argued that psychiatrists 'needed to change their role from that of expert psychotherapists to managers of acute and emergency care, and to carry out less direct treatment by becoming consultants to the mental-health community'. In Lehmann's vision, psychiatrists would not need to have much knowledge about therapy but would have in-depth knowledge of psychiatric symptoms. Paris (2005, p. 112) wonders if the pendulum has swung too far and psychiatrists are becoming 'DSM robots and pill-pushers'. This is not hugely dissimilar to the ethos of New Ways of Working (NWW; see CSIP and NIMHE, 2007, p. 12), described as 'a cultural shift' involving rethinking values, in that many of the psychiatrist's roles would be taken over by other, non-medical members of the multidisciplinary team (MDT) and the psychiatrist's involvement in the personal, daily therapy would be more light-touch. Unfortunately, the second half of Lehmann's prediction may not have materialized so much. What appears to be required of the psychiatrist nowadays is not so much increasing diagnostic knowledge and skills; on a practical level, it is information technology (IT) and admin skills that seem more and more relevant. There is a conflict of values implicit in these new ways of working: primarily management values versus clinician values. The declared drivers of NWW include relieving the psychiatrists with very high workload (and reducing the need for a very expensive locum psychiatrist workforce) by shifting some of their tasks to non-medical colleagues, for whom these activities might represent development opportunities, and thereby improving the sustainability of already overstretched healthcare systems. Although psychiatrists are trained to be therapists (and therapy is meant to include a broader concept here than just psychotherapy), the implementation guide is clear about the expectation that '[a]ll consultant practitioners will have to prove they are worth the investment made in them, and they will need to be flexible and adaptable in their roles in order to achieve this' (CSIP and NIMHE, 2007, p. 23).

Another important emerging issue is the strengths and weaknesses of IT. Notwithstanding the clear advantages when it comes to pulling out data for managers or researchers, most current electronic patient record systems are unnecessarily complicated, take longer to use, and offer few advantages over pen and paper. The change from paper notes to electronic could have freed up time if it had taken advantage of what cutting-edge

IT can offer nowadays; instead, it often replicates and multiplies the admin burden. Unlike pen and paper, electronic patient record systems almost invariably require a lengthy approval procedure and a significant amount of extra training just to be able to use them. They often have so many functions that no one in the hospital really knows how to use all of them. Clinicians are routinely required to enter a lot of data that will hardly ever be used for anything. Whilst there is no scientific evidence for the clinician clicking away at a computer for long hours improving patients' mental health, collectively we have allowed these record systems to take further time away from talking to patients or their relatives. What Deahl (2023) calls the 'functionalisation' of care (i.e. splitting the patient's journey within the healthcare system into many separate teams, such as inpatient, home treatment, community, primary care mental health) causes repeated unhelpful disruptions to continuity of care and the siloing of expertise and services. This type of division of labour increased productivity during the Industrial Revolution but doing it in psychiatry turns a blind eye to the important fact that human beings are very different from machines or other factory products that need to be assembled.

Another problem that psychiatrists acutely feel is the gradual, but by now almost complete, demolishment of the personal support we once had in our jobs. Most psychiatrists no longer have a medical secretary. People who used to provide this extremely important support have been huddled into impersonal 'admin hubs', often in geographical locations away from the team, expected to support many psychiatrists and therefore knowing none of them really well. In a clinical service dealing with people, this has had a devastating effect in many ways. Part of the problem is that the crucial contribution they provided, through talking to patients on the phone or on arrival at the clinic, helping the consultant sort out their busy timetable, taking care of annual and professional leave admin, and a myriad other things one needs in order to successfully function in a demanding person-centred job, is difficult to quantify or express in financial terms. The effect of taking them away is already reflected very visibly only a few years down the line in the plague-like retention problems in most systems.

In summary, clinical practice in psychiatry has changed very significantly over recent decades. Whilst some of these changes have been positive, an important lesson that can be distilled from a review of the values involved therein is that for any system to function well and in a sustainable way, there has to be some sort of alignment between the values of the stakeholders. Psychiatrists will be able to provide person-centred care only if their own needs, concerns, and preferences are also taken into consideration. The fact that it is when they are not that has the most important effect on recruitment and retention has been picked up by the Royal College of Psychiatrists, and it has now included well-being among the aspects it monitors when approving consultant job descriptions for the UK's National Health Service (NHS). To create a healthy alignment will require continual, genuine, and intelligent dialogue with the general public.

The Expectation of Managing Risk: Eliminating Suicide

Elizabeth Fistein

Healthcare systems do not always function safely; common adverse events include medication errors, hospital-acquired infections, and surgical complications. The World Health Organization (2019) estimates that the occurrence of adverse events, resulting from unsafe care, is likely to be one of the ten leading causes of death and disability worldwide. The principles of patient safety and healthcare improvement have been growing in influence in the two decades since the publication of the landmark report *To Err Is Human* (Donaldson et al., 2000). The belief that no patient should come to harm as a result of seeking healthcare is now so widely held that many consider it a core principle of healthcare delivery.

More recently, the call to apply the ideas of patient safety to the protection of users of psychiatric services has led to the development of the Zero Suicide movement. This movement is based on the belief that the suicide death of someone receiving psychiatric care is equivalent to death caused by medication error or hospital-acquired infection: a preventable event that should be eliminated using the principles of patient safety and quality improvement (Zero Suicide Institute, n.d.). The movement has become international, with representatives from twenty countries signing the 2018 Rotterdam Declaration (Zero Suicide International 4, 2018).

In this section, we will analyse the concept of suicide elimination, using the lens of values-based medicine (VBM). The conclusion that suicide elimination is a reasonable goal is based on the following premises:

- Suicide deaths are preventable.
- Suicide is a form of harm equivalent to other patient safety errors.
- Suicide should be eliminated.

Each of these statements is examined in turn in this section.

'Suicide Deaths Are Preventable'

The premise that suicide deaths are preventable is a statement of fact. It is worthwhile, therefore, examining the evidence that supports this statement.

People who are about to attempt suicide cannot be accurately identified: there is no single risk assessment tool that can accurately predict suicide (Lotito and Cook, 2015; Steeg et al., 2018); some people who are going to die by suicide will not be identified and some who are not will be identified as high risk (Nielssen et al., 2017). Suicide is not, therefore, *completely* preventable. This is acknowledged in Zero Suicide training materials: 'It is critically important to design for zero even when it may not be theoretically possible. When you design for zero, you surface different ideas and approaches that if you're only designing for 90 percent may not materialize' (Education Development Center, 2018, n.p.).

The use of language such as the statement 'suicide is preventable' has rhetorical force. It encourages people to think of suicide as a socially embedded phenomenon rather than simply the choice of an individual (Durkheim, [1897] 1966) and to take responsibility for reducing suicide rates. Setting such an ambitious objective challenges psychiatric healthcare providers to find ways of improving suicide prevention. The benefit, if they are able to rise to this challenge, is fewer people dying in despair.

The risks associated with this position manifest when a suicide is not prevented: if suicide is preventable, but nonetheless occurs, blameworthiness may attach itself to everyone who failed to prevent it. People involved in adverse events in healthcare are now called 'second victims' (Scott, 2019), referring to the impact of these events on healthcare workers. If a reduction in suicide rates is accompanied by an increase in the harm caused by the deaths that are not prevented, then the question of whether or not it is an acceptable risk to take is open for discussion. This is acknowledged in the Zero Suicide movement: whilst asserting that 'if depression care were truly perfect, no patient would die from suicide',

Coffey and Coffey (2016, article subtitle) acknowledge that pursuing perfection is most successful within a just culture. A just culture is a systems approach to patient safety that does not seek to blame and punish individuals when mistakes happen but holds everyone working in an organization accountable for monitoring the system, reporting 'near misses', and making things safer for all (Boysen, 2013).

The second issue raised by the fact that suicide risk assessment is an imperfect process is the question of how to respond to people identified as being at high risk of attempting suicide. This is especially pertinent if they are reluctant to accept help.

'Suicide Is a Form of Harm Equivalent to Other Patient Safety Errors'

Designing safer systems for psychiatric hospitals can be an effective means of reducing deaths from suicide. A well-known example is the reduction in rates of death by hanging among people receiving inpatient psychiatric care achieved by identifying and removing potential ligature points from psychiatric wards (Hunt et al., 2012).

The Zero Suicide movement has issued a call to action to improve safety and the quality of suicide care in psychiatric systems. One can think of this approach as the modern-day manifestation of one of the oldest values of medicine: 'First, do no harm' (Hippocrates of Cos, 1923).[1] However, some factors that place patient safety at risk in psychiatric units (e.g. self-inflicted harm, the use of physical restraint to prevent self-harm) differ from the kind of errors that lead to harm in the general hospital setting, creating a tension between maximizing patient safety and maintaining patient autonomy (Thibaut et al., 2019).

Prevention of hospital-acquired infections, medication errors, and wrong-site surgery is achievable through the design of safer systems and the training and management of staff to reduce human error, assisted by the fact that patients themselves do not want these events to occur. Inpatient self-harm and suicide differ from other patient safety issues in that they involve events that the patient (albeit in the context of disturbed mental state) wills and brings about through their own actions. Prevention of these critical incidents usually involves some degree of coercion, justified by the intention to protect patients from harm. Whether or not such paternalism is justifiable is a question of the relative value placed on the prevention of (self-inflicted) harm and on individual liberty. Furthermore, given that suicide risk assessment is imperfect and some people identified as high risk would not have gone on to die by suicide, some people will be deprived of their liberty in order to prevent a suicide that was never going to happen. The question of how many people it is acceptable to detain in order to prevent one suicide is a question of values, not fact (Szmukler, 2003), and is open to legitimate disagreement.

The Rotterdam Declaration sets a vision for Zero Suicide Healthcare where people who seek psychiatric treatment 'will experience that suicidality can be discussed openly, is treated directly and managed in a least restrictive, recovery-oriented way' (Zero Suicide International 4, 2018, p. 3). Nonetheless, a values-based decision to focus on inpatient safety may have unintended adverse consequences: creating a restrictive and 'clinical' environment in which people are reluctant to stay to receive treatment (potentially leading to increased rates of psychiatric detention); increasing use of sedation and restraint to prevent self-harm (potentially leading to increased rates of physical injury, increased psychological trauma in patients, and increased moral injury in staff); and fostering a risk-averse culture where inpatients are protected from death by suicide in the short term but may not learn the psychological coping strategies needed to resist suicidal ideation once they are re-exposed to access to lethal means in the community.

'Suicide Should Be Eliminated'

This is the most obviously value-laden premise in the argument for suicide elimination. Adoption of the goal of suicide elimination implies that (1) suicide is always a form of harm and that (2) it is a form of harm that outweighs the potential adverse consequences of its successful elimination. In other words, suicide is not only a tragedy but also the worst possible outcome, whatever the circumstances. If this reflects the values of everyone who will be affected, this is perhaps unproblematic. However, if suicide elimination imposes the values of one set of people onto another, it risks causing moral harm and undermining its own legitimacy.

The question of whether suicide is sometimes a legitimate response to a tragic conflict has been addressed in a variety of ways. In the non-Western traditions, a diversity of positions regarding the moral permissibility of suicide exists (Battin and Mayo, 1981). Ancient and Classical Western thinkers also differed in their views. Plato claimed that suicide is disgraceful and that those who die this way should be buried in unmarked graves. Aristotle argued that self-killing does not treat oneself unjustly so long as it is done voluntarily, but concluded that suicide is somehow a wrong to the state or the community. The Stoics argued that, in the absence of the 'natural advantages', such as health, considered necessary for flourishing and living a good life, it can be wise and appropriate to end one's own life (Cholbi, 2017). Early Christian thinkers opposed suicide, as a natural extension of the fifth commandment, 'Thou shalt not kill', and this became part of Christian doctrine and canon law – a ban on funerals for people who died by suicide was part of the legal code of the Catholic Church until the 1980s (Dine, 2020). Suicide was a criminal offence in many Western countries until liberalization in the modern era.

In recent years much work has been undertaken to de-stigmatize suicidality and mental ill-health (including the work of the Zero Suicide Alliance in the UK). People are encouraged to reach out to others if they experience suicidal ideas, and to access help and support, including psychiatric treatment for any underlying mental illness. Despite the lingering use of language such as the phrase 'commit suicide', suicide is no longer unlawful in the UK and people are free to end their own lives (Suicide Act 1961). In a democratic, pluralistic society, is it legitimate to aim to eliminate a lawful act?

There are numerous reasons why suicide may be evaluated as a serious harm which should be prevented, even if it is not criminalized: its irreversibility and the complete loss of potential for flourishing, especially in the context of disordered mental state; the grief of bereaved loved ones; the traumatization of witnesses; and the potential for increasing the likelihood that others will act on suicidal ideas.[2] However, there are also legitimate reasons why some deaths by suicide may be evaluated differently: as rational choices to escape unbearable suffering (physical or psychological) or simply as a response to life carrying on after the 'good life' has ended.

Given this plurality of values, the aim of eliminating suicide completely could be criticized for failing to recognize that it is value-laden – 'values blindness' (Fulford, 2007) – or that it is based on values that are not necessarily shared by others – 'values myopia' (Fulford, 2007).

In summary, the lens of VBM reveals that the fundamental principles on which Zero Suicide is based are not value-neutral. The values of Zero Suicide, some explicit and some hidden, may not be sufficiently widely shared to justify a universal goal of suicide elimination. Furthermore, a decision to prioritize suicide prevention over other activities could potentially reduce patient autonomy, prolong suffering, and impede recovery. Where a policy creates conflict between values, or where there is plurality of values held by those who will be affected by a policy, VBP suggests an alternative approach.

The Case for a Values-Aware Approach to Suicide Reduction

Target-driven approaches in healthcare management are widespread and bring with them both advantages and disadvantages. The old management adage 'You get what you measure' suggests that if you want to achieve an objective, you need to quantify it and monitor it, holding everyone in the organization accountable for the results. This creates a sense of shared purpose, enabling change. However, there are now numerous examples of target-driven healthcare initiatives distorting priorities (as the thing that is not being measured is no longer pursued) and even leading to harm, if the values of support for patient dignity are eclipsed in the pursuit of efficiency (Mid Staffordshire NHS Foundation Trust Public Inquiry, 2013).

The elimination of suicide makes an appealing target for health service improvement, as suicide rates are relatively easy to measure, especially in comparison with factors such as suicidal ideation or mental distress. However, target selection is a value-laden process and close attention to the values that underpin the choice of target is necessary to reduce the risk of creating perverse incentives and unintentionally damaging patient care (Fistein and Malloy, 2017).

The principles of VBP encourage a focus on process – the goal itself is less significant than the process followed to select it. The call is to focus on the perspective of patients and to balance legitimately different value perspectives by listening to and exploring the nature and extent of differences in values, aiming for mutual understanding and respect (Fistein and Malloy, 2017).

Someone who dies by suicide suffers the harm of losing their life – something that they had, presumably, ceased to value at the time of their suicide attempt, even though it may have been something that they would have come to value again had they not died. It is striking, however, that much of the harm associated with suicide is experienced by others, especially people who valued the life that has been lost. Balancing the different perspectives of the suicidal person, their future self, and those who would be affected by the suicide is no simple matter. Nonetheless, VBP calls on us to try.

One reason to be concerned about suicide is the evidence that it is often associated with severe mental illness – cognitive distortions such as beliefs that one is trapped, helpless, and hopeless (O'Connor and Kirtley, 2018) – and therefore may not represent a rational decision or the genuine, authentic will of the person who has died. What does seem clear is that behind the impulse to end one's own life lies a great deal of distress and suffering (O'Connor and Kirtley, 2018) and that both the suicidal person and those that would prevent their suicide place high value on ending that distress and suffering – they are simply choosing different means to achieve this end. Furthermore, to simply aspire to eliminate suicide rather than the suffering that drives suicidality risks arriving at an inhumane solution where people thought to be at risk of dying by suicide are deprived of their liberty in order to save their lives, but at the cost of their continued suffering.

A values-aware approach to suicide prevention would acknowledge the purpose of a Zero Suicide initiative: to strive to eliminate the distress and suffering that drives suicidal behaviour and that affects the 'second victims' of suicide. The focus would be on resourcing high-quality mental health care for all who would benefit from it and making this care accessible and acceptable to as many people as possible.

In comparison with a target-driven approach, underpinned by the values of management science, a VBP approach, underpinned by the values of psychiatry, has numerous advantages:

- By balancing the multiple values of patients and service providers, respect for autonomy can remain at the heart of medical care.
- Providing care that is consistent with the values of those who need to access it reduces the need for coercion and increases the scope for practice consistent with the rights, will, and preferences of patients.
- By concentrating on quality of care for all, rather than identifying high-risk individuals, the problems associated with imperfect risk-assessment tools (false positives and false negatives) are reduced.
- Reducing distress and suffering through the provision of effective, evidence-based treatment for mental ill-health should reduce the downstream consequences of that distress, including suicide.
- Reducing the likelihood of blame attaching to failures to prevent suicide should enable more focus to be placed on quality improvement in the context of a just culture.

Values Questioned and Debated

Robert B. Dudas

In medicine, in general, the sick and their carers place their trust in the doctor and the wider healthcare team to provide beneficial medical treatment. In psychiatry, this is often not the case. There is a much greater degree of value diversity and less alignment between how the doctor and the patient see the problem and the possible solutions for it. People with mental illness may deny that there is a problem even when others around them indicate this to them, disagree with the diagnosis, and decline treatment.

But it is not just patients who can disapprove of psychiatric practice; sometimes even people who have not been affected by mental illness personally or through their loved ones do so. Psychiatry is probably the only medical specialty that has a whole movement opposing it: *anti-psychiatry*. Academics and clinicians in other, often cognate, fields (and very occasionally within psychiatry), philosophers, journalists, and various others have questioned the validity of the concept of mental illness, identified the role of psychiatry in social control (as opposed to providing medical treatment), or called for the abolition of psychiatry.

A description of the history, possible causes, and various forms of these criticisms is beyond the scope of this section. From our perspective here, it may, however, be helpful briefly to examine the values attached to these viewpoints. What are their end goals or terminal values? Are these terminal values primarily personal or social? As we as humans always live in a social world, we also need to examine how these values relate to similar values of others in the immediate as well as the broader social environment of the person affected by mental illness. How and through what means do the proponents of various criticisms against psychiatry seek to achieve their terminal values? What are their instrumental values? What are the other values associated with the issue that need to be taken into consideration? And, crucially, do the instrumental values attached to these viewpoints help them attain their terminal values or end goals or detract from them?

One of the cardinal preferences of anti-psychiatry is for *the abolition of psychiatry*, at least in its current form. The main argument is often that psychiatry restricts the autonomy of the person by labelling them with a medical diagnosis and treating them (often against their will) because they do not fit societal expectations. Putting aside the question of whether we regard them as an illness, if we accept that presentations with mental symptoms, suffering, and functional impairment exist, we need to consider how they can be addressed. This is often accepted even by those advocating for the abolition of psychiatry; it is only the ways in which they believe that the individual and society should address it that differs (e.g. empowering people as opposed to giving them medical treatment).

As a thought experiment, we could look at what the effects would be if psychiatry ceased to exist completely. What would happen to those who are psychiatric patients in the current system? Would other medical specialties take over their care? Or would they be supported completely outside medicine? And would there be people left without any meaningful and reliable help as a result? It is more obvious with some patient groups than with others. People with delirium could perhaps be initially investigated by emergency doctors and then treated entirely by physicians or geriatricians, although these specialists often request input from psychiatrists to confirm the diagnosis (and exclude other, non-organic conditions that can present similarly) and also to advise on management, probably to a large extent because psychiatrists have much more experience with managing psychotic symptoms, aggression, and other behavioural symptoms. Mental disorders owing to a general medical condition are similar in that by treating the underlying physical condition one would expect the mental health symptoms to improve too. Of course, this is not always the case, and patients are often left with a psychiatric condition, for example post-traumatic stress disorder or depression, after recovery from their physical illness. Although geriatricians and neurologists could diagnose and treat dementia, they would need to expand their services and skills significantly if they were to look after dementia patients in the community with problematic behavioural and psychiatric symptoms of dementia (e.g. agitation, aggression, depression, hallucinations, delusions, wandering). These symptoms often lead to carer exhaustion and require the careful planning of a care package or consideration of various residential placement options. This work involves the skilful balancing of patient autonomy and quality of life with safety and other considerations. This work in the UK is done by psychiatrists specializing in old age psychiatry and encompasses a significant amount of mental capacity assessments and safeguarding work (prevention of abuse and neglect in this vulnerable population), interfacing with Social Services and care homes and care agencies. What would happen to people with schizophrenia, bipolar illness, or personality disorders is even less obvious. Psychological treatment services do not tend to take on patients with these conditions whilst they are still floridly psychotic, actively suicidal or violent, not eating and drinking, or unable to engage in talking therapy. Who would manage the risks in such cases? Any new subspecialty growing out of neurology or medicine would need to provide so much of the same type of support that it would become psychiatry in all but name.

Although psychiatry brings, as part of its medical approach, natural sciences methodology to the study of mental disorders, which are understood to have varying degrees of contribution from genetic and psychological components, what no other specialty or profession could do, or would want to do, it is not neuroscience. What uniquely enables psychiatrists to help those patients most in need of psychiatric help is the act of combining natural science and the social sciences. The criticism that we cannot ignore the fact that living circumstances and social and/or societal factors are crucially involved in the causation and recovery from most forms of mental illness has been justifiable. However, psychiatry, at its best, carefully considers biological, psychological, social, and existential aspects of mental illness and generates options relating to each of these aspects. And another important contribution: psychiatrists are experts at interviewing the patient and their family to explore their narratives and to help them make adaptive changes in their narratives in a way that promotes hope, agency, and recovery.

If psychiatry was abolished, important questions would remain from a values point of view. Would it really lead to more autonomy and personal freedom for people affected by severe mental illness? Would they achieve these important terminal values to a greater degree if they were left without psychiatric help? Would being supported only by other medical specialties, non-medical services, voluntary organizations, the police, or the criminal justice system enhance their autonomy and self-direction? Or is it that the appropriate instrumental value to achieve these is not the abolition of psychiatry?

Abolishing psychiatry could also contribute to an increasing (rather than a decreasing) conflict between the patient's own personal terminal values (e.g. retaining the autonomy to make one's own decisions even during severe mental illness versus having a healthy and comfortable life, both in the here and now and in the future). One of the value conflicts often discussed is that between personal versus social/communal values, such as in the context of detention to hospital for treatment: the autonomy of the patient versus the protection of society in the case of people who may become violent when ill, for example. Although detention often causes significant distress and whenever possible should be avoided, it can also be at the same time in the interest of the individual, not just society, as not being detained and acting violently in their social environment would also have (often long-term) negative consequences for them. These can range from retaliation by others and having to live with intense guilt feelings when they recover from the mental illness and realize what they have done and the impact of that, to being liable to pay a fine or compensation, losing a job or relationship, enduring various forms of exclusion from social participation, and/or incurring criminal charges. Not detaining to hospital for treatment those who trespass against the law during their severe mental illness leading to a gross distortion of reality testing, such as delusions and hallucinations, but treating them as criminals would go against the values of most people. Similarly, shall we abandon people when they are at great risk of harming themselves or being exploited or retaliated against by others? Shall we leave them to fend for themselves when they are very apparently not able to? Shall we leave them without treatment when that treatment has the potential to restore their mental capacity to make decisions for themselves and to improve their agency? This would conflict with the values of the majority of people living in the patient's community and also those of the relatives of most patients, and even many of the patients themselves when they are well. The approach of basing all treatment on consent by the patient, as advocated by some, fails when the person lacks the mental capacity to give that consent owing to severe mental illness, such as florid psychosis or mania, or severe depression. Personal autonomy is never absolute, even if we isolated ourselves from the rest of society (which is impractical), because within-person factors also do limit it for all of us. But coming back to balancing personal versus communal values, what may seem sensible from a personal perspective may not seem so from a communal perspective. For example, some may argue that the patient has the right to choose to remain psychotic. Notwithstanding the complex question of whether the patient has the capacity to make a choice in such a situation, this right is not absolute; when it starts impinging on somebody else's rights, it can become a problem. Indeed, it has been argued that for drawing the line between mental disorder and non-disorder, we must consider not just harmful-for-the-individual but also harmful-for-others evaluations (Brülde, 2007). Wanting a rather high degree of exemption from the complex web of rights and responsibilities inherent in living in society comes with a variety of consequences, too. True, it steers one away from a medical solution in this case, but what does it steer us towards instead? The criminal justice system or a pariah existence on the fringes of society? Would that not just mean that it all comes full circle? Surely, this would be very different from the originally declared terminal values.

Critical psychiatry does not call for the abolition of psychiatry – in fact, many of its proponents are practising psychiatrists themselves – but it draws attention to problematic areas in psychiatric theory and practice in order to provide constructive criticism (Middleton and Moncrieff, 2019). However, the ways it problematizes these is not always consistent with the methodology of mainstream psychiatry, and whilst some welcome it as a sort of reflective function of psychiatry, others feel that its approach is destructive (Tyrer, 2019).

Its scope is wide, ranging from the implications of using the biological model of mental disorder, through the overuse of medications, the power imbalance in the doctor–patient relationship, the role of the patient–therapist relationship in psychotherapy, the sick role, the tension between the patient's best interests and the (assumed) social control function of psychiatry, and epistemic injustice, to societal changes and social and political influences on psychological well-being.

But what are some of the values that drive critical psychiatry? One area that critical psychiatry concerns itself with is the overuse of medications in psychiatry. Critical psychiatrists tend to accept that medication can be helpful but call for more transparency about the limitations in our understanding of the pathomechanism of mental illness or how medications work. In this context, health appears as a terminal value and honesty as an instrumental value. Many critical psychiatrists see psychiatric medications as chemicals that alter brain function and human experience, which – coupled with other support – can be helpful in overcoming mental illness, but they feel that the decision about using them needs to be based on this understanding and made much more collaboratively with the patient than they see happening in current practice. They call this collaborative prescribing using a drug-centred (as opposed to a disease-centred) approach. According to this approach, the clinician should explain that the medication is not to correct some sort of abnormality but will alter both desired and undesired emotions, and can cause side effects and discontinuation symptoms; the clinician should also explore the patient's expectations around all of this. Critical psychiatrists take issue with portraying unwanted emotions or behaviour as the result of abnormal brain chemistry, among other reasons, on the grounds that this places the problem with the individual rather than with society. Many practising psychiatrists and trainee psychiatrists would recognize this as how they have been working already. Much of what critical psychiatry stood for has now been absorbed by mainstream psychiatry. Psychiatry as a profession has become rather critical of its own practices and is continually evolving. This self-reflective stance, being critical of our own theory and practice in a constructive way, plays an important role in keeping our profession on a sound ethical footing. Not unchallengeable, not universally viewed as something positive or perfect, but ethical. Psychiatry has been and is a broad church: some of us will call themselves critical psychiatrists; most will apply their critical ability as part of their professional good practice; and a few will continue to hold views that are now considered out of date.

In conclusion, any extreme position here that singles out one value or only a few values at the expense of considering all the relevant values ignores the complexity of values in psychiatry. Also, focussing on earlier practice that occurred in a context different from the current times or on exceptional cases that represent excess or abuse instead of examining typical clinical practice and training in psychiatry draws attention and resources away from addressing the main issues (Dudas, 2020). One of these is that there are conflicting terminal values here. Just one example of this is personal autonomy *versus* the rights and freedoms of others, including protection of the morals and health of others. There are also conflicting instrumental values with an impact on exactly how we should achieve the above terminal values and a balance thereof.

Is there a solution to this? A useful first step would be creating a framework within which these values can be made explicit, understood, acknowledged, and negotiated (i.e. represented, questioned, challenged) – and VBP can offer a methodological contribution for this work. Such a framework would need to enable decisions that affect the appropriate circle of stakeholders, neither unnecessarily wide nor unnecessarily narrow. An important component of this framework could be stakeholders' tribunals (see Chapter 4). Another useful step would be developing ways of handling dissensus in this context. The concepts that not all authority is necessarily harmful and that membership of a community involves accepting the attendant rights and responsibilities are germane to this. Honest public discussion facilitated through this framework needs to be an indispensable part of this process if we are to achieve progress and avoid harmful polemics.

Conclusion

Consistent with its immensely value-laden nature, psychiatry seems to be at risk of extreme positions. Unfortunately, taking extreme positions always runs the risk of ignoring or going against the values of a significant number of the stakeholders. With the changing values of society having an impact on the prestige and quality of working life in the profession, psychiatry has experienced recruitment and retention challenges. Psychiatry needs to make sure that it improves the quality of not just the neuroscience but also the social sciences and humanities content of its training programmes, if it wants to remain relevant to treating mental illness, to keep its identity, and to continue to attract and retain high-quality clinicians and researchers. This will also equip psychiatrists to make better decisions on how to take part in the work of the MDT, when to delegate, and what resources to request for the best outcome for patients.

Although demands on psychiatry to manage risk to self or risk to the public are continually made, VBP-informed analyses can help all stakeholders recognize what psychiatry can or should manage, where its remit ends, and why. Such analyses are also indispensable in laying bare essential misunderstandings about psychiatry and, of course, in accepting and responding appropriately to legitimate and constructive criticisms.

Notes

1. The Hippocratic Oath includes the promise 'I will abstain from all intentional wrong-doing and harm'.
2. If we accept that suicide elimination is a legitimate aim, a related question arises – is this aim always or solely the responsibility of psychiatric services? Should psychiatrists concern themselves with suicidality that is not a consequence of mental ill-health? And should wider society take greater responsibility for the social determinants of mental ill-health and of despair? These questions, however, are beyond the scope of this chapter.

References

Battin, M. P. & Mayo, D. J. eds. 1981. *Suicide: The Philosophical Issues.* London: P. Owen.

Beattie, S., Crampton, P. E. S., Schwarzlose, C., Kumar, N. & CornwalL, P. L. 2017. Junior doctor psychiatry placements in hospital and community settings: A phenomenological study. *British Medical Journal Open*, 7, e017584.

Boysen, P. G. 2013. Just culture: A foundation for balanced accountability and patient safety. *Ochsner Journal*, 13, 400–406.

Brülde, B. 2007. Wakefield's hybrid account of mental disorder. *World Psychiatry*, 6, 163–164.

Buchanan, A. & Grounds, A. 2011. Forensic psychiatry and public protection. *British Journal of Psychiatry*, 198, 420–423.

Care Services Improvement Partnership (CSIP) & National Institute for Mental Health in England (NIMHE) 2007. *New Ways of Working for Everyone: A Best Practice Implementation Guide.* https://shorturl.at/IM3D1.

Centre for Workforce Intelligence (CFWI) 2014. *In-Depth Review of the Psychiatrist Workforce.* London: CFWI.

Cholbi, M. 2017. *Suicide. In* Zalta, E. N. (ed.), *The Stanford Encyclopedia of Philosophy. Fall 2017 ed.* https://plato.stanford.edu/entries/suicide/.

Coffey, M. J. & Coffey, C. E. 2016. How we dramatically reduced suicide: If depression care were truly perfect, no patient would die from suicide. *NEJM (New England Journal of Medicine) Catalyst*, 2. http://catalyst.nejm.org/dramatically-reduced-suicide/.

Deahl, M. 2023. General psychiatry, still in no-man's land after all these years. *British Journal of Psychiatry*, 224(3), 86–88.

Dine, R. L. 2020. You shall bury him: Burial, suicide and the development of Catholic law and theology. *Medical Humanities*, 46, 299–310.

Donaldson, M. S., Corrigan, J. M. & Kohn, L. T. 2000. *To Err Is Human: Building a Safer Health System.* Washington, DC: National Academies Press.

Dudas, R. B. 2020. The discontents of psychiatry: What can the history of psychiatry and values-based medicine contribute to resolving them? In Marková, I. S. & Chen, E. (eds.), *Rethinking Psychopathology: Creative Convergences.* Cham: Springer International, pp. 145–152.

Durkheim, E. M. [1897] 1966. *Suicide: A Study in Sociology.* Translated by J. A. Spaulding & G. Simpson; edited by G. Simpson. New York: Free Press.

Education Development Center 2018. *Zero Suicide in Health and Behavioral Health Care.* https://zerosuicide.edc.org/sites/default/files/Transforming%20Systems.pdf.

Elton, C. 2019. Doctors can't care for patients if the system doesn't care for them: An essay by Caroline Elton. *British Medical Journal*, 364, l968.

Fistein, E. & Malloy, D. C. 2017. Healthcare leadership and applied philosophy: An essential resource. *Healthcare Management Forum*, 30, 218–220.

Fulford, B. (K. W. M.) 2007. Facts/values: Ten principles of values-based medicine. In Radden, J. (ed.), *The Philosophy of Psychiatry: A Companion.* New York: Oxford University Press, pp. 205–234.

Gibbons, R., Brand, F., Carbonnier, A., Croft, A., Lascelles, K., Wolfart, G. & Hawton, K. 2019. Effects of patient suicide on psychiatrists: Survey of experiences and support required. *British Journal of Psychiatry Bulletin*, 43, 236–241.

General Medical Council 2019. *The State of Medical Education and Practice in the UK.* The Workforce Report. London: GMC. www.gmc-uk.org/-/media/documents/somep-2019—full-report_pdf-81131156.pdf.

Goldstein, B. 2021. Decline of the humanities: Where does it STEM from? *Cornell Diplomat*, 24 November, 28–30. www.thecornelldiplomat.com/issue6/2021/11/24/decline-of-the-humanities.

Health Education England (HEE) 2020. *Supported from the Start; Ready for the Future: The Postgraduate Medical Foundation Programme Review*. https://shorturl.at/PRElf.

Hippocrates of Cos 1923. *The Oath*. Loeb Classical Library. Cambridge, MA: Harvard University Press. https://doi.org/10.4159/DLCL.hippocrates_cos-oath.1923.

Holdsworth, R., Browne, H., Ilsted, R. & Beezhold, J. 2023. Fish out of water: Junior doctors' experiences of psychiatry. *European Psychiatry*, 66(Suppl 1), S1122.

Hunt, I. M., Windfuhr, K., Shaw, J., Appleby, L. & Kapur, N. 2012. Ligature points and ligature types used by psychiatric inpatients who die by hanging: A national study. *Crisis*, 33, 87–94.

Insel, T. R. & Quirion, R. 2005. Psychiatry as a clinical neuroscience discipline. *Journal of the American Medical Association*, 294, 2221–2224.

Kerebih, H., Salelew, E. & Hailesilassie, H. 2019. Factors associated with medical students' choice of psychiatry as future specialty: A cross-sectional study. *Advances in Medical Education and Practice*, 10, 751–758.

Khajeddin, N., Riahi, F., Salehi Veysi, M., Hoseyni, H. & Izadi Mazidi, S. 2012. Do medical students' attitudes toward psychiatry and their intention to pursue psychiatry as a career change during psychiatric attachment? *Iranian Journal of Psychiatry and Behavioral Sciences*, 6, 53–61.

Lotito, M. & Cook, E. 2015. A review of suicide risk assessment instruments and approaches. *Mental Health Clinician*, 5, 216–223.

Mehta, N., Kassam, A., Leese, M., Butler, G. & Thornicroft, G. 2009. Public attitudes towards people with mental illness in England and Scotland, 1994–2003. *British Journal of Psychiatry*, 194, 278–284.

Mid Staffordshire NHS Foundation Trust Public Inquiry 2013. *Report of the Mid Staffordshire NHS Foundation Trust Public Inquiry: Executive Summary*. HC 947. London: Stationery Office. https://assets.publishing.service.gov.uk/media/5a7ba0faed915d13110607c8/0947.pdf.

Middleton, H. & Moncrieff, J. 2019. Critical psychiatry: A brief overview. *British Journal of Psychiatry Advances*, 25, 47–54.

Nielssen, O., Wallace, D. & Large, M. 2017. Pokorny's complaint: The insoluble problem of the overwhelming number of false positives generated by suicide risk assessment. *British Journal of Psychiatry Bulletin*, 41, 18–20.

O'Connor, R. C. & Kirtley, O. J. 2018. The integrated motivational–volitional model of suicidal behaviour. *Philosophical Transactions of the Royal Society B: Biological Sciences*, 373, 20170268.

Oliveira, A. M., Machado, D., Fonseca, J. B., Palha, F., Silva Moreira, P., Sousa, N., Cerqueira, J. J. & Morgado, P. 2020. Stigmatizing attitudes toward patients with psychiatric disorders among medical students and professionals. *Frontiers in Psychiatry*, 11, 326.

Pandian, H., Mohamedali, Z., Chapman, G. E., Vinchenzo, P., Ahmed, S., Mulliez, Z., Bruce, H., Burn, W., Korszun, A. & Tracy, D. K. 2020. Psych socs: Student-led psychiatry societies, an untapped resource for recruitment and reducing stigma. *British Journal of Psychiatry Bulletin*, 44, 91–95.

Paris, J. 2005. A shrinking perimeter. In *The Fall of an Icon: Psychoanalysis and Academic Psychiatry*. Toronto: University of Toronto Press, pp. 92–114.

Pescosolido, B. A., Tuch, S. A. & Martin, J. K. 2001. The profession of medicine and the public: Examining Americans' changing confidence in physician authority from the beginning of the 'health care crisis' to the era of health care reform. *Journal of Health and Social Behavior*, 42, 1–16.

Punton, G., Dodd, A. L. & McNeill, A. 2022. 'You're on the waiting list': An interpretive phenomenological analysis of young adults' experiences of waiting lists within mental health services in the UK. *PLoS (Public Library of Science) One*, 17, e0265542.

Royal College of Psychiatrists (RCPsych) 2019. Number of junior doctors choosing psychiatry at all time high. Press release, 11 July. www.rcpsych.ac.uk/news-and-features/latest-news/detail/2019/07/11/number-of-junior-doctors-choosing-psychiatry-at-all-time-high.

Royal College of Psychiatrists (RCPsych) 2023. Choose psychiatry: Choose to make a difference. www.rcpsych.ac.uk/become-a-psychiatrist/choose-psychiatry.

Schildkrout, B., Niu, K. & Cooper, J. J. 2023. Clinical neuroscience continuing education for psychiatrists. *Academic Psychiatry*, 47, 297–303.

Scott, D. A. 2019. Suicide and second victims. *Anaesthesia*, 74, 1351–1353.

Sebbane, D. 2014. Improving the image of psychiatry and psychiatrists: Results of a French national survey. *European Psychiatry*, 29, 624–625.

Shanafelt, T. D. & Noseworthy, J. H. 2017. Executive leadership and physician well-being: Nine organizational strategies to promote engagement and reduce burnout. *Mayo Clinic Proceedings*, 92, 129–146.

Steeg, S., Quinlivan, L., Nowland, R., Carroll, R., Casey, D., Clements, C., Cooper, J., Davies, L., Knipe, D., Ness, J., O'Connor, R. C., Hawton, K., Gunnell, D. & Kapur, N. 2018. Accuracy of risk scales for predicting repeat self-harm and suicide: A multicentre, population-level cohort study using routine clinical data. *BMC (BioMed Central) Psychiatry*, 18, 113.

Suicide Act 1961. An Act to amend the law of England and Wales relating to suicide and for purposes connected therewith. 9 and 10 Eliz. 2. c. 60. London: UK Parliament.

Szmukler, G. 2003. Risk assessment: 'Numbers' and 'values'. *Psychiatric Bulletin of the Royal College of Psychiatrists*, 27, 205–207.

Thibaut, B., Dewa, L. H., Ramtale, S. C., D'Lima, D., Adam, S., Ashrafian, H., Darzi, A. & Archer, S. 2019. Patient safety in inpatient mental health settings: A systematic review. *British Medical Journal Open*, 9, e030230.

Timmermans, S. & Oh, H. 2010. The continued social transformation of the medical profession. *Journal of Health and Social Behavior*, 51, S94–S106.

Tyrer, P. 2019. Critical psychiatry is becoming Luddite: Commentary on . . . critical psychiatry. *British Journal of Psychiatry Advances*, 25, 55–56.

World Health Organization 2019. Patient safety [10 facts]. www.who.int/news-room/facts-in-pictures/detail/patient-safety.

Zero Suicide Institute n.d. Zero suicide. https://zerosuicide.edc.org/.

Zero Suicide International 4 2018. *4th International Zero Suicide Summit, Rotterdam 2018: The Rotterdam Declaration*. www.zerosuicide.org/_files/ugd/686ed3_68bda2e0591c40acb9d6b7154f2cd3b5.pdf.

Chapter 11

Mapping the Value Changes in Depression and Recovery

Robert B. Dudas

Introduction

Depression has become the most important cause of disability globally (Friedrich, 2017). There are different types of depression, but, in most cases with depression, we do not really understand the pathomechanism. Most patients who are treated get treatment with antidepressant medications or psychotherapy, which are only moderately effective. Unfortunately, there have not been any major breakthroughs in this area for decades. Most cases are seen by their general practitioner (GP), that is, their primary care physician, and the severe cases, where the risks are felt to be unmanageable by primary care or where patients fail to improve, are seen by psychiatrists. How can a holistic approach in psychiatry that is based on both the natural and the human sciences contribute to a better understanding of this condition and better management of the complexity in the care of people with depression?

In this chapter, I will highlight some areas where philosophy (particularly, phenomenological psychopathology, enactivist theory, and hermeneutics) can make a useful contribution to our theoretical understanding of depression and improve clinical practice. I will demonstrate how much of what we actually do in psychiatry is making the values of the patient and those involved in the patient's care visible and negotiating these value perspectives. I will use a relatively common clinical scenario to illustrate how this clinical value-mapping can help us facilitate a good process for clinical decision-making. I will also make some observations about the challenges specific to working with the values of depressed patients.

A Philosophically Informed Approach to Understanding Depression

The Life World of the Depressed Patient

Depression is associated with characteristic subjective experiences and behaviours. Without studying the former, it can be hard to explain the latter. To do this most effectively from the perspectives of descriptive psychopathology and exploring values, the clinician needs to assess the patient's subjectivity carefully. As Giovanni Stanghellini and Milena Mancini explain in the introduction of their book *The Therapeutic Interview in Mental Health* (Stanghellini and Mancini, 2017, p. 1), there is a need for a philosophically enriched approach to the art of interviewing if we want to meet the epistemological and ethical challenges therein. *Phenomenological psychopathology* assumes a meaningful coherence between the various manifestations of depression, a meaningful whole in the depressive patient's life world. During the psychiatric interview, the psychiatrist tries to understand to the extent possible the form of life the depressed patient inhabits. A thorough and empathetic approach is used to explore the changes in the patient's experience and actions, and the emotions and personal values linked to these. The dimensions of this life world analysis include the lived body, lived time, lived space, selfhood, and otherness (Stanghellini and Mancini, 2017, p. 30). In addition to phenomenology, careful application of *hermeneutics* is necessary to aid the integration into the life narrative of the patient of any changes that may propel them towards recovery. Naturally, the connective medium between the patient's subjectivity and that of the clinician is language, which needs to be interpreted. Empathy is key in this, as it is with the help of empathy that the clinician 're-enacts' in herself the patient's experiences. The clinician attempts to understand the meanings and connections in them and to map the structures within the subjectivity of the patient.

Depression is a collective term within which melancholia is a certain type of depression. Stanghellini and Mancini (2017, p. 130) characterized patients with melancholic depression as experiencing a loss of feelings, not even being able to feel sad. This profound indifference is experienced as a source of suffering in itself and the patient may have a self-accusing, self-reprimanding attitude towards this as well as a sense of guilt. The whole experience of the melancholic patient is permeated by ethical worries. Depression brings with it a storm of values. At the height of their illness, the patient can constantly feel that they are transgressing important personal and group values. Transgression of personal values often elicits feelings of guilt, whilst transgressing social values is frequently associated with feelings of shame. In a non-psychiatric context, negative emotions caused by value transgressions were moderated by the presence of others and the values they were expressing (Fazel, 2012), and it is reasonable to assume that the same may hold true in depression. As the patient gets better and the values storm calms down, they have a tendency to deny their earlier negative sentiments for others. According to Stanghellini and Mancini (2017, p. 140), in the melancholic patient's *lived time*, the present does not weave into a future. Both the present and the future are dominated by the past which does not want to withdraw. There is often retardation or acceleration of subjective time and desynchronization between this and objective time. The person experiences a sense of unreality. There is no momentum to give one's experience a sense of aliveness. Patients describe a stagnation of bodily function: their organs are blocked or rotted away. In extreme cases, they may believe that they have no body. There is often guilt about the past and the feeling that they have to be punished for past misdeeds. There can also be a sense that one's identity cannot be modified. As regards the *lived body*, patients often say 'My body is dead', 'I cannot feel', or 'I am empty'. Some stop eating. They report a lack of energy, lack of strength, feeling cold, or having generalized pain. The body feels solid and heavy. There is overall bodily rigidity. Complaints of physical illness (nausea, numbness, etc.) are not uncommon. In terms of *lived space*, there is increased distance between oneself and things in the world that are experienced as inaccessible. This leads to inhibition, sometimes to the degree of depressive stupor. In melancholia, the *self* is also affected. Patients identify with a perspective not chosen by them and finite with stable characteristics. They experience themselves as guilty of not being able to love others or to feel compassion for them. *Otherness* is characterized by ethic depersonalization: an anguishing doubt about which of one's selves is the real one, the current one with the lost ability to love or the earlier one?

According to the *enactivist view* (for a description of this, see Chapter 4), in mental disorder a disordered pattern of sense-making leads to impaired functioning not just in terms of survival or reproduction but also in terms of 'faring well' in one's social-cultural environment and maintaining one's identity (Maiese, 2021). In depression, the patient shows heightened attunement to the negative features of herself and her environment. Many affordances and action-possibilities that are available appear to be closed off. Their interactions are too rigid and, therefore, they find it difficult to adjust their sense-making in response to the situation (Maiese, 2021). The depressed person's behaviour will elicit a certain type of reaction from others in their environment, leading to reciprocal loops (Haan, 2020, p. 197). These insights can help us generate novel ideas as to what may be helpful as treatment. For example, the deeply environmentally embedded and embodied nature of sense-making supports the use of dance-movement therapy (DMT) for depression. In DMT, the arrangement of the space, the positioning of the patients and the props, and particular movement sequences help to ignite motivation and facilitate interactive possibilities (Maiese, 2021).

Working with Narratives

Although checklist-like approaches are often used in medicine, in psychiatry the ability to work with the patient's narrative is essential (Gask, 2015, p. 15). This is because narratives are the ordinary form via which we try to order the meaning of our experiences and actions (Stanghellini and Mancini, 2017). It is narrative reasoning that enables us to raise above the level of the sentence, that is, above the level of single experiences. Narrative reasoning in the clinical context involves the creation of a story that is related to recovery (Mattingly, 1991).

Substituting a technical approach for having a conversation during interviewing, that is, only inquiring about the presence or absence of certain symptoms in a checklist-like fashion, runs several risks. One of them is misunderstanding each other by assuming that certain words mean the same to the patient and the clinician when this is not necessarily the case. The meaning of the word depression is a case in point: the patient using it (and laypeople in general) may be referring to a variety of things ranging from momentary low mood or normal sadness caused by the vicissitudes of everyday life, through grief or mood instability, to severe and life-threatening clinical depression. This is even more likely to happen in multicultural societies. Another major problem is preventing the patient from telling their own story and thereby suppressing their narrative. This will not only deprive them of the opportunity to achieve meaningfulness and coherence in their life story, which could have been therapeutic, but also deprive the clinician of the opportunity to understand more about the values of the patient. The patient's values have important implications for the treatment and the prognosis; 'to obtain a systematic knowledge of the patient's experiences in their peculiar feel, meaning, and value for the persons affected by them' (Stanghellini and Mancini, 2017, p. 28) is the main purpose of the therapeutic interview. This is done more easily if one is not influenced too much by a priori models. Standardized tools, which have become all the rage in primary care to screen patients, may have some logistical usefulness for identifying who needs a diagnostic interview or for charting treatment response at a later stage, but during the first encounter with the presenting problem, questionnaire measures would rather decontextualize the symptoms of the patient's personal history and personal narrative (Chen, 2020). Symptoms that do not fit with these instruments could simply be missed (e.g. disturbances of embodiment or time perception) or distorted to make them fit (e.g. subtle variations of mood disturbance).

Bruner (1984) distinguishes between 'life lived' (milestones, critical incidents, and key decision points), 'life experienced' (meanings, images, feelings, thoughts of the person), and 'life as told' (the unique personal narrative as influenced by cultural conventions of storytelling, audience, and social context). In a clinical encounter, 'the life experienced' is communicated through the 'life as told'. It is this that we are particularly interested in exploring, for it offers a window onto one's value systems (Dudas, 2022).

Arlene Bowers Andrews (2006) describes the process of taking social history. The health professional listens to the patient telling their story; contributes his or her own interpretations; supplements the personal narrative with other sources of information (other people's views, previous records, etc.); uses knowledge and skills from theory, empirical studies, past experience with other similar patients; shares his or her interpretations with the patient; and reflects carefully on his or her own interpretations in order to distinguish them from the client's interpretations. This is a joint hermeneutic activity, and, as Andrews (2006) points out, the practitioner becomes part of the story.

Values, Emotions, and Cognition

For practical use, when explaining what values are, we often say that values are things or actions that matter to the person; they are what is important to the person. Values can take the form of needs, desires, preferences, or virtues. One's values are a collection of one's personal, cultural, and historical values. Values arise from feelings, but it is possible to modify them by rational thinking. And, conversely, although we handle them cognitively, they always involve emotions. Making value judgements can activate negative or positive emotions such as guilt, shame, or pride, and attitudes such as caring, moral indebtedness, or responsibility (Horowitz, 2014). The person's values determine the meaning structure of the world they live in and regulate their actions: values are action-driving. Recognizing and acting according to one's own values is part of self-governance.

There are many human values and they are not chaotic; rather, they are organized into families. This *structure of values* appears to be fairly universal and tends to include the following types of values: self-direction, stimulation, hedonism, achievement, power, security, conformity, tradition, spirituality, benevolence, and universalism (Schwartz, 1992). Some values are more individual and situation-specific.

There is a certain *hierarchy among the values of the person* and this hierarchy is different from person to person. Cultures also place different emphasis on different values, and this will also have an impact on the clinical decision-making process in various ways. Milton Rokeach (1973) argued that values can be placed on a continuum from lower- to higher-order values according to Maslow's hierarchical theory of motivation, with values pertaining to self-actualization or psychological health being of the highest order. This value structure will motivate the person to act in a certain way in a given situation and is a crucial part of the person's identity. Importantly, the other person and the mutuality of my relationship with them is necessary for certain essential values to be realized, such as to be accepted, respected, and loved. Love is necessary for trust to develop in one's own self, in the same way as law is for self-respect, and solidarity in society is for personal integrity (Stanghellini and Mancini, 2017, p. 61). The need to be recognized as an individual person in such ways can be stronger than one's organic values relating to self-preservation, so much so that sometimes the struggle for this recognition can be a struggle *against* life (Ricoeur cited by Stanghellini and Mancini, 2017, p. 61). In other words, wanting to lead a good life may take precedence over basic biological needs and people may die for what they value (Haan, 2020, p. 181).

Values can conflict in various ways, for example when a patient has conflicting values about a particular situation or when their current values clash with their previously held values. Value conflicts are also typical when two or more people with different values are involved in a situation. *Conflict resolution* is important in values-based practice (VBP), but VBP recognizes that value conflicts cannot always be resolved and that often there is no one right solution but many. What is helpful in such situations is having institutions in which these conflicting values are tolerated, even honoured, where they can live together.

Emotions have often been thought to prevent people from seeing things objectively and thinking rationally, but the relationship between emotion and cognition is significantly more complex than that (for a philosophical treatment of the subject, see Charland and Zachar, 2008). Emotions are helping us appraise the world and ourselves in it. As their etymology (from the Latin *ex movere*) suggests, they move us in various directions and drive us to action. Words referring to emotion – uplifting, buoyant, high-spirited, downcast, crestfallen, dejected, longing, and so on – often reflect this. Emotions are relevant here because of their evaluative dimension (Hersch, 2008); at the most fundamental level they each represent a positive or a negative value. They act like a compass in decision-making and are therefore indispensable in this context. They give practical meaning and personal relevance to things around us. Our values also do this, but, unlike emotions, values transcend specific situations.

Both in health and in illness, some of our emotions are conscious, whilst others we experience only as vague feelings. Acting in line with our own values generally feels good. When we feel that we are forced to act against our own values, we experience negative emotions, often very strong ones. When we have conflicting values about a situation, our accompanying emotions may be mixed, but a feeling of cognitive confusion and a sense of unease (note the similarity to 'dis-ease') or anguish are often present. When we arrive at resolution, we experience a sense of relief. Similar relief can be experienced when conflicting values remain, but we manage to develop a new narrative that 'makes sense' of the situation and makes the dissensus between our values tolerable. For example, we can make the dissensus meaningful: 'I need to act in this way (come into the ward, even though I disagree) because it is good for my family (i.e. they will feel reassured that I am in a safe place).'

Values in Depression

Depression is not one condition but an umbrella term for a heterogenous group of conditions. This means that patients can have challenges in terms of living by their own values in various different ways. In some cases there is a clear history of a stressful life event or a number of such events in succession, whereas other people develop depression in the absence of any obvious stressful life event. Depression can be relatively mild or severe to the degree of being life-threatening. Some people have only one episode, some have recurrent episodes, and some never return to their baseline and suffer from chronic depressive changes interspersed with more severe bouts. When someone has suffered with depression, especially for a longer period, it may be difficult for them to remember what their life was like before their illness. As Linda Gask, a psychiatrist who herself suffered with recurrent depression throughout her life, put it, 'I sometimes struggle to remember how I felt a year ago, and what my worries were then, or perhaps I actively forget' (Gask, 2015, p. 15).

The milder forms may seem to be on the same spectrum in many respects with 'normal' sadness or a bad patch experienced in health, but the more severe forms appear to be qualitatively different and are more difficult to relate to without first-hand experience of them. Clinical depression is an illness in which the unhappiness is deeper and more powerful and interferes with the person's ability to go on with their life. Depression colours how one sees the world and themselves in it, and their options or action-possibilities. Melancholic depression is a particular type of depression which can be very severe. Both emotions and cognition are typically different from the way they are in normal times.

In this section, I will explore how depression can have an impact on the patient's values and their ability to work with these values in the context of clinical decision-making. This is something the clinician also does when treating depressed patients, although perhaps not in such a systematic way. The more complex the case is, the more this can be helpful. When things get really complicated, it is often when values have remained hidden (whilst very much active and leading to conflict) and/or when those involved in the situation lack the skills to reason about and negotiate the values at play.

Clinical Value-Mapping

Examining the values at play in the clinical care of persons with depression can be similar to creating a map. As part of this *clinical value-mapping* process, the clinician needs to

1. consider the needs, concerns, and preferences of every stakeholder;
2. explore what actions these values can drive; and
3. examine the relationship of these actions with their social context, such as the patient's immediate environment (e.g. their family) and the healthcare system, and see whether these actions are successful in terms of helping the person recover from their depression.

(If not, is that related to values? Are there any hidden values and, if there are, how can they be made explicit? Are there any value conflicts and, if there are, what would help resolve them? What is the way forward if the conflict is unresolvable? Can anything positive come out of the value conflict?)

Unlike ordinary maps, the clinical value map is three-dimensional. This is necessary in order to take into consideration

- the level of organization or the proximity to the primary stakeholders;
- the hierarchy of values; and
- the temporality of those values.

Level of Organization/Proximity to Primary Stakeholders

This refers to making sure that the values of all the stakeholders are recognized and treated at the appropriate level, starting from the patient, through their immediate social environment (the social support network of the patient, which is usually but not always their family and friends; the professionals involved in their care; other, more peripheral multidisciplinary team (MDT) members; the other patients on the ward; local peer groups; hospital management; etc.), to society level (the local community, patient organizations, professional organizations, the courts of law, citizens of the same country, government departments, Parliament, etc.).

The primary stakeholders are the patient and their clinician. This could be a doctor, a nurse, another MDT member, or a small team, but it is always the people who work the most closely with the patient and have a personal relationship with them. Detailed examination of the higher levels may be required only with the more complicated decisions where one's objective may be to flag up problems to or seek advice from professional organizations, courts of law, or lawmakers. In everyday practice, one usually takes into consideration the values of these through acting in accordance with their recommendations, previous rulings, and the law. However, mapping the values of all stakeholders carefully can enable the people involved in the decision-making to realize that, although rules and laws might exist for the good of the greatest numbers and to counteract utilitarianism and protect minorities with certain characteristics, the case in question is not covered by these or that the existing rules and laws work against the interests of one or more of the stakeholders.

Being mindful of this dimension helps us (1) avoid forgetting to consider the values of a legitimate stakeholder and (2) better see the distance between the patient and the stakeholder in question. The relative proximity of another stakeholder has an impact on how we perceive (or fail to perceive) their relevant values. An example would be the choice between following the recommendations set by a professional organization regulating the clinician or doing what the worried mother of the patient is asking us to do. Also, the consequences of an individual clinical decision are different according to the stakeholder's proximity to the patient emotionally, personally, legally, and in other important ways.

According to Shalom Schwartz (1992), values represent three universal requirements of human existence: (1) the needs of individuals as biological organisms, (2) the requisites of social interaction, and (3) the survival and welfare needs of the group. These three types of need can all be present in the clinical decision-making situation and lead to conflict within or between the stakeholders. Most publications consider only the values (needs, concerns, and preferences) of the patient, perhaps those of the clinician, very occasionally the values of wider social formations like the hospital or the National Health Service (NHS) trust, and exceedingly rarely those of the profession or society in relation to the specific case. Examining carefully the alignment of the patient's values with those of others is particularly relevant in mental illness, as these values can be misaligned temporarily or even chronically owing to the illness but also owing to other reasons. In some cases, this misalignment may constitute the mental illness.

Hierarchy of Values

There is always some hierarchy, an order of relative importance, among the values of every stakeholder. I am referring here not to any presumed hierarchy among the values of the various stakeholders but to the hierarchy among the values within the same, single person, group, or organization. Certain needs, concerns, and preferences can feel more pressing than others. This hierarchy may not always be clear even for the person holding these values. Nor is it necessarily stable or immutable, and changes in it may be necessary for successful collaboration between stakeholders as well as for the patient's recovery.

Temporality

People's values can change over time without any mental illness, but in depression, when the patient has limited access to their emotions, especially positive ones, this hierarchy can change dramatically and at a faster pace as the patient's illness is developing and when they are moving towards recovery. It often happens temporarily, but sometimes a new life situation or the experience of mental illness changes the patient's appraisal of themselves and their world in a lasting way. This can be confusing and difficult for the person and/or other people around them to accept and work with. The clinician needs to take this into consideration appropriately.

The values of others involved in the care of the patient change, too. This may be owing to their realization of the patient's changing mental state and the corresponding changes in the patient's needs. In the case of organizations or Parliament, value changes could be owing to representation from individuals or patient or professional groups demanding change (often after a scandal) or to macro-level changes such as those in the demographics or the economic environment. Scientific advances also often lead to value changes.

Using these three dimensions when mapping the values in a given clinical situation can be helpful in several ways. For example, it can enable *dissensus tolerance*. What may seem unacceptable initially might become more tolerable if the person realizes that a particular value is in fact less important to them than they previously felt, relative to some other values they also hold, that is, 'in the great scheme of things'. This is possible only if they are able to think about these values and reorganize relevant parts of their life narrative. Seeing the value hierarchies of other people around us can also help us achieve this: others, especially those who share in our values, taking certain stances influences our emotions associated with our own stance-taking. Mapping the values of the stakeholders can facilitate *realignment of relevant values* within and between the stakeholders.

I will now further elaborate on using clinical value-mapping in depression. For this, I will make use of the phenomenological psychopathology descriptions in the previous section, first-hand narratives by patients with depression, as well as my clinical experience as a clinician working with patients with depression over the last quarter of a century. I will also deploy the case history of a man with depression who believed that he was responsible for causing Covid. This story is fictional but typical of the illness.

The Values of the Primary Stakeholders

Proximity to Stakeholders

Many reports of depression, particularly those of severe episodes, describe an erosion of one's capacity to have moods and feelings or to find anything meaningful (Fernandez and Wieten, 2015). In this state, the depressed patient can be cut off from many or all of the values they would normally hold. This poses a significant clinical challenge as it also means that the clinician may not have access to these values either, or not until the patient gets better from their depression (Fernandez and Wieten, 2015). In some cases, the clinician can know some of the patient's values from previous encounters with the patient. For example, the patient may have expressed a preference in favour of or against a certain treatment in the past. A potential problem here is that the psychiatrist, especially in today's climate where follow-up of well patients is discouraged by management in healthcare systems, may meet the patient only when the patient is ill, or in a crisis, and their values may be already tainted by the illness. This is why it can be helpful routinely to inquire about the patient's values when they have recovered, so as to know what their preferences would be, should they become ill again. This is particularly relevant in depression in which relapses are relatively common.

The clinician can, of course, glean what the patient's relevant values might be from other sources. These sources would provide a less direct access to the patient's values and this information would be less specific to the concrete clinical situation. The clinician can, generally with the patient's consent, speak to people who know the patient well, such as their family and friends. A limitation of this approach is that people close to the patient are, in a different way, also affected by the patient's illness and will have their own feelings, interests, and agendas. Members of the wider clinical team, including the patient's GP (primary care physician), may be able to help. The clinician can also consult peer support workers working with the patient or other experts by experience not directly involved to learn about typical values of depressed patients in similar situations. This approach would not have the same biases as the previous one, but the elicited values would be less personally relevant and less specific to the patient and their social environment. Just as we go to a review of the evidence base for a certain diagnostic or treatment intervention if we are struggling with a particular case, we should go to a review of the values base. There are relevant secondary sources of information on the typical values of patients with depression, such as collections of first-hand narratives, ethnographic studies, and research from anthropology, history, law, and politics. The diversity of relevant values can also be grasped from media reports, literature, theatre, and film portrayal of depression. Lastly, there are also philosophical works using phenomenology, hermeneutics, or discursive analysis.

Box 11.1 Kieran, Part 1

Kieran was a thirty-eight-year-old builder, married with two teenage sons, who presented with a severe depressive illness. He had to stop working because he was consumed by constant anguish that he had caused Covid and he was responsible for the death of so many people in the world. He believed that he deserved punishment, and he was in constant fear that the police would turn up at his work and bludgeon him to death. A few weeks before his illness, Kieran had made an error at work and a wall in a house had to be partly demolished and rebuilt, which caused a minor delay in the completion of the job. Kieran went to see his GP (primary care physician) at the instigation of his boss at work. His wife was supportive of the idea of him seeking medical help, too. His GP referred him to the community psychiatric team where he was seen by the consultant, who recommended treatment with an antidepressant and a small dose of an antipsychotic. Kieran was afraid of taking psychiatric medication because a cousin of his had taken it in the past and he had experienced sexual side effects.

In this case, it was interesting how Kieran's relatively small mistake became magnified in his mind and came to affect the global population in a very negative way. This relates to the value types or domains of *security*, *benevolence*, and *universalism* (from here onwards I will indicate these in italics in parentheses). The weight of this enormous (perceived) responsibility was crushing him and caused him immense mental suffering: in a corresponding way he felt threatened in exactly these domains.

The primary stakeholders, the people who were most closely involved in the clinical decision-making here, were Kieran and his GP, and later on his consultant psychiatrist. Kieran was hardly able to think about anything other than the terrible things he thought he had done, even that with difficulty. As Linda Gask describes during her own depression, 'my mind seemed at last to disintegrate into small sharp-edged monochrome pieces. I was unable to think with any clarity' (Gask, 2015, pp. 170–171). In his spiritual autobiography *Memoir of the Early Life,* William Cowper (1731–1800) provides one of the earliest clear subjective descriptions of madness (Peterson, 1982). Cowper was an English poet and hymnist who suffered recurrent episodes of severe depression. He wrote:

> If it were possible that a heavy blow could light on the brain, without touching the skull, such was the sensation I felt. I clapped my hand to my forehead, and cried aloud through the pain it gave me. At every stroke, my thoughts and expressions became more wild and incoherent; all that remained clear was the sense of sin, and the expectation of punishment.
>
> (cited in Peterson, 1982, p. 65)

The decision to take a psychiatric medication is not an easy one for most people. Kieran had conflicting values in this regard, too. On the one hand, he had respect for the medical profession, and he thought it was important to follow the advice of his doctor (*conformity*). On the other hand, he did not think that he was ill; he thought he was guilty, for which he deserved punishment (*conformity* and *tradition*: accepting one's portion in life). His cousin's poor experience with antidepressants also made him cautious about medication. He felt that he needed protection or refuge (*security*), more than medication. In a way, he did value his own security, but the action this value was driving (search for *protection*) was not getting him the outcome he needed in order to get better.

His psychiatrist, Dr Wiseman, wanted to give Kieran the best evidence-based treatment to get him better from what he had diagnosed as severe psychotic depression. He felt that Kieran was too ill to be able to benefit from formal psychotherapy at this point. He was clearly suffering, and he needed to take medication if he wanted to get better. This was where things started to become complicated. Kieran had sought help via his GP and attended the appointment with the psychiatrist (*security*: maintaining one's own health); true, with a little persuasion from his boss and his wife. Dr Wiseman did not want to force any treatment onto Kieran because he respected his autonomy (*self-direction*) and did not want to compromise their therapeutic relationship (*benevolence*), but he was also aware of the increasing despair of Kieran's wife. Dr Wiseman agreed with Kieran that he would arrange for regular support from the psychiatric nurses of the MDT and a follow-up meeting with himself in two weeks' time. He also insisted upon Kieran and his wife agreeing to contact the team if his presentation changed. He still hoped that the nurses would be able to convince Kieran about taking medication. Even if he had wanted to treat Kieran with medications against his will, he knew that this was not possible under the current legislation. The relevant values of the elected representatives of society are enshrined in relevant parts of the law: the Mental Health Act (MHA – HM Government, 2007) specifies when treatment against the patient's will can be lawfully given (balancing, with *benevolence*, *self-direction* against *security*). Dr Wiseman carried out a risk assessment, looking at the risk to Kieran's health and safety and to the safety of others, and did not think that invoking the MHA (*power*) was necessary.

Kieran's boss and his wife were also involved and their values played a role in what course of action Kieran and his doctors took. His boss did not know Kieran's health-related values very well, but he knew Kieran as a good worker who took pride in doing his job well and was responsible for the safe running of a busy building site (*benevolence* and *security*). He had to make sure that Kieran got help and took some time off until he could safely return to work. Kieran's wife had known her husband for sixteen years and knew that he always looked after his health as well as he could. She was increasingly worried about him, as she felt that his thinking had become irrational, and she did not know what she could do to help him (*benevolence*), as trying to reassure him that he had done nothing wrong did not work at all. She felt that she was unable to appeal to his reason anymore.

Hierarchy of Values

Phenomenological psychopathology describes a loss of feelings that is a source of suffering and a reason to feel guilty (Stanghellini and Mancini, 2017). It is common for severely depressed patients to talk about themselves as being a burden to their loved ones. They do not experience pleasure on contact with their family members or friends and find it difficult to get involved in their lives. They often feel as though their family would be better off without them and attempts to convince them otherwise often feel futile. People in the patient's environment often try to encourage the patient to focus on all the good things in their life, but patients find it difficult to do that when they consider themselves to be completely worthless (Gask, 2015, p. 9). Anything that seems to offer an escape from this situation may become highly valued for the patient in this situation. Care for self-preservation diminishes as a value. In psychotic depression, the patient may believe that they have no body or that it is sick or rotting away. In such a context, values relating to meeting one's physical needs seem less important or even irrelevant. Unsurprisingly, it is often very difficult to persuade severely depressed patients to eat or drink or to maintain adequate hygiene. Explanation about their body's needs often feels fruitless. When the guilt is severe, they may feel that they need to be punished and can regard their depression or any illness they may be suffering from as punishment they deserve. Patients may feel actively suicidal, may not feel motivated to keep themselves safe, or may refuse treatment after a suicide attempt. Their value hierarchy is clearly warped; they feel differently from how they would usually feel about these things; and treatment may feel to them undeserved, inappropriate, or even contrary to their aims.

Although there are certain recognizable patterns, every patient is different and it may be difficult for the clinician to accurately predict the patient's values. This is why it is important for the clinician not to make assumptions but to regularly explore these values. William Styron (2001) describes in *Darkness Visible* the story of his own depressive illness, how Doctor Gold warned him about the possibility of impotence as a side effect of the antidepressant medication he was starting, after which Styron, who was feeling like a 'juiceless and ravaged semi-invalid', started to wonder if the doctor lacked any perspicacity.

At that point, looking after his diabetes (*security*) had very low priority for Kieran for a number of reasons. First, he thought that he was guilty of causing the loss of many lives and that he needed to be punished. He was convinced that he would die in a similar vein to how William Cowper described his feelings: 'No convicted criminal ever feared death more, or was more assured of dying' (cited in Peterson, 1982, p. 68). Second, he was preoccupied with saving people from Covid.

Not only had he by this stage lost his mental capacity to decide about whether to stay on the ward but he was also indicating that he wanted to leave. At this point, it would not have been possible to treat him safely in the community. The use of the MHA here also functioned as a safeguard to protect his liberty. Without it, Kieran would have had no formal recourse to appeal against being kept on the ward; that decision would have depended primarily on his consultant. This use of the Act reflected society's value of individual autonomy (*self-direction*). Although it removed the decisions from the primary stakeholders (if Kieran were to appeal, his case would be decided by a mental health

Box 11.2 Kieran, Part 2

Kieran was increasingly neglecting his own self-care. Dr Wiseman found out that Kieran used to take pride in his neat appearance but now he had stopped showering and changed his clothes only with a lot of encouragement. He started to say that his bowels were not working and he did not need to eat. He began to lose weight and his wife asked for him to be admitted to hospital, to which he agreed. This was further complicated by the fact that Kieran had diabetes. Although he knew he had to eat a regular diet, he often skipped meals, and when the nurses on the ward tried to encourage him to eat, he said he was not hungry.

Fortunately, Kieran accepted the antidepressant medication that was offered to him on the ward and shortly after that an anti-psychotic medication too, even though he thought that they were unlikely to help him, as his sin was unforgiveable and he would die. He felt that his life was completely doomed and he was convinced that he was never going to get better. In this context, the possibility of getting some side effects seemed much less important or relevant to him. He also felt relieved that people had stopped nagging him about medication.

When his wife, who was desperate for him to get better but struggled to motivate him to keep his diabetic diet and to take his diabetic medication, eventually admonished him about not looking after his diabetes, he started to say that he was only a burden on his family. She told him that she and their children needed him, but he felt that he was not a good husband or a good father to the children and that they would all be better off without him.

Kieran spent almost all of his time thinking about ways to save people from dying with Covid. Although he was not sure how he could achieve that, he felt that being on the ward was stopping him from doing it. After an assessment by a psychiatrist from a different team, his GP, and an approved mental health professional (AMHP) who was a social worker, he was detained to hospital under section 2 of the MHA, that is, he could not leave the hospital without authorization from his consultant.

tribunal, and not by him and his psychiatrist), it was a step in the right direction in terms of following a good process, reducing the arbitrariness of individual stakeholders, and drawing on the collective wisdom and sense of rightfulness of the wider community of the patient. It is also possible to appeal against the decision of the tribunal if an error on the point of law is suspected. His wife felt relieved as she had been worrying that Kieran's request to leave the ward might be granted and she would be unable to look after him and keep him safe at home. Her admonishment of him about his diabetic diet was motivated by her concern for his health (*security*) and her love for him (*benevolence*), and in the past when he was not depressed it worked, but on this occasion it seemed to backfire. Dr Wiseman also felt relieved as he felt that in this case his personal professional intuition of what would feel right happened to concur with the course of action dictated by the letter of the law. It is much more challenging for clinicians when that is not the case, especially if there is dissensus among the main stakeholders.

Kieran's value priorities, especially his wish to save people from Covid and to accept his punishment for having caused the pandemic in the first place (*benevolence*, *conformity*, *tradition*, and *universalism*), were clearly at odds with not just those of his psychiatrist but also those of others in his social environment, including his wife and his boss. If he had been allowed to act on his values at the time, he would not have got better and might even have died. In this case, the healthcare system had in place appropriate safeguards, including clinical governance and the MHA, to facilitate a good process. However, the law does not provide for every situation, and involving higher-level stakeholders can be more complicated than in Kieran's case (see Chapter 4).

Only discussing the facts of the situation and then deciding to invoke the MHA would have been callous and denying Kieran the dignity that we all deserve, whether we are in good health mentally or not. Carefully mapping the values involved in this case and discussing them with Kieran to the extent where he was able to participate in the discussion was the more humane and ethical approach that respected Kieran's agency. This reduced the traumatizing effect on him of his illness and the treatment for it. Clarifying all the values at play in the case also helped Dr Wiseman: he was able to practise medicine without significant moral injury.

Temporality

In depression, there seem to be four stages in terms of how the patient's values change: (1) getting ill, (2) the height of their illness, (3) recovery, and (4) post-recovery. Each stage has its own characteristics. During each stage, old values may become less important or disappear and new values may present. The hierarchy among them may also change in important ways. The patient (and thereby those around them) may have reduced access to these values owing to a variety of factors, such as extremes of low mood, restricted affect, difficulty concentrating, delusions of guilt or of a nihilistic or paranoid nature, or psychomotor retardation or agitation. This is why patients are usually advised not to make important decisions before they have recovered fully from their illness.

When they first seek help, patients may find it very difficult to articulate exactly what the problem is: 'They may not have yet matched words to the feelings they can sense in the hidden rooms of their mind' (Gask, 2015, p. 15). The present does not weave into the future, and the past is dominant – and anything offering escape from this situation may become valued. As the patient is recovering from depression, their experience of time changes; negative things start to seem not just less significant but also less immutable, and more positive action-possibilities start to appear more plausible. Linda Gask gives a vivid description of the recovery process: 'The terrible weight seemed considerably lighter and, while I could still sense its presence in the wings of my mind, something else was preventing it from taking centre stage: the sound of the birds, the smell of the grass and the brightness of the daylight. The world was singing to me. Life had returned' (Gask, 2015, pp. 181–182). William Cowper wrote: '[T]his change of sentiment gathered ground continually; yet my mind was in such a fluctuating state that I can only call it a vague presage of better things at hand, without being able to assign a reason for it' (cited in Peterson, 1982, pp. 70–71). Cowper's recovery from this episode of illness continued and he felt very happy and did not want to lose any time in slumber. The response of his doctor to this reminds us of this fairly common clinical concern: 'My physician, ever watchful and apprehensive for my welfare, was now alarmed, lest the sudden transition from despair to joy should terminate in a fatal frenzy' (cited in Peterson, 1982, p. 73). Fortunately, these concerns were unfounded.

The change in the value system of the patient brings about the opportunity for them to change their life narrative. Their social environment, including the professionals involved in their care, can facilitate (or sometimes hinder) this. Life history in this context is surprisingly *not* static: it changes over time as it is shared and retold (Gask, 2015, p. 15). Gask draws attention to how important it is to remain aware during this process that 'our vulnerability to depression does not mean that we are weak or lesser human beings in any way. This is sometimes difficult to remember but it is crucial to our survival' (Gask, 2015, p. 27).

Box 11.3 Kieran, Part 3

As Kieran was getting better, he became gradually less convinced about his role in the Covid pandemic. First, he said that he had not caused all of it, just contributed to it by passing on the infection to countless victims. As the days went on, his story changed, and it transpired that he had not been testing himself regularly and had only had a test done in a walk-in centre after he had started to feel really ill. The test was positive, and he felt extremely guilty because he had visited his elderly mother two days prior to that. Fortunately, she did not become ill, but he was very worried for several days as she suffers from advanced chronic obstructive pulmonary disease (COPD) and is on inhalers, so catching the illness at that stage could have been fatal for her.

Kieran stopped talking about the police coming to punish him and, when he was directly asked about this, he said that he'd never thought that would really happen. The nurses noticed that his eating improved and he was paying more attention to his diabetic diet. When the doctor asked him about this, he said that he had to be careful with his eating because he had diabetes and certain foods could make that worse. He wanted to stay as healthy as possible because he wanted to be there for his wife and his sons.

There was a palpable change in Kieran's values. It was a gradual change over weeks. Having mapped all the values of the stakeholders involved in the case, Dr Wiseman was able to sense any changes in the communal landscape of values. One could ask, 'But how did this help him make better decisions?' First, it made it possible for him to reason about values with more clarity, as they had been made explicit. Sometimes we are able to say only that we have done something in a certain way because it felt right that way, but in most cases of complex decision-making we would be left feeling that is not satisfactory. Being able to label values, identify their origins, examine their place in the hierarchy of other values of the same person, and compare this value structure with those of other stakeholders opens up new possibilities. Values are dynamic and maintaining an up-to-date version of the value map is particularly helpful when negotiating various treatment options. Second, when people have been involved in the process of making a certain decision, they will own it much more. This is not immaterial, as owned decisions are built into our personal narrative in a different way from those that have been imposed on us. This is particularly important in the context of mental illness where patients feel even more vulnerable and at the whim of others than in the case of most physical illnesses. In mental illness, others can call into question our mental capacity to make decisions for ourselves (or deem that we lack it), treat us against our will (sometimes even using physical force to do so), and deprive us of our liberty, for example by admitting and keeping us in hospital against our will.

The Values of Other Stakeholders

The patient's family and friends are often at a loss as to how to best support the patient towards recovery, which can be excruciatingly painful for them. This can be even worse if they also feel guilty about the patient's illness. Their needs, concerns, and preferences relate to security, hedonism, achievement, and self-direction in terms of value types. Normally, they would like their loved one to be well looked after in terms of their physical and mental health needs and to be kept safe from self-harm and self-neglect. They would like them to enjoy their life again and to return to their independent and capable self. In chronic depression, these concerns and preferences are slightly different, but those involved in the life of the patient would generally like the patient to have an exciting and varied life again. Regarding their values relating to themselves, they would like to be loving and supportive towards the patient but also to ensure that they themselves and their other family members continue to thrive.

No man is an island entire of itself. Psychiatrists work in a complex social environment. Professional organizations oversee their training, set their curricula and examinations to pass, and publish guidance for them, and thereby inculcate their values. Psychiatrists are medical doctors and their work is regulated and regularly appraised. Most of them work in an MDT and in the UK most MDTs are part of a mental health trust within the NHS. All of these groups and organizations have their relevant values. Most patients in the UK are seen by the NHS. The NHS Constitution lists six values that all staff are expected to demonstrate: working together for patients; respect and dignity; commitment to quality of care (safety, effectiveness, and patient experience); compassion (humanity and kindness); improving lives; and inclusiveness ('everybody counts') (NHS, n.d.). Respect and dignity includes valuing people as individuals, respecting their aspirations and commitments in life, and seeking to understand their priorities, needs, and abilities.

The values of the Royal College of Psychiatrists are summarized in *Core Values for Psychiatry* (Richards and Lloyd, 2017), a College document written by Veryan Richards, Patient Representative of the College and Keith Lloyd, Chair of the Royal College of Psychiatrists in Wales. Among other sources, it draws on VBP principles. The eight core values it lists are respect, trust, communication, dignity, empathy, fairness, honesty, and humility. One of the stated aims of this document is to '[provide] a basis for a skills-based approach to decision-making where complex and conflicting values are involved, and [serve] as a reference point and as a measuring tool for evaluating practice. It underpins the therapeutic relationship between the patient and the doctor, which in turn influences the quality of recovery' (Richards and Lloyd, 2017, p. 2).

All these stakeholders are influenced by the values of society as a whole, which come through via media coverage of mental illness and its treatment, blogs and vlogs about the subjects by members of the public, and depictions by artists, literature, films, and theatre.

Further Thoughts on Working with Depressed Patients' Values

People want to know the values of those they are in a relationship with. The therapeutic relationship is no different. When the therapist appears to be non-judgemental, the patient may feel that they are just withholding their criticism and may try to provoke the therapist to reveal their values (Horowitz, 2014). A very real risk at this stage is that if their values are too far apart, the patient may not persevere with the treatment (Vervaeke et al., 1997). However, if the therapist maintains equidistance between the sides of self of the patient regarding the patient's internal conflict, rather than value neutrality, and maintains their positive regard for the patient, the possibility of a new relational experience and a stronger therapeutic alliance arises (Horowitz, 2014, p. 677): 'the therapist is not neutral in terms of not taking any ethical position so as not to impose the therapist's values[;] instead, the therapist addresses the patient's latent and active ethics but does not him- or herself side with any particular value attitude, when there are contradictions'.

Many patients are frightened of how the therapist might judge their actions, real or fantasized (Horowitz, 2014). Asking them what they think the therapist might think of these is a good way to start exploring the similarities and differences between the values of the dyad. Apart from improving the therapeutic alliance, verbalizing these values helps to understand where these attitudes have come from and to examine the rationality of them. Conscious reflection and empathy may help the patient change their feelings and narrative about the persons and situations that contributed to the development of their values, which often act as a harsh and uncaring inner critic.

Returning to the fact that values are handled cognitively but also involve emotions, we can see that this is doubly problematic in depression because in depression both cognition and emotions are disturbed. As the depressed person is getting better from their depression, these cognitive and emotional disturbances gradually improve. This poses another challenge for us. How can we tell where exactly the person is in terms of their gradual return to their 'normal' values, that is, their values when they are not ill? This has strong relevance to the legal concept of mental capacity to make decisions, including treatment decisions. It is also possible that their illness will change their value system in a permanent fashion, meaning that they have different values post-recovery. Even so, a precise knowledge of the patient's values is essential. We need to differentiate, as much as this is possible, what is psychopathology and what their genuine values are, proper to the person, not the illness. This is an important distinction because, in practice, unusual choices are all too often attributed to one's mental illness. Yet another challenge is when the patient is chronically depressed and important treatment decisions need to be made.

Earlier, I mentioned that clinical value-mapping can help us tolerate dissensus better. Doctors do not like *dis*sensus and many aspects of clinical governance aim at identifying the single best solution and decision-making by *con*sensus. This chimes well with the natural scientific approach. Clinical value-mapping enables us to get to know the position of the other stakeholders. It encourages us to put ourselves in their shoes and to examine various action-possibilities from their perspectives. What may never even enter our minds as a potential solution may seem entirely plausible from their standpoint. The different stakeholders may also see the potential consequences of a particular solution differently. Only when all the relevant viewpoints have been given a fair hearing can the process truly qualify as shared decision-making. Appropriately involving the higher-level stakeholders can also help to share the responsibility, which can help the primary stakeholders to function at their optimum level even in high-pressure situations.

References

Andrews, A. B. 2006. *Social History Assessment.* Thousand Oaks, CA: SAGE.

Bruner, E. M. 1984. Introduction: The opening up of anthropology. In Bruner, E. M. (ed.), *Text, Play, and Story: The Construction and Reconstruction of Self and Society.* Washington, DC: American Ethnological Society, pp. 1–16.

Charland, L. C. & Zachar, P. 2008. *Fact and Value in Emotion.* Amsterdam: John Benjamins.

Chen, E. 2020. Recovering the Context in Psychopathology. In Marková, I. S. & Chen, E. (ed.), *Rethinking Psychopathology.* Cham: Springer, pp. 65–72.

Dudas, R. B. 2022. Values-based practice: How can history taking help psychiatrists explore the values involved in clinical decision-making? *British Journal of Psychiatry Advances*, 28, 153–162.

Fazel, H. 2012. Exploring the influence of social threat and value reinforcement on emotional reactions to value transgressions. Unpublished PhD thesis, University of Manitoba.

Fernandez, A. V. & Wieten, S. 2015. Values-based practice and phenomenological psychopathology: Implications of existential changes in depression. *Journal of Evaluation in Clinical Practice*, 21, 508–513.

Friedrich, M. J. 2017. Depression is the leading cause of disability around the world. *Journal of the American Medical Association*, 317, 1517.

Gask, L. 2015. *The Other Side of Silence: A Psychiatrist's Memoir of Depression*. Chichester: Vie Books.

Haan, S. D. 2020. *Enactive Psychiatry*. Cambridge : Cambridge University Press.

Hersch, E. L. 2008. A phenomenologist's view of the omnipresence of the evaluative in human experience. In Charland, L. C. & Zachar, P. (eds.), *Fact and Value in Emotion*. Amsterdam: John Benjamins, pp. 193–209.

HM Government 2007. Mental Health Act 2007, c. 12. London: National Archives. www.legislation.gov.uk/ukpga/2007/12/contents.

Horowitz, M. J. 2014. Clarifying values in psychotherapy. *Psychodynamic Psychiatry*, 42, 671–679.

Maiese, M. 2021. An enactivist reconceptualization of the medical model. *Philosophical Psychology*, 34, 962–988.

Mattingly, C. 1991. The narrative nature of clinical reasoning. *American Journal Occupational Therapy*, 45, 998–1005.

National Health Service (NHS) n.d. The NHS values [the six values of the NHS Constitution]. www.healthcareers.nhs.uk/working-health/working-nhs/nhs-constitution.

Peterson, D. (ed.) 1982. *A Mad People's History of Madness*. Pittsburgh, PA: University of Pittsburgh Press.

Richards, V. & Lloyd, K. 2017. *Core Values for Psychiatrists*. College Report CR204. London: Royal College of Psychiatrists. https://shorturl.at/78V2q.

Rokeach, M. 1973. *The Nature of Human Values*. New York: Free Press.

Schwartz, S. H. 1992. Universals in the content and structure of values: Theoretical advances and empirical tests in 20 countries. *Advances in Experimental Social Psychology*, 25, 1–65.

Stanghellini, G. & Mancini, M. 2017. *The Therapeutic Interview in Mental Health: A Values-Based and Person-Centered Approach*. Cambridge: Cambridge University Press.

Styron, W. 2001. *Darkness Visible: A Memoir of Madness*. London: Vintage.

Vervaeke, G. A. C., Vertommen, H. & Storms, G. 1997. Client and therapist values in relation to drop-out. *Clinical Psychology and Psychotherapy*, 4, 1–6.

Chapter 12

Dementia

More Than Just Memory

Tom Dening and Malarvizhi Babu Sandilyan

Introduction

Dementia is a collective term used to describe the effects of a range of disorders of the brain. It is a syndrome where one or more cognitive impairments, often with other symptoms, become severe enough to interfere with an individual's social and occupational functioning. The commonest cause of dementia is Alzheimer's disease, and other relatively common forms of dementia are vascular dementia, dementia with Lewy bodies, frontotemporal dementia, and dementia associated with neurological conditions (notably Parkinson's disease dementia). The prevalence and incidence of dementia increase exponentially with ageing, at least until about age ninety. However, not everyone with dementia is old – about 5% of cases present before the age of sixty-five and, rarely, cases may have their onset as early as thirty to forty years old.

Dementia is increasingly common in ageing populations across the world. Currently, it is estimated that there are 55 million people living with dementia globally, a figure set to increase to 139 million by 2050. Someone develops dementia every three seconds and the current annual cost of dementia is estimated at US$1.3trillion, a figure set to double by 2030 (Alzheimer's Disease International, 2024). Corresponding figures for the UK were an estimated total of 850,000 people in 2015 with an associated annual cost of £26 billion (Prince et al., 2014).

From the point of view of this book about values in clinical practice, dementia has several distinct features. First and foremost, dementia is generally a progressive condition. Cognitive and other impairments tend to worsen over time, so that eventually *a person may lose the ability to express their values* and may lose the mental capacity to make informed decisions about aspects of their life, including care and treatment. As a result, other people (most typically family members) are increasingly drawn into providing care and supporting a person with dementia. However, the complexities of health and social care are such that there are potentially *multiple stakeholders involved*, especially if the person with severe dementia has multiple care needs (see Box 12.1). Therefore, in dementia, the simple dyad of a doctor and a patient is uncommon, so considering values in dementia must encompass the possible impact of the values of all stakeholders.

A second feature of interest also relates to the progression of dementia over time. *It is possible that the person's values may change*, for various reasons. Simply the experience of having dementia and living with a diagnosis is likely to affect a person's world view. It may change some of the things that they prefer or that they aspire to do in the future; the changing pattern of their involvement with other people may also affect what matters most to them. An example is that a person newly diagnosed with dementia may choose to draw up an advanced care plan or establish a lasting power of attorney. It should also be considered

Box 12.1 Potential stakeholders in a case of dementia

This list is not exhaustive, but they include:

- the person living with the diagnosis
- family:
  - spouse or partner
  - children, including stepchildren – these may be middle-aged adult children, but they can also be young, e.g. school-aged
  - grandchildren
  - parents – e.g. in young-onset dementia or Down's syndrome dementia
  - ex-spouses and partners
  - other relatives – e.g. siblings, in-laws, etc.
- social contacts:
  - friends
  - neighbours
  - colleagues in paid employment or voluntary jobs
  - social media contacts – e.g. Facebook, WhatsApp, LinkedIn
  - personal and domestic help – e.g. hairdressers, gardeners, cleaners
  - other social contacts – e.g. community centres, faith groups, social clubs, shared interests
- health professionals:
  - medical – doctor/GP; specialists, e.g. for psychiatry, geriatric medicine, and other co-morbid conditions
  - nurses –in primary care/doctors' surgeries, hospitals, and nursing homes; modern matrons, community psychiatric nurses, Admiral nurses
  - other – occupational therapists, speech and language therapists, physiotherapists, psychologists, health care assistants, chiropodists
  - health services managers and commissioners
- social care:
  - social workers, safeguarding professionals, independent advocates, domiciliary care workers, staff in residential and nursing homes
- formal/legal:
  - police, banks, solicitors, DVLA, Court of Protection, patient advocates
- other:
  - voluntary organizations supporting older people or people with memory problems, e.g. Alzheimer's Society, Age UK, etc.

that the condition causing their dementia may have direct effects on their brain that also bring about changes in what the person seems to value. An example of this would be changes in eating behaviour that are often seen in frontotemporal dementia, where sudden cravings for sweet foods may arise, or even the ingestion of non-food items. Similarly, apathy and blunting of affect often occur in various forms of dementia, though it is a moot point whether this type of indifference represents changes in values or whether it is solely a change of behaviour. The point being made here is that for the person with dementia *their values may be at least in part organically driven as well as having social origins.*

A third important topic concerns two *significant recent shifts in how dementia is conceptualized.* The first of these is a change in the perception of the diseases, especially Alzheimer's disease, that cause dementia. With longitudinal studies and the emergence of biomarkers, it is clear that the antecedents of Alzheimer's disease lie many years before the onset of significant cognitive impairment and the clinical syndrome of dementia. This leads to a view that these disorders are long-term neurobiological entities, and therefore that it is the neurobiological changes that constitute the disease, not the clinical features (Jack et al., 2018). The second major change has been the move from a predominantly medical, cognitive deficit–based approach to person- or relationship-centred care, as introduced by Kitwood (1997) and refined by others, including Brooker and Latham (2016), Keady and Nolan (2021), and Nolan et al. (2004).

This chapter outlines some of the main features of dementia and then discusses the application of values-based medicine (VBM). We have approached this by considering some scenarios (illustrated by fictional case vignettes) of important issues that may arise during the course of the dementia journey. We have attempted to be illustrative rather than comprehensive and selected three topics from four different points along the way, as summarized in Table 12.1. Among other things, we wish to show that dementia is richer and more complex than simply being a memory disorder. Having said that, we begin with the problem of forgetting, as that is the commonest early manifestation of dementia.

Table 12.1 Issues discussed in this chapter

Theme	Issue
Early dementia	Forgetting
	How diagnosis happens
	Young-onset dementia
Changes in behaviour	Wandering
	Hoarding
	Self-identity
Legal and ethical	Driving
	Finances and wills
	Participating in research
Advanced dementia and care	Care at home – at any cost?
	Intimacy in care homes
	End-of-life care

Early Dementia

Forgetting

Why do we worry so much about memory and forgetting in relation to dementia? There are perhaps two main underlying reasons. One is that memory is an essential component of the current predominant mind model, that of the brain as a computer, notwithstanding that this metaphor has been much criticized (Cobb, 2020). The other is that memory is relatively easy to test. More accurately, it is deceptively easy, since the relationship of simple clinic-based tests to day-to-day functioning (ecological validity) is questionable (e.g. Dubreuil et al., 2007; Kumfor et al., 2014).

Box 12.2 Colin

Colin is seventy-eight and for more than a year has been increasingly forgetful. He can never find his spectacles; he mislays door and car keys; and he can't remember what he is supposed to buy at the supermarket. When things go missing, he gets very irritated and blames his wife. Doreen is generally tolerant, although she doesn't like being shouted at. Their daughter Tracey is growing increasingly concerned as she thinks that his memory is worse each time she visits. Colin doesn't think that there is a problem at all; Doreen ascribes it all to his age; and Tracey thinks her that father is getting Alzheimer's disease.

After much family debate, Colin goes to see his doctor. He is accompanied by Doreen and Tracey. The values and expectations that they bring with them are somewhat different. Colin expects that the doctor will tell him that he is fine and that nothing will ensue. Doreen is anxious that Colin will get defensive and not tell the truth to the doctor. Tracey thinks that her father needs to get his dementia seen to, whatever that may mean.

The doctor will also bring a set of values to the consultation. First and foremost, she needs to be attentive to what Colin (the patient) and his family say, whilst also responding to the different perspectives being expressed. Doing this follows both the 'patient-perspective' and the 'multi-perspective' principles of VBM. Part of her role is to introduce the scientific framework that is relevant to memory impairment and dementia (the 'science-driven' principle) and then to achieve some degree of consensus regarding the problem and the way forward, which is likely to be referral to the memory service. In order to help Colin realize that this would be a good idea, she needs to draw on her communication skills, with careful choice of language, and to use her own ethical reasoning to justify why the outcome should be a referral that Colin would probably not have wanted initially.

If VBM is successful here, then all four protagonists will emerge relatively content from the consultation. Colin feels that he has been taken seriously and that nothing terrible has happened to him. Doreen is relieved that he didn't blow up with the doctor or with her. Tracey is satisfied that action is being taken. The doctor considers that the outcome is scientifically appropriate and that access to a diagnosis will benefit the patient and the family in the longer term.

How Diagnosis Happens

The commonest route to diagnosis in the UK is through memory assessment services. A person notices a problem with their memory and consults their doctor (primary care physician), who refers them to a specialist service for assessment. Maybe, more often, it is not the person with the memory impairment who is concerned but someone close to them.

The individual (we will refer to them as the patient at this point) may be seen at a hospital clinic or, under some circumstances, at home by a nurse with special training in undertaking memory assessments, or by a doctor, sometimes by other professionals, too. The memory service is usually part of the local older people's mental health services, though this can vary.

The assessment consists, first, of history-taking, with a contribution from someone who knows the patient well to corroborate times and dates, and particular reference to medical history and medication alongside enquiry about the current problem, followed by mental state examination, including cognitive testing. The favoured cognitive assessment has changed over the years, though the Montreal Cognitive Assessment (MoCA; Nasreddine et al., 2005) and the Addenbrooke's Cognitive Examination (Mathuranath et al., 2000; Mioshi et al., 2006) are popular. Investigations performed include routine blood tests and neuroimaging, either computed tomography (CT) or magnetic resonance imaging (MRI).

After this, the relevant information is brought together to make a diagnosis, which is usually imparted to the patient and/or their family at the same or a subsequent appointment. There is a wide literature on communicating the diagnosis of dementia. Patients are not always informed that they have dementia (Low et al., 2018) or they receive a euphemism such as 'memory problem' or the patient may not even want to know the diagnosis.

Box 12.3 Mirza

Mirza is a Pakistani lady who is referred to the memory clinic. The doctor assessing her concludes that she has dementia. He attempts to explain the diagnosis to the patient and her family, armed with evidence-based scientific knowledge, only to be told by the patient that she does not wish to know her diagnosis. This may seem at face value that Mirza is rejecting her rights to know her diagnosis and to be treated with evidence-based medicine (EBM). However, the doctor understands that she grew up in a rural part of Pakistan where she had led her life not embracing modern medicine but with a preference for natural remedies. Mirza is exercising her autonomy by choosing her right 'not to know' and it is important that the doctor considers this along with other values in parallel. Her family wishes to know if the children will also develop dementia and seeks advice on a further course of action. It is worth bearing in mind that this right not to know – or medical ignorance itself – has been contested (Davies, 2020), particularly when it involves genetic information or harm to others.

In this situation, there is an interplay of values that could possibly be in conflict – those of the patient, shaped by her cultural beliefs; those of her family, founded by anxiety around diagnostic implications; those of the doctor, who is trying to apply evidence-based treatment methods. Using the 'two-feet principle' (Fulford, 2004) that all decisions are based on both values and evidence, the doctor offers Mirza cognitive-stimulation therapy but not cognition-enhancing drugs. He talks to the family members and addresses their queries around likely genetic susceptibility to developing dementia, alleviating their fears by drawing on his clinical knowledge and existing literature evidence.

At the time of diagnosis, there is an opportunity for questions to be asked, and for certain issues to be discussed, including prognosis, what to do about financial and other practical matters such as driving, and sources of support and further information about dementia. Here, EBM and VBM complement each other and enable the clinician to influence the outcomes by following the right process. The role of collaborating and establishing a partnership with all parties concerned – who may hold conflicting ideas – is vital in this process and pivotal to the values-based approach. This approach has been successfully incorporated into several training manuals, for example *Whose Values?* for front-line workers in mental health and social care (Woodbridge and Fulford, 2004).

People with dementia may present with other symptoms apart from memory loss, especially if they have non-Alzheimer forms of dementia, such as frontotemporal dementia (Warren et al., 2013), or if they present during the later stages of the condition. Alternatively, patients may receive a diagnosis of dementia for the first time when they are admitted to hospital with a co-morbid physical condition. Following a policy initiative, it appears that the recording of dementia diagnoses in general hospitals has improved in the last decade (Sommerlad et al., 2018).

Dementia in Young People

Young-onset dementia is described as dementia occurring in people under the age of sixty-five. It is estimated that this is 5% of all people with dementia, an estimated 3.9 million worldwide (Hendriks et al., 2021). Alzheimer's disease tends to be the commonest cause of dementia in young people, followed by vascular dementia and frontotemporal lobe dementia, with increased genetic preponderance in the family to develop the condition. The social and psychological stress on patients with young-onset dementia and their families is well recognized. The loss of independence, the unemployment, and the changes to their role within society and relationships can be challenging in these settings. High levels of anxiety and depression have been noted among carers of people with young-onset dementia (Lim et al., 2018).

Box 12.4 Martin

Martin is fifty years old and works as a production engineer. He lives with his wife Jane, who works as a teacher, and they have one daughter who has just started a new job and a son who is in the middle of his university studies. Martin's employer has referred him to the occupational health team as he appeared to be struggling with his work, especially since they computerized the system and he needed to adapt to new ways of working. The occupational health doctor does some preliminary tests and finds that Martin has difficulties in sustaining attention and carrying out some executive functions such as holding information in his short-term memory, planning his activities, maintaining attention during tasks, and switching between tasks. The doctor suggests to Martin that he requires full cognitive testing to investigate this further. Martin goes home and discusses his situation with his wife; the couple are obviously worried about the outcome of the appointment and the consequences if he gets diagnosed with dementia. Jane is also worried about the implications for her and how it will affect her job if she is required to take on a caring role for Martin. The couple discuss the financial strain they will be under if Martin's employer no longer requires him to work. They are wondering if they should get their children tested too, because, if Martin has dementia, they would like to know the possibility of the condition being inherited.

In this situation, the memory clinic doctor is in a unique situation not only to focus on the clinical (scientific) aspects of Martin's condition and get the relevant tests done, towards clarifying a diagnosis, but also to pay attention to other values that the family will be bringing into the picture. It becomes essential that the doctor takes on board the different sets of points that will be raised based on Martin and Jane's personal values (e.g. financial security, role reversal with Martin going from being the main provider to a receiver of care), societal values (e.g. employment laws governing safety in the workplace for people with dementia), scientific values (e.g. investigations, treatment options, genetic testing), and organizational values (e.g. the services available within that healthcare setting for young people with dementia and any relevant constraints, social services and what they offer in the area).

When taking a purely scientific approach in dementia assessment, it is easy to focus mainly on the brain functions and ignore the values that are important to the patient. This is where VBM becomes pertinent and enables the doctor to look at the broader picture from all perspectives. Historically, there has been a lack of literature on what people with dementia consider to be valuable to them; it is often represented by proxy reports from their carers or professionals, who tend to project their own experiences onto the person with dementia (Alzheimer's Society, 2010). However, more recently we see emerging qualitative research where collective views of people with dementia are being published (Pratt and Wilkinson, 2001; Williamson, 2008). This is a welcome trend towards placing importance on the values held by people with dementia and their carers. Being aware of and knowledgeable about what is important from the point of view of those affected with dementia is a key part of value-based practice: it supports better-quality care in these sensitive situations and puts the person affected with dementia at the centre.

Changes in Behaviour

Walking About

Walking aimlessly (wandering) is a common occurrence in dementia. Though it is often combined with agitated behaviour, it can be of therapeutic benefit to the person, providing physical exercise. Nevertheless, it is also associated with increase in carer burden and higher levels of anxiety for the families who worry about the potential harm their loved ones may run into (Cipriani et al., 2014). The wandering behaviour is often perceived as 'risky' in healthcare settings, implying that the behaviour is associated with vulnerability to harm, and is something that should be avoided or managed. Applying the principles of VBM to the process of risk management involves the collaboration of all the stakeholders who might hold competing conceptualizations of the risk and differing ideas as to how to manage it.

Box 12.5 Maureen

Maureen has dementia and has been living with her husband, Brian, in a retirement complex. As her condition has progressed, she increasingly forgets her way around and has been known to walk out of her home and get lost in the neighbourhood. There have been incidents where she has been brought back by the police, having been found on the main roads nearby. The memory clinic nurse comes to know about this situation and suggests to Brian that Maureen will be safer in a residential home under supervision. She is concerned that Maureen will come to harm by an accident on the busy main road nearby. Brian gets upset at the idea of a care home, as he had promised his wife that he would look after her till the end of her life. The nurse then calls for a multidisciplinary meeting to address the situation.

The situation is complex but also value-laden, and it is important to bring together all of the concerned parties and to listen to and acknowledge their views. All stakeholders must be mindful to balance Maureen's right to independence (patient perspective) with strategies to minimize harm to her. Brian, being both her carer and her husband, wishes them to remain together and he is anxious that she may be moved out of their family home. He holds the traditional husband–wife relationship dearly and feels that he cannot let down his wife. The nurse holds her organizational values related to risk management and feels duty-bound to protect Maureen from harm (beneficence). This is an opportunity to explore all of these potentially conflicting values from a multi-professional perspective, a process which VBM would facilitate.

Values-based practice advocates for collaboration and communication among all parties, to which the multidisciplinary approach lends itself. By acknowledging and respecting each person's wishes, preferences, and values, potential avenues and courses of action can be explored. The nurse can explain about assistive technology devices that may benefit Maureen and offer psychological strategies with which to analyse her walking behaviour, so that Brian can manage it better. She can explain how a care home can supervise Maureen and keep her safe from harm. Brian can relate the importance to him of being a husband and a carer to Maureen and what meaning it adds to his own life. Maureen can express her wishes to stay in her own home and remain closer to her husband. The point here is that they may not arrive at an imminent solution after the discussion, but the process will enable everyone's values to be considered and encourage a collaborative approach that underpins VBM. A combined systematic review and qualitative research (Robinson et al., 2007) into managing wandering behaviour in dementia, which involves seeking the various viewpoints of the stakeholders (formal caregivers, health professionals, patients, and family), also echoes the dilemmas involved in balancing patient autonomy with harm prevention and lobbies for capturing the differing perspectives and negotiating risk management strategies.

Hoarding

Hoarding is characterized by a person collecting a large number of things in their living areas to the extent where it starts to impede the person's functioning and ability to carry out activities of daily living. In fact, the Diagnostic and Statistical Manual of Mental Disorders – 5th Edition (American Psychiatric Association, 2013) has included hoarding as a specific disorder, and outlines the relevant criteria that are to be met for diagnostic purposes. Hoarding is also a behavioural symptom that occurs in dementia (Cohen-Mansfield, 2008), caused by a variety of cognitive deficits, in particular in executive functioning (Woody et al., 2014). The condition is associated with serious public health concerns, stress on families, and increased costs to the public (Vickers and Preston, 2014). Even though the possessions are often described in the literature on hoarding as useless or of trivial value, parting with them will cause significant distress to the patient and can create conflict between the values held by the professional and those held by the patient.

Box 12.6 Alan

Alan was diagnosed with Alzheimer's dementia seven years ago, and he lives alone in a council house. His neighbours are concerned that his house is overflowing with old newspapers, magazines, and clothes that he tends to buy from charity shops. They have called the social worker who visits Alan, add finds that the living areas are overfilled with his possessions and unfit for use. She deems the situation to be high-risk in relation to fire hazards and says that Alan must clear the house, which he resents. Alan regards his possessions as being dear to him and refuses to throw any of them away; he feels that he should be allowed to keep his private possessions in his own house.

In this situation, the social worker is concerned for Alan's safety and well-being and for the structural integrity of the house affecting the neighbours. If she were to enforce clearing out the house against Alan's wishes, it would be based purely on facts and evidence of hoarding-related health and environmental hazards. Instead, she applies the principles of VBM and attempts to understand and explore Alan's preferences and choices. She learns that Alan and his wife were keen cyclists and great fans of the Tour de France. She comes to know that he started collecting newspaper cuttings and memorabilia related to this interest, but when he developed dementia he could no longer ascertain which ones were cycling-related and which were not (impaired judgement), which resulted in him keeping everything. She understands the emotional significance behind these items, so she visits him regularly and helps him to sort out the things he wishes to keep and clear the rest.

The case illustrates the VBP principle of raising awareness of people's values in values-based practice. By understanding the emotional attachment that Alan has to his belongings and the cognitive deficits that impaired his decision-making skills and thus prevented him from sorting them out, we can combine evidence with values and approach the situation in a person-centred manner. With skilful communication and negotiation, his needs, wishes, and expectations are explored and matched with the evidence/science and clinical requirements. This enables shared decision-making between the patient and the health professional when there are potential conflicts in values. This approach also mirrors person-centred care in dementia (Kitwood, 1998), a philosophy of meeting a person's needs based on interpersonal relationships.

Self-Identity

The impact of dementia involves a complex interplay of neurological and psychosocial factors that often affect the person's sense of self. The loss of ability to communicate and understand speech, to recognize objects, and to orientate themselves in relation to to time, place, and people changes the person's view of their personhood itself. It goes without saying that all of this has a profound effect on those living with the person; they feel a sense of bereavement at having lost 'the person they once knew'. The previous concept of dementia as eroding the 'sense of self' owing to changing perceptions of the world and decline in cognitive functions (biological model) is now replaced with a sociological model where personhood is considered to be enhanced by social interactions with the person with dementia (Hampson and Morris, 2016). The 'sense of self' is a continuum throughout dementia, and role identities, though they diminish in importance with the progression of the condition, never disappear (Cohen-Mansfield et al., 2006). Therefore, understanding the past and the present self-identities of the person with dementia is crucial to enhance their experiences in healthcare settings.

Box 12.7 Jodie

Jodie has advanced dementia and lives in a sheltered home. She has carers visiting her daily to help her with her meals and personal care. Gradually, her cognitive abilities have declined and she now struggles to recognize her carers. One day, when the carer arrives, Jodie appears distressed and scared. She talks about an old woman living in the house who is trying to get rid of her. She is being reassured temporarily by the carer, but she continues to have moments of confusion that frighten her. The carer then notices that Jodie is catching her own reflection in the mirror and the windows but is unable to recognize her own self. Because of her memory impairment, she has an altered sense of her present self and tends to live in the past. She is unable to recognize the older image of herself in the mirror and feels threatened by this 'intruder' in the house.

If the carer rejects Jodie's notions because she is 'wrong' and 'lacks insight', it will be detrimental to their caring relationship. Person-centred care recommends taking a flexible and responsive approach towards people with dementia, acknowledging their experiences and validating their feelings. The carer instead listens to Jodie and understands that her experience comes from her attempts to make sense of her reality. She engages her with old photographs of Jodie from different years and tries to discuss with her about how she has aged in appearance over the years. People with dementia are said to remember events from their early life better than those events from the recent past and they are able to recall the emotions attached to events better than the actual facts (Klein-Koerkamp et al., 2012). When the carer goes through her old photographs, she is attempting to orientate Jodie back to reality, but also, by discussing the happy events in the photographs, she is triggering the pleasant emotions associated with the older image of Jodie in the pictures. This alleviates Jodie's anxiety and, even though Jodie still gets confused by her own mirror reflection, she is not so distressed anymore. By attempting to engage with Jodie, the carer is able to achieve a partnership with her and find some common ground, which underpins VBM.

Many studies, both quantitative and qualitative, have attempted to evaluate the role of personhood and self-identity in dementia. A systematic review of such literature concluded that almost all of these studies emphasized the preservation of self in all stages of dementia (Cadell and Clare, 2010). Enhancing communication, recognition, acknowledgement, and acceptance of their values around their own self-identity are some of the ways to strengthen the concept of self in people with dementia.

Legal and Ethical

Driving

Values guide actions . . . but because they are everywhere they also often go unnoticed. Values determine how people and organizations operate and are very relevant to the law of the society. Driving is one such aspect of life that is governed by local laws and policies to ensure safety. It is also a complex task that involves several cognitive domains working together efficiently. We see people with dementia develop changes in their cognitive domains that can result in impaired attention, executive function, memory, visuospatial orientation, and so on, all of which are vital to be able to drive safely (Duchek et al., 2003). Older drivers with mild to moderate dementia are more likely to show driving impairment and more likely to be

Box 12.8 George

George meets the doctor at the memory clinic where he is diagnosed with dementia. The doctor discusses the implications of George's cognitive impairment in relation to his ability to perform activities of daily living, including driving. George lives in a village where there is no frequent bus service and his wife doesn't drive. George and his wife are dismayed to learn that he will have to inform the driver and vehicle licensing agency (DVLA) about his new diagnosis; they immediately get concerned that he will have to stop driving. Driving is an essential part of George's independence; it enables him to be connected to the local community and to maintain his social activities. If he stops driving, then his wife is worried that it will put extra pressure on her to do the driving around for day-to-day chores. Clearly, driving is of significant value to George and his wife, who are now apprehensive about informing the authorities for fear that George will lose his driving licence and therefore his independence. The conversation is taking place between them and the doctor, who wants to protect the patient, but they must also look at the bigger picture and consider the overall safety of the public. The doctor explores the driving aspects further in detail, explains to George and his wife how dementia affects driving, and offers advice on alternative transport means. He also explains the legal obligations related to driving and gives suggestions about on-road driving assessment for older people, if George is interested. This ensures that George feels included and is part of the decision-making.

involved in accidents (Chee et al., 2017). Therefore, this is an important topic for discussion with the person with dementia and often not an easy one either!

The doctor has to take into consideration the best interests of the patient and the safety of the public, and must also adhere to his own professional standards. But what if George does not want to stop driving? What if he refuses to inform the DVLA about his diagnosis?

We can see the interplay of different sets of values here – George's equating of driving with social independence, the doctor's professional ethics and his moral duty to protect the public, and George's wife's worry about having to shoulder the burden of driving should the decision to stop driving be imposed on George and about the practicalities of transport for them. The Royal College of Psychiatrists (1996) and the General Medical Council (2017) clarify their expectations of doctors when dealing with such dilemmas, where there may be conflicting interests relating to protecting the patient and the public versus sharing confidential information with third parties such as a DVLA. The doctor must not only use his clinical assessment (of George's cognitive abilities, co-morbid conditions that affect driving, and level of insight into the problem) to advise the patient appropriately; he must also consider his duty to protect the public from dangerous drivers. There is also the issue of confidentiality if the doctor decides to overrule George's wishes and inform the driver and vehicle licensing agency himself about George's condition. Collaborating with the patient and the family and applying VBM is key in this sensitive situation. Depending on the level of cognitive decline, the doctor may advise the patient either to wait for the outcome of DVLA assessment or to stop driving straightaway. This decision may often come abruptly, causing anger and frustration for the patient. The doctor will have to discuss the legal and insurance implications for the patient if the patient chooses not to disclose the diagnosis to the DVLA. The doctor will also likely seek the support of the patient's family or carer in convincing the patient and suggest some practical strategies such as moving the car away to remove that visual cue for driving, and encouraging the use of safer alternative transport options such as taxis, buses, and so on.

There is also the option of referring the patient to an independent driving mobility centre for further assessment. George's wife will require some carer support as she may end up bearing the brunt of his frustration about not being able to drive. Having the patient's doctor as an ally is a valuable strategy as most patients have a long-standing relationship with their doctor and are thus more likely to take their views on board.

This kind of charged decision-making is advocated for by the National Institute for Health and Care Excellence (NICE, 2020) and is a vital aspect of putting VBM into practice, as people feel supported and empowered in the process. In this scenario, different perspectives are brought to the table and various options are explored; it is therefore conducive to person-centred care, where the care and the treatment are tailored to the patient's needs and circumstances.

Financial and Legal

The management of money and property for people living with a diagnosis of dementia also requires consideration of autonomy versus protection. In practice, this is usually determined by assessment of the person's capacity to manage their affairs. In most instances, this assessment is made by those closest to the person, and it is done informally and largely automatically. For example, a carer may decide that their spouse is no longer able to manage their bank account, and will take over, for example by creating a joint account and taking charge of any bank cards and online banking passwords. At a later stage, it may become clear that the person with dementia can no longer manage simple transactions with cash in shops. On other occasions, for more complex matters such as making a will, a formal assessment of capacity may be required.

Usually, matters proceed reasonably smoothly if the carer(s) is/are benignly motivated and there is no major disagreement as to the right course of action. However, under some circumstances, such as family conflict, difficulties can arise. This seems to be commoner when there is a substantial amount of money, property, or valuable items at stake.

Box 12.9 Wendy

Wendy had Alzheimer's disease of moderate severity. She lived alone. She had seven children, who did not get on with each other. Only one daughter, Teresa, lived locally, and was the main support for shopping and keeping the house clean. She would check that Wendy was eating regularly and taking medication. One day, one of the sons, who had not visited his mother for more than five years, turned up from more than 200 miles away and persuaded his mother to sign a lasting power of attorney (LPA) form, with him as the sole attorney. When she discovered this, Teresa was distraught as she felt that this was simply exploitation. She arranged an appointment with a solicitor to draw up a new LPA, and the solicitor thought that it would be prudent to invite an old age psychiatrist to assess Wendy's capacity to make a new LPA and to witness her signature.

The psychiatrist has to make their assessment based more on values than on scientific evidence. The overriding question concerns the patient's perspective: What does Wendy actually want? Would she genuinely prefer Teresa to manage her money? Or does she feel that finances are a man's job? Or maybe, if the son is the oldest child or perhaps even an accountant, she thinks that he is better qualified? Or that Teresa has enough to do for her already? And is she aware of the multiple perspectives in the family and the conflict arising from that?

The psychiatrist must draw deeply upon their values base because the situation has become more complex. There are at least four players already – Wendy, Teresa, a son, and the solicitor – and maybe the other five children will get involved later, too. The psychiatrist's communication skills will be tested because of Wendy's cognitive impairment and also because they will need to approach a sensitive subject with her and the others involved. They will have to understand Wendy's view of the situation and whether she has a consistent grasp on what is happening and what her preferences are. They will have to apply ethical reasoning to support their own clinical decision-making. This may generate ideas about other possible approaches, for example ways of avoiding conflict between Teresa and her brother. Perhaps there is scope for a joint LPA, or perhaps other siblings need to have a voice.

Of course, conflicts within the family are not the only areas where there can be financial and legal difficulties. Some conflicts can arise between the family and the paid carers of the person with dementia.

Box 12.10 Daphne

Daphne had a large collection of valuable porcelain figures. As her dementia progressed, her family employed a married couple to act as live-in carers. When the family visited at times over the next year or so, they noticed that there were fewer and fewer figures on display, and they questioned the carers about this. 'Oh, she gave them to us' was the answer. To the family, however, it looked like theft and the police became involved.

In the medical assessment of Daphne's mental state, the issues were around her capacity to make such valuable gifts. The main values involved were those of patient perspective (autonomy), her family's views about Daphne being exploited, and her carers' position on being scrutinized for the theft of items which they considered to be gifts. Eventually, it was concluded that it was impossible to prove that the items had not been willingly given, but the family was left with a very sour taste in the mouth after the experience.

Box 12.11 Gordon

Gordon, a retired army officer, made ten different wills in the last two years of his life. They alternated between favouring his family, who lived more than 100 miles away, and favouring Doreen, his resident carer. His solicitor, anticipating trouble in the event of Gordon's death, prudently made audio recordings of some of his later interviews with his client. When Gordon died, huge arguments ensued over the will and the family went to court to argue that he had lacked the capacity to make the will that favoured Doreen; the family insisted that she had influenced him improperly and tried to turn him against them. Doreen, in turn, claimed that the family had visited infrequently and that, when they did come, they had been hostile to her and had overlooked her good relationship with Gordon and the good care she had provided.

For the old age psychiatrist called as an expert witness, this was a serious clash of perspectives. The solution seemed to lie in recognizing the values of the conflicting parties, explaining to each side that Gordon had been unable to see the full picture at any one time. The psychiatrist suggested that when Gordon saw his family, he was inclined towards them, and would change his will accordingly. After they had left, he forgot that they had visited and lapsed into an unhappy state, where he felt that they didn't care and that the only person who did was Doreen. This would lead to another will, and so on. The psychiatrist therefore proposed a compromise that enabled the family and Doreen to resolve their differences according to the balance of legitimately different perspectives rather than seeking a single truth or 'right' outcome.

Participating in Research

Usually, the decision to take part in a research study is fairly straightforward. A competent adult reads the participant information for the study and gives, or declines to give, their consent. A person with dementia may or may not have the capacity to consent, and, around this, numerous issues arise. The Mental Capacity Act 2005 (Department of Health, 2005) specifically allows people who lack capacity to participate in research if the research can be done only on people in their situation (e.g. research on advanced dementia) and either if the person themselves may benefit or if other similar people may benefit in the future (as long as the research is not likely to cause serious harm to the person; Department of Constitutional Affairs, 2007). For drug trials, another person who knows the person with dementia can give consent, but for non-medicinal studies the researchers are required to consult a personal or a professional consultee (e.g. a relative or a care home manager, respectively) but they can give only advice, not consent as such.

Clearly, a person with mild cognitive impairment or very early dementia may well have the capacity to give consent. Even if they may have difficulty retaining information given to them, as long as they are able to process it and make a choice that they can communicate, their consent is as valid as anyone else's. Perhaps more complex are situations where a person has mild or moderate dementia and it is less clear whether they have capacity or not. Maybe the person's capacity fluctuates so that, as they get tired, they may be less able to understand about the research in the evening than they were in the morning.

Another consideration is studies that take place over time, for example interventional studies with follow-up intervals that are several months apart. Given the progressive nature of dementia, a person may start by giving valid consent but over the next year or two lose their capacity to keep consenting, in which case the researchers will need to seek the advice of a consultee about whether to retain the person in the study.

Anxieties about people with dementia participating in studies are quite common; for example, maybe the person will be distressed by being asked a lot of questions or having their memory tested repeatedly. Also, there is an understandable instinct to protect people who may lack capacity from being exploited by unscrupulous researchers. This can lead to a considerable amount of gatekeeping and protectionism, for example from carers who think that their loved one may be unnecessarily upset, or from organizations such as ethics committees or provider organizations. However, this needs to be balanced against the human right to participate in research.

Box 12.12 John

John is a retired engineer with early Alzheimer's disease. When first diagnosed with dementia, he and his wife signed up for the NIHR (National Institute for Health and Care Research) Join Dementia Research portal that would inform them of any suitable studies. He participated in a drug trial and a couple of studies with focus groups for people with dementia. He also signed up for a longitudinal study with annual follow-up reviews. Then his wife died and he was left living alone, his main carer being his daughter, Leanne, based twenty miles away. She was much less keen on him taking part in research, especially if it meant having to drive him around, and she took the view that he should no longer be disturbed. This led to an unfortunate scene when a research assistant called for the annual review. Although John seemed happy enough at the prospect of this visit, Leanne was not, so she made sure that she was at the house when the researcher called and was reluctant to let her in.

Here we see a clash of autonomy and choice against the wish to protect John from intrusion into his life. How the researcher reacts at this point is crucial to the outcome. They may simply withdraw and John is lost to the study, though this does not respect the fact that he was willing to continue. Also, this would be against the interests of the society that would benefit from the results of the research and has invested already into the project. If they are able to negotiate skilfully, the researcher may gain access to the house to talk things through with John and Leanne. Perhaps the researcher is able to acknowledge Leanne's concerns about John being disturbed, whilst at the same time pointing out that he does not actually seem to mind. They can also explain how the research is important for people with dementia in the future, and how developing new treatments needs the help of people like John.

Maybe they reach a compromise where it is agreed to undertake a shortened version of the full assessment, so thirty to forty minutes instead of the usual two hours, and to omit some of the test items that John is likely to fail on. In this scenario, in the end, all three parties are content. John has enjoyed the session, his daughter feels that she has been virtuous and protective of her father, and the researcher has some data and a continuing participant in the study. Whether this is successful depends on the researcher being nimble enough to maintain a dialogue, first on the doorstep and subsequently in the house. Acknowledging the conflicting perspectives and choosing language carefully are also crucial.

Advanced Dementia and Care

Care at Home – At Any Cost?

At the outset after diagnosis, people with dementia and their families are often committed to the idea of remaining at home for as long as possible. There are varying, but commonly negative, preconceptions about care homes and the quality of care that may be available there. Some people, as they age, will attempt to extract promises from their families that they will 'never put [them] into a home'. Such promises are quite easy to make at the time but, as the course of dementia unfolds, circumstances may change and care home admission may become inevitable, or the family may have to confront the dilemma of breaking the promise or not being able to cope themselves.

Box 12.13 Winston

Winston developed dementia at the age of fifty-seven. His wife Paulette, having retired as a dementia care nurse, expected to be able to handle his care, but things did not go to plan. Winston would often want to leave the house at inconvenient times, and she was concerned that he would get lost. Stopping him became confrontational. The local mental health crisis team was called owing to concerns that either Winston was hitting Paulette or perhaps vice versa, and the couple were referred to local safeguarding.

Assessing this situation has more to do with VBM than EBM, as only limited research evidence is likely to be helpful. For example, the literature on abuse of vulnerable people would tell us about the risk factors for abuse to occur, but many of these factors are already present in the case. It is only by drawing on values that a sensible plan for Winston and Paulette can be formulated.

Winston's awareness of his situation was limited. He knew that he lived with his wife and that she was his carer. However, his insight into the degree of his dementia and his functional impairment was limited. Whilst it might, thus, have appeared that the patient-led principle was not as relevant here as usual, this was not so; it remained paramount, but perhaps it was necessary to infer what Winston might have chosen had he had the capacity to make decisions and choices about his care. Paulette was clinically severely depressed and in need of antidepressant treatment. She had profound feelings of guilt and failure, and these were compounded by the scrutiny that is implicit in the safeguarding process. In her view, she had failed as a wife and failed as a nurse and carer, so her self-esteem had greatly diminished. The two daughters were angry with 'the services' for not doing more, though they had difficulty in articulating what should be done. The social worker and the psychiatrist responsible for Winston therefore had a challenging meeting on their hands. The social worker offered a needs-based assessment for Paulette followed by supporting them to procure care agencies, and advising them about short-term respite and long-term care home options. The Admiral nurse supported Paulette with one-to-one guidance on how to react when Winston got angry, as well as practical solutions for dealing with other difficult situations at home. The psychiatrist established whether there were any other underlying treatable psychiatric symptoms that Winston was experiencing. The psychiatrist had to consider the different accounts of Winston and his family and use these multiple perspectives to form a plan that protected not just the safety of Winston and Paulette but also their dignity and humanity.

Six months later, after Winston had settled into a home specialising in dementia, he was happier as he had regular company and could move around the home and its garden. Paulette could visit regularly but had also resumed her own hobbies and interests.

For some cultures, the idea of not caring for your elderly relatives is taboo and allowing a relative to enter a care home would attract opprobrium or even exclusion from your community. However, this set of values can lead to extreme circumstances, where it is VBM rather than EBM that suggests what might be done.

Box 12.14 Ahmed

Ahmed came from Bangladesh to live with his son in the UK. The house was crowded, accommodating several family members from the elderly to the babies. Having developed dementia, Ahmed became agitated, disorientated, and inappropriate, sometimes taking his clothes off in front of the family or urinating in inappropriate places. Ahmed's daughter-in-law, Fatima, was running the house and trying to manage Ahmed's care as well as her young family.

The family decided that Ahmed could not really mix with the children, so they hastily built an annex and contained him within it. The room was almost unfurnished as he would throw objects around, so he had a mattress on the floor. Encouraging him to eat and drink or providing personal care was almost impossible and put a lot of strain on his family, who strived to achieve this, and eventually led to carer burn-out, when a referral to old age psychiatry was made.

The clash of values was obvious. Here was a man with severe dementia, and possibly with a psychosis, too, spending his days in an environment of social and sensory deprivation. On the other hand, at least some of those in the household were exhausting themselves trying to provide care to a very disturbed family member. The main VBM discussion was with Fatima; it focussed on the various options and the reasoning behind them (challenging the values myopia imposed by the tenet 'you must care for family no matter what') and moving towards shared language about how to address the problem. This included identifying Fatima's own needs and showing her how helping herself would also help Ahmed and, indirectly, other members of the family. The discussion enabled Fatima to realize that, if she was responsible for his care, she was also the decision-maker in that area. As discussed in the previous case, there were discussions in collaboration with the local social services, a mental health team, and care agencies about how best to support Ahmed. As he had lost the mental capacity to make his own decisions, an independent mental capacity advocate (IMCA) was involved to iron out the cultural conundrums that surfaced during the care planning. Ahmed maybe would prefer a male carer to provide him personal care; perhaps he would prefer stimulating activities in his own native language; his food preferences could be different – all of these elements would be considered in ascertaining his needs.

Intimate Relationships in Care Homes

Box 12.15 Derek and Amy

Derek and Amy both live in a care home. Derek has dementia and Amy is quite forgetful but has never been diagnosed. Both of them are widowed. Over the last six months, they have struck up a friendship. They spend most of their time together. In the TV room they sit holding hands. He has sometimes been seen to kiss her. Last week they were found in bed together and this has caused some consternation among the staff and the families. Derek's son is not too worried; he thinks that his father is happy so the couple should just be allowed to get on with it. Amy's daughter is upset; her father died only eighteen months ago and the loss is still quite painful. She says that her parents were inseparable in life and that Amy wouldn't be behaving like this now except for the fact that (in the daughter's view) she is confused and doesn't really know what she is doing; therefore, the relationship should be stopped. The staff are happy with the friendship but have divided views about how intimate the relationship should become. They are unsure about the extent to which they should either facilitate or obstruct the couple's apparently growing intimacy.

Although this isn't ultimately a matter for doctors to decide, they are quite often asked to advise on situations like this. The important issues here concern autonomy and the ability and freedom to make decisions. To what extent do Derek and Amy know what they are doing, but also to what extent do they need to have much mental capacity to enjoy each other's company? To what extent does it matter that the relationship has taken a step change and apparently developed into a sexual one?

Clearly there are clashes of values here, not only between Derek's son and Amy's daughter but also within the staff group. The published literature on intimacy among people with dementia in care homes is somewhat limited. There is a tendency for staff and families to take a protective or defensive approach (Roelofs et al., 2015) and for sexuality and intimacy to be perceived as care needs, rather than a person's rights (Rowntree and Zufferey, 2015). Syme et al. (2020) explored the attitudes of mid-life and older adults towards sexual preferences in long-term care and found that approval of sexual expression among partners was high in care homes in this group. Whilst situational factors such as level of intimacy and assent behaviours seem to have influenced their preferences, the impact of cognition and relationship was more complex, in that the salience of relationship differences (married couples versus nursing home relationships) lessens in the light of increased cognitive impairment. Resolving the situation will require discussion with all of the interested parties, especially with Amy's daughter, to understand and show respect for her perspective. Hopefully, this may be sufficient to ameliorate her concerns and, specifically, to acknowledge that this does not mean disrespect to her late father.

Box 12.16 Nigel and Frances

In a care home two miles down the road, Nigel has become friendly in a similar way with Frances. Both of them have a moderate degree of dementia, but it is clear that they are not only fond of each other but also physically attracted to one another. There are two differences from the Derek and Amy case, though. First, Nigel is still married and his wife visits him quite often; and second, Nigel's wife and family are clearly unhappy that Frances is from an African Caribbean background. This emerges in the way that they refer to 'that black woman' and never seem to use her name. When Nigel receives his wife's visits, he is sometimes warm and affectionate ('like his old self') but on other occasions he scarcely recognizes her, which his wife interprets as 'she has turned him against me'.

Sometimes this can lead to distressing scenes between Nigel and his wife but often she simply leaves in tears. Staff have noticed that her visits have declined from daily to about twice a week, though of course this probably increases the chance of him not recognizing who she is. The clash of values here is harder to resolve, but the starting place in the communication process is trying to understand Nigel's perspective. Is he aware that he is still married? It seems that he may have conflated the two women, so that perhaps he is simply affectionate to the one who is nearest to hand. And if his wife is in a defensive frame of mind when she visits, perhaps that transmits itself to Nigel, which in turn may cause him to doubt that this is really his wife, because he doesn't recollect her being critical and jealous of him before.

Nigel's wife may need quite a lot of time spent with her so that she can understand more about how the world looks to him. It may be that eventually she finds a satisfactory approach, for example that it is possible for her to remain a loyal wife but for Nigel to have a 'girl-friend'. If she isn't able to contemplate alternatives, then visiting may become unbearable for her and she may simply stay away.

In both cases, the tenth principle of VBM ('who decides') suggests that the decisions about how to proceed should rest with the users and the front-line providers. In other words, the solutions will probably be negotiated between the families and the care home staff, with as much input as possible from the residents themselves (Royal College of Nursing, 2022).

End-of-Life Care

The last stages of a person's life with dementia are fertile ground for conflicts about values.

Box 12.17 Roy

Roy had been troubled with depression ever since he retired fifteen years ago and had increasingly taken to his bed. The psychiatrists and community mental health nurses had tried several different treatments, to no great effect. He had an admission under the Mental Health Act for assessment and on the ward his behaviour seemed fine. He went straight back to bed after he was discharged. His mood was flat and apathetic rather than profoundly depressed, but trying to get him out of bed was not successful. It also appeared that he was developing cognitive impairment, though testing this was impossible because of his apathy. Not surprisingly, Edie, his wife, found this very frustrating – even more so because twice in the last year he had got dressed and gone off into the town to buy something. These events proved a false hope, and he remained in bed, dozing most of the day. She increasingly resented having to bring his meals into his room, but he would not eat otherwise. She could not decide whether he was being wilful or this was part of an illness. Eventually she admitted defeat and he was admitted to a care home.

Was his wish to remain in bed and do nothing a valid choice? Was the fractious relationship a cause or a consequence of his behaviour? Should we think differently when we learn that a second MRI scan showed a frontal lobe tumour? Among the conflicting values were those of the psychiatrist and the nurse. The former saw the situation as being organically mediated apathy owing to brain disease, and the latter was more inclined to see the root as lying in the relationship. The psychiatrist was inclined to manage the situation conservatively and await events, whilst the nurse (under pressure from Edie) was looking for any treatments that could be offered. They had regular discussions with Edie to ascertain what entertained them previously in their relationship – were there any factors that would motivate Roy out of bed (sports, music, trips to football, etc.), and could Edie get any help from her friends and family? All of this was put into the mix and solutions were explored. The psychiatrist understood, by listening to Edie, the stress that she was under and was able to offer clinical explanations for Roy's unmotivated behaviour. Having an understanding of what underlay Roy's apathy made Edie feel less angry towards Roy and less guilty about the ups and downs of their own relationship. The nurse was able to take a more practical approach to the situation, having learnt that medication is not going to change his presentation.

Box 12.18 Harveen

Harveen was caring for her elderly father, Manraj, who had advanced dementia. She was determined to keep him at home as she felt that it was expected of her by her community. She had read somewhere that people with dementia often lose weight and can easily become dehydrated. Therefore, she decided that he should have three meals a day, plus high-calorie snacks, and drink at least two litres of water daily. This was quite a challenge to achieve. Manraj had little interest in food; he was unable to use cutlery and, even using his fingers, he would lose the food between his hand and his mouth. When he did put food in his mouth, he often did nothing with it, as he was as likely to spit it out as to swallow it. In addition to this, his swallowing reflex was impaired so he would often choke when drinking, so his fluid intake fell far short of the target. Harveen was in despair.

Eating and nutrition are common areas of tension and conflict, but the mental health team, aided by a community dietician, were able to help. Before giving their advice, they needed to understand Harveen and her family's values, which included family care and pride in the standard of care they were giving. The team could then proceed to explain the evidence, most importantly that Manraj was nearing the end of his life, as well as giving Harveen permission to change her regime of food and fluids so as to be more flexible. That would enable her to savour the last weeks of her father's life without the feelings of desperation and failure.

One of the most difficult things for families, and indeed for professionals, too, can be to recognize when someone is actually dying. And also the point at which interventions such as intravenous fluids or percutaneous gastric feeding have become futile. This may reflect confusion as to what the desired outcome really is. Is it about preserving and prolonging life at all costs, or is it more about ameliorating suffering and dying with dignity? Members of the same family can easily disagree among themselves. Most people say that they would prefer to die at home (Higginson et al., 2017), yet most end up dying in hospital, which suggests that as death approaches the impulse to transfer a dying person to hospital becomes very strong.

Box 12.19 Bill

Bill had chronic pulmonary disease and a history of bipolar disorder and alcohol abuse. He had lived alone but recently had moved into a care home. Over the last few days, his behaviour had been erratic and aggressive and he had been refusing food and fluids. His doctor could find no obvious cause of delirium, though of course only a limited examination had been possible, so the psychiatrist was called to consider a possible psychiatric admission. However, when he was seen, Bill was dehydrated, emaciated, and almost moribund. It looked as if he was dying, so admission to a mental health unit was clearly not appropriate. There followed a discussion between the care home manager, Bill's son, and the psychiatrist about what to do. The psychiatrist thought that an admission to the general hospital would probably be traumatic and futile, since it would involve moving Bill and performing multiple investigations, but with no likely effect on the outcome. The care home and the son waited until the next day and then called an ambulance. Bill died in the general hospital two days later.

Thus, despite trying to apply several principles of VBM, the psychiatrist was unsuccessful in preventing an admission that probably was of no benefit to Bill. This included taking time to understand the perspectives of the other parties, presenting the evidence base, being careful about use of language, and using ethical reasoning. Yet not everything works all the time! However, perhaps, although the psychiatrist saw this as a failure, the care home and the son may have felt that they did the right thing and that it was appropriate that Bill died in hospital, so they were not left with an awkward feeling that they should have done more.

Conclusion

Dementia, as we have shown, is a complex condition, the realms of which extend beyond the neurology of the brain. It touches upon several aspects of the personal values and traditions held by the person affected and those close to them. As a neurodegenerative condition, dementia affects a person's memory, language, and perception, but also extends onto their self-identity, relationships, independence, finances, and social status. Having a diagnosis of dementia brings to the forefront what is really important to that individual and their family and how society responds to them.

The various case scenarios that we have considered in this chapter illustrate some of the many challenges that dementia poses for a range of stakeholders – the person themselves, their family, healthcare professionals, and others. Despite their competing perspectives, they have to work as partners to provide the best solutions and outcomes. This requires awareness of, and respect for, the differing or even competing opinions of others. We have discussed some dilemmas that can arise from conflicting interests that relate to a person with dementia and how their values may differ from those who try to support them. We have also shown some typical values-based issues that can arise at certain stages of the dementia journey, from pre-diagnosis to the end of life.

We conclude that dementia care must take into consideration both scientific and values-based perspectives, in order to promote a person- or relationship-centred approach. This will also help health and social care workers to work together more closely to help those with dementia.

References

Alzheimer's Disease International 2024. *World Alzheimer Report 2024: Global changes in attitudes to dementia*. London: Alzheimer's Disease International.

Alzheimer's Society 2010. *My Name Is Not Dementia: Literature Review*. London: Alzheimer's Society.

American Psychiatric Association 2013. *Diagnostic and Statistical Manual of Mental Disorders*, 5th ed. Arlington, VA: APA.

Brooker, D. & Latham, I. 2016. *Person-Centred Dementia Care: Making Services Better with the VIPS Framework*, 2nd ed. London: Jessica Kingsley.

Brown, L. B. & Ott, B. R. 2004. Driving and dementia: A review of the literature. *Journal of Geriatric Psychiatry and Neurology*, 17(4), 232–240.

Caddell, L. S. & Clare, L. 2010. The impact of dementia on self and identity: A systematic review. *Clinical Psychology Review*, 30(1), 113–126.

Chee, J.N., Rapoport, M.J., Molnar, F., Herrmann, N., O'Neil, D., Marottoli, R., Mitchell, S., Tant, M., Dow, J., Ayotte, D., Lanctôt, K.L., McFadden, R., Taylor, J-P., Donaghy, P.C., Olsen, K., Classen, S., Elzohairy, Y. & Carr, D.B. 2017. Update on the risk of motor vehicle collision or driving impairment with dementia: a collaborative international systematic review and meta-analysis. American Journal of Geriatric Psychiatry, 25(12), 1376–1390.

Cipriani, G., Lucetti, C., Nuti, A. & Danti, S. 2014. Wandering and dementia. *Psychogeriatrics: Official Journal of the Japanese Psychogeriatric Society*, 14(2), 135–142.

Cobb, M. 2020. *The Idea of the Brain: The Past and Future of Neuroscience*. London: Profile Books.

Cohen-Mansfield, J. 2008. Agitated behavior in persons with dementia: The relationship between type of behavior, its frequency, and its disruptiveness. *Journal of Psychiatric Research*, 43(1), 64–69.

Cohen-Mansfield, J., Parpura-Gill, A. & Golander, H. 2006. Salience of self-identity roles in persons with dementia: Differences in perceptions among elderly persons, family members and caregivers. *Social Science and Medicine*, 62(3), 745–757.

Davies, B. 2020. The right not to know and the obligation to know. *Journal of Medical Ethics*, 46(5), 300–303.

Department of Constitutional Affairs 2007. Mental Capacity Act 2005 Code of Practice. London: Stationery Office.

Department of Health 2005. Mental Capacity Act. London: HMSO.

Dubreuil, P., Adam, S., Bier, N. & Gagnon, L. 2007. The ecological validity of traditional memory evaluation in relation with controlled memory processes and routinization. *Archives of Clinical Neuropsychology*, 22(8), 979–989.

Duchek, J. M., Carr, D. B., Hunt, L., Roe, C. M., Xiong, C., Shah, K. & Morris, J. C. 2003. Longitudinal driving performance in early-stage dementia of the Alzheimer type. *Journal of the American Geriatrics Society*, 51(10), 1342–1347.

Fulford, B. (K. W. M.) 2004. Ten principles of values-based medicine. In Radden, J. (ed.), *The Philosophy of Psychiatry: A Companion.* New York: Oxford University Press, pp. 205–234.

General Medical Council 2017. *Confidentiality: Good Practice in Handling Patient Information.* London: General Medical Council.

Hampson, C. & Morris, K. 2016. Dementia: Sustaining self in the face of cognitive decline. *Geriatrics*, 1(4), 25.

Hendriks S., Peetoom, K., Bakker, C., van der Flier, W.M., Papma, J.M., Koopmans, R., Verhey, F.RJ., de Vugt, M., Köhler, S. & Young-Onset Dementia Epidemiology Study Group. 2021. Global prevalence of young-onset dementia: a systematic review and meta-analysis. JAMA Neurology, 78(9), 1080–1090.

Higginson, I. J., Daveson, B. A., Morrison, R. S., Yi, D., Meier, D., Smith, M., Ryan, K., McQuillan, R., Johnston, B. M., Normand, C. & BuildCARE 2017. Social and clinical determinants of preferences and their achievement at the end of life: Prospective cohort study of older adults receiving palliative care in three countries. *BMC (BioMed Central) Geriatrics*, 17(1), 271.

Jack, C. R., Jr, Bennett, D. A., Blennow, K., Carrillo, M. C., Dunn, B., Haeberlein, S. B., Holtzman, D. M., Jagust, W., Jessen, F., Karlawish, J., Liu, E., Molinuevo, J. L., Montine, T., Phelps, C., Rankin, K. P., Rowe, C. C., Scheltens, P., Siemers, E., Snyder, H. M., Sperling, R. & Contributors 2018. NIA-AA Research Framework: Toward a biological definition of Alzheimer's disease. *Alzheimer's & Dementia: Journal of the Alzheimer's Association*, 14(4), 535–562.

Keady, J. & Nolan, M. 2021. Person- and relationship-centred care: Past, present, and future. In Dening, T., Thomas, A., Stewart, R. & Taylor, J.-P. (eds.), *Oxford Textbook of Old Age Psychiatry*, 3rd ed. Oxford: Oxford University Press, pp. 233–248.

Kitwood, T. M. 1997. *Dementia Reconsidered: The Person Comes First.* Milton Keynes: Open University Press.

Kitwood, T. 1998. Toward a theory of dementia care: Ethics and interaction. *Journal of Clinical Ethics*, 9(1), 23–34.

Klein-Koerkamp, Y., Baciu, M. & Hot, P. 2012. Preserved and impaired emotional memory in Alzheimer's disease. *Frontiers in Psychology*, 3, 331.

Kumfor, F., Hodges, J. R. & Piguet, O. 2014. Ecological assessment of emotional enhancement of memory in progressive nonfluent aphasia and Alzheimer's disease. *Journal of Alzheimer's Disease*, 42(1), 201–210.

Lim, L., Zhang, A., Lim, L., Choong, T.M., Silva, E., Ng, A., Kandiah, N. 2018. High caregiver burden in young onset dementia: what factors need attention? Journal of Alzheimer's Disease, 61(2), 537–543.

Low, L. F., McGrath, M., Swaffar, K. & Brodaty, H. 2018. Communicating a diagnosis of dementia: A systematic mixed studies review of attitudes and practices of health practitioners. *Dementia*, 18(7–8), 2856–2905.

Mathuranath, P. S., Nestor, P. J., Berrios, G. E., Rakowicz, W. & Hodges, J. R. 2000. A brief cognitive test battery to differentiate Alzheimer's disease and frontotemporal dementia. *Neurology*, 55(11), 1613–1620.

Mioshi, E., Dawson, K., Mitchell, J., Arnold, R. & Hodges, J. R. 2006. The Addenbrooke's Cognitive Examination Revised (ACE-R): A brief cognitive test battery for dementia screening. *International Journal of Geriatric Psychiatry*, 21, 1078–1085.

Nasreddine, Z. S., Phillips, N. A., Bédirian, V., Charbonneau, S., Whitehead, V., Collin, I., Cummings, J. L. & Chertkow, H. 2005. The Montreal Cognitive Assessment, MoCA: A brief screening tool for mild cognitive impairment. *Journal of the American Geriatrics Society*, 53(4), 695–699.

National Institute for Health and Care Excellence (NICE) 2020. *Shared Decision Making*. NICE guideline draft for consultation. December. www.nice.org.uk/guidance/ng197/documents/draft-guideline.

Nolan, M. R., Davies, S., Brown, J., Keady, J. & Nolan, J. 2004. Beyond person-centred care: A new vision for gerontological nursing. *Journal of Clinical Nursing*, 13(3a), 45–53.

Pratt, R. & Wilkinson, H. 2001. *Tell Me the Truth: The Effect of Being Told the Diagnosis of Dementia from the Perspective of the Person with Dementia*. London: Mental Health Foundation.

Prince, M., Knapp, M., Guerchet, M., McCrone, P., Prina, M., Comas-Herrera, A., Wittenberg, R., Adelaja, B., Hu, B., King, D., Rehill, A. & Salimkumar, D. 2014. *Dementia UK: Update*. London: Alzheimer's Society.

Robinson, L., Hutchings, D., Corner, L., Finch, T., Hughes, J., Brittain, K. & Bond, J. 2007. Balancing rights and risks: Conflicting perspectives in the management of wandering in dementia. *Health, Risk and Society*, 9(4), 389–406.

Roelofs, T. S., Luijkx, K. G. & Embregts, P. J. 2015. Intimacy and sexuality of nursing home residents with dementia: A systematic review. *International Psychogeriatrics*, 27(3), 367–384.

Rowntree, M. R. & Zufferey, C. 2015. Need or right: Sexual expression and intimacy in aged care. *Journal of Aging Studies*, 35, 20–25.

Royal College of Nursing. 2022. Older People in Care Homes: Sex, sexuality and intimate relationships, third edition. London, Royal College of Nursing.

Royal College of Psychiatrists 1996. Public Policy Committee guidance on medical aspects of fitness to drive. *Psychiatric Bulletin*, 20, 631.

Sommerlad, A., Perera, G., Singh-Manoux, A., Lewis, G., Stewart, R. & Livingston, G. 2018. Accuracy of general hospital dementia diagnoses in England: Sensitivity, specificity, and predictors of diagnostic accuracy 2008–2016. *Alzheimer's & Dementia: Journal of the Alzheimer's Association*, 14(7), 933–943.

Syme, M. L., Johnson, P. E. & Fager, M. 2020. Person-centered sexual expression: Determining preferences of future nursing home residents. *Gerontologist*, 60(4), 725–734.

Vickers, B. D. & Preston, S. D. 2014. The economics of hoarding. In Frost, R. O. & Steketee, G. (eds.), *The Oxford Handbook of Hoarding and Acquiring*. Oxford Library of Psychology. Oxford: Oxford University Press, pp. 221–232.

Warren, J. D., Rohrer, J. D. & Rossor, M. N. 2013. Clinical review: Frontotemporal dementia. *British Medical Journal*, 347, f4827.

Williamson, T. 2008. *Dementia: Out of the Shadows*. London: Alzheimer's Society.

Woodbridge, K. & Fulford, B. (K. W. M.) 2004. *Whose Values? A Workbook for Values-Based Practice in Mental Health Care*. London: Sainsbury Centre for Mental Health. https://valuesbasedpractice.org/wp-content/uploads/2015/04/Whose-Values-A-Workbook.pdf.

Woody, S. R., Kellman-McFarlane, K. & Welsted, A. 2014. Review of cognitive performance in hoarding disorder. *Clinical Psychology Review*, 34(4), 324–336.

Chapter 13

The Storm of Values in Borderline Personality Disorder

Challenges and Opportunities

Robert B. Dudas

Introduction

What is the special relevance of values in borderline personality disorder (BPD)? The importance of examining and working with values in BPD is supported by both theoretical arguments and empirical evidence. Values are closely linked to emotions and patients with BPD have significant difficulty regulating their emotions. Surprisingly, so far this has been relatively little explored or exploited for therapeutic purposes. An impact on clinical decision-making, in which values play a crucial role, is also to be expected. Values transcend individual situations and therefore de-emphasize attaining a specific goal; instead, they emphasize choosing behaviours that are consistent with a personal value at every junction: the focus is on process rather than on individual events within that, thereby allowing increased flexibility (Cameron et al., 2014). Early empirical evidence supports the usefulness of working with the person's values in therapy. A study of acceptance and commitment therapy (ACT), a modality focussing on acting in accordance with one's stated values, has shown efficacy for treating BPD (Morton et al., 2012) and Cameron et al. (2014) made the case persuasively that adding a component to dialectical behaviour therapy (DBT) that explores and works with the values of the patient may enhance motivation and treatment efficacy, reduce dropout rates, and – importantly – close the gap between improvement in symptoms (which many modalities can already demonstrate) and living a meaningful and fulfilling life.

In the first half of this chapter, I will explore the values of the stakeholders and some of the key conflicts among them in the context of BPD. In the second half, I will present ways of navigating this value complexity. In developing my argument, I will be drawing on four main sources: guidelines produced by UK governmental and professional organizations, qualitative research including that produced in collaboration with people affected by BPD, published first-person narratives, and philosophical analyses of BPD and related issues, including phenomenological psychopathology and enactivism.

Word choice matters. Although I will refer to the people seeking medical help in the healthcare system as patients, I am aware that this is not everyone's preference. All the alternatives have their pros and cons and entering the doctor–patient relationship presupposes an agreement that one abides by the rules of being a doctor or a patient. Similarly, I will use the term borderline personality disorder (BPD), but I provide critique of it and describe how a better choice could be found.

The Values of the Stakeholders: Conflicts and Their Roots

The Values of the Patients

Understanding what the experience of having BPD is like is essential for understanding our patients' values. In their handbook *Meeting the Challenge, Making a Difference: Working Effectively to Support People with Personality Disorder in the Community*, Bolton et al. (2014, pp. 10–11) describe how patients usually report long-standing emotional and relationship difficulties and finding themselves being let down, abused, or abandoned by others. They have rapidly changing emotions that can overwhelm both them and others with their intensity. Their presentation can include impulsive or self-destructive behaviour and maladaptive patterns in their relationships with others that keep repeating. They commonly recount a history of a range of extraordinarily traumatic or unhappy childhood experiences. Bolton et al. (2014) draw attention to difficulties in engaging with services, such as not being able to keep appointments, or becoming aggressive. There is also often a history of unsuccessful attempts at psychological treatment.

Giovanni Stanghellini and Milena Mancini give a description of BPD from the perspective of phenomenological psychopathology (Stanghellini and Mancini, 2017, p. 81). According to their findings, BPD patients oscillate between two life worlds: *the life world of dysphoria* and *the life world of anger*. Each of these life worlds has a corresponding set of possibilities for experience and action. The world of dysphoria is a painful experience of inner incoherence and emptiness, a sense of inauthenticity in relationships, and a feeling of the futility of life. Stanghellini and Mancini (2017, p. 103) also describe a 'desperate vitality' in dysphoria that leads to a need to satisfy the affective and biological values caused by the powerful feelings of being alive. As these values conflict with the ethical norms and social rules of others, they provoke a sense of frustration and worthlessness. In contrast, in the world of anger the person has a clear sense of 'good' (oneself) and 'bad' (the other), which helps them find their identity. In a similar vein, during anger the world also regains its structure and meaning. In terms of their lived time, the person lives in the 'absolute now' with no anteriority or posteriority, that is, no sense of self retained from the past or projected into the future.

Stanghellini and Mancini (2017) state that *our emotions are closely linked to our values* which orient our experience of the world, other people, and ourselves. This is key to our understanding of how patients' values can fluctuate so much. People with BPD often respond with unusually strong emotions to life events and other triggers. Not only can they often take much longer to return to baseline, but their emotions can also fluctuate rapidly. This can be very confusing and exhausting for both them and those involved in their care. Whilst dysphoria can be both a permanent trait and a state, anger is primarily a state. In BPD, they combine in a particular way, usually accompanied by feelings of shame and humiliation (Stanghellini and Mancini, 2017, p. 83). Disgust-related emotions are more common (Buchman-Wildbaum et al., 2021) and have different brain connectivity in BPD compared to healthy people (Dudas et al., 2017).

As regards the self, BPD patients find it difficult to integrate the good and the bad in themselves and others (Stanghellini and Mancini, 2017, p. 95). This leads to a shifting view of the self with shifting roles, such as victim and victimizer, and a sense of inner emptiness. The integrity of the self can be damaged by trauma; especially, responses can be invalidated, for example when other people discourage, disregard, or trivialize the person's private experiences (Stanghellini and Mancini, 2017, p. 96). In our own empirical research (Evans et al., 2015), we found that greater BPD severity was associated with less positive and more negative content of the self-concept, and this was driven by depressive symptoms. Also, positive content was more diffuse and negative content more interconnected at greater BPD severity, but for positive content this was clearly linked to co-morbid depression symptoms. Greater BPD severity was associated with a more fragmented self-concept, consistent with the body of literature on the incoherence of the narrative self across time and context (Liu et al., 2023).

Patients with BPD often develop depression. However, this depression is different from melancholic depression. It is characterized by emptiness, loneliness, desperation, and labile affectivity as opposed to guilt, which is more typical of classical depression (Gunderson and Phillips, 1991; Stanghellini et al., 2006; Westen and Cohen, 1993). Patients can also have very short depressive periods, often multiple times during the day, which can be accompanied by intense depersonalization.

Acknowledging the role of patients' existential stances towards themselves and their situation, including their disorder, is a vital aspect of treatment (de Haan, 2020). As the majority of BPD patients are victims of childhood abuse or neglect, in this sense their typical appraisal that how they present today is somebody else's fault is, in most cases, correct. The problem is when this generalizes to other relationships and becomes maladaptive and unhelpful to such a degree that it repeatedly brings the patient into conflict with others, including those who are trying to help them.

People with BPD, like most people, wish for intimacy: to belong, to be accepted, to have an emotional relationship with another. This is, however, often very hard to attain for them for a variety of reasons. The other needs to be present and validating, but also to be spontaneous and act 'according to the vital impulses of the present moment' (Stanghellini and Mancini, 2017, p. 104). The main related values of people with BPD are *authenticity* (absolute emotional fusion with the other), *immediacy* (the instantaneous satisfaction of one's needs and desires), and *need for recognition* (attention and acceptance by the other) (Stanghellini and Mancini, 2017, p. 108; Mancini and Stanghellini, 2020). The values of people with BPD are directed at achieving a sense of being a person through belonging, reciprocated sensuous experiences, and being forgiven (Mancini and Stanghellini, 2020).

To successfully partake in coordinated social interaction, whether in one's own family, at work, or in the healthcare system, and to navigate the cultural world, people need to develop a 'feel for the game', which includes behaving in line with what others expect (Maiese, 2021). In BPD, this is made difficult by several factors, including distrust, shame, and impaired empathy at times of intense emotions (Salgado et al., 2020). Stanghellini and Mancini (2017, p. 105) warn about the gaze of the other person (in a clinical context, the clinician) that reveals the part of their self that elicits shame. This shame is painful, and it can make them feel the victim of an unjust accusation and activate a victim–perpetrator reciprocal role pair. This, in turn, can prevent them from focussing on their own actions, taking responsibility for them, and having a sense of agency.

The Values of the Clinicians and Healthcare Organizations

The principal aim of the clinician is to help the patient and there is plenty of evidence showing that people with BPD can improve significantly with treatment (Choi-Kain et al., 2017; Katakis et al., 2023; Storebø et al., 2020). Apart from the skills needed to deploy the procedural elements and techniques of various treatment modalities, what are the other important factors in creating effective clinical services? In their description of the therapeutic environment, Bolton et al. make reference to the atmosphere or *culture of the service* (Bolton et al., 2014, p. 53), which people with BPD have identified as a factor in their recovery (Castillo et al., 2013). Patients with BPD may have had few positive experiences of engaging with other people, including professionals. They may not often have seen other people engaging with each other consistently in a positive way, either. Trust, confidence, and agency (concepts related to recovery that I will return to in the second half of this chapter) can be fostered only in services where both the patients and the clinicians can feel listened to, respected, and safe. Patients can be extremely acute observers and notice how the professionals treat them and also each other. Bolton et al. (2014, p. 53) provide a list of words that describe a positive therapeutic environment: 'welcoming, warm, informal, friendly, safe, open, easy-going, belonging, non-judgemental, humane, – and not: stuffy, stiff, strict, harsh, bureaucratic, secretive, scary, intimidating or rigid'. Other relevant characteristics may include respectful, caring, validating, duly praising, tolerant, non-blaming, and democratic – and not infantilizing, gaslighting, procrastinating, neglectful, authoritarian, shaming, or punitive. Of course, clinicians cannot be expected to display all the dos and none of the don'ts if their employers, managers, and colleagues do not create the same positive environment for them. Regularly assessing the degree to which these values are perceived by both patients and workers within the organization and having appropriate governance systems to address any obstacles to creating such work environments is essential. Selecting the right organizational values and creating a healthy organizational culture can benefit all primary stakeholders enormously (Braithwaite et al., 2017; Morris et al., 2007). The Royal College of Psychiatrists' *Enabling Environments Standards* (RCPsych, 2023) consider the values necessary to create such positive environments from the perspective of both those running the services and those in receipt of them. They highlight as key values *belonging, boundaries, communication, development, involvement, safety, structure, empowerment, leadership*, and *openness*. The standards recognize the importance of having a set of expectations of behaviour and processes to maintain and review them.

Different psychiatric illnesses elicit different feelings in the people around the sufferer. As Bolton et al. (2014, p. 67) describe, most clinicians come across BPD patients in relation to whom they feel confused, anxious, frustrated, hopeless, or angry. They may have feelings of guilt about not offering enough for their patient or anger if the patient seems ungrateful. These are difficult feelings and clinicians need time and support to understand and process them. Supervision, multidisciplinary team (MDT) meetings, and Balint and reflective practice groups are opportunities for this. But working with patients with BPD also has the potential to help clinicians with their own self-discovery. Every now and then, a clinician notices parallels between their life and that of the patient. They may feel guilt and/or relief that their life is not as troubled as that of the patient. Clinicians also have a lived experience of the condition they work with that needs to be respected and taken into consideration.

Team members need to be able to clarify and manage expectations and provide consistent care. They need to have an understanding of the nature of the problems specific to this patient group and what is helpful in resolving them. For example, the clinician doing more and more for the patient as a reflex when the patient keeps sending signals of distress is usually the right response in most other psychiatric conditions, but it can be counterproductive and reduce agency in BPD. This creates an apparent value conflict between the clinician and the patient, and resolving this without causing too much of a sense of rejection in the patient requires great skill and the ability to build trust. Another difficult balance between conflicting values is safety versus actively promoting change, which – when done well – increases patients' motivation and facilitates their recovery (Katsakou and Pistrang, 2018).

Turner et al. (2011) describe the interesting issue of two kinds of expertise in the context of personality disorder. They feel that the idea that 'experts by experience' could sometimes be the same or even more knowledgeable than 'experts by profession' is still anathema to many; professionals find this difficult and service user trainers, who would be best placed to inform professionals of the needs, concerns, and preferences of this patient group, struggle to find their identity in the system. Turner et al. (2011) believe that there are competing interests here that can be damaging to the recovery of the patients.

Dilemmas and Value Conflicts

Values in the Diagnosis of BPD

The prevailing psychiatric classification systems are far from perfect in defining homogeneous groups with shared underlying pathology or a uniform response to treatment, but they do serve functions that are of value to the stakeholders (Dudas, 2014), such as aiding communication between clinicians, providing access to treatments that can lead to improved outcomes by narrowing down which treatments might offer the most promising risk:benefit ratio, managing expectations, and guiding research.

But what are the values associated with the diagnosis of BPD at a deeper look? Although patients do not want to be labelled, they are often well aware that diagnosing has the potential to be helpful (Nehls, 1999). *Diagnosis offers an explanatory scheme for the patient and their relatives*, which can serve as a starting point for the patient's journey of recovery. Patients (and sometimes their families) can report disbelief, shock, denial, or anger after diagnosis, especially initially, but there are also many patients who describe feelings of relief that they are not mad or alone with their difficulties, and also feelings of hope (Bolton et al., 2014). This is particularly so for those who experienced a long delay before receiving a diagnosis (Proudfoot et al., 2009).

From a theoretical point of view, diagnosis can take several forms. Medical diagnoses tend to be *categorical*, sometimes with qualifiers of severity such as mild, moderate, or severe. Using a *dimensional* approach for personality disorders, describing the person in terms of severity along various continua of personality characteristics, has been suggested. It was not adopted by the Diagnostic and Statistical Manual of Mental Disorders (DSM) working group during the most recent revision, but ICD-11 (the eleventh revision of the International Classification of Diseases; WHO, 2022) has moved into this direction by doing away with the various categories of personality disorder, although allowing for a 'borderline pattern' specifier and introducing four graded levels of severity. This is consistent with the idea that we all have personalities that vary on similar dimensions (Bolton et al., 2014). Psychologists use a different, *formulation-based* approach, usually drawing on various theories to explain the person's history and presentation, maintaining and precipitating factors and possible avenues for improvement. Each of these approaches can have its place and various patients may benefit from each to varying degrees at different times in their lives. Although there is an apparent value conflict here, in clinical practice a combination of these three approaches often works best (as they are to a significant degree complementary) and most services are indeed organized in such a way.

Accurate diagnosis is regarded as important by every stakeholder. However, *misdiagnosis* still occurs: some patients who do not have BPD get diagnosed with it, and some patients who do have it never receive the diagnosis or receive a different one instead. The presence of self-harming or repeated suicide attempts often leads to the former, whilst the latter can happen when the person with BPD does not want to be diagnosed or the clinician for some reason does not want to make the diagnosis. This could be for fear of a negative effect on the patient or of ruining the therapeutic relationship, waiting for the crisis or a co-morbid condition to settle first, or fear of causing stigma or other difficulties for the patient. There seems to be a striking dearth of patients diagnosed with BPD in old age services and an abundance of patients diagnosed with atypical depression instead.

The problem of diagnosis is overshadowed by *stigma*. The view that mental health diagnoses lead to stigma and not seeing the patient as a person but as a label is fairly common among both laypeople and mental health professionals. As Linda Gask, a psychiatrist with a lived experience of mental illness, points out, '[a] lifelong difficulty in relating to others is called a "personality disorder", but [she is] always unhappy about using this label, particularly in the case of a young person, as it can be very "sticky" and serve as a convenient excuse to blame the patient for the problems they are experiencing' (Gask, 2015, p. 158). Stigma is likely to reduce in the same way as it has in the case of many types of cancer or infectious disorders if – through research and psycho-education – ignorance is replaced by an understanding of the pathomechanism and the development of effective treatments (Sheehan et al., 2016). But emphasizing to the public the biological differences alone can be counterproductive.

Giving no diagnosis when there is illness and the patient is seeking diagnosis would be wrong for many reasons. For example, it deprives the person of understanding their illness and receiving effective treatments, as seen in some cases (Little, 2024). The choice of either neglecting a whole group of people who are suffering or harming them through medicalizing 'normal' emotional suffering, overdiagnosis, and causing stigma is a false dichotomy: a scientific approach combined with compassion and humanity, which is the true medical approach, should mean staying clear of both (Dudas, 2014).

We also need to consider how BPD patients experience *the care they receive as a result of being diagnosed*. What are their needs, concerns, and preferences in this regard? A number of themes emerge from published first-person narratives and professional clinical experience. One of them is communication often being unhelpful or disrespectful. One patient described an important aspect of the gross misunderstanding of the needs of this patient group that still occurs in places: 'please don't tell me I know exactly what I am doing because if I knew what I am doing I wouldn't be in hospital being held down by a policeman' and 'please don't say to me "I've got patients who are sick"' (McAdam, 2024). Patients often report difficulty getting help with this diagnosis: 'With panic disorder and depression I received help. With personality disorder I was treated differently, I had no help' (Bolton et al., 2014, p. 23). Bolton et al. (2014, pp. 10–11) draw attention to how healthcare providers often respond to the individual with an unusual reaction, which may be owing to the clinician's own shortcomings or to how the patient perceives themselves or others. But lack of skills or capacity is only part of the explanation; less satisfactory treatment can also be the result of values and attitudes: 'I was treated less sympathetically because of personality disorder. They believe it's not mental illness but something you've brought on yourself'

(Bolton et al., 2014, p. 24). However, the picture would be very skewed without also mentioning the descriptions of gratitude in response to understanding and respect, as illustrated by what another patient said: 'thank you to the nurses and doctors in intensive care six years ago that fought to keep me alive' (McAdam, 2024). There are many services where clinicians are empathetic and respectful of diversity and differences, and show unconditional positive regard. They are interested not in abusing their power but in working collaboratively and in ways that promote the patient's personal autonomy. So, maybe we are seeing a turning of the tide. Training has improved significantly in recent decades, as has service planning. In some areas in the UK, specialized personality disorders services are also available now. Professional organizations, like the Royal College of Psychiatrists, very much embrace BPD as a diagnosis that is within their remit. The national policy environment in the UK and other countries has changed significantly (Gunderson, 2009; NIMHE, 2003). The fact that now there are new, effective psychological treatments for BPD, as well as evidence-based scalable generalist approaches, has a lot do with this.

Finally, I would like to discuss briefly the term 'borderline personality disorder' which has been criticized by all stakeholder groups. (Emotionally unstable personality disorder is only a little bit better in that it brings to focus a crucial aspect of the condition.) For the purposes of my argument here, I will mention only two problems with it. First, although some of the symptoms in BPD do concern personality traits, to many people the term 'personality disorder' seems to convey a summative value judgement about the whole person, overshadowing the many positive traits and abilities the person with BPD may have. Second, it is at best confusing, potentially even misleading: most people are unaware of the original meaning of the word 'borderline' as rooted in psychoanalytic thinking and to some it seems to suggest that the person does not really have the problem and is instead on the borderline between health and illness.

I would argue that any renaming, if it is done, should be based on values, not just on facts, and preferably should be co-produced. One of the reasons for this is that at the moment we do not have all the relevant facts: we do not know enough about the causal mechanisms and they are also likely to be multi-factorial. So, any name based on that would be imprecise. Names based on descriptive features of the illness would be arbitrary and could easily be perceived or used as blaming or derogatory. If we want to find a term that is most helpful to our patients, a needs-based approach seems better suited, for example 'complex emotional and interpersonal needs'. Values are action-driving and terminology creates expectations and shapes attitudes. This name would draw attention to what people with BPD need help with.

Do We Need a Separate System to Support People with BPD?

In psychiatry, personality disorder is considered to be different from other major mental illnesses such as major depression, schizophrenia, and bipolar disorder (Bolton et al., 2014). Much of this distinction is based on the fact that whereas personality disorder is developmental (it develops gradually over childhood and adolescence and is then present for years or decades, or is possibly lifelong), the above-listed classic forms of mental illness tend to have, with the exception of treatment-resistant, chronic cases, an episodic (although potentially recurrent) nature with a clear onset and recovery. They also tend to respond better to medication and, in the majority of cases, there is some form of a return to a previous, healthy level of functioning. Except in rare cases when their illness developed later in adulthood, people with BPD do not have a 'healthy self' as such to return to. Qualitative research with service users has shown that patients can find the word 'recovery' problematic (Gillard et al., 2015; Katsakou et al., 2012; Larivière et al., 2015) and some patients feel that 'discovery' describes their journey more accurately (Gillard et al., 2015).

It would not be unreasonable to argue that not all forms of mental distress fit neatly into the current model of mental health provision and BPD may be one of those conditions: instead of forcing a one-size-fits-all recovery model, a separate new system could foster principles that are distinctively helpful for this specific group. However, one needs to be careful not to throw the baby out with the bathwater. *First*, the medical model and clinical psychiatry have a lot to offer to many people with BPD in terms of effective treatments. *Second*, for a long time it was only psychoanalysts who showed any interest in the condition (Paris, 2005, p. 109) and it took a lot of effort from leading figures in the field to achieve the acceptance of BPD in psychiatry. I still remember that when I was a trainee some consultants felt that BPD was not a psychiatric illness, 'just women misbehaving' who were not to be admitted to hospital under any circumstances. Although childhood emotional abuse and neglect, which is very common in the histories of BPD patients, is associated with rejection sensitivity (Foxhall et al., 2019), which may contribute to how patients perceive their care, it is important to acknowledge that rejection and exclusion undoubtedly still do occur (Gunderson, 2009). For example, specific personality disorder services have different barriers to access to help. Some of this is owing to there being limited resources and efforts to direct patients to care pathways that are believed to be therapeutically effective and appropriate for them. In the wider psychiatric system, there are also prejudices and fears about BPD treatment being resource-intensive, particularly challenging, and of limited efficacy. An optimal support system for BPD would make full use of evidence-based scalable generalist approaches where patients would not need to be excluded from services owing to lack of capacity. *Third*, typically, these patients have had difficult relationships with others, often including those who were supposed to look after them. Owing to these experiences, many patients find it difficult to trust people in authority, including clinicians. They may also have had negative experiences in the past when their views were dismissed because of their diagnosis. This can perpetuate feelings of invalidation and mistrust (Bolton et al., 2014, p. 60). Consequently, their interactions with clinicians can be fraught and problematic. *Fourth*, to argue that BPD is not a psychiatric illness or that it should not be looked after in the psychiatric system would generate a strong sense of rejection and abandonment in many people suffering from BPD.

Therefore, I am going to argue that BPD patients would benefit from a new support system, or a support system running on a new set of principles, *within* the healthcare system. In addition to the reasons explained just now, I will do so mainly on the basis that BPD patients need a different therapeutic approach and follow a different path in terms of their recovery compared to patients with other major forms of mental illness. Caring for them requires a different skill set. Approaches that work for patients with other types of illness may even be harmful to them. This is consistent with evidence finding that personality disorder services are perceived by patients as better at counteracting the hopelessness associated with the diagnosis (Morris et al., 2014). A significant proportion of people with BPD feel that they are not ill in the same way as people with other major mental illnesses but that they need help and support. A meta-synthesis of qualitative studies exploring patients' experiences (Katsakou and Pistrang, 2018) identified ten main themes that are important to BPD patients: (1) self-acceptance; (2) new ways of relating to others; (3) taking control of emotions and thoughts; (4) implementing practical changes and developing hope; (5) safety and containment in treatment; (6) being cared for and respected; (7) not being an equal partner in treatment; (8) focussing on change in treatment; (9) having an open-ended journey; and (10) having a series of achievements and setbacks. Although many of these apply to several or all mental health conditions, individual sub-themes within these – such as reconciling the internal and external worlds; the struggle to be understood as a person; recovering by refusing to be violated; fearing relations whilst longing for love; emotion and impulse regulation; conquering suicidal and self-harm impulses; learning boundaries; maintaining healthy attachment; and recovery not being the best term to name patients' experience – appear to be more specific to this patient group and argue for a separate system.

Navigating Values in BPD

Agency, Emotions, and Values

In order to elucidate how the clinician can successfully negotiate the various challenges relevant to the value conflicts discussed in the first half of the chapter, I need to first explicate the links between agency, emotions, and values, at least to some degree.

As Bolton et al. (2014) note, the most effective forms of therapy address personal *agency*. For this to happen, the clinician needs capabilities above and beyond their core capabilities in order to create a non-blaming, non-judgemental, and compassionate milieu within which they can enable the patient to take responsibility for their actions. They need to be neither overly supportive, which would thwart the development of the patient's agency, nor overly demanding, as that would likely trigger an angry reaction and, potentially, disengagement.

But how do people develop agency in general? According to Michelle Maese (2021), people develop certain *habits of mind as to what they notice* of their environment, *what sources they trust as evidence*, and *how they gauge the significance of things or events*. Unfortunately, BPD patients often have difficulty in all these. If my attention is somehow more attuned to things in my environment that keep me stuck in a maladaptive vicious cycle, and I find it difficult to trust the people who try to teach me how not to do that, my sense of agency is unlikely to grow, and my life will be unlikely to improve. Regrettably, I may even jump to the conclusion that ending my life is the only way out of my repeated failure at building a meaningful life and my perpetual suffering. According to Fonagy et al. (2015), one of the main problems BPD patients have is the significant impairment in their ability to develop *epistemic trust*, that is, the willingness to accept new information from the other person as generalizable and relevant to us. Consequently, they cannot benefit from social interaction, which they call epistemic petrification (Fonagy et al., 2015). The role of psychiatric treatment should be to help the patient develop this trust, to help them discover their self for themselves, and to build positive relationships. The person can develop their agentic strength only in such a therapeutic environment.

Emotions are important in gauging the significance of things and events, and when they are running high, this becomes skewed. Strong emotions (in either party) can often get in the way and BPD is associated with interpersonal hypersensitivity (Gunderson and Lyons-Ruth, 2008) and heightened emotional reactivity (Dixon-Gordon et al., 2017). Often, BPD patients grew up in environments where caregivers displayed very strong emotions and / or in neglectful environments in which only the most extreme cries for help were answered.

Emotions and attitudes in the other person generate corresponding emotions and attitudes in us: caring – feeling cared for, idealizing – feeling idealized, critical – feeling criticized, abusive – feeling abused, to name but a few. These internalized templates about the social world are called reciprocal roles in cognitive-analytic therapy (CAT; Denman, 2001). This has important implications for our attempts to foster agency in patients with BPD. If, for example, the patient becomes very angry and critical, the clinician may overreact and risk doing too much for the patient and thereby take away the patient's opportunity to develop their own agency. In such situations, it is helpful to be aware that there are strong feelings in the room and to take a step back to give ourselves a little bit of thinking space. Furthermore, extreme situations may lead to extreme degrees of curtailing the patient's agency. For example, at times of extreme emotional arousal, when the patient is felt to be unable to keep themselves safe, clinicians may feel that they need to use the powers of the Mental Health Act (HM Government, 2007) to detain the patient to hospital for assessment or treatment. Although necessary at the time in order to protect the patient, it is a real challenge to help them process this experience in a way that promotes, rather than reduces, their sense of agency in the future.

Emotions are linked to *values* (Conte et al., 2023; Stanghellini and Mancini, 2017). Both orient our attention and make us likely to respond to the situation in a certain way, but whilst emotions are for the moment, values transcend concrete situations. When we act against our values for some reason, we experience negative emotions. A particular challenge in BPD is that certain key values, such as having a warm, intimate, loving relationship, may often be linked to trauma and pain (Cameron et al., 2014).

Research suggests that people with BPD rate their values across various life domains, especially relationships with family, friends, and romantic partners as well as health and well-being, as highly important, but they report significantly lower levels of value commitment, desire to improve, and success in living in line with their values (Mohi et al., 2018). Depression and experiential avoidance (the unwillingness to stay with aversive experiences such as painful thoughts or emotions) predict the discrepancy between desire to improve and success (Mohi et al., 2021).

Psychological intervention focussing on the patient's values (see, e.g., Cameron et al., 2014) has the potential to influence what they notice of their environment and how they gauge the significance of things or events. It can improve their psychological flexibility and widen their range of behavioural responses. Thus, values-based interventions can improve agency. They can also increase motivation and help the patient find *meaning*, which is negatively associated with depression, suicidality (García-Alandete et al., 2014), and self-harm in BPD (Marco et al., 2015). There is empirical evidence from longitudinal observation that an increase in agency in the patient's life narrative is part of the recovery process (Lind et al., 2019).

Therapy always occurs in complex interactions among the various stakeholders. Thus, the three dimensions of the *clinical value-mapping* procedure I described in Chapter 2 on depression can help us work more effectively with their values.

Working with Values

Clinical Value-Mapping in BPD

Hierarchy of Values

Key features of the illness, such as the mood fluctuations, the intense and unstable relationships, and the unstable sense of self, can all have an impact on the hierarchy of values in

BPD. At times of extreme emotions, one's values or the *hierarchy* between them can become warped temporarily. This is a major challenge in BPD where executive functioning is affected in certain ways during these periods, with an impact on memory, the perception of time, and central coherence (Cox et al., 2019). Certain values that we take to be paramount, such as self-preservation, may get surpassed momentarily by other values, such as the patient's need for the other person to realize how much they are suffering or the need to avoid being abandoned by them. Consistent with the phenomenological description of BPD (Stanghellini and Mancini, 2017, p. 108), for the patient in that moment nothing is more important than that the other person be present and validating. Explaining to the patient about these value hierarchy changes should form part of the psycho-education.

Patients' value hierarchies can also clash with those of the government or the mainstream psychiatric system. Members of the service user movement have expressed concerns about and dissent with applying the same recovery model to BPD as to the rest of mental illness on the grounds that 'any proscriptive, "one size fits all" notion of "recovery" is not only inappropriate but unrealistic because it fails to acknowledge the ongoing challenges of living with such a chronic disturbance of "being": it risks excluding whilst seeking to include' (Scanlon and Adlam, 2011, cited in Turner et al., 2011, p. 342). Turner et al. (2011) articulated that recovery, as part of mainstream mental health provision, has intrinsic links with 'social inclusion' and ties in with the government's reliance on the 'Big Society', which is its hypothetical route to society's 'recovery' from the financial troubles and the welfare and social care burden on the state. According to Turner et al. (2011), the mainstream 'recovery' doctrine and 'social inclusion' with the expectancy of engaging with the outside world, playing by its rules, and being accepted accordingly were felt by some members of the community to be decidedly harmful. They argue that the disruption in the attachment system means for many that they find being with others overwhelming and they avoid social contact. They assert that creative activities, such as art, can, however, distract people away from the pain of 'being together' (Turner et al., 2011), but, unfortunately, services that provide these are often the first to be cut during times of financial difficulty. The opportunities for people to inhabit the creative world are stepping-stones to personal 'internal' well-being and also a link to the outside world, that is, an avenue to social inclusion and acceptance. Turner et al. (2011) feel that the ingredients for what many people with this diagnosis would consider a pathway to a meaningful recovery are stripped away. This is particularly lamentable as research evidence shows that pharmacological treatments, at least in their current forms, are ineffective, and long-term residential treatment facilities are being replaced with time-limited treatment pathways.

Proximity of Values

When we are highly emotionally aroused, we tend to focus on the person or situation that is associated with our emotional arousal and we find it difficult to think about the values of those (or our own values relating to those) whom we perceive as less directly involved in the situation, even when they also have a legitimate stake in it. Our family, community, employers, Social Services, or courts of law get banished to the periphery of our attention. This is even more so for people with BPD. Impaired executive function during periods of high emotional arousal plays an important role in this. Having unstable relationships with switching between idealization and devaluation is also a common contributing factor, for example when a relationship that previously acted as a protective factor breaks down. The most important early relationships of patients with BPD were often broken and, as a result, they struggle to calibrate other relationships in terms of attachment, suffer from rejection sensitivity (Foxhall et al., 2019), and struggle to develop epistemic trust. Additionally, many patients become progressively socially isolated. This means that they need to meet their social needs through their remaining few social connections. The focus is often on one or very few individuals. Therefore, they cannot benefit from the perspectives and advice of a greater number of people who know them and their life situation.

This is when it helps to have a clear and robust structure that promotes a good process. Such structures include the MDT meeting, multi-professional meetings, clinical supervision, or potentially in the future the stakeholder tribunal I described in Chapter 4. They give the primary stakeholders what they need at that point: the *perspective* to notice all the actual and potential stakeholders and their relative proximity and *time* for the warped hierarchy of values to realign itself.

Temporality of Values

Just like their emotions, the values of BPD patients can also fluctuate surprisingly quickly. Depending on their current mood state, people with BPD can declare different, sometimes opposing, values in relation to the same subject. Urgent new priorities can suddenly completely trump ones that are usually important to the person. This can involve relatively reversible situations or decisions with a longer-lasting or irreversible effect. As their values fluctuate rapidly, so do the action-possibilities and actions these values drive. This is often very frustrating for them too and contributes to their sense of fragmented self, shame, and humiliation. People with BPD tend to act impulsively and then regret what they did when they were emotionally aroused. The reason for this, at least in part, could be that they cannot project themselves into the future and many of the reasons why one would not act in certain ways just do not feel relevant to the patient. At times of heightened emotions, sometimes there is a struggle between their conflicting values that is obvious to the observer or even the person with BPD. Sometimes the person is even able to verbalize what their preferred course of action would be, but the values driving this healthier course of action appear to be less accessible or less powerful at the time, and those driving a riskier or less adaptive course of action win. This is consistent with both the enactivist view that the value of various affordances depends on the organism's needs at the time and the phenomenological psychopathological description of BPD with switching between the life worlds of dysphoria and anger that comes with different needs.

A particular case in point is euthanasia and (physician-)assisted suicide (EAS): EAS solely on the basis of mental disorder has now been legalized in a number of countries and a large proportion of people who have requested it had personality disorder (Kim et al., 2016; Thienpont et al., 2015). The aim of the legislators was to make it possible to end what is considered to be unbearable, untreatable, and unnecessary suffering in people with incurable illness (Mehlum et al., 2020). It has been pointed out that, although there are treatments with proven efficacy to reduce personality disorder symptoms, including suicidality, the majority of those requesting EAS had had some form of psychotherapy, but very few had been treated with these evidence-based treatments specific to their personality disorder (Mehlum et al., 2020). This begs the question of how the criterion of the illness being incurable was explored in the majority of the cases. Mehlum et al. (2020) also argue that suicidal behaviour in BPD is often linked to the patient's wish to seek help, to communicate an interpersonal problem, or to have a sense of control or relief, that is, it is not necessarily a lasting wish to die. Relevant to the assessment of untreatability, patients also often feel disappointed or rejected by their therapists and disengage from treatment. Pertinent to temporality, in BPD the suicidal wishes, though they frequently emerge, in most cases fluctuate rapidly. Patients with BPD often experience strong painful emotions, and thinking about death and suicide ('If I can't bear this suffering anymore, I can terminate it by ending it all') can offer a sense of control and relief and become habitual. Although there is a surprising dearth of research on death anxiety in BPD (Liu et al., 2023), Mehlum et al. (2020) note that people with personality disorders tend to contemplate death more often and may have a stronger wish for death for more extended time periods than people without these conditions. However, relevant to the hierarchy of values, as one spends some time exploring these thoughts with the patient, it is often possible to identify other values that may be more important to the patient than dying. For the above reasons, assessing 'true' suicidal intent – that is, when the person really wants to irreversibly die because their suffering is unbearable, and their wish is not fluctuating but stable and permanent and not a way of communicating interpersonal distress that is amenable to change and therefore temporary – and whether someone's condition is untreatable and incurable is extremely difficult. Yet, it has been argued that excluding people with mental illness as a blanket rule would be discriminatory (Braun et al., 2024), and to say that if someone has a diagnosis of BPD they should never be allowed to have access to EAS could be seen as an example of that. This is another situation where the stakeholder tribunal (see Chapter 4) with experts on BPD would be required for good process. A careful examination of the proximity, the temporality, and the hierarchy of the patient's values and a review of which evidence-based treatments have been tried and with what result could go a long way to negotiating this complexity, that is, avoiding the death of people for whom there is a realistic chance of improvement, but still allowing the ending of suffering where all reasonable interventions have been tried. A whole raft of specific value conflicts will be inevitable in this context, as suggested by a recent survey on this issue by the Royal College of Psychiatrists (2024), so it appears to be crucial for psychiatrists to engage with philosophers, ethicists, and law experts for a broader multidisciplinary perspective. Although this is certainly time-consuming and costly, it is human lives that are at stake. Making it part of psycho education to talk about the hierarchy, proximity, and temporality of values may offer an opportunity to reduce impulsivity and increase hope in patients with BPD.

Mechanisms of Improvement: The Example of 'Service User' Involvement

Improvement in the patient's illness is usually associated with a lasting shift in their values. Life becomes more valued and so can certain areas in one's living. There can be many routes to this, acting in isolation or together. A special case is getting involved in designing and running the health services for one's own care. This may be particularly relevant to BPD in which taking control and assuming responsibility is a key task during recovery. Whereas in the previous section ('Clinical Value-Mapping in BPD') we looked at the hierarchy, proximity, and temporality of mainly individual values, recovery usually involves changes to a whole set of values within the individual.

Service user involvement can have many benefits for the patient. As one patient put it, '[p]utting something back into the system that had helped me gave me a sense that what I'd been through was not in vain' (Bolton et al., 2014, p. 58). It also gives focus to the patient. Having this new role means that their system of relevant values can be pulled away from the pathological and in the direction of health. Value systems are like a web of nodes connected by rubber strings, in which the nodes are individual values. Nodes (values) that are currently distant from each other can become close when the whole web is pulled and thereby reshaped through one or a small group of values being dragged in a certain direction by an important issue or event in the patient's life. This can lead to a change in the relative distances of nodes and result in new clusters within the web (i.e. a new configuration of values in the person), sometimes leading to a new, stable configuration. Values are action-driving and this new configuration can reveal and facilitate new affordances, new action-possibilities for the patient and, thereby, for their social environment, too. This is where the therapeutic value of service user improvement comes from. As patients are getting better clinically and old ways of coping and parts of identity are left behind, co-production can provide an opportunity to explore new roles and new ways of relating to people and improve self-esteem, self-confidence, and sense of agency.

References

Bolton, W., Lowell, K., Morgan, L. & Wood, H. (eds.) 2014. *Meeting the Challenge, Making a Difference: Working Effectively to Support People with Personality Disorder in the Community*. London: Department of Health. www.newhamscp.org.uk/wp-content/uploads/2016/11/Meeting-the-Challenge-Making-a-Difference.pdf.

Braithwaite, J., Herkes, J., Ludlow, K., Testa, L. & Lamprell, G. 2017. Association between organisational and workplace cultures, and patient outcomes: Systematic review. *British Medical Journal Open*, 7, e017708.

Braun, E., Scholten, M. & Vollmann, J. 2024. Assisted suicide and the discrimination argument: Can people with mental illness fulfil beneficence- and autonomy-based eligibility criteria? *Bioethics*, 38, 61–68.

Buchman-Wildbaum, T., Unoka, Z., Dudas, R., Vizin, G., Demetrovics, Z. & Richman, M. J. 2021. Shame in borderline personality disorder: Meta-analysis. *Journal of Personality Disorders*, 35, 149–161.

Cameron, A. Y., Palm Reed, K. & Gaudiano, B. A. 2014. Addressing treatment motivation in borderline personality disorder: Rationale for incorporating values-based exercises into dialectical behavior therapy. *Journal of Contemporary Psychotherapy*, 44, 109–116.

Castillo, H., Ramon, S. & Morant, N. 2013. A recovery journey for people with personality disorder. *International Journal of Social Psychiatry*, 59, 264–273.

Choi-Kain, L. W., Finch, E. F., Masland, S. R., Jenkins, J. A. & Unruh, B. T. 2017. What works in the treatment of borderline personality disorder. *Current Behavioral Neuroscience Reports*, 4, 21–30.

Conte, B., Hahnel, U. J. J. & Brosch, T. 2023. From values to emotions: Cognitive appraisal mediates the impact of core values on emotional experience. *Emotion*, 23, 1115–1129.

Cox, C., Bulluss, E., Chapman, F., Cookson, A., Flood, A. & Sharp, A. 2019. The Coventry grid for adults: A tool to guide clinicians in differentiating complex trauma and autism. *Good Autism Practice*, 20, 76–87.

De Haan, S. 2020. An enactive approach to psychiatry. *Philosophy, Psychiatry, and Psychology*, 27, 3–25.

Denman, C. 2001. Cognitive–analytic therapy. *Advances in Psychiatric Treatment*, 7, 243–252.

Dixon-Gordon, K. L., Peters, J. R., Fertuck, E. A. & Yen, S. 2017. Emotional processes in borderline personality disorder: An update for clinical practice. *Journal of Psychotherapy Integration*, 27, 425–438.

Dudas, R. B. 2014. What is it like to be diagnosed with bipolar illness, borderline personality disorder or another diagnosis with mood instability? *British Journal of Psychiatry*, 204, 178–179.

Dudas, R. B., Mole, T. B., Morris, L. S., Denman, C., Hill, E., Szalma, B., Evans, D., Dunn, B., Fletcher, P. & Voon, V. 2017. Amygdala and dlPFC abnormalities, with aberrant connectivity and habituation in response to emotional stimuli in females with

BPD. *Journal of Affective Disorders*, 208, 460–466.

Evans, D., Dalgleish, T., Dudas, R. B., Denman, C., Howard, M. & Dunn, B. D. 2015. Examining the shared and unique features of self-concept content and structure in borderline personality disorder and depression. *Cognitive Therapy and Research*, 39, 613–626.

Fonagy, P., Luyten, P. & Allison, E. 2015. Epistemic petrification and the restoration of epistemic trust: A new conceptualization of borderline personality disorder and its psychosocial treatment. *Journal of Personality Disorders*, 29, 575–609.

Foxhall, M., Hamilton-Giachritsis, C. & Button, K. 2019. The link between rejection sensitivity and borderline personality disorder: A systematic review and meta-analysis. *British Journal of Clinical Psychology*, 58, 289–326.

García-Alandete, J., Marco Salvador, J. H. & Rodríguez, S. P. 2014. Predicting role of the meaning in life on depression, hopelessness, and suicide risk among borderline personality disorder patients. *Universitas Psychologica*, 13, 1545–1555.

Gask, L. 2015. *The Other Side of Silence: A Psychiatrist's Memoir of Depression*. Chichester: Vie Books.

Gillard, S., Turner, K. & Neffgen, M. 2015. Understanding recovery in the context of lived experience of personality disorders: A collaborative, qualitative research study. *BMC (BioMed Central) Psychiatry*, 15, 183.

Gunderson, J. G. 2009. Borderline personality disorder: Ontogeny of a diagnosis. *American Journal of Psychiatry*, 166, 530–539.

Gunderson, J. G. & Lyons-Ruth, K. 2008. BPD's interpersonal hypersensitivity phenotype: A gene-environment-developmental model. *Journal of Personality Disorders*, 22, 22–41.

Gunderson, J. G. & Phillips, K. A. 1991. A current view of the interface between borderline personality disorder and depression. *American Journal of Psychiatry*, 148, 967–975.

HM Government 2007. Mental Health Act 2007 Explanatory Notes. London: National Archives. www.legislation.gov.uk/ukpga/2007/12/notes/division/6/1?view=plain.

Katakis, P., Schlief, M., Barnett, P., Rains, L. S., Rowe, S., Pilling, S. & Johnson, S. 2023. Effectiveness of outpatient and community treatments for people with a diagnosis of 'personality disorder': Systematic review and meta-analysis. *BMC (BioMed Central) Psychiatry*, 23, 57.

Katsakou, C., Marougka, S., Barnicot, K., Savill, M., White, H., Lockwood, K. & Priebe, S. 2012. Recovery in borderline personality disorder (BPD): A qualitative study of service users' perspectives. *PLoS (Public Library of Science) One*, 7, e36517.

Katsakou, C. & Pistrang, N. 2018. Clients' experiences of treatment and recovery in borderline personality disorder: A meta-synthesis of qualitative studies. *Psychotherapy Research*, 28, 940–957.

Kim, S. Y., De Vries, R. G. & Peteet, J. R. 2016. Euthanasia and assisted suicide of patients with psychiatric disorders in the Netherlands 2011 to 2014. *Journal of the American Medical Association Psychiatry*, 73, 362–368.

Larivière, N., Couture, É., Blackburn, C., Carbonneau, M., LacombE, C., Schinck, S.-A., David, P. & St-Cyr-Tribble, D. 2015. Recovery, as experienced by women with borderline personality disorder. *Psychiatric Quarterly*, 86, 555–568.

Lind, M., Jørgensen, C. R., Heinskou, T., Simonsen, S., Bøye, R. & Thomsen, D. K. 2019. Patients with borderline personality disorder show increased agency in life stories after 12 months of psychotherapy. *Psychotherapy*, 56, 274–284.

Little, B. 2024. Part of the world again [recording]. Patient Voices®, 29 April. ® Pilgrim Projects, www.patientvoices.org.uk/flv/0586pv384.htm.

Liu, C. T. X., Menzies, R. E. & Menzies, R. G. 2023. A systematic review of existential concerns in borderline personality disorder. *Journal of Humanistic Psychology*. https://doi.org/10.1177/00221678231165792.

Maiese, M. 2021. An enactivist reconceptualization of the medical model. *Philosophical Psychology*, 34, 962–988.

Mancini, M. & Stanghellini, G. 2020. Values in persons with borderline personality disorder:

Their relevance for the therapeutic interview. *Research in Psychotherapy*, 23, 48–55.

Marco, J. H., Garcia-Alandete, J., Pérez, S., Guillen, V., Jorquera, M., Espallargas, P. & Botella, C. 2015. Meaning in life and non-suicidal self-injury: A follow-up study with participants with borderline personality disorder. *Psychiatry Research*, 230, 561–566.

McAdam, M. 2024. Can you hear what I say? [recording]. Patient Voices®, 29 April. ® Pilgrim Projects, www.patientvoices.org.uk/flv/0750pv384.htm.

Mehlum, L., Schmahl, C., Berens, A., Doering, S., Hutsebaut, J., Kaera, A., Kramer, U., Moran, P. A., Renneberg, B., Ribaudi, J. S., Simonsen, S., Swales, M., Taubner, S. & Di Giacomo, E. 2020. Euthanasia and assisted suicide in patients with personality disorders: A review of current practice and challenges. *Borderline Personality Disorder and Emotion Dysregulation*, 7, 15.

Mohi, S., Deane, F. P., Mooney-Reh, D., Bailey, A. & Ciaglia, D. 2021. Experiential avoidance and depression predict values engagement among people in treatment for borderline personality disorder. *Journal of Contextual Behavioral Science*, 20, 94–100.

Mohi, S. R., Deane, F. P., Bailey, A., Mooney-Reh, D. & Ciaglia, D. 2018. An exploration of values among consumers seeking treatment for borderline personality disorder. *Borderline Personality Disorder and Emotion Dysregulation*, 5, 8.

Morris, A., Bloom, J. R. & Kang, S. 2007. Organizational and individual factors affecting consumer outcomes of care in mental health services. *Administration and Policy in Mental Health and Mental Health Services Research*, 34, 243–253.

Morris, C., Smith, I. & Alwin, N. 2014. Is contact with adult mental health services helpful for individuals with a diagnosable BPD? A study of service users views in the UK. *Journal of Mental Health*, 23, 251–255.

Morton, J., Snowdon, S., Gopold, M. & Guymer, E. 2012. Acceptance and commitment therapy group treatment for symptoms of borderline personality disorder: A public sector pilot study. *Cognitive and Behavioral Practice*, 19, 527–544.

National Institute for Mental Health in England (NIMHE) 2003. *Personality Disorder: No Longer a Diagnosis of Exclusion*. www.nimhe.org.uk/downloads/PDFinal.pdf.

Nehls, N. 1999. Borderline personality disorder: The voice of patients. *Research in Nursing and Health*, 22, 285–293.

Paris, J. 2005. A shrinking perimeter. In *The Fall of an Icon: Psychoanalysis and Academic Psychiatry*. Toronto: University of Toronto Press, pp. 92–114.

Proudfoot, J. G., Parker, G. B., Benoit, M., Manicavasagar, V., Smith, M. & Gayed, A. 2009. What happens after diagnosis? Understanding the experiences of patients with newly-diagnosed bipolar disorder. *Health Expectations*, 12, 120–129.

Royal College of Psychiatrists (RCPsych) 2023. Values and standards: What are enabling environments? www.rcpsych.ac.uk/improving-care/ccqi/quality-networks-accreditation/enabling-environments-network-ee/what-are-they.

Royal College of Psychiatrists (RCPsych) 2024. RCPsych comments on vote for assisted dying bill in England and Wales. www.rcpsych.ac.uk/news-and-features/latest-news/detail/2024/11/29/rcpsych-comments-on-vote-for-assisted-dying-bill-in-england-and-wales.

Salgado, R. M., Pedrosa, R. & Bastos-Leite, A. J. 2020. Dysfunction of empathy and related processes in borderline personality disorder: A systematic review. *Harvard Review of Psychiatry*, 28, 238–254.

Scanlon, C. and Adlam, J. 2011 . Cosmopolitan minds and metropolitan societies: Social exclusion and social refusal revisited. *Psychodynamic Practice*, 17(3) 241–254.

Sheehan, L., Nieweglowski, K. & Corrigan, P. 2016. The stigma of personality disorders. *Current Psychiatry Reports*, 18, 11.

Stanghellini, G. & Mancini, M. 2017. *The Therapeutic Interview in Mental Health: A Values-Based and Person-Centered Approach*. Cambridge: Cambridge University Press.

Stanghellini, G., Bertelli, M. & Raballo, A. 2006. Typus melancholicus: Personality structure and the characteristics of major unipolar depressive episode. *Journal of Affective Disorders*, 93, 159–167.

Storebø, O. J., Stoffers-Winterling, J. M., Völlm, B. A., Kongerslev, M. T., Mattivi, J. T., Jørgensen, M. S., Faltinsen, E., Todorovac, A., Sales, C. P., Callesen, H. E., Lieb, K. & Simonsen, E. 2020. Psychological therapies for people with borderline personality disorder. *Cochrane Database of Systematic Reviews*, 5, CD012955.

Thienpont, L., Verhofstadt, M., Van Loon, T., Distelmans, W., Audenaert, K. & De Deyn, P. P. 2015. Euthanasia requests, procedures and outcomes for 100 Belgian patients suffering from psychiatric disorders: A retrospective, descriptive study. *British Medical Journal Open*, 5, e007454.

Turner, K., Lovell, K. & Brooker, A. 2011. '... And they all lived happily ever after': 'Recovery' or discovery of the self in personality disorder? *Psychodynamic Practice*, 17, 341–346.

Westen, D. & Cohen, R. P. 1993. The self in borderline personality disorder: A psychodynamic perspective. In Segal, Z. V. & Blatt, S. J. (eds.), *The Self in Emotional Distress: Cognitive and Psychodynamic Perspectives*. New York: Guilford Press, pp. 334–360.

World Health Organization (WHO) 2022. *ICD-11: International Classification of Diseases 11th Revision: The Global Standard for Diagnostic Health Information*. https://icd.who.int/en.

Chapter 14

A New Way of Doing Research in Psychiatry

Including Values

Robert B. Dudas

Introduction: The Need for a New Research Approach

Psychiatric research has made great strides over the last hundred years or so in many areas, including the epidemiology and social determinants of mental illness, (epi)genetics, psychological treatments, pharmacological and other somatic treatments, and new ways of studying the neural correlates of mental illness, such as brain imaging, to mention but a few. Developing a satisfactory explanation of the pathomechanism of mental illness, developing biomarkers to aid diagnosis, developing an aetiological classification system, and developing effective treatments that reliably lead to symptom elimination and functional recovery or a cure in most patients has, however, remained the holy grail of psychiatry for most conditions. As Leichsenring et al. (2022) conclude, 'After more than half a century of research, thousands of RCTs [randomized controlled trials] and millions of invested funds, the effect sizes of psychotherapies and pharmacotherapies for mental disorders are limited, suggesting a ceiling effect for treatment research as presently conducted. A paradigm shift in research seems to be required to achieve further progress.'

A major challenge in psychiatry is knowing how to integrate elements of knowledge originating from admixtures of biological, psychological, and sociocultural components. Only focussing on one dimension risks missing the root causes of mental illness. If, for example, the dimension studied is distal in a causal chain, the changes in it may be only correlational and not causal in relation to the mental symptoms or clinical outcome measures, or they may represent consequences as opposed to causes. Integration in psychiatry requires a strong grasp of both natural and social scientific methodology as well as solid and well-worked-out epistemological foundations. Although these are essential for mapping the structure of our object of inquiry, which is essential if we are to do reliable and useful empirical research, unfortunately, currently only a very small proportion of research is aiming at this. The scientific community has been becoming increasingly aware of this. The lack of recognition of the limitations of natural scientific (logico-empirical) methodology on its own for studying psychotherapy, for example, has been a major source of the criticism of psychotherapy research (Spinelli, 2006). Major funders have begun to shift their priorities reflecting this understanding as well, which is positive because doing things differently would require significant investment into setting up multidisciplinary research centres and courageously bringing together researchers to create the required skill mix. What we can offer in this chapter is an attempt at outlining how the role of values could be incorporated into such cross-disciplinary research.

An important part of the solution would be going back to the person level. What is required here is empathetic and imaginative identification with the patient, and investigation and interpretation of meaning, that is, 'the whole gamut of both explicit and implicit beliefs, assumptions, biases, attitudes, and values, together with their concomitant affective and behavioural components, that are maintained by a person' (Spinelli, 2006, p. 2). This means that the person of the therapist becomes a research tool, and the 'data' come from the conversational interaction between them and the patient. The smallest 'units of analysis' are the individual personal experiences of the patient, for example hearing their deceased father's voice beckoning them to join him in heaven. These can, of course, form larger units, composed of several individual experiences linked by meaning, for example an episode of clinical depression after losing a parent. This example shows how highly contextualized this type of data is and how hard it is to capture it with standardized rating scales or other questionnaire measures (Chen, 2020).

Measuring variables relating to abstract concepts in an impersonal way, which is how much of current research is done, comes at a high price; it introduces a significant degree of indirectness and risks missing important correlational or explanatory relationships. Nomothetic approaches, in which data cannot be traced back to or analysed at an individual level, can provide only probabilistic findings relating to groups and 'construct people who never were and never could be' (Smith et al., 2022, p. 25, quoting Datan et al., 1987, p. 156). This brings us back to our starting point: what is the best way to use the findings of evidence-based medicine (EBM)? Interestingly, research has shown that decisions made by individual clinicians did not reflect recommendations based on EBM, and, apart from the paucity of relevant research, distrust of the research in terms of whether or not it reflected the complexities of real clinical situations also played a role (Smith et al., 2022, p. 182). Until we manage to close the currently rather large gap between research and clinical practice by coming up with new ways of doing research, this will remain a constant obstacle to a smooth translation of research into practice. What is required for success is an approach that is capable of integrating methodologies from different disciplines, including ethics, and that can combine natural scientific explanation, social scientific and humanistic understanding, and clinical care (Stanghellini and Broome, 2014). This would make psychiatric research not less but more evidence-based.

Research Themes and Directions

Value-related research themes can be grouped into two main areas: (1) the role of values in the causation of mental illness, its prevention, and recovery from it in general; and (2) specifically value-laden issues in clinical practice.

As regards (1), values are inevitably involved in all forms of mental illness in some way, but they are more likely to play a particularly important role in those that are more clearly psychiatric problems (i.e. not caused primarily by a general physical health or neurological condition). Examples are:

- ongoing existential distress, adjustment disorder, or depression, with its attendant symptoms and functional impairment when someone is 'not in the right place', the right relationship, the right job and so on, for them
- mental illness in the aftermath of abuse and neglect
- mental illness in the aftermath of psychological trauma
- sliding into addiction
- mental disorder with increasingly paranoid or otherwise delusional interpretation of the world.

Values are also heavily involved in a whole raft of factors associated with mental illness, such as unhealthy habits, making poor life choices, self-defeating behaviour, maladaptive vicious cycles, the untoward effects of migration, natural disaster, war, climate change, and other man-made catastrophes. Finally, values are important in major challenges in psychiatry, such as poor treatment adherence and self-harm and suicide. These together are responsible for the brunt of mental illness and the question is how we can capture the value component in them. If we manage to do this effectively, we will stand a much greater chance of achieving major breakthroughs in both research and treatment. For all of these situations, there are a number of questions that can help us better understand the role of values.

Pathomechanism

- What is the role of values in individual mental illnesses? How can they be predisposing, precipitating, or maintaining factors?
- Is this more of a problem of the person's values becoming maladaptive (failure of adaptation) as the situation changes or is their illness rooted in a problem with their original constellation of values, or a combination of these?
- Where did these values of the person come from? Was it their immediate social environment, the wider society, their entire culture, or a result of living in two or more cultures at the same time?
- How are these values mediated? Is it via one-to-one conversations, social media, the wider media, 'toxic' memes, or some other channel?
- What else, if anything, is necessary for the development of mental illness (in addition to the value 'problem')?
- What is the timeline of events like? For example, did the person start off having vulnerability factors then become exposed to certain value situations, such as a new life situation, that created conflict between core values within the person or between the person and their environment? Does the order of events or the time between them matter? Are there any mitigating or exacerbating factors?

Prevention, Mechanism of Improvement, and Recovery

- Are there any ways to work with values to prevent mental illness? What are these and how do they work?
- Is there a road to recovery once illness has developed? If so, what can help to resolve value conflicts? Are there any 'side effects' to these solutions in the short and the long term for the person and for their environment?
- What helps when the value conflict cannot be resolved? Is there a good process for handling dissensus?
- What is the role, if any, of pharmacological, psychological, and social intervention in this?
- What are the best ways of exploring the patient's narrative to help them make adaptive changes in a way that promotes hope, agency, and recovery?
- What features are important and helpful to patients when designing services? Where are the opportunities for successful co-production?

As regards (2), there are a number of research themes that relate to clinical practice in which values play a primary role and VBP could be instrumental. These themes include, for example:

- the interface between the Mental Capacity Act and the Mental Health Act and the dissensual decision-making that exists in clinical practice (relating to mechanisms and what does and does not work; similarities to political democracy; specific situations, e.g. patients wanting further treatment despite treatment appearing more harmful than helpful?)
- implementation of values-based principles at scale (involving effective engagement of stakeholders, system-level challenges, potential gains and losses, the creation and evaluation of mental health policy, etc.)
- deciding what are the transferable insights from VBP for the rest of medicine, public health, and health policy
- economic and sustainability analyses of exploiting the full capacity of VBP principles in clinical care.

VBP-Informed Research Methodology

What follows from our exploration in the previous chapters is that for psychiatry (academic and clinical) to remain relevant and to be able to make progress and for psychiatry to keep its identity, it will be essential to incorporate and work with values more effectively. This would help us identify novel, hitherto unexplored solutions for our currently limited understanding of pathomechanism, the mechanism of improvement with treatment, and limited treatment efficacy. Table 14.1 includes some questions that could be used in research for value mapping.

Qualitative, and only later quantitative or mixed-method, studies could use these questions to gather data that could then be linked to other variables in the same person from the neurobiological, psychological, social, and existential dimensions. In the initial, qualitative phase, phenomenological (Larsen et al., 2022; Ritunnano et al., 2023), hermeneutic, and other idiographic approaches could contribute to better understanding of the particulars of the symptom, treatment, or life choice studied. Phenomenology offers sound empirical methodology with which to study the person's subjective experience. Phenomenological input can help us increase the granular resolution of our psychopathological description and improve the accuracy of diagnostic, prognostic, and therapeutic subgroup identification (Ritunnano et al., 2023). In the context of disorders affecting subjectivity, enriching the data with more exploration of subjective experience could also enhance the path analyses that are so crucial to understanding pathomechanism and the mechanism of improvement.

Interpretative phenomenological analysis (IPA; Smith et al., 2022) is an established method used in the study of lived experience of mental distress. It is particularly suited to examining how individuals make sense of major events in their lives and it has been demonstrated that IPA can be used to understand even experiences that do not easily lend themselves to empathic inquiry, such as psychosis (Smith et al., 2022, p. 169). It is important to note that using an idiographic approach does not mean that patterns that apply to more than a single individual cannot be identified. More general claims with applicability to other persons presenting with the same symptom can be developed using analytic induction and quasi-judicial approaches (Smith et al., 2022, p. 26).

Table 14.1 Questions for value-mapping studies

Aspect studied	Sample questions to help exploration
Exploration of the values involved	What is important to you about [x symptom / treatment / life choice]? What else is important to you about it? What is most important?
Cognitive, affective, behavioural context and strengths of associations	What do these values mean to you? Why are these the most important things to you? Is this related to anything else about [x symptom / treatment / life choice]? Is there a conflict between any of your relevant values? When you have a conflict between your own values, how do you feel? What do you do?
Proximity of values / levels of organization (interrelational / embedded / 'in-the-world' aspects)	How do your values regarding [x symptom / treatment / life choice] fit with those around you? Your family members / friends / peers / boss / colleagues / neighbours / (ethic/religious) community / country / humankind? How important is it to you that your values fit with those of these other people? Whose values are the most important to you? What happens when you have a conflict between your values and the values of other people? How do you feel? What do you do? If there was a value conflict, which one would be hardest/easiest for you to tolerate (one between you and your family, one between you and your peers, etc.) and why?
Hierarchy of values	Do you see this [understanding about a symptom/illness/decision] as a simple, clear-as-daylight, easy one or as a complicated, multifaceted one? Do you feel that part of you would want to decide one way and part of you another way? If so, why? Do you hold any values that guide your decisions in similar situations? What are these? How do your values regarding [x symptom / treatment / life choice] fit with your other values? Are some of these values more important to you than the others? What happens when you have conflicting values? How do you feel? What do you do?
Temporality of values	Do you find that what matters to you about this particular [symptom/illness/decision] can change over time? How rapidly does this happen? How stable is this change (temporary/fluctuating/permanent)? What causes the change usually? Context? Meaning? Do you have any control over the change? Did you use to have values about this that you no longer hold? How did that change in your values happen? How did those close to you react to the changes in your values? What was the impact of this on you?

Table 14.1 (cont.)

Aspect studied	Sample questions to help exploration
Thought (or actual) experimentation	How much are you already living out the values that matter most to you? If you are not at all / not fully, – what stops you from living out your core values fully? – what if you could (/ could never) live them out? How would that change the situation? – is there any other way for you to live out your important values more fully? – what changes would you have to make to live out these values more fully? How do you form your values? What could change your values relevant to your [x symptom / treatment / life choice]? Do you think you yourself could change your values relevant to your [x symptom / treatment / life choice] somehow?
Comprehensive phenomenological understanding of the person's relevant values	What would be a precise psychopathological phenomenological description of the person's value system related to this particular situation?
Multidisciplinary (combined natural and social scientific) understanding	How would a philosopher approach this situation / ask the questions in this context? An anthropologist / sociologist / social worker / psychologist / historian of psychiatry / pharmacist? A peer researcher with lived experience? A group of experts by lived experience co-producing the research?

The data elicited this way could then be linked to other variables from the neurobiological, psychological, social, and existential dimensions to develop an understanding of the psychiatric symptom / illness / clinical decision that is relevant to the person in their social environment.

Last but not least, history of psychiatry research could contribute valuable insight into how the studied mental symptom or syndrome has travelled across epistemes (hinting at how it may have more or less stability) and manifested in different social, cultural, and political contexts, and whether changes in it have been associated with any changes in those contextual factors. This historical information could be particularly useful as factors at higher levels of organization often cannot be experimentally manipulated owing to ethical reasons or logistical limitations.

Research could uncover how the proximity, hierarchy, and temporality of values change in the context of different treatment modalities, including both pharmacological and individual or group psychological interventions and how these changes correlate with clinical improvement at symptom, syndrome, and functional levels. This would be a methodology that includes the biological dimension but is radically different from our current way of doing psychiatric research, resulting in a new, more direct and more precise way of generating knowledge about mental illness and the recovery from it.

References

Chen, E. 2020. Recovering the context in psychopathology. In Marková, I. S. & Chen, E. (eds.), *Rethinking Psychopathology: Creative Convergences*. Cham: Springer, pp. 65–72.

Datan, N., Rodeheaver, D. & Hughes, F. 1987. Adult development and aging. *Annual Review of Psychology*, 38, 153–180.

Larsen, R. R., Maschião, L. F., Piedade, V. L., Messas, G. & Hastings, J. 2022. More phenomenology in psychiatry? Applied ontology as a method towards integration. *Lancet Psychiatry*, 9(9), 751–758.

Leichsenring, F., Steinert, C., Rabung, S. & Ioannidis, J. P. A. 2022. The efficacy of psychotherapies and pharmacotherapies for mental disorders in adults: An umbrella review and meta-analytic evaluation of recent meta-analyses. *World Psychiatry*, 21(1), 133–145.

Ritunnano, R., Papola, D., Broome, M. R. & Nelson, B. 2023. Phenomenology as a resource for translational research in mental health: Methodological trends, challenges and new directions. *Epidemiology and Psychiatric Sciences*, 32, e5.

Smith, J. A., Flowers, P. & Larkin, M. 2022. *Interpretative Phenomenological Analysis: Theory, Method and Research*, 2nd ed. London: SAGE.

Spinelli, E. 2006. The value of relatedness in existential psychotherapy and phenomenological enquiry. *Indo-Pacific Journal of Phenomenology*, 6(suppl), 1–8.

Stanghellini, G. and Broome, M. R. 2014. Psychopathology as the basic science of psychiatry. *British Journal of Psychiatry*, 205(3), 169–170.

Conclusion

Robert B. Dudas

When we set out to write this book, we wanted to examine values in psychiatry from two main directions. Firstly, we were curious to explore the role of values in mental illness and the recovery from it. Secondly, we were interested to showcase the valuable contributions of psychiatry to the diagnosis and treatment of mental illness.

Our historical analysis revealed some interesting facts and trajectories that still have their effect on how we understand mental illness today. Madness was transformed into a medical object by the nineteenth century. This was the result of the convergence of social, economic, and political factors. Putting medicine in charge has had profound consequences on many levels, including what has come to be regarded as legitimate ways of generating knowledge. The concepts of mental symptom and of madness with its varieties as clusters of symptoms led to the need to explain what keeps these symptoms together. What is the nature of this glue? In an era where medicine was making great strides in identifying the causes of disease, the search for a biological cause was intense and led to the gradual reclassification of conditions in which brain lesions have been identified as clearly neurological as opposed to psychiatric. When the search for 'objective' signs of illness in psychiatric conditions, unlike in other branches of medicine, did not reveal any biological markers, alienists borrowed from the social sciences their primary criteria to differentiate normal from abnormal, such as deviance from what was considered proper, ethical, and socially acceptable. This, combined with (mainly speculative) neuroscientific claims concerning brain pathology, provided a 'hybrid' natural and social scientific conceptual platform for psychiatry from the beginning. The currently predominant view originated in the nineteenth century when madness started to be regarded as a natural kind located in the brain, resulting from brain factors and influenced by external ones. An alternative view could be that although madness is always manifested and observed in the person (or persons, as in the case of *folie a deux*, for example), the 'disease' (the pathological constellation of causes that results in madness) is located in the combination of the person with their environment rather than in the person's brain per se, although of course the brain will always be implicated as the organ involved in perceiving, thinking, feeling, moving, and so on (and therefore it will be possible to demonstrate some brain 'differences'), even when the brain may have nothing fundamentally wrong with it. The fact that a change of environment often helps in these conditions would be consistent with this.

Interestingly, at its inception psychology also placed itself between the natural and the social sciences, which was reflected in its conceptual and methodological choices. This is unlikely to be accidental. The leading minds who created the discipline of psychology also intuited that mental phenomena are fundamentally different from physical phenomena and the social dimension was important. Drawing on the social sciences and humanities is necessary to grasp them fully. The usefulness of any psychological approach for psychiatry has appeared to be determined to a large degree by how much they managed to incorporate person-centredness and agency into their theory and research. This is an area where psychology has also benefited from more (rather than less) social science and humanities input during its history, as these anchor psychology at the person level and above.

The fact that psychiatry has its roots in medicine and its practitioners first train as medical doctors explains to a large degree psychiatry's fascination with neuroscience. In recent decades, psychiatric training and research development have focussed on neuroscience almost exclusively, without much regard for other approaches. This is not without risks, though, because if it turns out that madness is something more complex than a disorder at the organizational level of the brain, other disciplines with more adequate conceptual and hermeneutic capabilities will likely take over. Such a shift could lead to not just gains but also significant losses, in terms of both our ability to understand mental illness and our ability as a society to look after and treat effectively those who do benefit from the medical approach.

Although social and cultural historians have tended to accept the inevitability of a close relationship between psychiatry and the values of the era in which it was practised, the precise nature of this relationship has received surprisingly little attention. History tells us that the broader values of society can be just as important as those of psychiatry itself in shaping the way people with mental illness are treated. Historical scholarship also alerts us to the need to be circumspect about taking society's self-declared values at face value, an example being the humanitarian reform of the care system for the mentally ill during the Victorian era where harsh and discriminating morality and a growing intolerance of society towards the marginal were also demonstrated. Historically, in the UK, doctors have repeatedly found themselves limited in their ability to build a person-centred, therapeutic relationship with their patients by circumstances that were beyond their control, for example the overcrowding of the asylums and the strict legalism of the asylum system. Inclusion of the mental health system in the UK's National Health Service (NHS) during the post-war period did not change the inadequate staffing and resourcing or the overcrowding.

From the twentieth century onwards, there have been periods when society has turned to psychiatry for advice about normal life, for example during the inter-war period and at the time of national crisis during the Second World War, in relation to how to bring up children to become good citizens and how to create a mentally healthier society. Psychiatry extended beyond mental illness and into mental health. The emergence of anti-psychiatry in the 1960s and 1970s happened during a period when the idea that psychiatry could be a tool for social adjustment was under growing criticism; individual freedom began to be prized over conformity, and the service user movement started. One important legacy of anti-psychiatry is that psychiatry has become much more cautious about taking a public stance on values. Being aware of the boundaries of one's remit is, of course, important, but so is the continual dialogue with society about our respective relevant values in a field as value-laden as psychiatry. How society and the profession will respond to the growing prevalence of mental health problems in our current era will be the subject of future research.

***

The proper integration of values into our models of mental illness still has not happened. This is an outstanding task for psychiatry, and one that, if completed, could lead to significant improvement in our ability to understand mental illness and recovery. Values are crucial to our understanding of psychiatry at the person and the social levels. They play a role in symptom formation, help-seeking, and treatment adherence, and also, at societal level, in what is considered mental illness and what is not or how we should treat it. Integrating values into our theorizing and research would be an important step in developing a fully-fledged epistemology of psychiatry, which could lead to real advances after a long period of stagnation.

A fascinating (and largely unacknowledged) feature of today's psychiatry is that its various stakeholders – included among whom are the patient and their carers, the various clinical professions involved in clinical care, and researchers in psychiatry – all use different coexisting models of mental illness or combinations thereof. This has a significant impact on how they each see the duties and responsibilities of each other and on the communication among them, and contributes to the rather large gap between research and practice. The neuroscientific model, which currently dominates research and training, has produced an impressive amount of relevant knowledge, but without fully integrating other relevant dimensions, such as the experiential, the social, and the existential; it is too reductionistic to fulfil the expectation of explaining mental illness and recovery. More holistic models are required. Engel's biopsychosocial model (Engel, 1977), Leigh's genetic-memetic model (Leigh, 2010), the enactive model (one of the most comprehensive expositions of which can be found in de Haan, 2020), and the hybrid model by Berrios and Marková (2015) all foreshadow a new epistemology that, when worked out fully, will be able to provide the robust theoretical foundations required for psychiatry. For this to happen, we will need a genuine multidisciplinary approach in research as in clinical practice; such a multidisciplinary team (MDT) would include a philosopher and a values-based practice (VBP)-trained clinician, as well as optional collaborators with expertise relevant to the research problem, such as a sociologist, an anthropologist, or a journalist.

A daily practical test of our ability to become aware of, reason, and communicate about values is MDT working. The different needs, concerns, and preferences of the professions constituting the MDT reflect the hybrid nature of the subject matter of psychiatry and the knowledge base and skill mix required for good clinical practice, drawing on both the biomedical and the social sciences. Although training can improve MDT working, currently, professionals receive relatively little specific training on this. Traditionally, medicine sat at the top of the hierarchy in the professions of the MDT. This hierarchy has become more horizontal in recent decades, but MDTs are situated primarily within healthcare. Several ways of integrating health and social care have been attempted over the last forty years, but none has been completely satisfactory. Working closely together is clearly beneficial, but advantages and disadvantages have been described for both integrated and separate services. Importantly, VBP can provide a good process for care decisions in both systems but especially so when working together.

Working skilfully with values is also key to the prevention of mental illness. We have a great deal of evidence about environmental factors associated with good mental health and also those associated with mental illness. This could, in theory, allow us to choose or shape our values appropriately at the person as well as the societal levels. However, psychiatry needs to be transparent not just about these factors but also about the fact that it is only one of the players, and if the values that are instrumental to good mental health are to be fully realized, public health, government, and the public will need to work collaboratively. This requires constant and genuine dialogue between them, and, happily, VBP can be instrumental in creating appropriate vehicles for this. Psychiatrists of the future will need to be equipped to communicate about values in this way, too.

Another major way in which values feature in psychiatry is in how the profession sees its own professional values and its contribution to improving the lives of those suffering with mental illness. The other side of the coin is how psychiatry is seen by society. Personal history and culture have a strong influence on the values of individual practitioners, as do current practice in the specialty and the history of psychiatry. Most psychiatrists have a strong medical identity but recognize that to be a good clinician they need more than just their biomedical knowledge and skills. The psychiatry training curricula in the UK have seen a major shift, with values featuring much more prominently in the new versions. Pertinent aspects explicitly incorporated into the new curricula include: VBP principles, such as practice being based on both evidence and values; a model of the person that draws on the social sciences, neurosciences, and the humanities; clinicians needing to be cognizant of and to have the ability to work with the impact of culture, religion, and social systems; partnership with the patient, their carers, and other professionals; person-centred care; and multidisciplinary working. The new curricula reflect the changing value landscape in the profession, shifting away from the biological and the psychological, and putting more emphasis on safeguarding. Value-laden concepts – such as the power imbalance between doctor and patient, co-production, protected characteristics, the relevance of the history of psychiatry, and sustainability – appear as new, important additions.

How society sees psychiatry is reflected in the media portrayal of psychiatry, but the latter has many other functions, too. Among others, it helps the public to understand mental illness and psychiatry, shapes public attitudes and stigma, influences treatment-seeking, scrutinizes how people with mental illness are treated by psychiatry and wider society, and has the potential to protect but also, when done carelessly, to harm people. Although overall there has been some improvement in recent decades, more with some conditions than with others, there are still examples of media coverage that maintains negative stereotypes about people with mental illness or psychiatric treatment. Appropriate guidelines are needed. The use of social media changed the nature of communication from one-to-many to many-to-many and many-to-one – and also from experts to opinion leaders, in many cases. Crucially, however, the media offer a forum that we can use to explore and negotiate the different values among the stakeholders.

Art can help us understand and communicate about our history, culture, and lives, and the experiences of others in ways that are different from those used in science, for example. That art can offer benefits to psychiatry has long been recognized and art is used as a form of therapy. Art offers ways to explore and communicate concepts, emotions, and values. It is capable of expressing both universal and highly personal subjective content. Literature, for example, can help us understand the impact of disease on the person and their life. Literature can also open our eyes to the fact that the concerns of our patients do not necessarily coincide with our own concerns. One of the specific challenges of mental illness is that the sufferer can have experiences that are highly subjective and out of the ordinary, to the degree that they are hard to communicate. They may be impenetrable and difficult to describe in ordinary language, and literature, through using images, metaphors, and other literary tools, can facilitate understanding that would not be possible otherwise. Literature offers us an opportunity to learn about and experience, as much as this is empathetically possible, a wide range of mental states, illnesses, and lives that we do not have direct experience of. It also opens a private window into the unspoken inner commentary of those involved in the clinical situation. But literature is not only a medium through which patients and psychiatrists can communicate about mental illness and its treatment; their loved ones and the general public can also resort to it.

Portrayals of psychiatrists and psychiatric treatment are relatively common in literature and provide important feedback for clinicians on how they are perceived by their patients and for the public on how those afflicted with mental illness perceive their position in society. This feedback is often negative, but there are positive examples, too. Those in receipt of psychiatric care often write about the humanity of the psychiatrist and appreciate their being versed in a range of disciplines, including art and music. Literature also offers an opportunity for the patient to show compassion for the doctor.

Literature is about weaving a narrative, which is an important part of recovery in psychiatry. In literature we are perhaps afforded more licence to use our imagination and are less bounded by the limits of reality. Literature opens up possibilities. Psychiatrists (and other clinicians involved in the care of the mentally ill) can in literature express many of their thoughts, feelings, and values that could be seen as 'unprofessional' or inappropriate were they expressed in any other context.

Literary works contain many details that are illuminating regarding the values involved. Furthermore, they can lay bare those aspects of the cultural and moral context of practice that we may not think about otherwise, including the origins of the societal and professional value context that, though generally unacknowledged, always influences doctor–patient interaction.

As we mentioned before, the environment within which we work has a major impact on our values. Unfortunately, working conditions in psychiatry have worsened in many healthcare systems. Care is spread more thinly, allowing little time to get to know the patient and to provide person-centred care. There is a conflict of values in these new ways of working: primarily management values versus clinical values. Information technology carries great potential in psychiatry, but many current systems fail to free up time for human-to-human contact. Personal support for clinicians from admin and other important ancillary services has been dwindling, with clear deleterious effects on retention.

Importantly, there has been a strong expectation towards psychiatry to prevent suicides. In recent years, in some places, this has been taken to mean complete elimination of all suicides. This is problematic for several reasons: suicide is not completely preventable; it is not a form of harm equivalent to other patient safety errors; and there is plurality of values regarding suicide. Prioritizing suicide prevention over other activities has the potential to reduce patient autonomy, prolong suffering, and impede recovery. For example, in some cases, suicide can be evaluated as a rational choice to escape unbearable suffering. The unintended consequences of an extreme focus on suicide elimination can include creating a restrictive environment in which people are reluctant to stay and receive treatment, increased use of restraint and sedation, and a risk-averse culture in which inpatients are protected from suicide in the short term but may not learn the coping strategies needed to resist suicidal ideation after discharge back into the community. Sadly, victimization of the professionals affected by the case is also an important issue.

Owing to its relatively undeveloped conceptual foundations, psychiatry has often struggled to defend itself against various criticisms, for example those from anti-psychiatry. A VBP-based analysis of the terminal and instrumental values of anti-psychiatry can be helpful in highlighting some of the weaknesses of its arguments against psychiatry. One important value conflict in this context, for instance, is that between personal and communal values. Critical psychiatry also draws attention to problematic areas of psychiatric theory and practice, but with a different aim: constructive criticism. Remarkably, much of what critical psychiatry stood for has now been accepted and adopted by mainstream psychiatry. Psychiatry as a clinical activity has become rather critical of its own practices and is continually examining itself. This self-reflective stance, being critical of our own theory and practice in a constructive way, plays a very important role in keeping our profession on a sound ethical footing. Focussing on earlier practice that occurred in a context different from the current times or on exceptional cases that represent excess or abuse instead of examining typical clinical practice and training in psychiatry draws attention and resources away from addressing the main issues. A genuine dialogue about values among practitioners, patients, carers, and wider society is needed for constant calibration.

The picture about values and psychiatry would not be complete without mentioning some of the progressive developments in psychiatry in recent decades. These may turn out to be instrumental in overcoming the challenges of integrating the different dimensions of mental illness and developing new treatments. One such development is the revival of psychopathological phenomenology, which will help us improve the precision of our descriptive psychopathological characterization of symptoms and syndromes. This, in turn, could lead to improvement in the classification of mental disorders and correlational and causal modelling in observational and experimental designs. Ideally, theory and practice feed from each other, and, indeed, developments in existential psychotherapy have been meaningfully adding to our theoretical understanding of the influence of our position in our social world and in history.

Some psychological treatment modalities have an explicit focus on values. Motivational interviewing has many similarities to VBP and is designed to increase the person's agency by enabling them to draw out the personal meaning and importance of change. It targets ambivalence, which is also often present in value conflicts. A crucial insight from it relating to good process in VBP is the observation that putting in words and saying out loud what our own values are can greatly enhance our understanding of them. Conflict between one's own core values can be crippling. Treatment may mean improving the patient's ability to recognize their environment's affordances so that they realize they can live out their core values to a greater degree, that is, demonstrating that their core values may not necessarily need to remain in a paralysing conflict. Alternatively, the therapist can help the patient improve their sense-making and, as a result, alter their values.

Psychiatry has been pioneering among the medical specialties in embracing alternative meanings of recovery. In addition to the traditional medical meaning, that is, recovery from illness with successful treatment, recovery can also mean recovery from impairment through rehabilitation, or recovery from invalidation. In psychiatry, the most important consequence of this different interpretation of the word was that it enabled discussions about recovery as something that is actually possible with mental illness. Although in the more severe and enduring forms this would not normally mean being free of symptoms, these alternative meanings allowed for new frames of reference and energized thinking about supporting people with mental illness and their inclusion in society.

Psychiatry was also one of the first specialties to adopt co-production, which has some of its roots in service user involvement, which itself has both the civil rights movement and consumerism in its genealogy. For co-production to be truly progressive, it needs to start with a change in how society sees mental illness and apply a public health approach that draws on expertise from both living with mental illness and professional experience.

Importantly, for co-production to work well in this way, we need systems of accountability that protect everyone from poor practice but do not stifle progress or leave psychiatrists as the scapegoats for society's failings.

***

Our exploration of values in three different clinical conditions demonstrated to us how closely developments in theory and practice go hand in hand in psychiatry. It also further confirmed our premise that a truly multidisciplinary approach is required for genuine progress. These three conditions represent three different scenarios in terms of the challenges in accessing and working with the patient's values.

In depression, the patient's values tend to change dramatically, but relatively slowly, over weeks, and usually return to normal. At the height of their illness, the patient can constantly feel that they are transgressing important personal and group values. The former often elicits feelings of guilt, whilst the latter is frequently associated with feelings of shame; both are commonly elicited in depression. The person's values determine the meaning structure of the world they live in and regulate their actions: values are action-driving. Importantly, the other person and the mutuality of the relationship with that other person is necessary for certain essential values – such as to be accepted, respected, and loved – to be realized. The need to be recognized as a person in such ways can be stronger than one's values relating to self-preservation. Because of this, sometimes the struggle for this recognition can be a struggle *against* life, more commonly in the form of self-neglect, self-defeating or socially destructive behaviour, and sometimes even suicidality.

Examining the values at play in the clinical care of persons with depression can be similar to creating a map with three-dimensions: (1) the level of organization or the proximity to primary stakeholders, (2) the hierarchy of the values, and (3) the temporality of the values. The first one of these is about making sure that the values of all the stakeholders are recognized and treated at the appropriate level, starting from the patient, through their immediate and wider social environment, to the society level. Examining carefully the alignment of the patient's values with those of others is particularly relevant in mental illness, as the patient's values can be misaligned temporarily or even chronically owing to the illness but also because of other reasons. In some cases, this misalignment may constitute the mental illness. Value-mapping can facilitate realignment within and between the stakeholders.

There is always some hierarchy, an order of relative importance, among the values of every stakeholder; certain needs, concerns, and preferences can feel more pressing than others. However, changes in the hierarchy may be possible and also necessary for successful collaboration between stakeholders and for the patient's recovery. In depression, when the patient has limited access to their emotions, especially positive ones, these hierarchy changes can be dramatic and happen at a faster pace whilst the illness is developing and during recovery.

Another specific challenge in depression is that with the erosion of one's capacity to have moods and feelings or to find anything meaningful, the depressed patient can be temporarily cut off from many or all of the values they would normally hold. This poses a significant clinical challenge as it also means that the clinician may not have access to these values, either. It is important to recognize that in addition to records of the former wishes of the patient and collateral information from those who know the patient, there are important other sources of knowledge about relevant value changes, including peer support workers with experience of the same illness, or first-hand narratives, ethnographic, anthropology, history, law, and political studies, as well as media reports, literature, theatre, and film portrayals of depression. Philosophical descriptions and methodologies, using phenomenology, hermeneutics, or discursive analysis, are also available. Philosophy has further usefulness in understanding narrative reasoning. This is crucial because changes in one's life narrative are essential for the creation of a story that is related to recovery. The changes in the patient's value system during recovery enable them to make these changes. This is helpful in order to come to terms with the illness episode and, potentially, to make important changes in one's life to build resilience against another episode. Life history is surprisingly not static: it changes over time as it is shared and retold. The patient's social environment, including the professionals involved in their care, can facilitate (or sometimes hinder) this.

Dementia is a progressive condition, and the person may gradually lose the ability to express their values. With this diagnosis, the simple scenario of the dyad of a doctor and a patient is uncommon; considering values in dementia must encompass the possible impact of the values of all stakeholders. In dementia, the changes in the patient's values may be at least in part organically driven as well as having social origins. The experience of having dementia in itself is likely to affect a person's world view. The condition causing their dementia may have direct effects on their brain that also cause changes in what the person seems to value. Historically, there has been little literature on what people with dementia consider to be valuable to them, and it has often been represented by proxy reports by their carers or professionals. However, now there is emerging qualitative research describing the views of people with dementia. Being aware of and knowledgeable about what is important from the point of view of those affected is a key concept in VBP, as this supports better-quality care in sensitive situations and situates the person with dementia in that context.

Interestingly, there have been two significant recent shifts in how dementia is conceptualized, seemingly pointing in opposing directions. First, the fact that antecedents of Alzheimer's disease are present many years before the onset of cognitive impairment and the clinical syndrome of dementia has led to a view that these disorders are long-term neurobiological entities, and therefore it is the neurobiological changes that constitute the disease, not the clinical features. Second, there has been a move from a predominantly medical, cognitive deficit-based approach to person- or relationship-centred care. The previous concept of dementia as eroding a 'sense of self' owing to changing perception of the world and decline in cognitive functions (biological model) is now replaced with a sociological model where personhood is considered to be enhanced by the social interactions with the person. Understanding the past and present self-identities of the person with dementia is crucial to improving their experiences in healthcare settings. Enhancing communication, recognition, acknowledgement, and acceptance of their values around their own self-identity are some of the ways to strengthen their concept of self.

Borderline personality disorder (BPD) presents with yet another set of challenges from a values point of view. Values are closely linked to emotions, and patients with BPD have significant difficulty regulating their emotions. At times of extreme emotions, one's values or the hierarchy among them can become warped temporarily. And just as the values fluctuate rapidly, so, too, do the actions these values drive. Making it part of psychoeducation to talk about the hierarchy, proximity, and temporality of values offers an opportunity to try to reduce impulsivity and increase hope in patients with BPD. Team members need to have an understanding of the nature of the problems specific to this patient group and what is helpful in resolving them. For example, what is usually the right response in most other psychiatric conditions can be counterproductive and reduce agency in BPD. Team members need to be neither overly supportive, which would thwart the development of the patient's agency, nor overly demanding, as that could trigger an adverse reaction. This, however, can create an apparent value conflict between the clinician and the patient, and resolving this without causing too much of a sense of rejection in the patient requires significant clinical skills and the ability to build trust with the patient. Another difficult balance between conflicting values is ensuring safety versus actively promoting change.

Most effective forms of therapy address personal agency. For this to happen, the clinician needs to create a non-blaming, non-judgemental, and compassionate milieu within which they can enable the patient to take responsibility for their actions. Values-based interventions can improve agency. They can also increase motivation and help the patient find meaning, which in turn is negatively associated with depression, suicidality, and self-harm in this patient group. Values transcend individual situations and therefore reduce the pressure to attain a specific goal; instead, they emphasize choosing behaviours that are consistent with a personal value in general: the focus is on process rather than on individual events, which gives the person increased flexibility. Expectedly, early empirical evidence supports the usefulness of working with the patient's values in therapy using acceptance and commitment therapy (ACT), a modality focussing on acting in accordance with one's stated values. Empirical evidence from longitudinal observation suggests that an increase in agency in the patient's life narrative is part of the recovery process.

Patients with BPD follow a different path in terms of their recovery compared to patients with other major forms of mental illness. Patients with BPD can find the word 'recovery' problematic and many feel that 'discovery' describes their journey more accurately. A significant proportion of people with BPD feel that they are not ill in the same way as people with other major mental illnesses although they do need help and support.

***

Although psychiatric research has made great strides over the last 100 years or so, developing a satisfactory explanation of the pathomechanism of mental illness, finding biomarkers or other tests to aid diagnosis, creating an aetiological classification system, and producing effective treatments that reliably lead to symptom elimination and functional recovery or a complete cure for most conditions have remained the holy grail of psychiatry. One of the greatest potential benefits of including values would be to be able to fully map the objects of psychiatric inquiry, be they symptoms; various forms of mental illness; predisposing, precipitating, and maintaining factors; or treatments. Value-mapping, as shown in this book, as well as phenomenological and other social scientific methodologies are available to do this work. This would require a different, genuinely multidisciplinary scientific approach and significant investment, but it would greatly enhance the precision of any quantitative approach afterwards.

***

Over the last two decades, VBP principles have become part of the narrative of health and social care practice in many places (Woodbridge-Dodd, 2012). The need to embrace patient-centred care, cultural competence, and co-production is very much present in current thinking in the UK National Health Service (NHS England, 2017, 2020). The curriculum for core training set by the Royal College of Psychiatrists and approved by the General Medical Council (GMC) lists many of the VBP principles among the intended learning outcomes and the curricula for specialist training require trainees to demonstrate an understanding of VBP (RCPsych, 2022). Correspondingly, an increasing number of publications is now available to facilitate learning (e.g. Fulford, 2007; Fulford et al., 2012; Woodbridge & Fulford, 2004). Additionally, VBP principles are part of the fundamental standards set by the Care Quality Commission (CQC, 2020) and a report commissioned by the GMC also recognizes the ability to navigate conflicting values as a senior medical leadership quality (Shale, 2019). Psychiatrists at consultant level are senior clinicians who are expected to have the ability to recognize, communicate about, and resolve conflicts related to values. However, we are still very far from exploiting the full potential of studying values in psychiatry. We hope that this volume will be useful for those who set out to do so for the benefit of those affected by mental illness.

References

Berrios, G. E. & Marková, I. S. 2015. Towards a new epistemology of psychiatry. In Kirmayer, L. J., Lemelson, R. & Cummings, C. A. (eds.), *Re-visioning Psychiatry*. Cambridge: Cambridge University Press, pp. 41–64.

Care Quality Commission (CQC) 2020. The fundamental standards. www.cqc.org.uk/what-we-do/how-we-do-our-job/fundamental-standards.

De Haan, S. 2020. *Enactive Psychiatry*. Cambridge: Cambridge University Press.

Engel, G. L. 1977. The need for a new medical model: A challenge for biomedicine. *Science*, 196, 129–136.

Fulford, B. (K. W. M.) 2007. Ten principles of values-based medicine. In Radden, J. (ed.), *The Philosophy of Psychiatry: A Companion*. New York: Oxford University Press, pp. 205–234.

Fulford, B. (K. W. M.), Peile, E. & Carroll, H. 2012. *Essential Values-Based Practice: Clinical Stories Linking Science with People*. Cambridge: Cambridge University Press.

Leigh, H. 2010. *Genes, Memes, Culture, and Mental Illness: Toward an Integrative Model*. New York: Springer.

NHS (National Health Service) England 2017. *Co-production for Personal Health Budgets and Integrated Personal Commissioning – Summary Guide*. www.england.nhs.uk/publication/co-production/.

NHS (National Health Service) England 2020. Developing patient centred care. www.england.nhs.uk/integrated-care-pioneers/resources/patient-care/.

Royal College of Psychiatrists (RCPsych) 2022. Curricula documents and resources. www.rcpsych.ac.uk/training/curricula-and-guidance/curricula-implementation/curricula-documents-and-resources.

Shale, S. 2019. How doctors in senior leadership roles establish and maintain a positive patient-centred culture. www.gmc-uk.org/about/what-we-do-and-why/data-and-research/research-and-insight-archive/how-doctors-in-senior-leadership-roles-establish-and-maintain-a-positive-patient-centred-culture.

Woodbridge, K. & Fulford, B. (K. W. M.) 2004. *Whose Values? A Workbook for Values-Based Practice in Mental Health Care*. London: Sainsbury Centre for Mental Health. https://valuesbasedpractice.org/wp-content/uploads/2015/04/Whose-Values-A-Workbook.pdf.

Woodbridge-Dodd, K. 2012. Values-based practice in mental health and psychiatry. *Current Opinion in Psychiatry*, 25(6), 508–512.

Index

For EU product safety concerns, contact us at Calle de José Abascal, 56–1°,
28003 Madrid, Spain or eugpsr@cambridge.org.

www.ingramcontent.com/pod-product-compliance
Lightning Source LLC
LaVergne TN
LVHW022202200926
848481LV00006B/1815

* 9 7 8 1 1 0 8 7 9 3 1 1 7 *